THE SHAKERS AND
THE WORLD'S PEOPLE

Gift drawings like this 1859 watercolor by Sister Polly Collins of Hancock, Massachusetts, were unknown to the world until the 1930s. Photographed by John McKee from the collection of the United Society, Sabbathday Lake, Maine.

THE SHAKERS
AND THE
WORLD'S PEOPLE

By FLO MORSE

Illustrated with Photographs and Drawings

University Press of New England
Hanover and London

To the memory of my Mother

UNIVERSITY PRESS OF NEW ENGLAND

Brandeis University   Dartmouth College
Brown University   University of New Hampshire
Clark University   University of Rhode Island
University of Connecticut   Tufts University
University of Vermont

Printed in the United States of America

LIBRARY OF CONGRESS CATALOGING-IN-PUBLICATION DATA

Morse, Flo.
    The Shakers and the world's people.

    Bibliography: p.
    Includes index.
    1. Shakers—United States—History—Sources.
I. Title.
BX9766.M67   1987   289'.8   87–8223
ISBN 0–87451–426–6 (pbk.)

    5   4   3   2

Thanks are due to the following for permission to use the material indicated: Jonathan Aldrich: for the poems "The Millennial Laws" and "Fruitlands" from his *Croquet Lover at the Dinner Table* (© 1977 by Jonathan Aldrich; pub. by University of Missouri Press). American Historical Association: for excerpt from *Backwoods Utopias* by Arthur Bestor (© 1950 by the American Historical Association; pub. by University of Pennsylvania Press). Faith Andrews: for excerpt from *Fruits of the Shaker Tree of Life* (© 1975 by Faith Andrews; pub. by Berkshire Traveller Press, Stockbridge, Mass.). The Magazine ANTIQUES: for excerpt from the article "The Coming Shaker Exhibition in Manhat-
Permissions continued on page 379

Contents

The Shakers, who are best known today for the furniture they produced and the handiwork to which they lent their genius, were in the eighteenth and early half of the nineteenth century so exciting and challenging as a religious group that their name became known throughout the length and breadth of the land. Shakers might be looked upon as strange people but not as unhappy or unsuccessful people. They were among the most vibrant and vital people in the new world.

—V. F. Calverton, *Where Angels Dared to Tread*, 1941

In the story of Shakerism there are the
dark views and the bright views that interweave
and are often in dialogue with each other.

—Henri Desroche, *The American Shakers*, 1955, 1971

About This Book

Shaker life has been richly recorded, by the Shakers themselves, by ex-Shakers, and in both expected and unlikely places in literature and journalism. Most observers were confounded.

Charlotte Cushman, our first American stage star, cried in an ode, "Mysterious worshippers! Are you indeed the things you seem to be, /Of earth—yet of its iron influence free. . . ?"

Charles Dickens found the Shakers "grim." He called the elder who received him "a sort of calm goblin."

But many others considered them saints—more honest than most of their countrymen, original, peaceable, and pure.

This book excerpts writings of the Shakers and of the world's people about the Shakers, and places them in the general context of Shaker history. Much of the material comes from rare and out-of-print books in generous libraries and in my own collection. It has not been gathered before into a single source for the general reader, the student of American religions and American communities, and the Shaker specialist. The extracts weave back and forth in time, and have been fitted together like a mosaic or collage, with the author's comments in italics.

The material divides itself naturally into three parts, three centuries: the eighteenth, when the Millennial Church was established in America; the nineteenth, when Shakerism reached the height of its influence and renown; and the twentieth, when Shakerism (although still active and productive) suffered a decline, was rediscovered, and is now cherished.

To see the Shakers as the world's people saw them and wrote of them, errors and all, it was necessary to include a wide variety of opinion. Among anti-Shaker selections is a long excerpt from Valentine Rathbun's narrative, *Some Brief Hints of a Religious Scheme Taught & Propagated*

vii

by a Number of Europeans, published in 1781. This is the embittered work of an early apostate, who wrote from the "sorrowful experience" of only three months. But it renders a vivid picture of the exuberance and zeal of the first Believers in post-Revolutionary America, when they were at their all-time "high."

The first descriptions of the Shakers come from books like this, which had an enormous circulation. The Shakers did not begin to explain themselves until 1790. In the nineteenth century, however, they defended their foundress and their faith in a series of distinguished books.

To omit the prejudiced pieces from a record of the relationship between the Shakers and the world's people would distort its character. That the Believers survived prejudice, ridicule, and misunderstanding is evident from their long and wonder-filled presence.

My views are the bright views in this dialogue. I have been enriched by the friendship of the Believers of today and by the study of the Believers of the past.

ACKNOWLEDGMENTS

It is a pleasure to thank those who have helped me in my long study. I am indebted to the following people now or formerly at these libraries and institutions: the Bedford, New York, Free Library: Jane Grimason and Miriam Marschner; the Case Memorial Library of the Hartford Seminary Foundation: Duncan Brockway; the Detroit Institute of Arts: Mary Jane Jacob; the Fruitlands Museums: William Henry Harrison and Richard Reed; Hancock Shaker Village, Pittsfield, Massachusetts: Robert Meader, Amy Bess Miller, John Harlow Ott, and June Sprigg; the Historical American Buildings Survey: Deborah Burns; the William H. Lane Foundation: John Driscoll; the Mount Vernon, New York, Public Library: Mary Brooks; the City of Manchester (England), Cultural Services: D. Taylor; the Museum of American Folk Art: Dr. Robert Bishop; the New Hampshire Historical Society: Mary Lyn Ray; the New York State Library: Mildred Ledden and Melinda Yates; the New York State Museum: John Scherer and Peter Shaver; the Petersham, Massachusetts, Memorial Library: Delight Haines; the Shaker Library and the *Shaker Quarterly*, Sabbathday Lake, Maine: Br. Theodore E. Johnson; the Shaker Museum, Old Chatham, New York: Jean Anderson, Peter Laskovski, and Claire Wheeler; Shakertown at South Union, Kentucky: Deedy Hall and Julia Neal; Shaker Village of Pleasant Hill, Kentucky: Jane Brown and James C. Thomas; Shaker Village of Canterbury, New

Hampshire: John E. Auchmoody; the United Institute: Father Robley Edward Whitson; the Virginia Historical Society: John Melville Jennings; and the Western Reserve Historical Society: Virginia Hawley and Kermit Pike.

Among other libraries, museums, institutions, and organizations to which I am grateful for access to their Shaker resources, research facilities, special services, and hospitality are: the American Antiquarian Society; the Briarcliff College Library; the Brown University Library; the Cleveland Public Library; the Connecticut Historical Society; the Darrow School; the Baker Library of Dartmouth College; the Fox Lane School, Bedford, New York; the Massachusetts Correctional Institution at Shirley, Massachusetts; the Index of American Design, National Gallery of Art; the Library of Congress; the Dance Collection of the New York Public Library at Lincoln Center; the Rare Book Division and the Manuscripts and Archives Division of the New York Public Library; the Sarah Lawrence College Library; the Shaker Historical Society in Shaker Heights, Ohio; the Warren County Historical Society in Lebanon, Ohio; the Westchester Library System; the Williams College Library; and the Henry Francis du Pont Winterthur Museum.

Singling out individuals from the many to whom I owe thanks is difficult, but I wish to express special gratitude to: Alva Adams, Jonathan Aldrich, Faith Andrews, Olive Austin, Charles and Mary Grace Carpenter, Mary Lou Conlin, Nancy Melcher Diemand, A. Donald Emerich, Robert Emlen, Dorothy Filley, Roger Hall, Ed Horgan, Jane Hutton, Jay Johnson, Susan Jackson Keig, Steven Kistler, Lyn Lifshin, Mary Jane McCauley, Garnett McCoy, William Mahoney, Marilyn Marlow, Daniel Melcher, Goldie Satterlee Moffat, Barbara Morgan, Charles R. Muller, Harold Nestler, Daniel W. Patterson, Robert Peters, William Randle, Mary L. Richmond, Berton Roueché, David Serette, Frank Sierra, Mrs. Charles Sheeler, Patterson Sim, Norman Simpson, David Starbuck, Ernestine Stodelle, Thomas Swain, Suzanne Toomey, Virginia Weis, Gerard C. Wertkin, and Frank Wood.

Special thanks go to photographers Richard Hong and Elmer R. Pearson. And I am most appreciative to naïve painter Kathy Jakobsen for the privilege of using on this book's cover her striking recreation of a Massachusetts mob's attack on the Shakers in 1783.

I also take pleasure in thanking my editors at Dodd, Mead and Company, Allen Klots and Genia Graves; my "editor" at home, my husband Joe; and my family, for its patience and support.

The deepest debt of all is to my friends among Believers, the extended families at Sabbathday Lake, Maine, and at Canterbury, New Hampshire. Without their largesse of love and inspiration, coupled with practical contributions like facts, photographs, bed and board, this book would never have been undertaken or completed.

With Canterbury's growth into a museum-village, Eldress Bertha Lindsay, Eldress Gertrude Soule, and Sister Ethel Hudson remain serene in the midst of projects and planning. I recall Eldress Gertrude in her role in my first overwhelming experience of a Shaker meeting, at Sabbathday Lake in October 1967. Later on that same long ago, life-changing Sunday, Eldress (then Sister) Bertha, the late Sister Lillian Phelps, and Eldress Marguerite Frost first welcomed me to Canterbury. The spiritual insights I gained from that visit have been renewed over the years, and Eldress Bertha and Eldress Gertrude have continued kind and helpful in their quiet Shaker way.

I am especially beholden to the Believers at Sabbathday Lake. I thank Sisters R. Mildred Barker, Frances Carr, Elsie McCool, Marie Burgess, Elizabeth Dunn, Minnie Green, and Brothers Theodore Johnson, David Serette, Arnold Hadd, and Wayne Smith for the warmth and friendship I "come home" to wherever they are—in Maine or Worcester, New Haven or New York. Like Mother Ann and the Elders, they carry about the Shaker spirit. They live with the gift to be simple and simply what they are: the last hopeful practicing Shaker community in the world. They have been a source of comfort, spiritual guidance, and education.

FLO MORSE

Lyme, New Hampshire
1979

Preface to the New Edition

Nineteen eighty-six marked the 250th anniversary of the birth of Mother Ann Lee, who led eight English Shakers to the New World in 1774. Now "Mother Ann's children" are down to almost the same number from a peak of about five thousand before the mid-nineteenth century. But modern Shakers in two remaining communities in New England are not concerned about their numbers. At Canterbury Shaker Village in New Hampshire, Eldress Bertha Lindsay, Eldress Gertrude Soule, and Sister Ethel Hudson are comfortable, in their nineties, watching their museum home come to new life. At Sabbathday Lake, Maine, the Shakers still maintain an active, open religious community as well as a museum. "We're not history yet," says Sister Frances Carr.*

Interest in these Believers and their foresisters and brethren has soared since this book was first published in 1980. In 1986 more than 300,000 people visited Shaker museums and museum-villages in Maine, New Hampshire, Massachusetts, New York, and Kentucky. Eight million watched a public television documentary film about the Shakers. And over 160,000 stood in awe of a hundred objects gathered for an exhibition of Shaker design at prominent museums in New York and Washington, D.C.

In addition, new books, a stream of stories in the media, auctions of costly Shaker furniture, study groups across the country, and a host of Shaker reproductions have all drawn the world's people to the Shakers more than to any other American folk group.

What better time for a new edition of this book, which many readers, including Shaker historians, teachers, students, tour guides, and writers for television and the theatre, seem to have found useful. My hope continues to be that it will contribute to a broader understanding of the durable Shakers and their communal faith, the source of their famous art and invention.

FLO MORSE
LYME, NEW HAMPSHIRE
MARCH 1987

---

*Active in publishing, the Maine Shakers have launched a new series of the scholarly *Shaker Quarterly*, edited from 1961 to 1974 by Brother Theodore E. Johnson, who died in 1986.

xi

THE SHAKER COMMUNITIES

1	Watervliet, New York	1787–1938
2	Mount Lebanon, New York	1787–1947
3	Hancock, Massachusetts	1790–1960
4	Harvard, Massachusetts	1791–1918
5	Enfield, Connecticut	1790–1917
6	Tyringham, Massachusetts	1792–1875
7	Alfred, Maine	1793–1932
8	Canterbury, New Hampshire	1792–
9	Enfield, New Hampshire	1793–1923
10	Sabbathday Lake, Maine	1794–
11	Shirley, Massachusetts	1793–1908
12	Gorham, Maine	1808–1819
13	West Union (Busro), Indiana	1810–1827
14	South Union, Kentucky	1807–1922
15	Union Village, Ohio	1806–1912
16	Watervliet, Ohio	1806–1900
17	Pleasant Hill, Kentucky	1806–1910
18	Savoy, Massachusetts	1817–1825
19	Whitewater, Ohio	1824–1916
20	Sodus Bay, New York	1826–1836
21	Groveland, New York	1836–1895
22	North Union, Ohio	1822–1889
23	Narcoossee, Florida	1896–1911
24	White Oak, Georgia	1898–1902

Introduction

Who Were and Who Are the Shakers?

For more than two hundred years the American Shakers have lived in simplicity and unity in Christian communal families. They liberated women, welcomed all races, opposed war, perfected their quiet arts and crafts, worshipped God as Mother and Father, and expressed religious joy and love of each other by dancing and singing.

Their faith is one of the few religions founded by a woman. She was Ann Lee, an English blacksmith's daughter and a blacksmith's wife. Those who followed her to the New World in 1774, on the eve of the American Revolution, called her Mother Ann. "Put your hands to work and your hearts to God," she told them, inspiring the rise of nineteen industrious societies* in eight states during the eighteenth and nineteenth centuries. These unique homesteads, so strange to "the world's people," as Shakers called outsiders, were heaven on earth to thousands of American converts who strove for perfection within them.

Like angels, Mother Ann's "children" did not marry, or, like her, they gave up marriage. They confessed their sins to their elders, and in "the kingdom come" lived as brethren and sisters, enjoying equal rights, sharing in their common property, and working for the common good. At first their chastity was suspected, and their withdrawal from the world was feared. But in time hard work, high principles, true charity, and honest trading earned both prosperity and respect for the United Society of Believers in Christ's Second Appearing.

Then the quaint Shaker village-communes, which flourished like carefully tended garden patches from Maine to Ohio and Kentucky, be-

---

* plus five of short duration

came a national wonder. They were famous for the revolutionary social and economic advancements that resulted from their communal religion. "Shakertowns" had no poverty, no crime, no jails. They were governed by women as well as by men. Customs odd to the world's people prevailed, like wearing old-fashioned costumes, separating the sexes, and singing, dancing and whirling about in worship. On the Sabbath the dancing and shaking that gave these Believers their name made the plain white meetinghouses a mecca for visitors. The Marquis de Lafayette went to see the Shakers worship. So, in the next century, did Presidents Jackson and Monroe, and Charles Dickens.

Many besides Mr. Dickens left their frank impressions of the Shakers, who reached their peak in an age of great writers. Among American authors who called and commented were Cooper, Hawthorne, Emerson, Melville, Howells, and Greeley. Nathaniel Hawthorne published two dark tales with a Shaker background. Herman Melville worked a chapter in *Moby Dick* around a mad seaman who "had been nurtured among the crazy society of Neskyeuna Shakers where he had been a great prophet." Ralph Waldo Emerson often considered the Shakers in his journals and essays, giving them credit when credit was due. Kinder, personally, and in four novels and an essay, was William Dean Howells. He was not the first to put the Shakers into a novel. In *Redwood: A Tale*, published in 1824, Catharine Maria Sedgwick subplotted the rescue of a young woman who had "been befooled by the Shaking Quakers."

The Believers were often caricatured, once by humorist Artemus Ward, who called them "the strangest religious sex" he ever met. He wondered, "Why this jumpin up and singin? . . . this anty-matrimony idee?"

Curiosity sent the world's people to see plays like *The Shaker Lovers*, and to watch unethical performances of Shaker dancing by ex-Shakers. Other apostates found readers eager for sensational testimonies "exposing" and "unmasking" Shakerism. For a while Shaker doings were the talk of the times.

The Shakers' fame spread overseas. In England poet and critic Matthew Arnold doubted the "magnetic power" they were said to wield over American thought. John Stuart Mill found the influence, whatever its proportion, a healthy one. In Germany, Friedrich Engels, co-founder with Karl Marx of "scientific socialism," hailed the impact of the Shaker system. Despite "the religious humbug" that he underestimated, he welcomed proof that communism worked. Years later in Russia Count Leo

Tolstoy, writing *The Kreutzer Sonata*, was impressed when he read of Shaker abstinence from "the flesh."

To the end of the nineteenth century Shakerism was a newsworthy, controversial, incomprehensible American institution. *Shaker* itself was a household word, thanks to the broad distribution of superior products like garden seeds, herbs, medicines, slat-backed chairs, oval boxes, household brushes, and the efficient flat broom that Shakers invented. Even so, it grew difficult in a less religious era to attract converts into "Christ families." Most of the orphans and children raised among Believers did not remain. Membership slumped, even as the united societies survived a civil war, an industrial revolution, the growth of cities, strikes, panics, and depressions.

With the gift to persist, fourteen Shaker communities "traveled" into the twentieth century. Believers went on putting their hands to work and their hearts to God, adjusting as Shakers have always done to God's changes and continuing revelations. This meant renting or selling the once model farms, hiring outside help, closing family homes, and dropping industries once ahead of their times in the face of factory competition and for lack of manpower.

Woman power took over more and more of the production of Shaker goods as the brethren, whom sisters had long outnumbered, aged or went to the world and were not replaced. The sisters' workshops hummed as they turned their own long cloaks into the latest style for fashionable women. In their bonnets and gowns with prim covered bodices, the sisters carried their handwork, their woven poplar baskets and lined boxes, to resorts and country fairs, where they became a familiar sight.

The cloak industry ended in the 1930s and the last Shaker chair was manufactured in the 1940s. The Shaker schools closed, and while girls were still growing up in some Shaker families, most of the societies had dissolved by the fifties, and the surviving members clustered in a few communities. Collectors gathered up the furniture and objects and books left in the big deserted buildings, as the Shaker story was considered to be nearing the end. Soon museums would make themselves at home in some of the forlorn villages.

But in the 1960s a revival of communalism swept across the land. Young people especially were drawn to that other American way practiced by thousands in the nineteenth century, when the nation was dotted with small independent communes living according to an amazing variety of new social and economic systems. It was only natural that interest flared in the longest-lasting, most original, and most influential of those old "utopian" communities. And so the Believers themselves, by now all women, were finally appreciated. New friends gathered around them to share the peace and serenity they sensed in the ongoing Christian calling. Shakerism seemed so meaningful to the times, with its inherent human potential movement, its feminism, its freedom from racial prejudice, its pacifism, its respect for work, its concern for natural foods, hygiene, and conservation, its ecumenism, and its joyful personal worship.

In 1974 a knowing public helped the Believers celebrate the two hundredth anniversary of the Shakers' arrival in America. Bicentennial conventions and meetings were held in Ohio as well as at the Shaker homes in New England. The media overflowed with articles, and Sister R. Mildred Barker became the first Shaker to appear on the cover of a national magazine. Many readers were astonished to discover that Shakers are alive and well and living in the last two Shaker villages in the world, at Canterbury, New Hampshire, and Sabbathday Lake, Maine.

The Believers in Maine—once considered "the least of Mother's children in the East"—are concerned with the continuance of the Shaker way of life. They regret that the public is more interested in Shaker antiques than in the faith that inspired them, and Sister Mildred protests, "I don't want to be remembered as a piece of furniture!" Over the issue of admitting new members a sad controversy has arisen with the Canterbury kin.

And so mixed opinion about Shakerism—even among the Shakers—follows Mother Ann's work into its third century. Diminished but not yet done, peculiarly relevant to today, it has outlived all other religious and social "utopias" founded in early America. "This gospel will go to the end of the world," Mother Ann predicted, "and it will not be propagated so much by preaching, as by the good works of the people."

PART

I

IN THE
EIGHTEENTH
CENTURY

•

Mother of Zion

At Manchester, in England,
This blessed fire began,
And like a flame in stubble,
From house to house it ran:
A few at first receiv'd it,
And did their lusts forsake;
And soon their inward power
Brought on a mighty shake.

The rulers cried, "Delusion!
Who can these Shakers be?
Are these the wild fanatics,
Bewitched by *Ann Lee?*
We'll stop this noise and shaking.
It never shall prevail;
We'll seize the grand deceiver,
And thrust her into jail."

—From "Mother," a hymn,
Millennial Praises, 1813

Mother of Zion

On November 9, 1769, a colonial newspaper, the Virginia Gazette, *published the following story from England in the lower right-hand corner of the front page.**

Our correspondent at Manchester writes a very strange account of a religious sect who have lately made a great noise in that town. They took their rise from a prophet and prophetess who had their religious ceremonies and tenets delivered to them in a vision, some years ago. They hold theirs to be the only true religion, and all others to be false. They meet constantly three times a day, at the house of some one of their society, and converse in their own way about the scriptures, a future state, other sects of religion, &c. until the moving of the spirit comes upon them, which is first perceived by their beginning leisurely to scratch upon their thighs or other parts of their bodies; from that the motion becomes gradually quicker, and proceeds to trembling, shaking, and screeching in the most dreadful manner; at the same time their features are not distinguishable by reason of the quick motion of their heads, which strange agitation at last ends in singing and dancing to the pious tunes of Nancy Dawson, Bobbin Joan, Hie thee Jemmy home again, &c. These fits come upon them at certain intervals, and during the impulse of the spirit they disturb the whole neighborhood for some considerable distance, and continue sometimes whole nights in the most shocking distortions and commotions, until their strength is quite exhausted, from which uncommon mode of religious worship they have obtained the denomination of *Shakers.*

Ten and a half years later, a small band of English Shakers was discovered in this country. They had arrived quietly in New York in 1774 and gone their separate ways to earn a living. In 1776 they gathered together upstate at Niskayuna, later called Watervliet, about eight miles

---

* Author's commentary appears throughout in italics.

from Albany. "Put your hands to work and your hearts to God," their leader, Mother Ann Lee, told them.

Unknown and unnoticed for the first three and a half years of the American Revolution, they worked on their land and at their trades as blacksmiths and weavers, and they worshipped in the unusual shaking and "laboring" that gave them their name. Be patient, said Mother Ann, and lay up provisions. She prophesied, "They will come like doves."

And lo! they did come, Yankees weary of war and sick of sin and sorely disillusioned at the end of a nearby religious revival at New Lebanon, New York. When they heard of a singular people who praised God night and day and never sinned, they went to see them with new hope of finding salvation. The Shakers took the pilgrims in, taught them to confess their sins, forsake the marriage bed, and "travel" in the way of the Lord and the Primitive Church. Many Americans set out in the faith. Others feared and mocked it.

Valentine Rathbun, a "minister of the gospel" in Pittsfield, Massachusetts, warned the public about "a new and strange religion" spreading "like wild fire" through Massachusetts and New York. The leaders and teachers, he said,

consist of five males, and seven females: three of the males, and two females, profess to be perfect . . . the other seven not perfect yet, but very far advanced.

From "sorrowful experience," apostate Rathbun wrote a twenty-four page pamphlet attacking the Shakers, entitled Some Brief Hints of a Religious Scheme, Taught and Propagated by a Number of Europeans Living in a Place Called Nisqueunia, in the State of New York. *Published in 1781, it was a vivid and vicious portrait.*

When any person goes to see them, they all meet him with many smiles, and seeming great gladness; they bid him welcome, and directly tell him they knew of his coming yesterday. This sets a person wondering at their knowledge, and presently they get the person some victuals; then they sit down and have a spell of singing; they sing odd tunes and British marches, sometimes with words, and sometimes without words, and sometimes with a mixture of words, known and unknown. After singing, they fall to shaking their heads in a very extraordinary manner, with their eyes shut and face up; then a woman, about forty years old, sits and makes a sort of prayer, chiefly in an unknown tongue, (if I may so call it;) then one of the men comes to the person, and pretends to interpret the woman's prayer; after which they tell the person he has come to the right place to be instructed; they inquire the person's name, and ever after call him by his christian-name: they use no compliments, but their language is *yea* and *nay*.

With the visitor's consent, says Rathbun, they cut his hair. After it is done,

they come round him, and touch him with their fingers here and there, and give him a sly cross, and in a very loving way put their hands on his head, and then begin to preach their doctrine to him.

They begin with many good words, "saying we must hate sin, love God, take up our cross &c." A new dispensation is taking place, they tell the visitor, and add that they have "entered into it" and have all the apostolic gifts.

When he comes again they tell him that he must confess his sins to them, from his childhood, that they may take his case, and travail for him, that he may be born again. . . .

They tell him, they have got a mother; and that she speaks seventy-two tongues and that when she speaks in unknown tongues, the living people cannot understand her; yet the dead understand her, for she talks to them.

They say, that the fore-sighted woman . . . is the woman spoken of in the xiith chapter of the Revelations of John, who was clothed with the sun, having the moon under her feet, and on her head a crown of twelve stars. . . . Further, that she is the mother of all the elect; and that she travails for the whole world. . . .

The "mother's" role in the Shakers' worship is described.

Their manner of worship is entirely new, and different from all others. . . . While they are . . . shaking, one will begin to sing some odd tune, without words or rule; after a while another will strike in; and then another; and after a while they all fall in, and make a strange charm. . . . The mother, so called, minds to strike such notes as make a concord, and so form the charm. When they leave off singing, they drop off one by one, as oddly as they come on. In the best part of their worship, everyone acts for himself, and almost every one different from the other . . . dancing . . . hopping . . . turning around, so swift that if it be a woman, her clothes will be so filled with the wind, as though they were kept out by a hoop. . . .

Then all break off, and have a spell of smoaking, and sometimes great fits of laughter. . . . They have several such exercises in a day, especially on the sabbath.

But it is impossible, says Rathbun, founder of the Baptist Church in Pittsfield, to point out any exact form in which the Shakers worshipped. They constantly varied it, and seldom did the same thing twice.

When they meet for their worship, they fall a groaning and trembling . . . one will fall prostrate on the floor; another on his knees and his head in his hands . . . some will be singing, each his own tune; some without words, in an Indian tone; some sing jig tunes; some, tunes of their own making, in an unknown mutter, which they call new tongues; some will be dancing, and others stand laughing, heartily and loudly; others will be druming on the floor with their feet, as though a pair of drum sticks were beating on a drum head; others will be agonizing, as though they were in great pains; others jumping up and down; others fluttering over somebody, and talking to them; others will be shooing and hissing evil spirits out of the house; till the different tunes, groaning, jumping, dancing, druming, laughing, talking, and fluttering, shooing and hissing, makes a perfect bedlam: This they call the worship of God.

Above all else, the Shakers denounced sex.

When any person goes to them to be instructed . . . they tell him he must renounce and abstain from all works of the flesh; telling him that the first fall of our first parents, was carnal copulation and that this ruined the world; and that every one that has any thing to do with man or woman, in the work of generation, is acting Adam and Eve's sin over again: They tell the man to abstain from his wife, the woman from her husband. . . . They tell young men and young women, if they marry, and have any thing to do with the work or lusts of the flesh, they can never be born again. . . . They dwell more on this part of their instruction than all the rest. . . .

They prophesy, that this gospel (as they call it) must be preached to all the world, and all those that do not fall in with it, will be damned. . . .

The effect of this scheme is such, that men and their wives have parted, children ran away from their parents, and society entirely broke up in neighbourhoods; it makes children deny and disown their parents, and say they are full of devils. . . .

They meet together in the night, and have been heard two miles by people, in the dead of the night; sometimes, a company of them will run away to some house, get into it, raise a bedlam, wake up all in the house, and the neighbours round about for a mile: They run about in the woods and elsewhere, hooting and tooting like owls; some of them have stripped naked in the woods, and thought they were angels, and invisible, and could go about among men and not be seen, and have lost their clothes, and never found them again.

"It is as impossible to fully set forth the power and effects of this new religion," says Rathbun, *"as to trace the airy road of the meteor."* He concludes:

I am very sensible, that the spirit which leads on this new scheme, is the spirit of witchcraft, and is the most powerful of any delusion I ever heard or read of. . . . Multitudes have fallen in with this dreadful scheme, and are so infatuated in their senses, that they are deprived of their reason, and past recovery, unless God interpose for them, while the leaders of this dreadful catastrophe, like the bowels of Aetna, are ever vomiting up their sulphur; like wild fire it flies, and catches at a distance, and spreads like a plague. For such a delusion to take place in the land, loudly proclaims the judgment of God. —Valentine Rathbun, *Some Brief Hints of a Religious Scheme, Taught and Propagated by a Number of Europeans Living in a Place Called Nisqueunia in the State of New York,* 1781 (American Antiquarian Society)

ANOTHER WARNING

When we consider the infant state of civil power in America, since the revolution began, every infringement on the natural rights of humanity, every effort to undermine our original constitution, either in civil or ecclesiastical order, saps the foundation of Independency. To see a body of more than two thousand people, having no will of their own, but governed by a few Europeans conquering their adherents into the most unreserved subject, argues some infatuating power. . . .

There are few people in this land no doubt but what have heard of the contents of VALENTINE RATHBUN'S Narrative, in which some gross absurdities in point of doctrine and worship are pointed out. But since this people have increased in numbers, they have established such orders and

An apostate warns of their "infatuating power" in an attack against the Shakers published in 1782. Photograph of the title page, courtesy of the Western Reserve Historical Society.

founded such institutions among themselves as renders it very easy to trace them in their discipline to the seat and foundation of their power. For this purpose the writer thinks proper to lay open to the learned world, more particularly, the whole body of their discipline. . . .

The predominant principle in the heart of man is the love of dominion and preeminency. Pride is the root of all sin. From this principle the whole fabrick of that religion is founded. These people are artful, designing men, especially their leaders. The common people who are imposed upon are many of them sincere. . . . Their discipline is founded on the supposed perfection of their leaders: The Mother, it is said, obeys God through Christ; European elders obey her; American labourers obey them: The common people obey them while confession is made of every secret in nature, from the oldest to the youngest. The perpetual labours of which gives their teachers experience and skill. By this means the people are made to believe themselves to be seen through and through in the gospel glass of perfection by their teachers, as they express themselves, for hundreds of miles in an instant, and that they are arrived to that state of glory by which they behold not only the state of the living, but of the dead, with innumerable worlds of spirits good and bad.

—Amos Taylor, *A Narrative of the Strange Principles, Conduct and Character of the People Known by the Name of Shakers*, 1782

God, declared the Shakers, had sent them from Great Britain, to call in His elect. They had left behind to wither away the remains of the small Manchester society described in 1769 by the **Virginia Gazette**. That germinal group had drawn its inspiration from the French Prophets, persecuted Protestants who fled to England for religious liberty early in the eighteenth century. In France the Prophets were known as Camisards, from the shirts they drew over their armor in holy wars to distinguish themselves from their foe.

The mystical trances and twitchings, prophecies and postures of these French enthusiasts influenced the first Shaker leaders, tailors named James and Jane Wardley. They may have been Quakers, and the group that grew around them, dissidents from the Anglican and Methodist churches, were often called in derision "Shaking Quakers." Their worship began with Quakerlike silence but progressed to a crescendo of strange movements and outcries under what they called "operations of the power of God."

With the Wardleys and their expectation of "the end of all things,"
the story of the Shakers begins. It is told here in the often conflicting
words of the Shakers and of those outside the faith called by the Shakers
"the world's people," and considered in the early days "the wicked." A
minimal history laces the selections together, even as they crisscross time.

About 100 years ago a poor woman, living at Bolton-on-the-Moors, a
bleak and grimy town, in the most stony part of South Lancashire, announced that she had received a call from heaven to go about the streets of
her native town and testify for the truth. . . . Her husband, James, a tailor,
with gifts of speech, had become her first convert and expositor. These
poor people had previously belonged to the Society of Friends; in which
they had been forward in bearing testimony against oaths, against war,
against formality in worship. Living in a hard and rocky district, in the
midst of a coarse and brutal population, Jane had seen about her, from her
youth upwards, a careless church, a Papist gentry, a drunken and fanatical
crowd. Going out into the marketplace, she had declared to these people,
that the end of all things was at hand, that Christ was about to reign, that
his second appearance would be in a woman's form, as had long ago pre-
figured in the Psalms. —Hepworth Dixon, *New America*, 1867

In 1758 a young woman with spiritual promise became a follower of
the Wardleys. She was Ann Lee, a poor blacksmith's daughter, then
twenty-two. The second of eight children raised on Toad Lane in the
Manchester slums, she had worked fourteen-hour days in a factory from
an early age and never attended school. As a child she was given to visions
of "heavenly things." She later recalled that the prophets and apostles
"used to look after her very wishfully, and she wondered at it."

When the time was fully come, according to the appointment of God,
Christ was again revealed . . . in England . . . and in the person of a female.

This extraordinary female whom God had chosen . . . was ANN LEE.
She was born in the year 1736 in the town of Manchester, in England.
Her Father's name was John Lee; by trade a blacksmith. She had five
brothers . . . and two sisters. . . . Her father, though poor, was respectable
in character . . . and industrious in business. Her mother was counted a
strictly religious, and very pious woman.

Their children, as was then common with poor people, in manufacturing towns, were taught to work, instead of being sent to school. By this

means, Ann acquired a habit of industry; but was very illiterate; so that she could neither read nor write. She was employed, during her childhood and youth, in a cotton Factory, in preparing cotton for the looms, and in cutting velvet. It has been said, that she was also employed as a cutter of hatters fur. . . .

From her childhood she was the subject of religious impressions and divine manifestations. She had great light and conviction concerning the sinfulness and depravity of human nature, and especially concerning the lusts of the flesh. . . .

It is remarkable that, in early youth, she had a great abhorrence of the fleshly co-habitation of the sexes; and so great was her sense of its impurity, that she often admonished her mother against it; which coming to her father's ears, he threatened and actually attempted to whip her; upon which she threw herself into her mother's arms and clung round her to escape his strokes.   —Rufus Bishop and Seth Y. Wells, eds., *Testimonies of the Life, Character, Revelations and Doctrines of Our Ever Blessed Mother Ann Lee, and the Elders with Her: through whom the word of eternal life was opened in this day of Christ's second appearing: collected from living witnesses, by order of the ministry, in union with the church,* 1816

But not having attained that knowledge of God which she early desired, and finding no one to strengthen and assist her in the pursuit of that true holiness which she sought after, nor even to encourage her to withstand the powerful examples of a lost world (her mother having deceased while she was yet young,) she grew up in the same fallen nature with the rest of mankind.   —Calvin Green and Seth Y. Wells, *A Summary View of the Millennial Church, or United Society of Believers (commonly called Shakers),* 1823

Urged against her conscience to marry the blacksmith Abraham Stanley, or Standerin, in 1762, Ann soon felt remorse for her sexual sin. Three children died as infants, a fourth arrived as reluctantly as her mother had married and lingered only a few years. Ann agonized between her marital obligations and her spiritual longings. She battled the depravity of mankind—and Mr. Stanley.

[Abraham Stanley was] a kindly man, who loved his beef and beer, his chimney corner and seat in the village tavern.
          —Anna White and Leila S. Taylor, *Shakerism: Its Meaning and Message,* 1904

Parish record of the marriage of Ann Lees, spinster, and Abraham Standerin, blacksmith.

1

My husband doesn't intend
the pain.

Carnality is an incredible
thwarting of the spirit, of *my*
spirit.

I hardly allow myself to
feel tingling in my fingers
without shame. I avoid my
reflections in water, pewter, or tin.
The mind subdues, translates
the body's aches into the blaze
of God.

2

My gentle husband: his supple body
has the fragrance of oaks and maples.
It savors of forest ponds. His hairs
cling to his body. His back and thighs
are smooth pewter. I like the brush
and feel of his hair. But
when I see his gaze color with
lust and see his throat pulse
I pray for our guardian angel
to save us . . .   —Robert Peters, "Abraham Stanley," from *The Gift*
                to Be Simple: A Garland for Ann Lee, 1975

Ann begged Mother Jane Wardley to help her. Jane said, "James and I lodge together but we do not touch each other any more than two babes. You may return and do likewise."

In obedience to Jane, Ann said in afteryears, "I went to bed with my husband; but could not sleep, seemingly, any more than if I had been in a bed of embers. I quitted the bed in great tribulation, and continued laboring and crying to God, for the space of twelve days and nights, to know how the creation was falled, and how the restoration should take place."

But Ann was destined to still deeper sufferings, in order to prepare her for a far greater work. . . . In watchings, fastings, tears and incessant cries to God, she labored, day and night, for deliverance from the very nature of sin. And under the most severe tribulation of mind, and the most violent temptations and buffetings of the enemy, she was often in such extreme agony of soul as caused the blood to perspire through the pores of her skin. . . .

By such deep mortification and sufferings, her flesh wasted away till she became a mere skeleton. . . . Her earthly tabernacle was so reduced that she was as weak as an infant.

—Rufus Bishop and Seth Y. Wells, eds., *Testimonies of the Life, Character, Revelations and Doctrines of Mother Ann Lee, and the Elders with Her,* 1888

At last, after a long struggle of body and soul, Ann was purified of all worldly feelings. Her soul, she said, "broke forth to God," and she was "newborn." When her strength returned, her zeal increased, and she went out into the world to testify against sin. She became more active in the Wardley group, warning at the long, powerful meetings of the sins of the flesh and the worldliness of the churches. Sometimes the meetings were raided by police and the members cast into prison. Once Ann Lee, charged with "Sabbath-breaking," languished in a cold, dark cell in the Manchester jail. There she had the vision that changed the course of her life and led to her founding of an American religion. She saw the fall of man and woman in the Garden of Eden, and she felt divinely called to help them find redemption through a life without sin.

ACCOUNTS OF THE CONSTABLE, MANOR OF MANCHESTER, ENGLAND

		Shillings	Pence
July 1772	To apprehending 5 Shakers on Sunday last 24 Persons 6^d each for Assistants ...	12	
May 1773	To Ann Lees a shaker apprehended for disturbing the Congregation in the old Church detaining her in the Prison room two days 2^s maintaining her with meat & drink and her attendant 2.3. wages 2^s ...	6	3
July 1773	To attending Ann Lees two whole nights	3	

On Saturday laſt ended the Quarter Seſſions here, when the following perſons were tried, viz. John Crowder, for obtaining by falſe pretences, as much cloth as would make him a coat and waiſtcoat, the property of Mr. North, was ordered to be tranſported for 7 years. George Ware, for ſtealing wearing apparel, the property of Mr. Thomas Barlow, was ordered to be whipped. John Townley J. Jackſon, Betty Lees, and Ann Lees, (Shakers) for going into Chriſt Church, in this town, and there willfully and contemptuouſly in the time of divine ſervice, diſturbing the congregation then aſſembled at morning prayer in the ſaid church, were ſeverally fined twenty pounds each.

An extract from records of the Quarter Sessions from *Prescott's Manchester Journal*, July 31, 1773.

While she was lying in prison—old Bailey prison, on the Irwell—she said a light had shone upon her, and the Lord Jesus had stood before her in the cell, and become one with her in form and spirit. Jane Wardlaw [Wardley] had never yet pretended to have wrestled with so high a power; and when Ann Lee came out of prison, the little church of six or seven persons to whom she told her story, had raised her to the rank of Mother, in place of their foundress, the tailor's wife.

A feminine church had been now openly proclaimed in Manchester and Bolton, with Mother Ann that queen who was described by David, as that Bride of the Lamb who was seen in the Apocalypse by John. Christ had come again; not in His pomp and power, as the world expected Him, but in the flesh of a factory girl, who could neither read nor write.

—Hepworth Dixon, *New America*, 1867

After she was released from prison, Ann hurried to share her vision and the revelation of the root of evil with members of her sect. And they were joyful and believed themselves witnesses to the quiet Second Coming of the spirit of Christ to a woman, as the Wardleys had predicted. Now James and Jane Wardley stepped aside, sensing with the others the charismatic gifts Ann bore and seeing the radiance of heaven in her blue eyes. From that time Ann was called Mother. Her disciples rejoiced not in her divinity, but in her role as the first of many pure daughters and sons of God in a New Dispensation.

The Second Appearing of Christ is in his Church. Christ has come to put away sin from his people.

—(Ann Lee) *Testimonies*, 1816

From that time she never faltered in her calm assurance of knowledge that to her had been given the revelation of the Maternal Spirit of God.

—White and Taylor, *Shakerism*, 1904

We do not pretend that Jesus Christ has made his second appearing in a woman, or in any other way *literally*, nor do we believe he ever will; but we testify that there has been—not a second appearing of Christ, but a SECOND REVELATION of the Gospel first revealed by Jesus, the Christ; and that revelation was made through a woman. . . . I should like to have our testimony presented to mankind on this subject in this way.

—R. W. Pelham, *The Shaker*, Sept. 1872

By the immediate revelation of Christ, she henceforth bore an open testimony against the lustful gratifications of the flesh, as the source and foundation of human corruption. . . . She testified in the most plain and pointed manner, that no soul could follow Christ in the regeneration, while living in the works of natural generation, and wallowing in their lusts. —*Testimonies*, 1888

Those who are any way inhibited from a normal, satisfying sexual life easily make a virtue of their misfortune, and achieve a compensation by means of the so-called supernormal or superhuman exaltation of their spirituality. . . . This is accomplished by the simple trick of adopting a new and spiritual explanation for the commonplace facts. . . . The victims of this sort of self-deception may become very vehement in their denunciation of the normal relation.

> —Theodore Schroeder, "Shaker Celibacy and Salacity Psychologically Interpreted," *New York Medical Review*, 1873

After Mother was received and acknowledged as the spiritual Mother and leader of the society, the manner of worship and the exercises in their public assemblies were, singing and dancing, shaking and shouting, speaking with new tongues and prophesying, with all those various gifts of the Holy Ghost known in the Primitive Church. These gifts progressively increased until the establishment of the church in *America;* by which, those who were in the spirit of the work, were convinced . . . that it was the beginning of Christ's reign upon earth.

> —Benjamin Seth Youngs, *The Testimony of Christ's Second Appearing*, 1808

In 1770, when Ann Lee experienced the immediacy of the presence of Christ—not as one remote from man in a far-off Heaven, but as totally involved here-and-now in all of human life—she quite naturally identified the experience with the longed for *parousia* [Second Coming]. And as she bore witness to her sudden transformation in Christ, the others gathered with her themselves experienced the same transformation: they experienced Christ come again as they experienced that now their many lives were one in Union with him and with each other. And, most important, the experienced Second Coming in the Union of men and women was not terminal as had been expected, but was to be a progressive unfoldment of Christ in the continuing process of history. . . . All of Shaker life is devoted to the living and understanding of this revolutionary interpersonal experience.   —Robley Edward Whitson, *Shaker Theological Sources*, 1969

There are men and women . . . who have dared to say to one another: why not have our daily life organized on Christ's own idea? Why not begin to move the mountain of custom and convention? Perhaps Jesus' method of thought and life is the Saviour,—is Christianity! For each man to think and live on this method is perhaps the second coming of

Christ. . . . We have hitherto heard of Christ by the hearing of the ear; now let us see him, let us be him, and see what will come of that.

—(Elizabeth Peabody) "A Glimpse of Christ's Idea of Society," *The Dial*, Oct. 1841

The first full and public testimony which was borne by Mother, against the root of human depravity, was about the year 1770. And the convincing power of God which attended it, caused the formal denominations to raise and stir up tumultuous mobs, by which she was often shamefully and very cruelly treated; and was a number of times imprisoned. —Benjamin Seth Youngs, *The Testimony of Christ's Second Appearing*, 1808

The House of Correction, Hunt's Bank, where Mother Ann was imprisoned. From a drawing of 1766 by Thomas Barritt of Manchester.

What Mother Suffered at the Hands of the Wicked, on Account of Her Testimony

They put me into the stone prison, and there kept me fourteen days, where I could not straiten myself. The door was never opened through the whole time. . . . I had nothing to eat nor drink. . . .

After I had been there a while, one of the Believers came and whispered to me, through the key-hole, (for he durst not speak a loud word, for fear of being heard,) and said, *"Put your mouth to the key-hole, and I will give you drink.*" I did so, but the pipe-stem was so big that he could not get it through the key-hole: So I got no drink that night. The next night he came again, and put the stem of a pipe through, so that I could just take it into my lips; and I sucked through the pipe-stem till I felt refreshed. It was wine and milk, poured through into the bowl of the pipe. This I received as a favor of God. I had no one to look to, but God, for help. I bore testimony against their sins, and told them of their wicked lives; which was the reason of their hating me so. . . .

I was released in God's time. . . . They let me out, and I found I could walk off, spry and nimble, and felt as well as I did before. So they did not get their design accomplished: for they meant to kill me.

—(Ann Lee) *Testimonies*, 1816

The world were astonished at it, and said it must be a supernatural power that attended her; and that they did not believe it was right to confine or oppress her.   —(Father John Hocknell) *Testimonies*, 1816

I suffered great persecution, in England, on account of my faith. Sometimes the power of God operated so mightily upon me, that numbers would try to hold me still; but the more they tried to withstand the power of God, the more I was operated upon.

One of my brothers, being greatly enraged, said he was determined to overcome me. So he bought a staff, about the size of a large broom handle; and came to me, while I was sitting in my chair, and singing by the power of God. He spoke to me; but I felt no liberty to answer. *Will you not answer me?* said he.

He then beat me over my face and nose, with his staff, till one end of it was very much splinter'd. But I sensibly felt and saw the bright rays of the glory of God, pass between my face and his staff, which shielded off the blows, so that I did but just feel them. He continued beating me till he was so far spent, that he had to stop and call for drink.

While he was refreshing himself, I cried to God for his healing power. He then turned the other end of his staff, and began to beat me again. While he continued striking, I felt my breath, like healing balsam, streaming from my mouth and nose, which healed me, so that I felt no harm from his strokes; but he was out of breath, like one who had been running a race.   —(Ann Lee) *Testimonies*, 1816

While we were in England, some of us had to go twenty miles to

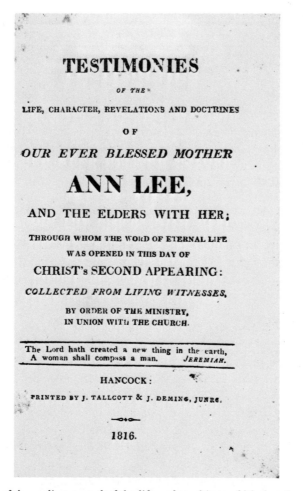

Title page of the earliest record of the life and teachings of Mother Ann and the formative events in Shaker history. Another volume of testimonies and recollections was published in 1827, and the 1816 *Testimonies* was re-edited and reissued in 1888.

meeting. We travelled a-nights, on account of the persecution. One Saturday night, while on our journey, we sat down by the side of the road to eat some victuals. While I was sitting there I saw a vision of America; and I saw a large tree, every leaf of which shone with such brightness as made it appear like a burning torch, representing the Church of Christ which will yet be established in this land. After my company had refreshed themselves, they travelled on, and led me a considerable distance before my vision ceased.   —(James Whittaker) F. W. Evans, *Shakers. Compendium of the Origin, History, Principles, Rules and Regulations, Government and Doctrines of the United Society of Believers in Christ's Second Appearing*, 1859

Since persecution, fines, or jail had been the Shakers' lot in England, Mother Ann looked to the New World to carry out her mission. She said God had a chosen people in America. She had seen them in vision and they would help her build the Millennial Church. For to Mother and her "children," the Millennium had begun.

Previous to our coming we called a meeting, and there were so many gifts (such as prophecies, revelations, visions, and dreams) in confirmation of a former revelation for us to come, that some could hardly wait for others to tell their gifts. We had a joyful meeting, and danced till morning.
                —(Ann Lee) F. W. Evans, *Shakers. Compendium*, 1859

Eight of the society followed their visionary leader to America. Among them was her rejected husband, Abraham Stanley, who soon "fell away." Others included her brother, William Lee, a handsome former Royal cavalry officer; her niece, Nancy Lee, who later defected; a pious young weaver, James Whittaker, who had fed her through the pipe in jail and who would be her successor; and one man of means, John Hocknell, who paid everyone's passage on the ship Mariah.

It was a rough voyage. Nevertheless, the Shakers went forth on deck in their way of worship—singing and dancing, shaking and shouting— and shocking Captain Smith and his crew. The captain threatened to throw them overboard if they did not stop. But when a storm arose and a leak developed, all hands were needed to pump out water that poured through a loose plank. Mother Ann assured the frightened captain that they were not doomed. "Two bright angels standing at the mast" had promised her their safe arrival in New York. As she comforted him, a towering wave slapped the plank into place, and the ship traveled soundly on its way.

The Shakers arrived in America on August 6, 1774.

Landing in New York on a Sabbath afternoon, they marched in a body up the middle of Pearl Street, until they came opposite to a house where a family by the name of Cunningham resided, who were sitting outside their door at the time. Here they halted, and Ann Lee, going up to the woman and calling her by name, said,

"I am commissioned of the Almighty God to preach the everlasting Gospel to America, and an Angel commanded me to come to this house, and to make a home for me and my people."

Without any words, she was immediately taken in and kindly cared for.　　　　　　　　—F. W. Evans, *Shaker Communism; or, Tests of Divine Inspiration*, 1871

In the latter part of the summer of 1775, Abraham Stanley was visited with a severe sickness. . . . On regaining his health . . . he began to associate with the wicked at public houses, and soon lost all sense and feeling of religion, and began to oppose Mother Ann's testimony in a very ungodly manner, and urged her to renounce it, and live in sexual cohabitation, like the rest of the world. She replied . . . she should never consent to violate her duty to God. . . .

He continued his vicious practice, instead of returning to his occupation, and left Ann to provide for herself. At length, he brought a lewd woman into the house to her, and declared that, unless she would consent to live in sexual cohabitation with him, he would take that woman for his wife. . . . He soon went off with the woman. . . . Thus ended the connection between Mother Ann and Abraham Stanley.

　　　　　　　　—Green and Wells, *A Summary View of the Millennial Church*, 1823

It is not a little astonishing that Ann Lee—or "Mother Ann," as the Society calls her—who laid the foundation of the Association in celibacy, was a married woman, and the mother of four children, all of whom died young. This latter circumstance, it is thought, soured her disposition, and led her to separate from her husband, who, however pure her motives, thought himself badly treated, and consoled himself by pursuing a course diametrically opposite to the one she had adopted in this respect.

　　　　　　　　—*Frank Leslie's Illustrated Newspaper*, Sept. 13, 1873

After passing through many trying scenes, Mother Ann and those who stood faithful with her, were collected together, and in the month of September, 1776, took up their residence in the woods of Watervliet, near Niskeyuna, about seven miles north-west of Albany. The place being then in a wilderness state, they began, with indefatigable zeal and industry, and through additional sufferings, to prepare the way for a permanent settlement, where they could enjoy their faith in peace, amid the tumults of the war, in which the country was then involved. . . . Here they occupied themselves in improving their new settlement . . . and here they held their solemn meetings, and offered up their devotions to God, full three years and a half, until the way was prepared for the commencement of their testimony to the world.

—Green and Wells, *A Summary View*, 1823

Six years after their arrival in the New World, the Shakers moved into the public eye. They "opened the testimony" on the dramatic "dark day" of May 19, 1780. The scene was awesome, as Issachar Bates, a Revolutionary War fifer who later became a prominent Shaker, described it.

That day was as dark as night—no work could be done in any house, without a candle! and the night following was as dark accordingly, although there was a well grown Moon. . . . The people were out wringing their hands, and howling, "the day of judgment is come!"—for darkness covered the whole face of the land of New England!

And what next!—Right on the back of this—On came the Shakers! and that made it darker yet—for they testified, that an end was come on them; and proved it, by their life of seperation from the course of this world; and by the wicked persecutions they endured, from this adulterous generation.

Now, wrote Issachar Bates, there was such confusion of body and mind as he had never witnessed before.

On the part of the Shakers, it was singing, dancing, shouting, shaking, speaking with tongues, turning, preaching, prophesying, & warning the world to confess their sins & turn to God; for his wrath was coming upon them. . . . On the other part it was cursing, blaspheming, mocking, railing, lying, threatening, stoning, beating with clubs & sticks, & firing pistols.   —Issachar Bates, "A Sketch of the Life and Experience of Issachar Bates," *Shaker Quarterly*, Winter 1961

Bates saw the work of God among these pure people (though he had "married a wife" and would father eleven children before he joined them). His neighbors saw the hand of the devil. They raised the cry of witchcraft.

"There is no witchcraft but sin!" said Mother Ann. But she was feared as the daughter of Satan, as well as a lewd and drunken impostor and blasphemer who pretended gifts of healing and tongues. When she preached against the flesh, she was often attacked and abused, even though she said that, "of all lustful gratifications," a faithful marriage was "the least sin." Sometimes, say early Shaker accounts, "she kneeled down and wept, and groaned and said, 'They do not know who I am, nor my calling.'"

Many conjectures were in circulation concerning these strange people, and especially concerning their female leader. By some she was strongly suspected of witchcraft, and the old accusation was in substance revived: "She casteth out devils by Beelzebub."
—Green and Wells, *A Summary View,* 1823

In the spring of 1780, I heard of a strange people living above Albany, who said they served God day and night and did not commit sin. . . . I went to see these remarkable strangers. . . . When I arrived, Mother Ann met me at the door, took hold of my hand and led me into the house. Her first salutation to me was in these words: "Being a daughter of Zion, how camest thou hither without a cap on thy head?"

She sat down in a chair, and I sat by her side. Her eyes were shut, and it appeared that her sense was withdrawn from the things of time. She sung very melodiously, and appeared very beautiful. . . . Her countenance appeared bright and shining, like an angel of glory. The graceful motions of her hands, the beautiful appearance of her countenance, and the heavenly melody of her voice, made her seem like a glorious inhabitant of the heavenly world, singing praises to God.

As I sat by the side of her, one of her hands, while in motion, frequently touched my arm; and at every touch of her hand, I instantly felt the power of God run through my whole body. . . . Could I then dispute the work of God in this woman? Nay, in no wise.
—(Thankful Barce) Seth Y. Wells and Calvin Green, *Testimonies Concerning the Character and Ministry of Mother Ann Lee and the First Witnesses of the Gospel of Christ's Second Appearing,* 1827

I have not been following a drunken woman nor a harlot. . . . Can an evil tree bring forth good fruit?
—(Hannah Cogswell) *Testimonies,* 1827

Because of their pacifism, the Shakers were also accused of being British spies.

Every one, as soon as they fall in with this new religion, immediately throw down their arms, and cry out against the means of defence made use of against the common enemy, and appear the most obstinate against all of the country. . . .

When any person goes to them to be instructed . . . they inquire of him, whether he has given his vote and money for the defence of the country? And presently tell him, it is contrary to the gospel to bear arms; saying, Christ's kingdom is not of this world: They labour to convince him, that it is a great error to have any thing to do with war and fighting.

—Rathbun, *Some Brief Hints of a Religious Scheme,*
      1781

We are firmly persuaded that those who subject themselves to the cross of Christ, and after his example, subdue those evil propensities which lead to war and strife, render more essential service to their country than they possibly could do by bearing arms and aiding war.

—*A Declaration of the Society of People (Commonly Called Shakers) Shewing Their Reasons for Refusing to Aid or Abet the Cause of War and Bloodshed, by Bearing Arms, Paying Fines, Hiring Substitutes, or Rendering Any Equivalent for Military Services,* 1815

In the summer of 1780, Mother Ann and a number of the "leading characters" were arrested and jailed for treason. Through the prison grates in Albany and Poughkeepsie, they preached to curious crowds and continued to win converts. Eventually, they were released as harmless by New York's first governor, George Clinton, and they emerged better known than before.

As *David Darrow* was on the way between *Lebanon* and *Albany,* with a flock of sheep, which he was driving to *Water-vliet,* he was followed by a company of evil-minded men, who pretended to have authority to arrest him. Accordingly, they brought him back, with his sheep, to *Lebanon,* and had him before the court, under pretence of treason. But finding no just ground of accusation against him, to answer their purpose, these hungry wolves, after dividing the sheep among them, sent their owner, (accompanied by *Joseph Meacham*) under guard, to be tried by the Commissioners at *Albany*.

—Benjamin Seth Youngs, *The Testimony of Christ's Second Appearing*, 1808

Having received Information that Daniel Green, Joseph Potter and David Darrow were collecting a Number of Sheep in King's District with an intention of driving them to the westward and as there is the greatest reason to suppose from their disaffection to the American Cause that they mean to convey them to the Enemy or at least bring them so near the Frontiers that the enemy may with safety take them that therefore [a Justice of the Peace informs us] he had caused them to be apprehended & conveyed to us.... David Darrow on his examination denying the Authority of this Board and all Civil Jurisdiction in this State and pretending that by his religious principles he is restrained from taking up Arms in defence of the Country and that he does not intend to do any kind of Military duty whatsoever nor does not in any instance intend to abide by the Laws of this State, and John Hocknear [Hocknell] of Nistageune [Niskayuna] and David Macham [Meacham] of New Lebanon ... acknowledging a Concurrence of Sentiment with him and declaring that it was their determined Resolution never to take up arms and to dissuade others from doing the same and as such principles at the present day are highly pernicious and of destructive tendency to the Freedom & Independence of the United States of America—

It is therefore resolved that the said David Darrow, John Hocknear and Joseph Macham stand severally committed.

—Victor Hugo Paltsits, ed., *Minutes of the Commissioners for Detecting and Defeating Conspiracies in the State of New York, Albany County Sessions, 1778–1781*, 1909

Albany Nov'r 19th 1780

D'r Sir, The Bearer William Lees, of the Denomination of shaking Quakers, who has been confined on suspision by the Commissioners here and has been inlarged, has made application to me respecting his sister, Ann Standivin, who, he informs me, has been confined some time past in or near Pughkeepsie, on a similar account.

You are better acquainted with the circumstances relating to her, than I can be; you can best determine what is to be done with her, and if nothing material has been proven against her, I shou'd suppose she may

The Baltus Van Kleek house in Poughkeepsie, where Mother Ann and Mary Partington were held prisoner when the Shakers were accused of being British spies. From an 1835 sketch by Benson J. Lossing in his *Pictorial Field Book of the Revolution*, 1859.

[be] released agreeable to their requisition. . . . I am, with perfect Esteem, Dear Brother, yours sincerely

JAMES CLINTON

—Letter to Governor George Clinton from Lieutenant General James Clinton, *Public Papers of George Clinton, First Governor of New York*, 1902

Jonathan Slosson received a measure of faith and confessed his sins, while Mother was at Poughkeepsie; but was bound in his affections to a young woman, who was in a similar condition: for which reason neither of them were able to gain any gospel strength. . . . Jonathan, having never seen Mother, went to Watervliet to see her, just after she returned from Poughkeepsie.

Shortly after he entered the house, Mother came into the room. Jonathan, with his back to the fire and the skirts of his coat drawn forward, asked, "How does Mother do?" To which she replied, "if I am your Mother, young man, I'll teach you to turn your face to the fire, not your back: for heating your backside by the fire enrages lust. It shows ill breeding and bad behavior, for people to stand heating their backsides by the fire." Jonathan received the admonition, and took his seat facing the fire.

Mother then spoke to him as follows: "God will bring down the haughtiness of man, and stain the pride of all flesh. Jonathan, do let that woman alone. . . . God will break in pieces the man and maid. If you want to marry, you may marry the Lord Jesus Christ. He is my husband, and in him I trust."

After a little pause, she said, "I see the glory of God, both in visions and revelations! I hear the angels sing! I see the dead arise and come to judgment!" Turning to Jonathan, she said, "Jonathan Slosson, forsake your lust and that woman, and you shall be my son. The marriage of the flesh is a covenant with death, and an agreement with hell; forsake it and be my son. I have seen you and all your father's family in the visions of God." —Bishop and Wells, *Testimonies*, 1816

After Mother Ann and her companions were released from prison, they returned to Watervliet . . . and were constantly visited by those who had embraced the testimony, and also by many others. . . . And tho many came from motives of curiosity; yet no honest soul, who . . . viewed the wonderful operations of the power of God which prevailed in their meetings, could go away without a full conviction that the work of God was among them. But they were often afflicted with mockers and scoffers . . . such were ever ready . . . to fix the stamp of evil upon whatever they saw among the people. Hence arose those numerous evil reports which have been so industriously circulated, by reprobate characters, to the present day. —Green and Wells, *A Summary View of the Millennial Church*, 1823

In May of 1781, Mother Ann and the Elders set out on a missionary trip. For more than two years they traveled about New England and New York, visiting thirty-six towns and hamlets where Shaker converts lived. Everywhere they faced what William Dean Howells called "the foolish mob which helps to establish each new religion."

For their headquarters they paid $568.48 for the mysterious Square House in Harvard, Massachusetts, where another prophet had recently lived and died. Shadrach Ireland had claimed to be immortal. After his death and failure to rise "on the third day," many of his disillusioned disciples "embraced the testimony" of Mother Ann.

From the Square House, Mother Ann and the Elders made side trips to nearby villages. Along their way they were cruelly persecuted, and nowhere with more violence than in Petersham, Massachusetts. There, as elsewhere, many people of "the world" came to attend their meetings.

Among them was "a company of lewd fellows who stiled themselves the Blackguard *Committee."*

As their object was to seize Mother, the candles had been previously concealed to prevent them finding her. But this did not hinder them: they seized fire-brands and searched the house, and at length found her in a bed-room. They immediately seized her by the feet, and inhumanly dragged her, feet foremost, out of the house, and threw her into a sleigh, with as little ceremony as they would the dead carcase of a beast, and drove off, committing at the same time, acts of inhumanity and indecency which even savages would be ashamed of.

In the struggle with these inhuman wretches, she lost her cap and handkerchief, and otherwise had her clothes torn in a shameful manner. Their pretence was to find out whether she was a woman or not. In this situation in a cold winter's night, they drove nearly three miles to Samuel Peckham's tavern, near Petersham meeting house.

Father William, feeling great concern for Mother's safety, he and David Hammond, followed the sleigh. He told the ruffians that she was his sister, and he would follow her; and attempting to hold on by the hind part of the sleigh, they gave him many blows with the butts of their sleigh-whips. He and David, however, followed to the aforementioned tavern. Elder James, being badly wounded, was not able to follow them.

It appears from information that Samuel Peckham, who was a captain of militia, had previously agreed with the ruffians who seized Mother, to give them as much rum as they would drink, upon condition that they would bring her to his house. After their arrival, Father William and David Hammond remonstrated against the ungodliness and brutality of their behavior. David represented to them the unlawfulness of such conduct, and how they had exposed themselves to the penalties of the law.

Being, by this time, ashamed of their conduct, and fearful of the consequences, they promised to release Mother, upon condition that David would sign an obligation not to prosecute them. . . .

This being done, they released Mother, and some time in the night, some of them brought her, and those with her, back to David Hammond's. She came in, singing for joy, that she was again restored to her children. . . .

Of those who persecuted Mother and the Elders in Petersham, we will remark, that Samuel Peckham, captain of militia, to whose house Mother was carried, run out his interest, was reduced to poverty, and obliged to leave the town.... Doctor Bridge undertook to build a large house, and having got the frame up, there came a violent whirlwind, and rent it from the foundation....

Jonathan Hunter had his house consumed by fire, and came to poverty.... Aaron Fisk was killed by the falling of a tree. Jonathan Grout came to nothing, and many others.

—*Testimonies*, 1816

From Petersham history come these recollections:

About the year 1783, the singular sect called Shakers made their appearance here. Some persons of substance joined them, and large numbers attended their meetings.... Their proceedings were scarcely better than the orgies of Pandemonium. So excited was the opposition at length aroused against them ... that a mob collected about their place of resort, and they were violently assaulted. Mother Ann Lee is said to have fought valiantly against the assailants in person. The Shakers, though at one time considerably numerous in the vicinity, obtained no permanent foothold in Petersham.... (One of your aged citizens ... remembers "when there was more Shaker travel by his house, than all the present travel!")

—*An Address Delivered in Petersham, Massachusetts,*
July 4, 1854, in Commemoration of That Town, by
Edmund B. Willson, 1855

When I was about 17 years of age, the people called Shaking Quakers came into our neighborhood (1783). One family with whom I was quite intimate, joined that society; the man was possessed of handsome property, had a large house so there they held their meetings. People flocked to hear the new and strange religion, and I went among the rest a few times. One time in particular the woman called the Elect Lady or Mother of the Church and a number of the Elders who came from Ireland were there. More than 200 gathered together that day and their exercise was reading in the Bible, explaining and bringing proof in support of all they did. They professed to work miracles, speak in unknown tongues which I heard a number of them attempt.

—Diary of Sarah How, in Mabel Cook Coolidge, *The*
History of Petersham, 1675–1947, 1948

The famous matron known as "The Elect Lady" ... is generally attended by a number of her Elders. The select company that attends her are emphatically called "The Church." She frequently removes from town to town, and constantly sends forth "laborers" as she calls them, to preach and teach her religion to the world. In some towns mobs have abused and insulted them; this they call persecution, and a proof of their being the true followers of that religion which is not of this world.

—William Plumer (1783), "The Original Shaker Communities in New England," edited by F. B. Sanborn from the Plumer Papers, *New England Magazine*, 1900. (Plumer was later governor of New Hampshire and U.S. senator.)

After Daniel Wood had confessed his sins before Mother and the Elders, she said, "Daniel, your faith is like the faith of John the Baptist, the forerunner of Christ. You must go and prepare the way of the Lord; go and preach the gospel to the ends of the earth. Go and testify your faith to those that you call brethren."

—*Testimonies*, 1816

Incidents Related by Jemima Blanchard of Her Experience & Intercourse with Mother and the Elders

Daniel Wood (says Sister Jemima) was the first person from whom I obtained any knowledge respecting the Believers. He came to my Father's house one evening when I was there on a visit (I lived at Isaac Willards). He said they confessed their sins, and were operated upon by the power of God. My brother Joseph and myself were all the children who were there, the rest being out on an evening visit.

I listened to the conversation as long as I could bear it, it affected my feelings so, and then went out. Joseph soon followed me and we talked about it together. He said he would take me up to see them; but I did not agree to this, yet there was always a fear in my mind after this, that they were the only people of God.

Joseph seemed to feel it more than I did. Daniel said he did not know but they would come here, and I feared it. This was in the winter.

The next April or May Joseph came home and told me he had heard that they were coming, and that he intended to go to sea to get away from them. I tried to disuade him but to no purpose. I never saw him afterwards. The next June I went to Hollistown to work for a family by the name of Cutler. My friends were anxious to have me go, I suspect, for fear

I should get taken in with the Shakers, and I was willing to get away for the same reason.

While I was there, Daniel Wood visited Cutler: I was at that time absent with a neighbor of his. . . . And being afraid myself to see Daniel I staid away. When I returned to Cutler's, I urged him to go and see the Shakers; his wife joined me and we persuaded him to go.

On his return he spoke favorably of the people. . . . We prevailed on him to go again and carry us.

We went first to Zacceus Stephen's in Harvard, where I saw some who had set out. . . . They appeared so solemn and Heavenly, that it struck my feeling very much. . . . I looked at them with wonder, and saw the power of God visible on their faces, and even on the clothes of the believers. It looked perfectly white and run in veins. I noticed it mostly on those young persons whom I knew. . . .

In the morning I started off alone to go to the Square House, passed by Jeremiah Willards, where I was well acquainted. . . . I went in and found them all Believers. They spoke kindly to me, yet they seemed so solemn and strange that I soon came out, and went on to Isaac Willard's where I used to live. Here I found the same change in the appearance of the family yet they looked pleasant, and were kind to me, said they were glad I had come and asked if I was going to meeting etc.

I soon left them and thought I would go and see for myself, what had wrought such a change in all my acquaintance.

Sister Jemima found two of her friends, Deliverance and Beulah Cooper, working in the kitchen of the Square House. There she also saw Mother Ann.

Mother was in the kitchen washing herself. She turned and looked at me with such a pleasant heavenly countenance, that it absorbed my whole soul, so that I scarcely heard what my companions said to me. She took me by the arm and said, "Will thou be a Daughter of Zion, and be searched as Jerusalem with candles?" I answered not for I knew not what to say. Her voice seemed to me like the voice of God.

She then took me into meeting, and it seemed all day that her eyes were upon me, and that she could see thro me. . . .

The young women before mentioned got dinner for us, and when it came to the table they informed me that it was their manner to kneel before eating and insisted upon my uniting with them: but I objected saying that I did not want any dinner . . . there being many of the world looking on with countenance expressive of scorn and contempt. Mother then came to me and said, It is becoming in all people to render thanks to God. This bound my feelings so that I kneeled with her. . . .

It was not my intention to stay over night, but . . . Mother told Cutler's wife she had better stay and let me visit my acquaintance so we consented and staid. In the morning we met Mother in the hall; she spoke very lovingly to us, and invited us to stay to breakfast but Cutler's wife excused herself by saying, We must be a making our visit as fast as we can etc.

Mother said "Why do you want to get this young woman away? You cannot help her soul to God. All we want is to help her soul to God; and you cannot do this, for you have not found Him yourself." She took offence and went away charging me to come soon. I told her I would, and that I would be to my father's to breakfast. As soon as Mother left me I went into the kitchen and took my leave of my acquaintance, leaving my compliments for Mother with them, and then made the best of my way out of the house and hastened homeward. . . .

I had gone about as far as where the first house now stands when I distinctly heard Mother come down stairs, go into the kitchen and say, "Where is that young woman." They replied "She is gone." "Gone!" said Mother, "what did you let her go for? Go and call her back, tell her she had not bid me farewell yet; and it was *I* that invited her to stay and she has not treated me with good manners."

I stopped as it were voluntarily and turned around, saw Mother standing on the door steps and the young women coming after me. They told me what Mother had said and I went back to excuse myself for I abhored the idea of treating any one with ill manners & especially such a beautiful and Godlike woman as Mother.

I told her I could not stay, that I liked them very much but that I could not be like them . . . that perhaps I should come again—

Mother said "Oh, oh, nay, you did not mean to come again." I knew this was my very thoughts, so I knew not what to say, but still kept excusing myself. . . . I kept trying to get my arm away, but as soon as I did this she would take me by the other, while she advanced still nearer to the house.

When we got to the door I resisted going in, as much as I could civilly; and after I got in I kept striving to get away but Mother would have another and another word to say, and I kept speaking in behalf of the people, how well I liked them, and how well they had done by me, meaning every sentence should be the last, until Mother said don't you want the people of God to pray for you? I replied that I did.

In an instant her arms were around my waist, and we were both on our knees. I shook so that the windows clattered, but I did not know what it was for some moments.

Mother said, "James, did I not tell you that the time had come that we must go into the highways and hedges and compel them to come in?"

After this I thought no more of going home, being exercised, all most constantly by the power of God for many days.

Cutler and his wife staid at my father's about a week to see if I would not return; then they came to the Square house to see if they could not get me; and as I was laboring by the east door, Cutler's wife catched me by the clothes, and told me that Cutler wanted to speak with me.... So I went with her as far as the South door, when the Believers saw me, and a company came out and took me into the house while another company raised a war and drove them off. It was thought there was a plan laid to take me away by force.

Jemima stayed at the Square House for about a month, attending the meetings and sometimes helping out in the kitchen. There were meetings most of the time until one or two in the morning, she said, except for meals.

At one time, Sister Jemima recalled, in the winter, there were so many at the meeting that the brethren went out into the woods to cut timber to prop up the meeting-room floor. Mother Ann had all the children under fourteen sent home. Then she and some of the young sisters next to her went out into the dooryard, and, said Sister Jemima, "we labored around there with her." They flocked out after Mother Ann until there was more than enough room in the house.

When I had been there about a month I spoke of my home at Isaac Willard's. There was so much company all the time at the Square House, that I could not feel at home in any place except in meeting or the kitchen. Mother told me they would labor upon it, and they concluded I might go.

So I went home; but I used to go to meeting every night. I do not think I was left home but one night, and then Mother told Jeremiah he must not do it again, as my brothers (who were very much opposed) might come and take me away by force....

The next winter I believed, my Brother went to Jeremiah Willards and told him that my Mother was sick and wanted to see me. It was thought best for me to go. . . . I found Cutler there, my Mother was knitting. He tried to persuade me to go home with him, said his wife could not be pacified without trying once more to get me. He was a minister and wealthy. They had often talked to me of the property, as if it was as much mine as theirs, if I would only stay with them;

And now he brot up all his arguments afresh. My relations, except my Mother were very much against me, but I stood against them all. I had a real gift to speak to Cutler . . . and when I had done speaking, I left the house immediately.

I heard from Cutler several times afterwards, and learned that he run out all his property and became poor, which seemed like a real judgment as there was no apparent cause for it.

> —Unpublished manuscript, "Sayings of Mother Ann and the First Elders, Gathered from Different Individuals at Harvard and Shirley Who Were Eye and Ear Witnesses, the Divine Word of God, Revealed thro Them at Different Times and in Various Places," Collected Together by Roxalana L. Grosvenor, 1845 (Case Memorial Library, Hartford Seminary Foundation)

Now the Square House was full to overflowing and hundreds camped in the woods near by. The present village street was then a mere wood road, but soon it bore the imprint of innumerable feet as day and night the brethren and sisters would go forth in the worship of God. Songs of Zion . . . shouts of joy reverberated from hill to hill. Much care fell upon Mother Ann and the Elders, and in an extract from one of the old journals a quaint description of it is given by Sister Jemima Blanchard to Eldress Roxalana Grosvenor who reports it:-

"At a time when Mother and the Elders were greatly pressed with company and had very heavy labors so that they had slept very little for some weeks, Jemima saw Father James going to the barn. Mother called him and told him of some labors she wished to have him perform. Father said, 'This is the third time I have started to go to the barn and lie down.' Mother replied, 'James, you are faithful, you shall have rest, but you cannot have it now.'"

"Sister Jemima once heard Mother reprove one of the brethren for going without his victuals for the sake of mortification and asked where he got his gift [inspiration]. She said Mother taught them to eat as much as they needed for the support of the body, and then serve God by the

The Square House, remodelled, is probably the second building from the left in the upper left corner of this "Plan of the First Family, Harvard" by George Kendall (1836). Courtesy of Fruitlands Museums, Harvard, Massachusetts.

strength of it. She always showed a concern that all should have what they needed. She took special care of Jemima in this respect as she was bashful, and had but little appetite."

> —Clara Endicott Sears, *Gleanings from Old Shaker Journals*, 1916

At Harvard in April of 1783, Mother Ann was warned in a vision a few days before of a "new and trying scene, which overtook them about the first of June. Mother said to Elder James, 'There is going to be a great persecution; for I saw a man come and look in at the window, and he was as black as a negro.'"

Sarah Turner . . . had married a deaf and dumb man of Leominster, by the name of Jude Carter. Sarah had embraced the testimony of the gospel, and her husband, appearing friendly and pliable, she had labored to gain his feelings to the way of God, and had induced him, by signs, to make some confession of his sins.

Being at Elijah Wild's, in Shirley, in company with her husband, and wishing to have him conform to the faith and practice of Believers, she endeavored to prevail with him to have his hair cut, and to sell his silver buckles, to buy things more necessary. He replied, by signs, that if he would have his hair cut, people would laugh at him, and, as to his buckles, other people wore buckles, as well as he.

The next day they went together to the Boston market, for the purpose of getting some family necessaries; and Sarah prevailed with her husband to sell his buckles, and buy something more necessary. On their return they came to Nathan Kendal's, in Woburn, where she also prevailed with him to have his hair cut; but, Jude not being willing to have it cut so short as some, and seeing a man the cut of whose hair suited him, he consented to have it cut like that man's, which was accordingly done.

Jude appeared much pleased with his new friends, and passed the time in much harmony till bed time, when he strenuously insisted on lying with his wife. This being utterly inadmissible in a family of Believers, was as strenuously opposed. Being highly offended with this treatment, he set off early the next morning, for home, and left his wife, who, afterward, followed on, with some other company. In passing through Harvard, Jude made a grievous complaint, by signs, that the Shakers had robbed him of his silver buckles, cut off his hair, and got away his wife.

The motions and gestures of this deaf and dumb man furnished a sufficient occasion, for those who were always watching for occasion, to persecute, without inquiring into the true state of the matter. Secret measures were now taken to raise a mob, of which the Believers had no knowledge, till the mob appeared. This tumultuous assembly from Harvard, came to Elijah Wild's, in Shirley, on Sabbath evening, June 1st, 1783, and beset the house at every door and window, and forbade any person going in or out.

Mother and the Elders, having very early that morning gone from Harvard to Shirley, were at this time in the house, with many other Believers, who had assembled there, and who were, at this time, in the worship of God. The leaders of the mob were . . . all of Harvard, with a considerable company of the baser sort from Harvard, Roxbury, and Bolton. Like the men of Sodom, they attempted to enter the house by pressing hard against the door; but were prevented, by the Brethren within. . . .

One of the sisters . . . obtained liberty to return home to her young child. Having got home, she immediately dispatched a messenger to ac-

A deaf and dumb man's complaint that the Shakers cut his hair and refused to let him lie with his wife was the excuse for a mob to attack the Believers at Elijah Wild's house in Shirley, Massachusetts. A modern painting of the 1783 scene by Michigan naïve artist Kathy Jakobsen, 1978. Oil on canvas, 16″ × 20″. Courtesy of Jay Johnson, America's Folk Heritage Gallery.

quaint the Grand Juryman of the town, of their situation. The mob continued to surround the house all night, with much railing and savage behavior; but committed no personal injury till next morning.

Mother said, "We must feed our enemies, and so heap coals of fire upon their heads." Four came in and ate breakfast. Elijah Wild carried bread and cheese to the mob outside.

After this Elder James said, "I must go and speak the word of the Lord to them." . . . The mob broke forth in a rage, and seized Elder James by the collar and arms . . . he would have been choked to death, had not one of the Brethren unclinched the ruffian's hands.

About this time . . . the Grand Juryman of the town, and a Peace Officer, arrived, who immediately commanded the peace, and ordered the mob to desist from troubling the people . . . but still the tumult continued, and the mob continued to increase from Harvard. A number of the Brethren and sisters, being at this time in the street, kneeled down to pray, at which some of these ungodly ruffians, who were on horseback, attempted to ride over them, but were not able.

The leaders of the mob wanted to carry off Mother and the Elders, but they agreed to leave Mother if William Lee and James Whittaker would go with them to Harvard. They promised no one would be hurt. The elders set off with them, followed by some of the Believers.

The Elders, being mounted on good horses, outrode the mob, and arrived at Jeremiah Willard's before them. Jeremiah, who then professed the faith, sat in the door of his house to keep the mob from entering. . . . But . . . they violently drew him, feet foremost, out of the house, with his head thumping against the steps. . . . They then broke into the chamber, and furiously dragged the Elders out, and carried them back about half a mile, where they met the main body of the mob.

Here they made a stand to execute their savage designs, and said, "James Whittaker, and William Lee, should be tied to a tree, and whipped."

But first they threw down on the ground the two brothers who had followed the Elders. They held them down

until their barbarous deed was accomplished. They then seized Elder James, tied him to a limb of a tree, near the road, cut some sticks, and . . . began the cruel work, and continued beating and scourging till his back was all in a gore of blood, and the flesh bruised to a jelly. They then untied him, and seized Father William Lee; but he chose to kneel down and be whipped, therefore they did not tie him; but began to whip him as he stood on his knees. Notwithstanding the severity of the scourging which Elder James had already received, he immediately leaped upon Father William's back, Bethiah Willard, who had followed from Jeremiah's, leaped upon Elder James' back; others . . . followed the same example. . . . But . . . those who attempted to manifest their love and charity in this manner, were inhumanly beaten without mercy.

Mother Ann, standing in Elijah Wild's garden, at Shirley, seven miles away, said to Hannah Kendal, "The Elders are in great tribulation, for I hear Elder William's soul cry to Heaven."

After the mob left the ground, the Elders, and those few Believers with them, retired a few rods, and all kneeled down; and Elder James had a new song of praise put into his mouth, which he sung on the spot, as he was kneeling. They ... returned to Shirley the same evening, and were received by Mother and the Elders, with great joy.

"Did they abuse you, James?" said Mother. "I will show you, Mother," said James, and kneeling before her, he ... showed his wounded back, which was covered with blood.... When they came to wash, and dress it, they found his flesh black and blue from his shoulders to his waistband, and in many places, bruised to a jelly, as though it had been beaten with a club....

Mother Ann and the Elders, with all the Brethren and Sisters, then kneeled down and prayed to God, to forgive their bloody persecutors.... "James, this is the life of the gospel,'" said Mother. After this Mother and the Elders were very joyful, and thankful that they were worthy to suffer persecution for Christ's sake....

Such were the transactions of a malicious and cruel mob, raised under the pretense of avenging the alleged abuse to a deaf and dumb man.

—*Testimonies*, 1888

It is not now more than six months ... since in company with Mother and my dear brethren, the other Elders, I returned off an itinerant ministry of somewhat more than three years continuance, during which time I faithfully preached the gospel; and for it I have been imprisoned, beaten, mocked, calumniated, etc., and have been pursued by cruel and desperate mobs, night and day. And once last summer past, I was whipped in the most cruel manner, being stripped naked, (to the waist,) and my two hands tied up, being stretched above my head. However God hath preserved me in a wonderful manner....

The sound of the gospel hath been preached far and wide, and thousands of people have obeyed the gospel call. Considering we hold up a whole cross to men, even to deny themselves of the very thoughts of sensual gratifications of every kind ... it is wonderful that such multitudes have gathered ... into obedience.

I now live with my kind Mother in Israel, Ann Lee, formerly so called, and the rest, and have all things in common with others that have come in to us, and we live in great joy, love, and union.

—James Whittaker, from a letter to his parents and friends in England, Feb. 10, 1784

A marble shaft in the woods marks the spot where Father William Lee and Father James Whittaker were beaten in Harvard, Massachusetts. A passing Shaker places a stone on the cairn in their memory. Photograph, courtesy of the Fruitlands Museums.

A year after the Shaker leaders returned to Niskayuna from their long journey, Mother Ann's brother William, once her strongest protector, died. Mother Ann herself was worn out by years of persecution and exertion. She worried about the still scattered state of the Believers, and she prophesied:

The time will come when the church will be gathered into order; but not until after my decease. . . . After my departure there will come grievous wolves, who will destroy many of the flock.

It will not be my lot, nor the lot of any who came with me from England, to gather and build up the church; but it will be the lot of Joseph Meacham and others. . . . Joseph Meacham is my first-born son in America; he will gather the church into order; but I shall not live to see it.

Mother Ann soon followed her brother to rest. In a final vision she saw him coming to fetch her in a "glorious chariot." Father John Hock-

nell, who had financed the Shakers' voyage to America, was said to have witnessed her exodus on September 8, 1784. He saw her "wafted away" in a golden chariot drawn by four white horses.

Ann Lee was only forty-eight when she died, yet her accomplishment was great. In a few years' time she had inspired thousands of men and women to become brothers and sisters in a new unselfish relationship and way of life. The gospel of Christ's second appearing in the spirit of the Shaker Church had indeed swept "like wild fire" even farther than apostate Valentine Rathbun had warned. It had seared through eastern New York, into Massachusetts and Connecticut, and up to New Hampshire and Maine.

Greater power will never be on the earth than now is.

> —(Father James Whittaker) Roxalana L. Grosvenor, "Sayings of Mother Ann and the First Elders," 1845

Sister Jemima told me she had turned from the Square House to the South House passing over fences or whatever came in her way without touching them, or making the least effort to clear them; that she would, at times, be entirely supported by the power, without touching any material thing.

> —Roxalana L. Grosvenor, "Sayings of Mother Ann," 1845

They say their number in America is now near 7,000.

> —William Plumer (1783), "The Original Shaker Communities in New England," *New England Magazine,* 1900

Those who often saw frenzied women "whirling" along the public road for long distances, and dancing with rhythmic shaking of heads, hands and arms dignified into a ceremonial of worship, were tempted to jeering comment and ridicule; and when they saw happy homes broken up, families impoverished, the acutely nervous made insane, affianced girls frightened into rejection of their sweethearts, it is hardly to be thought strange that sometimes in wrath they sought to scourge out of town the promoters of such distractions.

> —Henry Stedman Nourse, *History of the Town of Harvard, Massachusetts,* 1894

Many of the new converts, as might be expected, were filled with great power and zeal; but for the want of experience and understanding, they were not able, at all times, to exercise their zeal according to the dictates of wisdom. Many times they exhibited a degree of wildness and enthusiasm in their conduct, which, to the beholders, appeared like the greatest inconsistency and delusion, and especially to such as trusted in the forms of religion, while they were ignorant of its internal power. To the natural man, such views of a new and singular manifestation of religion, were very natural; especially as its light and testimony struck at the very root and foundation of the fallen nature of man. . . .

The work was all new to those who embraced it, and the leaders being few in number, and the work extensive, irregularities could not always be foreseen nor prevented.

—Green and Wells, *A Summary View*, 1823

About four years she labour'd
With the attentive throng,
Confirm'd the young believers,
And help'd their souls along.
At last she clos'd her labour,
And vanish'd out of sight,
And left the Church increasing,
In the pure gospel light.

How much are they deceived,
Who think that Mother's dead!
She lives among her offspring,.
Who just begin to spread;
And in her outward order,
There's one supplies her room,
And still the name of *Mother*,
Is like a sweet perfume.

—Seth Y. Wells, ed., from "Mother," Hymn II, Part II, *Millennial Praises*, 1813 (first Shaker hymnbook)

From the revealing and the endowment of the Divine Maternal Spirit that rested upon Ann Lee to the present time, Shaker faith looks to see the anointing of the Mother Spirit rest upon each successive occupant of the office of leader. The Visible Head is regarded as a sacred vessel to be filled with the unction of the Mother Spirit; not an incarnation of God to be worshipped, but a human being called to be the channel of divine life to all in her charge. The degree of endowment must perforce depend upon the capacity of the vessel, but its abiding richness is manifest in the long line of noble and saintly women, who, in each society and family, have borne the name and fulfilled the functions of Eldress and Mother.

—Anna White, *The Motherhood of God*, 1904

Departed this life, at Nisquenia, Sept. 7, Mrs. Lee, known by the appellation of the *Elect Lady*, or *Mother of Zion*, and head of that people called Shakers. Her funeral is to be attended this day.

—*Albany Gazette*, Sept. 9, 1784

Mother Ann's grave in the Shaker cemetery, now bordered by Heritage Park, a sports stadium, in the Town of Colonie, New York. Photograph ca. 1930, courtesy of the New York State Museum.

When I heard of Mother's decease I felt so distressed and sorrow-stricken that I thought it was impossible for me to live. I retired in secret and lay prostrate upon the floor, expecting to breathe out my soul in sorrow—for the more I tried to refrain the deeper my sorrow became. This continued without cessation, until I saw the appearance of Mother Ann, about the size of a child three years old. This beautiful messenger held something in each hand that appeared like a wing which she waved inward, and advancing toward me said: "Hush! Hush!" This took away my sorrow, so that I was able to attend to my duty.

—(Sister Jemima Blanchard) Clara Endicott Sears, *Gleanings from Old Shaker Journals*, 1916

In her was first wrought the complete redemption of the female; and through her ministration a way was opened for the restoration of the female character to its proper lot and dignity, from which it had been degraded by the transgression of the first woman.

—Green and Wells, *A Summary View*, 1823

A poor, illiterate, uneducated factory woman has confounded the wisdom of all *men*—reformers, legislators, & scholars, who have come to nothing as promoters of human happiness.

—Elder Frederick W. Evans to Count Leo Tolstoy, 1891

Out of thee, O England, shall a bright star arise, whose light and voice shall make *the heavens* to quake and knock under with submission to the blessed Jesus.   —Christopher Love, 1618–1651. (Elder Frederick Evans applied this prophecy to Mother Ann.)

Ann Lee arose in the dawning of the morning and took upon herself the spirit of Christ, the same spirit that baptised the man Jesus. He was the first among many Brethren. She is the first among many Sisters. . . .

The women of the nations are following in her wake, asserting themselves equal to their brothers, both in the sciences and governments. They will acknowledge her and confess her name when they find out the spirit that is leading them. —Sister Aurelia Mace to Count Leo Tolstoy, 1891

It has been asserted by some writers that she styled herself the *Elect Lady;* but this is a groundless charge: that title was given her by her enemies in derision.   —Green and Wells, *A Summary View*, 1823

Mother was boldly pronounced by them to be immortal. But after *she was taken out of their sight in the ordinary way of all living,* this magnificent story, of which she was undoubtedly the author, was told no more. Had Christ uttered such a declaration concerning himself and it had terminated in the same manner, it would have ruined all his pretensions in a moment. But this event has never disturbed the faith of the Shakers at all. Of her they plainly think as favorably as if she had been actually immortal.   —Timothy Dwight, *Travels in New-England and New-York,* 1821

Mother Ann Lee, in her personal appearance, was a woman rather below the common stature of woman; thick set, but straight and otherwise well proportioned and regular in form and features. Her complexion was light and fair, and her eyes were blue, but keen and penetrating. . . . Her manners were plain, simple and easy; yet she possessed a certain dignity of appearance that inspired confidence and commanded respect. By many of the world, who saw her without prejudice, she was called beautiful; and to her faithful children, she appeared to possess a degree of dignified beauty and heavenly love, which they had never before discovered among mortals.   —Green and Wells, *A Summary View,* 1823

When Mother first came here, she had twisted strings in her cap, yet she looked very neat. —(Jemima Blanchard) Roxalana L. Grosvenor, "Sayings of Mother Ann and the First Elders," 1845

In the presence of Timothy Hubbard, Mother was overshadowed with the power of God. She stood erect on the floor for the space of an hour. Her countenance was angelic, and she seemed to notice nothing of the things of time. She sung, chiefly in unknown tongues.
—*Testimonies,* 1816

Sarah Barber of New Lebanon, in the spring of the year 1784, saw Mother in vision. She saw a bright spot on the top of her head, which gradually spread all over her, till she seemed to be a clear glory, and it seemed as though God . . . dwelt in her. Sarah afterward related the vision to Mother, and Mother said, "It is a great gift of God. I have nothing in me, to my knowledge, but what is of God. If I have, I do not know it."
—*Testimonies,* 1816

Once Mother Ann reproved the men and brethren for their "hard-

ness of heart and unbelief in the second appearance of Christ." She spoke of the unbelieving Jews, in his first appearing.

Even his own disciples . . . would not believe that he had risen, because he appeared first to a woman! So great was their unbelief, that the words of Mary seemed to them like idle tales! His appearing first to a woman, showed that his second appearing would be in a woman!

—*Testimonies*, 1816

I will tell you a vision I saw of myself. I saw a great gulf, fixed between God and the world of mankind; and I had two great wings given to me; and my work was to go up that gulf and fan it away. . . . And, speaking in a very joyful manner, she said, I did go up the gulf with my two great wings, and did fan it away . . . so that poor lost souls could come to God.   —(Mother Ann) *Testimonies*, 1816

If I owned the whole world, I would turn it all into joyousness; I would not say to the poor, "Be ye warmed, and be ye clothed," without giving them wherewithal to do it.

—(Mother Ann) *Testimonies*, 1816

As I was tossing—tumbling—rolling—jumping—throwing myself against the wall—the chimney—the floor—the chairs, in fact everything that did not keep out of the way, I felt that my blood was boiling, and every bone in my body was being torn asunder, my flesh pinched with hot irons, and every hair on my head were stinging reptiles. I had laid me down to die, when Mother Ann came along, saying, "Why, Abijah, there is some of the worst looking spirits on your shoulder I ever saw in my life."

I crawled along and laid me down at her feet and prayed her in mercy to help me; she raised me up and made a few resolute passes from my head to my feet, with her hands, and I was relieved at once,—and I have never doubted since. That . . . was the power of God in Mother.

—(Abijah Worster) Anon., *Extract from an Unpublished Manuscript on Shaker History*, 1850

It is often said, "The Shakers do not worship God, or Christ, but Ann Lee instead." This idea is wrong and absurd. It would be just as sensible for us to worship Ann Lee as it would be for the whole world to worship Columbus, because he discovered America.

> —Sister Gennie Coolbroth, *Facts about the Shakers,*
> *1794–1933,* 1933

Souls that go out of this world, and have not heard the gospel, do not know God, nor where to find him. I have seen them wandering about, weeping and crying, until, to appearance they had worn gutters in their cheeks, as large as my fingers.

I have seen the poor negroes, who are so much despised, redeemed from their loss, with crowns on their heads.

> —(Ann Lee) *Testimonies,* 1816

As Mother Ann was one day viewing an apple tree in full blossom, she said, "How beautiful this tree looks now! But some of the apples will soon fall off; some will hold on longer; some will hold on till they are full half grown, and then fall off; and some will get ripe. So it is with souls that set out in the way of God. Many will set out very fair, and soon fall away; some will go further, and then fall off; some will go still further, and then fall; and some will go through."

> —Green and Wells, *A Summary View,* 1823

Though our blessed Mother was a woman of few words, yet her soul was filled with divine wisdom. . . . Many precious sentences were occasionally spoken, which had a powerful effect, and left a lasting impression.

> —*Testimonies,* 1816

Sayings of Mother Ann

Put your hands to work, and give your hearts to God.
Beware of covetousnous, which is as the sin of witchcraft.
If you have anything to spare, give it to the poor.
You ought not to waste the least thing.
The devil tempts others, but an idle person tempts the devil.
You must not lose one moment of time, for you have none to spare.
If you improve in one talent, God will give you more.
Do all your work as though you had a thousand years to live, and as you would if you knew you must die tomorrow.
You should make the way of God your occupation. The way of God

is to be learned as much as a trade. You learn to have faith, learn to believe. A man that has a trade is industrious to work at it and get a living. And you ought to be as industrious and as much engaged in the way of God.

Remember the cries of those who are in need and trouble, that when you are in trouble, God may hear your cries.

You can never enter the Kingdom of God with hardness against any one; for God is love; and if you love God, you will love one another.

You have had the privilege of being taught the way of God. And now you may all go home and be faithful with your hands. Every faithful man will go forth and put up his fences in season, and will plough his ground in season; and such a man may with confidence look for a blessing. But the slothful and indolent will say, *tomorrow will do as well.* . . . Such a man never finds a blessing.

OF CHILDREN

You ought not to cross your children unnecessarily: for it makes them ill-natured; and little children do not know how to govern their natures. . . . But when they are disobedient, then let them feel your severity.

You ought never to speak to your children in a passion; for if you do, you will put devils into them.

When I was a child, my mind was taken up with the things of God, so that I saw heavenly visions, instead of trifling toys.

You must bring up your children in the fear of God; and never give them playthings; but let them look at their hands and fingers, and see the work of God in their creation.

And when your daughters are grown so large that men will lust after them, you must put caps on their heads, and not build them up in pride.

Do not allow dogs to be in your houses: without are dogs and sorcerers. Do not let your children play with them; if they do, they will catch evil spirits, and be stubborn and wicked.

You must keep them to work: nor allow them to be idle; for if you do, they will grow up just like the world's children.

You ought not to talk about the flesh before them; lest it corrupt their minds.

Little children are nearer to the Kingdom of Heaven than those of riper age. Little children are simple and innocent; they should be brought up so, and they ought never to be brought out of it. If they were brought up in simplicity, they would receive good as easily as they would evil.

When children are put to bed, they ought to be made to lie straight, to prevent them from growing crooked.

FOR WOMEN

Let the moles and bats, that is, the children of this world, have your gold necklaces, jewels, rings, silver buckles and ornaments: for they set their hearts upon such things; but the children of God do not want them.

[The mother then warned them of the danger of pride, the great sin of following the foolish and vain fashions of the world; and after having fleeced them of their jewels, ear-rings, necklaces, buckles, and every other thing which might feed their pride, or rather enrich herself . . . would then admit them into her fraternity.

—*Theological Magazine*, 1795]

Dress yourself in modest apparel, such as becomes the people of God, and teach your family to do likewise. Be industrious and prudent. Labor for a meek and quiet spirit.

See that your family is kept decent and regular in all their goings forth, that others may see your example of faith and good works, and acknowledge the work of God in your family.

Keep your family's clothes clean and decent. See that your house is kept clean and your victuals prepared in good order, that when the brethren come home from their hard work, they can bless you, and eat their food with thankfulness.

Don't speak harsh; but let your words be few and seasoned with grace.

Never put on silver spoons, nor table cloths for me; but let your table be clean enough to eat from without cloths, and if you do not know what to do with them, give them to the poor.

You ought to be neat and clean, for there are no slovens or sluts in heaven.

Mother's Way

Mother Ann's life was so closely intertwined with the lives of her followers that her own acts and characteristics as an individual merge with

Mother Ann's rocking chair is preserved at the Fruitlands Museums, Harvard, Massachusetts.

those of the group. Her spiritual emotionalism, her courage, her practicality were prototypes of the emotionalism, the courage and practicality of all the Shakers. She herself would have preferred it thus. The submergence of the individual in the group was what Shakerism wanted. Yet one quality of Ann's was hers alone: her warm, passionate love for humanity, not humanity in the abstract, but little children, puzzled adolescents, worried men and women, who came to her for help. She listened to them, she yearned over them, she showed them that she really cared as a mother cares when her children are in trouble. She was in deed as she was in name Mother to all the Believers.

—Marguerite Fellows Melcher, *The Shaker Adventure,* 1941

MOTHER ANN'S BIRTHDAY CAKE
(From several Shaker communities)

1 cup best butter (sweet butter, fresh if possible)	3 teaspoons baking powder
	1 cup milk
2 cups sugar	2 teaspoons vanilla
3 cups flour, sifted	12 egg whites, beaten
½ cup cornstarch	1 teaspoon salt

Beat butter and sugar into a smooth cream. Sift flour with cornstarch and baking powder. Add flour mixture in small amounts alternately with milk to butter mixture. Beat after each addition, about 200 strokes in all. Add vanilla and lightly fold in the beaten whites of eggs to which the salt has been added. Bake in three 8 inch greased tins in a moderate 350° F. oven for 25 minutes. When cool fill between layers with peach jelly and cover the cake with any delicate icing. Makes one 3 layer cake.

Mother Ann's birthday fell on February 29, but was celebrated on March 1. The above cake was served at supper, following the afternoon meeting commemorating the life of the Shakers' beloved founder, Ann Lee (1736–1784). The original recipe reads: "Cut a handful of peach twigs, which are filled with sap at this season of the year. Clip the ends and bruise them and beat cake batter with them. This will impart a delicate peach flavor to the cake."

—Amy Bess Williams Miller and Persis Wellington Fuller, *The Best of Shaker Cooking*, 1970

From the first, Ann Lee has been a controversial figure. Her obsessions regarding "lust" and her messianic pretensions should not, however, obscure the fact that she instituted a movement deeply religious in aspiration and essentially democratic in practice. Her advocacy of equal rights (and responsibilities) for women in the Shaker society anticipated the feminist movement in America. Her belief in an equalitarian order, in the dignity of labor, and in the rights of conscience accorded with American idealism. Principles such as these, spoken with what seemed to her followers like divine authority, inspired them in their efforts to establish a truly Christian community, in many respects the most successful experiment in religious communitarianism in American history.

—Edward Deming Andrews, "Ann Lee," *Notable American Women: 1607–1950*, vol. 2, 1971

The odd Shaker dogma about Christ "reincarnated as a woman" was perhaps not as outlandish in its original meaning as it later came to be. The root idea is that of the "maternal" aspect of God's love, and man's, an aspect too often ignored: the view which sees love as tenderness and care for all living beings (compare the Buddhist meditation on the "four un-limiteds") and indeed for life itself. Such love is one of the deepest forms of respect for the creative tenderness of God whose merciful Spirit of Love broods over all beings.

—(Thomas Merton, Introduction) Edward Deming and Faith Andrews, *Religion in Wood*, 1966

A feminine redeemer! A Female Christ! *Was* the merciful, all-loving spirit of the first Redeemer really visited upon a woman? Perhaps yes, perhaps no, for there are those who can legitimately advance the argument of course that Jesus Christ died at the hands of others, whereas Ann Lee died by natural means. This fact in itself would tend to destroy the comparison of a male Christ leading men out of sin and a female Christ leading women out of sin. To be consistent, for comparison's sake, perhaps both should have died as human sacrifices—if we are going to use the argument at all.

Be that as it may, one thing is *sure*. In this day and age it would hardly be out of order to honor the Shaker leader's sweet pledge: "More love, brother, more love!"—would it?

—Arthur F. Joy, *The Queen of the Shakers*, 1960

The circumstances of Ann's death are as shrouded in mystery as the early years of her life. She died one year after the conclusion of an arduous mission through parts of New York and New England, a journey marked by constant hardship, persecution, and at times physical mistreatment. Was her death a natural one? One wonders. For when the remains were disinterred for removal to the Shaker cemetery, there was evidence that her skull had been fractured and that she may therefore have died from wounds suffered on that mission. There may be corroboration in the fact that in the eventful year following her successful tour, no record exists of her part in what by that time was a burgeoning movement.

—Edward Deming and Faith Andrews, *Fruits of the Shaker Tree of Life*, 1975

The *Phrenological Annual* is out. Among other matters, we find a purported portrait of Ann Lee, together with our letter to S. R. Wells. Very few Shakers coincide with the Spirit Artist; but it is very interesting to observe what artists attempt, and phrenologists determine from such attempts. —*The Shaker*, March 1872

We have presented to us a portrait purporting to be that of Mother Ann Lee, as she is reverently and affectionately called. It is what is called a psychometric portrait, and the manner of its procurement will be found in a note at the close of this article. We have caused an engraving to be made of the picture, and if it really were a true likeness of her, we might readily understand that she could conscientiously and very naturally adopt the sentiment or doctrine of celibacy, and release herself from the marriage relation. . . .

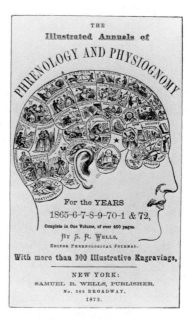

Not a portrait of Mother Ann, but only a "psychometrically drawn" image considered by a nineteenth-century medium to be her likeness. From the *Illustrated Annals of Phrenology and Physiognomy for the Years 1865–1872.* Photographs, courtesy of the Western Reserve Historical Society.

Right: Phrenology, Mythology, Mesmerism, and such sciences as are foreign from Believers duty, may not be studied at all by Believers. *Millennial Laws*, 1845.

This portrait shows a large amount of reflective intellect, and an excessive development of the organs of Benevolence, Veneration, and spirituality. It also evinces very large Ideality and Sublimity, with large Cautiousness. Such a head, if Ann Lee resembled it, could hardly do otherwise than be lifted up into the realm of sympathy, spirituality, and imagination far above the affairs of common life. But it is an abnormal head.

If she had so small a base of brain, and such an immense top-head, it is no wonder her children died, and that she inclined to devote herself to a life of spirituality. How little animal vitality is evinced in that small, delicate face! She was apparently all brain; and nothing but the life and health of her children to divert her from it could have spared her from a career of fanaticism in some direction. . . . Does not her early constitutional aversion to the commerce of the sexes explain why she regarded this commerce as the original sin, and the source of all other sin? Does it not explain why she dissolved her marriage ties, and established celibacy as a religious tenet?

The adherents to the sect are, as a class, not a coarse, animal, passional people. . . . They do not believe it necessary or desirable that all should adopt their views and practices—nor do they think it wrong for the people of the world to marry,—celibacy they hold to be a higher state of life—a kind of sanctification of the body and mind to a pure and holy life.

In reference to the portrait, we have received the following explanation from Geo. A. Lomas, editor of THE SHAKER, a monthly journal published in the interest of the Shakers near Albany.

Office of the Shaker,
Shakers, Albany Co., N.Y.
May 9th, 1871

My dear Wells:

The picture is a copy from a crayon purported to be psychometrically drawn by one Milleson, of New York. The picture, while in the hands of the artist, was not recognized by him nor by any of his friends, but they supposed the same to be the likeness of some of the nobility of England. An individual named Trow, also of New York City, took the picture to a test medium, or psychological expert, and before presenting the picture, the medium began moving round the room after the marching manner of the Shakers, singing a genuine Shaker song at the same time; at the conclusion of the exercise the medium asserted that the likeness of Ann Lee, mother of the Shakers' faith was in the possession of the inquirer!

There are several descriptions of Ann Lee in our Society differing somewhat; and one of these descriptions agrees very uniformly with the portrait, and is believed to be genuine by many of our people. I think the head of the picture represents a most extraordinary personage.

History, today, gives Ann Lee an important niche in the temple of fame for exaggerated spirituality and beauty of disposition; and these you find very palpably displayed in the picture. The features of the lower face I do not admire, the mouth looking as though capable of scolding—chin too pointed; the nose begins to add beauty to the form, and the brain-house is surpassing beautiful. I express my doubts of its genuineness solely on the ground of its extreme mentality: for Mother Ann Lee was an ignorant woman, so far as letters were concerned, though speaking above sixty languages while under spirit control.

I am, very truly

G. A. LOMAS

The First Famous Visitor

On September 26, 1784, eighteen days after the death of Mother Ann, the Marquis de Lafayette, the twenty-seven-year-old French hero of the American Revolution, called at the Shakers' first American settlement at Niskayuna. He was on his way to Fort Schuyler with a party including the Marquis de Barbé-Marbois, French chargé d'affaires in America, to help negotiate a treaty of peace with the Indian tribes of New York State.

Shaker tradition dates the Frenchmen's visit within the lifetime of Mother Ann. It even records her conversation with Lafayette and her generous rejection of him as a would-be Shaker until his lifework as a soldier was done. Lafayette's interest was flattering to the Shakers, and they elevated his visit to a legend. But his fascination with them seems to have stemmed from an enthusiasm of his own: mesmerism. He was a registered student of the guru of Paris at that time: Dr. Franz Anton Mesmer, who pioneered the development of hypnotism.

To Lafayette they furnished a possible example of the workings of animal magnetism, particularly since they healed disease by the laying-on of hands. He tried to "mesmerize" one of the community but was interrupted by an elder who asked whether he acted in the name of a good or bad spirit. "Certainly in the name of a good spirit," Lafayette replied. Marbois did not think Lafayette had much success, however. Except that

Marie Joseph Paul Yves Roch Gilbert du Motier, Marquis de Lafayette (1757–1834), Major-General of the American Army, after a drawing by A. Chappel. From the Bettmann Archive.

the Shakers were as favorably impressed that so fine a gentleman should take them so seriously, nothing came from these observations of Mesmer's disciple.
—Louis Gottschalk, *Lafayette Between the American and the French Revolution (1783–1789)*, 1950

It is a curious fact, that *fifteen days before* Lafayette's death [in 1834] was published in the United States, the same was made known by himself to a medium at Watervliet, N.Y., and was a matter of common conversation among our people. He, at the same time, referred to his visit to Mother Ann, when on earth.
—*The Shaker*, Sept. 1872

Brother Abijah [Worster] . . . was at Watervliet at that time, and entered the room where Lafayette was just after Mother left it. . . . Abijah was under the operations of the power of God, and Lafayette would keep near him and touch him, as if with a view to receive it from him.

Abijah said to him, "You love this power, don't you?" He replied, "It seems desirable." He followed him out to the barn and kept close to him sometime. —Roxalana L. Grosvenor, "Sayings of Mother Ann," 1845

According to Shaker legend, Lafayette was determined to learn what "power" caused such strange actions in Brother Abijah. He followed him from room to room and from barn to cellar, emerging finally into the presence of Mother Ann and the Elders. Then, for the first time

Lafayette found voice enough eagerly to ask of them what manner of man he had encountered, and what was the nature of his malady? He was informed that it was wholly of a religious type, and that such dwelt among them. The tenet of their religion was then explained to him, when he enquired to know why he could not share it as well as others; but Mother Ann informed him that his mission was of the world, and on the great earth plane before him; that in the soldier life which he had chosen, he had a work to do of vast importance.

—From a pamphlet, *The Shakers* (East Canterbury), quoted in *Gleanings From Old Shaker Journals*, by Clara Endicott Sears, 1916

We had heard a great deal about the American "convulsioners" . . . and to the ordinary motives of curiosity M. de Lafayette joined that of desiring to examine at close range phenomena which have a great similarity to those of "Mesmerism." . . .

An old woman,—and it was their prophetess, the "elect lady,"—was, they believed, immortal. Her death, which happened about six weeks ago, embarrassed them a little. They explained it in so ridiculously mystical a way . . . that, a place having become vacant in heaven, through some promotion, it was necessary to fill it. . . . These enthusiasts were persuaded that this holy matron sat in the Council of the Almighty three times a week. . . .

The Shakers are seized with their movements at any time, on any occasion, while they cultivate the earth, while they are cutting trees, while traveling on foot, or on horseback. We saw them in this condition during their rest, and during conversation. The convulsion does not interrupt anything; the most usual movement is to turn the head from left to right, with eyes closed or raised toward the sky, with an expression which proclaims ecstasy, anguish, and pain. We noticed that the women shed tears, were pale and downcast, and that their face reanimated itself only when the convulsion was at an end. The men raised their arms, trembling; their knees gave way and knocked together. Often while all their members shook, they would seem to have a seizure under which they would succumb, but it was the end of the ecstasy. The head turned less rapidly, and when the crisis was over, they sighed deeply, like people relieved at length of excessive anxiety, or coming out of a painful swoon.

> —Eugene Parker Chase, *Our Revolutionary Forefathers: The Letters of François, Marquis de Barbé-Marbois During His Residence in the United States as Secretary of the French Legation 1779–1785,* 1929

LAFAYETTE JUMBLES

Nearly half a cupful of milk, one half a cupful of butter, one cupful of sugar, three cupfuls of flour, two eggs, one half a teaspoonful of soda, half a nutmeg. Roll out and dust with the white of an egg. Sprinkle with sugar.

> —Recipe from *Mary Whitcher's Shaker House-Keeper,* reprinted in William L. Lassiter, *Shaker Recipes for Cooks and Homemakers,* 1959

Surprising Worship

The men were strong and virile and it is possible that the excitement of the dance led to spontaneous emissions, giving them a kind of sexual satisfaction that could be rationalized as "immaculate." I do not know enough about women to be able to guess at the nature of their physical gratifications.

> —Robert Melville, "Shaking Grace," *New Statesman,* May 23, 1975; a review of "The Shakers," an exhibition at the Victoria and Albert Museum in London

Though they had cautioned me against being surprised at their worship, yet their conduct was so wild and extravagant that it was some time before I could believe my own senses. . . . Near the centre of the room stood two young women, one of them very handsome, who whirled round and round for the space of fifteen minutes, nearly as fast as the rim of a spinning-wheel in quick motion. . . .

The house trembled as if there were an earthquake. After this several young women embraced and saluted each other; two men embraced and saluted each other; a third clasped his arms around both, a fourth around them, and so on, until a dozen men were in that position, embracing and saluting. I did not observe any man salute or embrace a woman, or any woman a man. . . .

After their meeting was done, I was invited by the Elders to take lodging at their house. . . . The young woman who had whirled the most began to shake and tremble astonishingly. She told me this was not a voluntary motion, but that she was acted upon by a supernatural impulse. I asked whether a man could, by his strength, prevent her shaking and whirling. She said it would be blasphemy against God to attempt such a thing. . . . When she was whirling with great velocity, I rose and advanced gradually towards her, clasped her in my arms, and in the course of a moment held her still, though she exclaimed against me as very rude and indecent.
    —William Plumer (June 17, 1782), "The Original Shaker Communities in New England," *New England Magazine*, 1900

The idea I had formed of the folly & ridiculousness of these infatuated people fell very far short of the reality. . . . When we arrived they were singing . . . in this unknown language a very solemn tune, at the end of which they always begin with Oh! & in such a loud & hollow note accompanied with a catching of the breath as if they were strangling & the most violent contortions of their whole body as cannot fail to shock every one who first sees them. . . .

One of the men who appeared the most decent & sensible & who I am informed was formerly a preacher in New England [probably Joseph Meacham] began a lecture evidently for us. . . . He said that he knew their religion was despised but . . . that they were supported under all their trials & persecutions by visitations from heaven. . . .

He mentioned Davids dancing before the Ark in honor of his God . . . he then began to hum the Soldiers Joy a country dance tune & the whole assembly . . . began a violent dancing without any kind of order the men keeping on one side of the room & the women on the other . . . four began to turn around with a velocity that is really inconceivable to any one who has not been a witness to it . . . for the space of eighteen minutes they went round, until they were called off by a clapping of hands in which they all joined for the space of five minutes; they then began their solemn singing, then their jig & then claped hands & continued at that kind of worship for some time—a likely young girl fell into such a fit of shaking as exceeded any convulsion fit I had ever seen. . . . The old man then came up to us and told us to observe and admire the powerful working of God in his people.

After having proceeded for some time, the men got together in a cluster holding out both hands, as if supporting something, then one of them spoke to this effect, the rest all repeating as by way of response, "This is our altar & our altar is love & none can build this altar or sacrifice upon it but the pure in heart & such are we—therefore we will sacrifice on our altar & we will love one another—they then began to shout & clap their hands the women joining them & renewed their jig—presently after they repeated something like this "The dead should be buried, yes we will bury the dead but we are alive & we will sacrifice on our altar, communion, union, love, we will love one another . . ." They then continued their shouting &c.   —Anonymous letter, dated July 25, 1785, in the collection of the Connecticut Historical Society

As Mother Ann foretold, it fell to American-born leaders to gather her "children" into independent village-communes, where worldly goods were held in common and daily life was service to God. The foundation for communal living had been laid by Mother Ann's immediate successor, the English weaver James Whittaker. He journeyed as far as Maine and New Hampshire to strengthen the faith of Believers and keep them from falling back into the world. His fanatic zeal, second only to Mother Ann's, consumed his strength, and he died in 1787 at the age of thirty-seven.

Leadership of the Believers then passed to Joseph Meacham, whom Mother Ann called her "first-born son in America." A former Baptist minister and native of Enfield, Connecticut, he was the leader of the disappointed New Lebanon revivalists who found the English Shakers living "without sin" in the woods near Niskayuna.

Father Joseph was the great organizer of the long-lived Shaker way. When he invited Lucy Wright to be his counterpart "in the female line," he set the pattern for a dual order of government with equality of the sexes far in advance of the times. Mother Lucy was twenty-eight-years old, a handsome, intelligent, and wellborn matron who had followed her husband into the Shaker ranks and resumed her maiden name.

After Lucy Wright came to Watervliet to see the Church, as Mother and the Elders were called, and had received faith, a number of the Brethren and Sisters being there, Mother Ann passed through the room, and, with a smile, said, "We must save Lucy, if we can, for, if we save her, it will be equal to saving a nation."

—Bishop and Wells, *Testimonies*, 1888

Mother Lucy and Father Joseph formed the parent ministry at New Lebanon, New York. That society became "the centre of union" and church headquarters for the United Society of Believers in Christ's Second Appearing, the formal name of the Shakers.

They gradually gathered the people from their scattered condition into families, having their property in common. Orders, rules, and regulations, in temporal and spiritual things, were framed, appropriate to the new relations they were then coming into as a body of people. Elders and deacons of both sexes were appointed, and set in their proper order; and a Covenant was written and entered into for the mutual understanding and protection of the members.

—F. W. Evans, *Shakers. Compendium*, 1859

"Gospel order" required severing connections with kinfolk for greater union among Believers.

My Father was the greatest opposer I ever had. . . . He opposed me as long as he could, or untill he saw it had no effect on me, & then he tried to turn me by flattery . . . but it never touched me.

After I had loaded my things to come away, I went in & said "Father, I must bid you farewell." He reached out his hand, turned up his eyes & cried. Said he "John, you are my youngest son, & all the rest are gone away"; & intimated that if I would stay, I should heir his property.

—Daniel W. Patterson, "Bearing for the Dead: A Shaker Belief and Its Impress on the Shaker Spiritual," *Shaker Quarterly*, Winter 1968

Love not self, that must be hated,
Love not satin, love not sin;
To the flesh, tho' you're related,
Love not flesh, nor fleshly kin.
Love not riches, honor, pleasure,
Love no earthly vain delight:
But the gospel's hidden treasure,
You may love with all your might.

—*Millennial Praises*, 1813

From the administration of Joseph Meacham, the affairs of the brotherhood have been formed into a system. The love of domination appears to have taken a final possession of the elderhood; and absolute submission, of the brethren. . . . The spirit of proselyting is now very evidently the controlling principle. . . . Their excesses will from time to time be pruned away . . . the inconveniences which obstruct their prosperity removed. . . . For all this they are furnished with the most convenient of all pretences. It is only for the principal elder to say that he has a gift, i.e. a revelation, for any change; and the thing is accomplished.

> —Timothy Dwight, *Travels in New-England and New-York*, 1821

We believe and do testify . . . that the present display of the work and power of God, will increase until it is manifest to all . . . and none can stand in sin . . . but in that righteousness . . . obtained by . . . denying all ungodliness and worldly lusts; by confessing all sin, and taking up the cross of Christ against the world, flesh, and devil; we desire therefore, that the children of men would believe the testimony of truth, and turn from their sins . . . before it be too late.

> —Joseph Meacham, *A Concise Statement of the Principles of the Only True Church*, 1790. (This was the first published statement of Shaker theology.)

Father Joseph died in 1796, having charted the course Believers would travel for more then two hundred years. Mother Lucy survived a "falling off" of members and served alone for twenty-five years longer.

The Shakers in the neighborhood of New-Lebanon Spring and Hancock, are of late in a great fermentation, which seems to indicate an approaching revolution among them. . . . Their young people, on whose industry depends principally the prosecution of their lucrative manufactories, are deserting them one after another, and recovering wages for their past services. . . .

This hath however been expected by many of their neighbours, who considered how little inducement their young manufacturers and labourers have to remain with them, after arriving to mature years. When placed, by accident, or by their parents or guardians, under the Shakers, they were mostly too young to have any rational choice; nor does it appear that they were ever wrought into that religious enthusiasm which is so far cooled that very little precept or example of their religion is exhibited even by the Elders. . . . The common rank of their church are steadily at work on weekdays and are allowed no religious books on Sunday, nor may they of late years, go to their Meeting-house. But in order to stimulate them to industry, they are taught to excel the world's people in their works as much as in their faith. . . .

Artful as their rulers are . . . as nothing but the frantic enthusiasm which actuated them at first could therefore impel them to stem the current of nature and reason, they might have foreseen that as soon as this blind zeal had spent its force (which was too intense to be durable) their former zealots would begin to warp off as seems now to be coming the case. . . .

Who of the old inhabitants of their neighborhoods but can recollect the wild vagaries of their first setting out, the drunkenness of their old first mother and foundress, whom they held to be immortal; her known lasciviousness; their once crowding and kneeling around her, when she was drunk, to kiss the hem of her garment, in presence of most of the neighbours. . . . The Bacchanalian dances she instituted, of naked fathers, mothers, brothers, and sisters, through each other in the same room; men running after their hands, which were extended and guided by the Spirit, through quags, briars, hedges and over mountains, their agonizing groans, twitchings, whirling around, talking in unknown tongues, prophesying, working miracles, &c. while excessive drinking was countenanced among them, and industry quite discarded.

The artful refugees from Europe, who formed and led them, with the mother at their head, perceiving that by the mode of procedure sustenance would soon be lacking, ordained now the collection of their persons and estates under a spiritual head. This done, they taught the body of them industry, economy, sobriety, dependence, and implicit devotion to the Chief, who, with a few favorites, seems thence forward to have secretly monopolized the various excesses which their institutions favoured.

—From the Western Star (Stockbridge, Mass.), reprinted in the Connecticut Gazette, Feb. 11, 1796

THE UNION IS THE GIFT

To my sense, Believers are held together in union, by a golden chain, this chain is composed of the gifts and orders of God; and every order is a link in this chain; and if you break any of these orders you break this chain and are exposed to be led astray. But while you are careful to keep the gifts and orders of God, you are surrounded by this golden chain and are secure from all.   —(Mother Lucy Wright) "Mother Lucy's Sayings," ed. by Sister Frances Carr, *Shaker Quarterly,* Winter 1968

Well before 1800 eleven Shaker settlements had been established in "gospel order." Besides the early New York colonies of New Lebanon and Niskayuna, later called Watervliet, they were: Harvard, Hancock, Tyringham, and Shirley in Massachusetts: Enfield in Connecticut; Canterbury and Enfield in New Hampshire; and Alfred and New Gloucester, later called Sabbathday Lake, in Maine.

The Shaker brethren in their broad-brimmed hats were already on the road in America's first one-horse wagons, peddling their surplus produce and garden seeds and later, well-made house and farm utensils. The quality and ingenuity of these products, and the Shakers' growing reputation for honest dealing, gradually won the respect of those outside the faith called by the Shakers "the world's people."

A ministration ceased, and persecution ceased also; and the Believers worshipped God, in their appointed habitations, unmolested by the wicked.   —*Testimonies,* 1816

A nice wagon, loaded with fine vegetables, often passed before our door. It belonged to the Shakers, who were located at a distance of six or seven miles. The driver of the wagon always stopped at our house, and I never failed to talk with him about their manner of life, their customs, and their belief. He urged us to visit their estabishment, and we decided to go there some day. . . .

[They] were then protected on all sides by a forest several miles deep. They therefore had no reason as yet to fear their neighbors. Their establishment was bounded on one side by woods which covered 20,000 acres, belonging to the city of Albany, and on the other by the river Mohawk. . . . This establishment was a branch of their headquarters at Lebanon, which was located in the large forest through which we passed in going from Boston to Albany.

Our negro, Prime, who knew all the routes in our neighborhood, conducted us to their place. At the start we were at least three hours in the woods, following a road which was hardly laid out. Then after having passed the barrier which marked the limits of the Shaker property, the road became more distinct and better marked. But we still had to pass through a very thick forest, broken here and there by fields where cows and horses were pastured at liberty. Finally, we came out in a vast clearing traversed by a pretty stream and surrounded on all sides by woods. In the midst was erected the establishment, composed of a large number of nice wooden houses, a church, schools, and a community house of brick.

The Shaker, whose acquaintance we had made, greeted us with kindness, although with a certain reserve. They showed Prime the stable in which he could put up his horses, for there was no inn. We had been advised that nobody would offer us anything, and that our guide would be the only one to speak to us. He first led us to a superb kitchen-garden perfectly cultivated. Everything was in a state of the greatest prosperity, but without the least evidence of elegance. Many men and women were working at the cultivation or the weeding of the garden. The sale of vegetables represented the principal source of revenue to the community.

We visited the schools for the boys and girls, the immense community stables, the dairies, and the factories in which they produced the butter and cheese. Everywhere we remarked upon the order and the absolute silence. The children, boys and girls alike, were clothed in a costume of the same form and the same color. The women of all ages wore the same kind of garments of gray wool, well kept and very neat. Through the windows we could see the looms of the weavers, and the pieces of cloth which they were dyeing, also the workshops of the tailors and the dress-makers. But not a word or a song was to be heard anywhere. . . .

When the Shaker who came to sell vegetables and fruits passed before our farm, I always bought something. He was never willing to take money from my hand. If I remarked that the price which he asked was too high, he replied: "Just as you please." Then I placed upon the corner of the table the sum which I thought sufficient. If the price was satisfactory, he took it; if not, he climbed into his wagon, without saying a word. He was a man of very respectable appearance, always perfectly dressed in a coat, vest and trousers of gray homespun cloth of their own manufacture.

—Marquise de la Tour du Pin (1795), *Recollections of the Revolution and the Empire,* 1920

About the year 1785, the testimony was withdrawn from the world; so that for a number of years, there was no public manifestation of the faith of the Society to those without. The great and important work which was then progressing in the Church, rendered this cessation of the testimony essentially necessary; for while the believers were gathering themselves into Societies, and establishing gospel order, they found enough to do, without testifying their faith to others. As this was an important change, and absolutely necessary for the protection and permanent establishment of the Society, it required all the energies of soul and body to accomplish it.   —Green and Wells, *A Summary View*, 1823

Here we relate the incident which seems to have produced a lasting impression upon the mind of Sir William Satterlee, toward the "Shakers," near whose village he was about to settle. It was known that the route which the family were to travel lay directly through the settlement of the Shakers, in Columbia Co. N.Y. It has been represented that they were a peculiar people, and many of their doings had been related in his hearing, which fixed the impression upon his mind, that they are witches, and possessed power also to molest others. This produced such a serious alarm as to lead him to ask protection from "Him who careth for all" that he might safely pass the Shakers settlement.

It was a new country, so that the family were obliged to travel on horseback. As they neared the Shaker village, the fear of them became more exciting among the children. One of the horses stumbled and fell, which one of the girls was riding, the family was obliged to halt. Shakers immediately approached and offered help, a house was thrown open and every hospitality proffered to them; yet, when the refreshments were prepared, William refused to eat, lest by so doing he might become deluded. But from the kind treatment rendered, his mind was changed, and a friendly relationship formed with some of the members of that community, which lasted through life; but he regarded them deluded.

—Goldie Satterlee Moffatt and John L. Satterlee, *Satterlee & Allied Families Genealogy*, 1970

Sunday, Oct. 10, 1796. Having heard various accounts of the very singular mode of worship practised by the people called Shaking Quakers, I this day went to visit them. I found the house at which they were assembled, situated 9 miles NW. of Albany, and 2 miles from the Mohawk river; it is built of logs, neatly squared, and is 50 feet in length, and 25 in width, with a chimney at each end. When I entered this building, I beheld 24 men dancing at one end of the room, and 20 women at the other. They appeared to be from the age of 14 to 80 years; and were formed four deep. Two of their elders were singing a song tune, called the rose tree. They kept good time, though frequently trembled as if much convulsed—this they call the working of the spirit. After continuing in this way for about an hour and a half, the elders stopped singing; this stopped the dancing for the present. The men then put on their coats, and they all retired to a house, but a short distance from that in which they had been dancing; where they partook of some refreshment; but soon commenced singing a kind of gibberish, which they call an unknown tongue. They say they can speak several different languages, and though the living cannot understand them, they are intelligible to the departed spirits, with whom they say they hold frequent converse. After about an hour's intermission they assembled again and formed two deep; they then all sang in their unknown tongue, appearing, at times, to be very much convulsed; after a continued dancing and trembling for half an hour, they ceased singing, and after many heavy sighs and groans, and much twisting and trembling, one of their elders, in broken accents, muttered out, let us, my dear friends, endeavour to praise God in the dance; prepare yourselves by throwing off your garments. The men then put off their coats and waistcoats; then after opening their collars, and tieing up their sleeves, they formed four deep, the women also forming in the same manner. One of their elders then, after groaning and trembling for a few minutes, said, my dear friends, you that are blest with the gift of songs, I hope will praise God by singing a few tunes for us. Immediately two young men stepped out from the ranks, and began to sing, at which time they all commenced dancing. In this way they continued about an hour, appearing, at times, very much agitated. They then all stopped dancing, and one of their elders, after violently shaking his head and arms, thus addressed them— My dear friends, I hope you will endeavour to walk worthy the vocation wherewith you are called; and praise God for separating you from the wicked world; for in like manner as Lot escaped out of Sodom, so have you, my friends, escaped, and have been separated from the wicked world. He was soon seized with a very violent shaking of the head, after which, he, with a heavy sigh and groan, told his trembling audience that they might put on their garments and retire, which they soon did.

—Moses Guest, *Poems on Several Occasions, to Which Are Appended, Extracts from a Journal Kept by the Author While He Followed the Sea, and during a Journey from New-Brunswick, in New Jersey, to Montreal and Quebec*, 1823

"SHAKERS near LEBANON state of N York, their mode of Worship. Drawn from Life." A lithograph ca. 1830–40 often misattributed to Anthony Imbert. Courtesy of the Library of Congress.

There is a beautiful villa within sight of Lebanon-pool, inhabited by a society of that newly risen sect, called, by every body, but themselves, the Shakers, or Shaking Quakers.

If it be true, that "by their fruits ye shall know them," they are not a people to be derided.

Their houses have a neatness beyond any thing I have yet seen in our country. Their farms, their gardens, their manufactories in iron, in brass, and in tin, bear traits of order and neatness, as well as marks of good heads for contriving, and good hands for executing. Their agriculture and horti-culture are beyond any thing I have seen in my journey. They themselves are plain, decent, and grave in their dress, language, and deportment. As to integrity, their character is established among all considerate people in this quarter, but the very vulgar still entertain idle and shameful stories of this virtuous, honest, and industrious society. The contortions, grimaces, and promiscuous dancings, which marked and disgraced their conduct, when they first rose among us, have given way to a mode of worship, which tends to inspire sentiments of solemnity, rather than derision.

They have a regular, solemn and uniform dance or genuflecions, to as regular and solemn a song, or hymn, which is sung by the elders, and as regularly conducted as a proper band of music, and a well trained company of soldiers.

I never saw any worship that appeared to carry a more solemn aspect of devotion than I saw among these people in the retired vale of Lebanon.

—By "A Traveller," Cambridge (Mass.), Jan. 1796,
Theological Magazine, 1796

Ann's Vision of a Shaker World

Come, life, Shaker life!
Come, life eternal!

    Ann, I am a community of white houses
and buildings, three and four-storied,
impeccably plain, with stairs to the
sisters' and stairs to the brothers'
lodgings. I face a hill crammed with
orchards, and fields of wheat and
vegetables and maize. Blossoms perfume
the land.

Shake, shake out of me
all that is carnal.

    Ann, I am a hill, green and fertile,
with apple, cherry, plum, and pear
trees. Grass covers me. Fat cattle
browse beneath the trees. The air
is filled with chanting angels, their
melodies urge the finest fruit to
grow, and the foraging cattle
give the finest milk and cream. To
walk here is to walk in the Spirit.

I'll take nimble steps,
I'll be a David

    Ann, I am a field of maize
bordering a field of wheat. My
ears are plump and sweet. The
shiver of fall reaches the huge

orange pumpkins and the
meaty yellow squash.

I'll show Michael twice
how he behaved!
    Ann, I am a field of wheat
in a flourishing valley. My
yield is greater per acre
than that of any of the World's
fields. Breezes
shake the heads of the ripe
wheat. Brothers with their
scythes are whistling and
singing as they cut neat
swathes through me. I am
bread, I am flour, I am cake.

Come, life, Shaker life!
Come, life eternal!
    Ann, I am a sawmill standing
on a foundation of granite
boulders. A stream flows through
me for cooling saws and floating
timbers. From me emerge the
truest planks for our buildings,
and for our furniture. My machines
are superbly honed, efficient, and
clean.

Shake, shake out of me
all that is carnal.
    Ann, I am a spare, high room where
herbs and garden seeds are gathered,
processed, and packaged, and sent
throughout the World.

I'll take nimble steps,
I'll be a David
    Ann, I am the long workroom where
chairs are made, and clocks
and buckles, buttons, pails, tubs

casks, barrels and churns, whips
and cheese hoops, baskets, sieves
and oval boxes, pipes, and writing
pens. Here, too, clothes are cut
and sewn, bonnets and shoes designed,
and brooms and brushes.

I'll show Michael twice
how he behaved!
    Ann, I am the Church, rectangular, hip-
roofed, two and a-half stories high,
set back from the road, with a green
lawn in front, an avenue of maples,
each tree named after a young sister
who must tend her tree until she dies.

I have two doors: on the left the
brethren enter, on the right the sisters.
My windows are plain: three windows between
each of the main doors, and a window set
in each facade, plus dormer windows. The
entrances face two gates, exactly opposite,
tied in with a white picket fence.

Inside, I boast a large hall paneled
with wood up to the sills, with beams
crossing the ceiling, and wooden pegs
all around the room for hanging chairs
out of the way, and for hats and cloaks.

I am the center,
I am the center of the Community.

                —Robert Peters, *The Gift to Be Simple: A Garland*
                for Ann Lee, 1975

The Gift of Community

Many years ago as she walked and rode along the byways of rural
New York and New England, Mother Ann Lee, both by her life and
teaching, paid witness to what was for most of her contemporaries a star-
tlingly new way of looking at the world. That millennial anticipation

which had grown out of the Great Awakening still held the northeastern seaboard in its grasp, yet for Mother Ann and her followers anticipation had reached rich fulfillment. Christ as spirit had come to establish the millennium, not on clouds of righteousness, not in glory on the Mount of Olives, but unobtrusively, quietly, as the scriptures had foretold, "like a thief in the night." Mother and her earliest followers realized as Benjamin Seth Youngs was later to write, that "Christ in His Second Appearance had come in them." It is this concept of the indwelling presence of Christ in an active, ongoing way that lies at the heart of all Shaker teaching. Yet it is not the teaching in itself that has constituted the uniqueness and the greatness of Shakerism, but the way in which that teaching has through the daily activity of men and women expressed itself as a way of life, a way of life that shaped a community, and was consonant with community by its very nature.   —Theodore E. Johnson, "Life in the Christ Spirit," *Shaker Quarterly*, Summer 1967

Only with the Shakers did communitarianism make a real impact upon American opinion at large. From the time of their coming in 1774, no barrier of language separated these English sectarians from their new neighbors. Persecution was quickly visited upon Mother Ann Lee and her followers, but this was at least a positive reaction, indicating (as indifference would never have done) that the new sect was making its impression. The missionary journey that Ann Lee and the elders of her church made through Massachusetts and Connecticut in the years 1781–83 was a momentous event in the history of communitarianism. American converts quickly outnumbered the original immigrants, for the first time in the history of such sects. The groups of believers that were won to the new faith in the various towns of New England therefore constituted the very first communitarian colonies of native-born, English-speaking Americans. Americanization of the Shaker sect proceeded rapidly. . . . In less than fifteen years a small revivalistic band of dissenters in Manchester, England, had transferred their activities to the New World and had become a fully Americanized and growing sect.

—Arthur Bestor, *Backwoods Utopias*, 1950

PART

II

IN THE NINETEENTH CENTURY

•

Kingdom Come

The prophets saw most clear,
That Christ would come again,
And in the woman would appear,
And thus begin his reign:
The time is come, the work begun,
And by the Lord's command,
We now possess the promis'd rest,
And dwell in Zion's land.

—"The Kingdom of Zion,"
Millennial Praises, 1813

Kingdom Come

THE SHAKERS

Come, ye children of the Kingdom,
You that have been gather'd in,
Bring an off'ring of thanksgiving,
For you have been sav'd from sin.

—*Millennial Praises*, 1813

THE WORLD'S PEOPLE

    Probably there never was a sillier enthusiasm than this; yet, by a singular combination of circumstances, it has become to society the most harmless and in some respects the most useful perhaps of all the mental extravagances of this nature recorded in history. The doctrines are so gross that they can never spread far, while the industry, manual skill, fair dealing, and orderly behavior of the brotherhood render them useful members of society.... I believe that they are more decent than they were in the earlier periods of their establishment.

—Timothy Dwight, *Travels in New-England and New-York*, 1821

THE SHAKERS

The kingdom of heaven is far out of sight,
Until with each other we learn to unite;
And when into union our spirits do run,
We find that our heaven on earth is begun.

—Philos Harmoniae (Richard McNemar), *A Selection of Hymns and Poems for the Use of Believers*, 1833

THE WORLD'S PEOPLE

If the women demand votes, offices, and political equality, as an Elder and Elderess [sic] are of equal power in the Shaker Families, refuse it not. 'Tis very cheap wit that finds it so funny. Certainly all my points would be sooner carried in the state if women voted.

—Ralph Waldo Emerson, *Journals*, July 1855

THE SHAKERS

This is the lovely Kingdom,
Which we have listed in;
It is remote from evil,
'Tis separate from sin;
'Tis blest of God, 'tis known abroad,
And will forever stand;
The angels too, in passing through,
Do bless Mount Zion's land.

—*Millennial Praises*, 1813

THE WORLD'S PEOPLE

The sketch which has been introduced of the society of Shakers would have been withheld if we could have supposed that it would wound the feelings even of a single individual of that obscure sect.... The representation is deemed just, and it is hoped would not be thought offensive; and besides, there is little danger that these light volumes will ever find their way into a sanctuary from whose pale the frivolous amusements and profane literature of the "world's people" are carefully excluded.

—Catharine M. Sedgwick, preface to *Redwood: A Tale*, 1824, the first novel in which the Shakers appeared

THE SHAKERS

It is not expected that the people of God will ever be confined, in their mode of worship, to any particular set of hymns, or any other regular system of words—for words are but the signs of our ideas, and of course, must vary as the ideas increase with the increasing work of God.... As the work of regeneration is an increasing work, and there can be no end of the increase of Christ's government and Kingdom; so all that his people have to do is, to keep in the increasing work of God, and unite with whatever changes that increase may lead to, which, to the truly faithful, will be a continual travel from grace to grace, and from glory to glory.   —Preface, *Millennial Praises*, 1813

THE WORLD'S PEOPLE

Emily makes a first-rate wife, which I take to be partly owing to her having learnt many prudent and prospering ways among them shakers; and I do think if they could be prevailed on to turn their settlement into a school to bring up young folks for the married state, they would be a blessing to the world, instead of a spectacle to show how much wisdom and how much folly may be mixed up together.
                          —Catharine M. Sedgwick, *Redwood*, 1824

THE SHAKERS

It was said that the world's people about them would attend their religious services on Sunday evenings and watch them go round and round in their dance and consider them the most impractical visionaries on earth. The next morning at sunrise, these same neighbors, who had business at the mill would find them hard at work warping logs to the saw frame, and carrying away boards, and their conversation and deportment were as grave and serious as their religious exercises had been strange and inexplicable the night before.
                          —Sister R. Mildred Barker, "History of Union Branch,
                          Gorham, Maine," *Shaker Quarterly*, Summer 1967

THE WORLD'S PEOPLE

There is no fear that this or any other religious sect that is founded altogether on fanaticism and folly, will ever arrive to the smallest importance.   —James Fenimore Cooper, *Notions of the Americans,
                          Picked Up by a Travelling Bachelor*, 1828

THE SHAKERS

I'll walk with Christ in valleys low
Where streams of living waters flow
Where Saints in garments white as snow

Rejoice in full redemption.
'Tis here the tree of life is seen.
And here in verdure ever green
Elysian fields in beauty gleam,
Here in God's new creation.

> —"Tree of Life," song by Maine Elder Otis Sawyer,
> about 1876

MOTHER'S GOSPEL IN THE WEST

The next opening of the gospel will be in the Southwest. It will be at a great distance and there will be a great work of God.

—Mother Ann Lee

The great Kentucky Revival in the first five years of the nineteenth century was like an early American Woodstock. It drew thousands of young pioneer families and frontiersmen to mass camp meetings in the forest, where they listened night and day to one impassioned preacher after another. Caught up in a contagious frenzy for righteousness and salvation, many were moved to strange "exercises," barking and baying, rolling, jerking, falling down stiff as corpses. Others were set rejoicing, Shakerlike, singing and dancing their praise to the Lord.

From eastern revivals with the same powerful "manifestations," the Shakers had gained many members. It was not surprising, then, that they sent three missionaries 1,200 miles on foot to gather in some of the troubled souls in Ohio and Kentucky. One of the missionaries was Issachar Bates, who first encountered the Shakers on the famous "dark day" of 1780 when they "opened the testimony" in the New World. Now nearly fifty, he and his wife, with nine of their children, were new Believers, and he was eager for the task.

Like God's hunters we went through this wild wooden world . . . hunting up every soul that God had been preparing for Eternal Life . . . which life to obtain, they must honestly confess all their sins, thing by thing; and forsake them by taking a final cross against the world, flesh & all evil in their knowledge; and by righting all their wrongs with their fellow creatures; and to subject themselves to those appointed from time to time to minister unto them.... This was our gospel.

—Issachar Bates, "A Sketch of the Life and Experience
of Issachar Bates," *Shaker Quarterly*, Winter 1961

"Thank the God of heaven that salvation is come!" cried a Shaker convert. "Here goes wife & child, houses & land for the kingdom of heavens sake!"

The very woods may have clapped at the entrance of the Shakers, as Bates suggests, but not everyone was jubilant. Hostile mobs threatened the Shakers, as they had in the East, when once more they broke up families and unsettled churches, and gathered new Believers into celibate colonies. Bates and two brethren tarried for three weeks in Indiana, successfully "preaching, singing and dancing." But on the next visit to the Wabash country, he recorded,

a mob of 12 men came upon us on horseback with ropes to bind us, headed by [one] John Thompson. He stepped up to me and said, Come prepare yourselves to move—Move where? said I—Out of this country, said he, for you have ruined a fine neighborhood and now we intend to fix you—Your hats are too big, we shall take off part of them, and your coats are too long, we shall take off part of them, and seeing you will have nothing to do with women, we shall fix you so that you can not perform.

Well, said I—have you any precept? Yes, precept enough for you— Well, you must show it—Damn you, get your horses for you must go— Well, I tell you up and down we shall not go with a mob. Then John Hadden spoke, if you do not go and get your horses I will get them, for you *shall* go. Where are they? They are in William Berry's stable ... but if you get them, we shall not get on to them—Well then, we will put you on—Well then, we shall get off again—Well then, we will tie you on— Well, you will have a hard job before you get thro'—and by this time all the rest of the mob were a-laughing and said, come let us go—So they started, but John Thompson looked back and let off these words: If you ain't gone before Saturday night, I'll be d—d if you don't go—dead or alive—Verry well, said I.

Now on Saturday was their muster day at Vincennes and we expected that a number of them would come along drunk on Sabbath and trouble us, so one of the brethren went to the Governor [of the Indiana

Territory] and informed him, and on Sabbath morning he sent a magistrate and constable, and they stilled them very quick; and so he was always ready at anytime to help us.

> —(Issachar Bates) "Sketch of the Life and Experience of Issachar Bates," from a Mount Lebanon manuscript copy, Shaker Museum, Old Chatham, New York

The ill-fated outpost at Busro, Indiana, was also beset by Indian problems and disease, and lasted only until 1827.

Issachar Bates, Sen., was getting his horse shod at a smith's, in a western state, when he, as usual opened a sermon on man's fallen fleshly nature, and assured the company present that Christ had come again, and that he was a representative of the new gospel. He then showed the necessity of a man's confessing his sins, and living a new life like Jesus, and he should then be enabled to do greater works than even Jesus. While preaching to his motly hearers, he was annoyed by one who kept demanding a miracle! "What shall I do for you?" he finally asked. "Turn that cart-wheel into a horse!" replied his annoyer. "That's just like the evil one," he remarked, "to leave the owner of that cart with only one wheel to go home with."   —*The Shaker*, Sept. 1872

One of the most important converts in the Southwest was Richard McNemar, the scholarly Presbyterian minister who was a leader of the Kentucky Revival. A New Light pastor who had left the established church, Richard knew that his congregation would follow him a second time, into Shakerism. But he pondered his decision carefully. He was pacing up and down in his garden, praying for guidance, when, it is said, he received a sign: a woman's arm stretched beseechingly from the heavens. "I will follow thee forever!" he cried to his vision of Mother Ann.

Richard, like Issachar Bates, devoted many talents to his calling as a Believer. The father of Shaker literature and journalism, he wrote a history of the Kentucky Revival with a description of the Shaker missions to the Shawnee Indians. This was the first bound book by the Shakers. He was also a great versifier, and wrote most of the early Shaker songs. As Believers were gathered into "society order," he cast even the sober Shaker convenant into a spirited hymn.

Come ye souls that are sincere, the gospel to pursue
Now your faith you may declare, & what you mean to do

Are you pleas'd with what is done,
    To introduce Emanuel's reign?
Yea I am, and each for one, may freely say—Amen.

Can you in this work rejoice, because it saves from sin?
Was it your delib'rate choice that freely brought you in?
    Is it your good faith alone
    That holds you like a golden chain?
Yea it is, and each for one, may freely say,—Amen.

Does the cov'nant you have sign'd a right'ous thing appear?
Is it your unwav'ring mind, in it to persevere?
    In its bonds however tight
    Are you determin'd to remain
Yea I am,—Then we'll unite and jointly say Amen.

You have promis'd and agreed, a daily cross to bear,
And obey your gospel lead, with faithfulness and care
    Do you think it just and fit,
    A due subjection to maintain?
That's my faith, and I'll submit—and all may so, Amen. . . .

Can you part with all you've got, & give up all concern,
And be faithful in your lot, the way of God to learn?
    Can you sacrifice your ease,
    And take your share of toil and pain?
Yea I can, and all that please, may freely say,—Amen.

Can you into union flow, and have your will subdu'd,
Let your time & talents go, to serve the general good?
    Can you swallow such a pill—
    To count old Adam's loss gain?
Yea I can, and yea I will, and all may so, Amen. . . .

I set out to bear my cross, and this I mean to do:
Let old Adam kick and toss, his days will be but few.
    We're devoted to the Lord,
    And from the flesh we will be free;
Then we'll say with one accord, Amen, so let it be.

—"A Covenant-Hymn," Union Village, Ohio, 1813, in
    J. P. MacLean, *A Bibliography of Shaker Literature*,
    1905

In relation to our building a new Meeting House & the causes thereof: how that the old M.H. was So Shattered, that it would take much labour to repare it & besides it did not Stand So much in the centre as the Believers wished. Therefore, the Ministry at Union Village [Ohio] gave us union in building a new one & makeing a work Shop of the old one and it answers a valuable purpose for that use. The new M. House is 60 by 44 feet, & very Strong, Substantial Frame it is, and neatly finished off . . .

The Brethren Started into the woods, about 3½ milds off, to cut the timber for this House, the 3rd of January, 1820 and pronounced it done, the last day of the next October, which was 10 months in the building, lacking two days.   —Pleasant Hill journal, quoted by Samuel W. and
James C. Thomas, *The Simple Spirit: A Pictorial
Study of the Shaker Community at Pleasant Hill,
Kentucky,* 1973

*By 1827 the roster of western Shaker societies was complete: Union
Village (the New Lebanon of the West), Watervliet, North Union, and
Whitewater had been gathered in Ohio; South Union and Pleasant Hill
in Kentucky. The worst mob scenes and terrorism were past, and the
Shakers were regarded as excellent farmers and well-meaning neighbors.
Among many accomplishments, they were noted for their livestock and
for introducing the culture of silkworms and the manufacture of silk.
Their seedsmen and salesmen went down the Kentucky, Ohio, and Mississippi rivers in flatboats and steamboats with garden seeds, cattle, and
hogs for markets as far as New Orleans. The first bound Shaker books
were published in Ohio. And there and in Kentucky, ministries established in detail the order and institutions that characterized Shaker societies everywhere.*

Despite its complexity, the Shakers' closed system was not unique, but replicable. It could be created anywhere that new members gathered to form "a living building."
    —Dolores Hayden, *Seven American Utopias,* 1976

*With the rousing songs of the Kentucky Revival coming readily to
their lips, the western Believers rejuvenated the style of their new worship, and influenced the development of Shaker song.*

In May 1836 a party of Ohio Shakers sat at sunset on the deck of a canal boat traveling between Columbus and Cleveland. The evening was "still, & serenely calm." Most of their fellow travelers had gone off to bed, but they were still accompanied by "a grave old high Sherif" who had made it his aim to fall into their company whenever he "handsomely could." He at last "began to conclude he must hear a Shaker hymn, before he could go to rest" and asked that they sing one, "if it was agreeable" to their feelings. A brother struck up "Vain World." Immediately all the other travelers "came scampering out like so many mice," one poor old woman "so enamored, that she came with her night cap on!" After several hymns and an anthem or two, the Shakers went off to their own "little plank beds" with the cordial thanks of their audience.

From such chance meetings or from attending a service, Worldlings naturally picked up few Shaker songs, but it may seem surprising that songs were rarely taken into the World by people raised among the Shakers or resident for a time in one of the communities. Some, like Mary Dyer, left of course in bitterness and sang the songs, if at all, only to ridicule them. But many others probably refrained out of simple decency and a respect for religion in general or the Shakers themselves. The apostates from the community at Savoy, New York, for example, were never known to ridicule or speak against the Shakers. "Some of them," said Calvin Green, "when asked by the world to sing Shaker songs, would answer 'How shall I sing the Lord's songs in a strange land?' "

VAIN WORLD

Farewell! farewell! vain world farewell! I find no rest in thee.
Thy greatest pleasures form a hell too dark and sad for me.
Alas! alas! I have too long prefer'd thy sinful croud:
I listen'd to your Syren song, while mercy call'd aloud.

Farewell, vain world! I say once more, I'm bound for Canaan's land.
I see a happy world before—prepar'd at God's right hand.
On life's tempestuous sea I sail, while countless billows roll;
But Christ my pilot will not fail, with him I trust my soul.

He can command the roaring tide, and silence all my foes:
With courage safely I can ride through ev'ry wind that blows;
Then as I daily homeward steer toward the land of peace,
This world does less and less appear and all its charms decrease.

The shining millions sail'd before, who gain'd the port above—
Found nothing in old Babel's store that they could prize or love.
That everlasting glory bright will tarnish all below,
Just as the sun's meridian light forbids the stars to glow.

> —Excerpt and Hymn No. 31 from Daniel W. Patterson, *The Shaker Spiritual*, 1979

Sept 1847

23rd . . . We took the steamboat Milwaukie for Cleveland . . . slept none.

24th   At day break we found Elder Samuel Russel on the dock with a very nice carriage to take us out 9 miles to North Union . . . where we were made welcome by our beloved gospel kindred.

27th . . . There are about 160 in the society, they are simple and kind, loving and near feeling, true hearted and well tried, subject and obedient to their visible lead, yea, in short I think they are worthy heirs of the kingdom. They are not yet so well accommodated for buildings as they are in some places among believers.

> —"Prudence Morrell's Account of a Journey to the West in the Year 1847," *Shaker Quarterly*, Fall 1968

In 1818, it was thought best to call home from the western societies most of those who had been sent out to do the work of organization. These societies were now believed to be strong enough and sufficiently well grounded in the principles of the Gospel to care for themselves. Of the three pioneer missionaries, John Meacham was a native of New York State, born in 1770. Returning from the west in 1818, he passed from earth in 1854. Benjamin Seth Youngs, also from the State of New York, returned from his western home in November, 1836, and passed away in March, 1855. Issachar Bates was a native of Hingham, Mass., an old hero of the Revolution. He was born January 29th, 1758. Recalled in his old age to Mount Lebanon, he withdrew with great reluctance from his hard won fields in the west, mournfully sounding his "retreat." Returning on June 9th, 1835, he passed to his heavenly home on March 17th, 1837.

> —White and Taylor, *Shakerism*, 1904

It is interesting to note that every dollar expended Western Shakers in the early years of their organization by the Mt. Lebanon ministry in New York, and by the Hancock, Mass., Enfield, Conn., and Canterbury, New Hampshire Communities was returned in full to the Eastern brethren.

When Benjamin Seth Youngs was recalled from South Union, Kentucky, in 1835, he took $500. to cancel the last donation to that area.

The last payment of $1,640 was made by Union Village in 1841 before they started to build the large center building in 1844.

—Hazel Spencer Phillips, *Richard the Shaker*, 1972

Far as the gospel spirit reigns,
  Our souls are in communion,
From Alfred to South Union's plains,
  We feel our love and union.
Here we may walk in peace and love,
  With God and saints uniting,
While angels smiling from above,
  To glory are inviting.

—*Hymns and Poems for the Use of Believers*, 1833

THE SHAKER WAY

No Dirt in Heaven

In 1850 a chain of peaceful and polished Shaker societies with a population of 6,000 stretched across the country almost to the Mississippi. Most of the sisters and brethren in the fifty-eight "families" that composed the societies were Millennialists. They believed God's kingdom had come, and they were living in it, unmarried and unsullied as angels. Christ's spirit filled them, as it had Mother Ann, and they labored as she'd taught, to make the way of God their own. It was their occupation.

Mother Ann taught too that there was "no dirt in heaven." And there was none in a Shaker village. Even the dust in the road seemed pure to one observer. "Gospel order" meant not only cleansed souls but model farms and well-scrubbed shops, carefully tended grounds, and clean rooms in airy dwellings.

The world's people, who had looked askance at the Shakers' theological heresy, looked again at this effective social and economic union.

They are an orderly, industrious sect, and models of decency, cleanliness, and of morality, too, so far as the human eye can penetrate. I have never seen, in any country, villages so neat, and so perfectly beautiful, as to order and arrangement, without, however, being picturesque and orna-

"The Village of the United Society of Shakers, in Canterbury, N.H." From the *American Magazine of Useful and Entertaining Knowledge*, November 1835. Courtesy of the Library of Congress.

mented, as those of the Shakers. At Hancock, the gate-posts of the fences are made of white marble, hewn into shape and proportions. They are manufacturers of various things, and they drive a considerable trade with the cities of New-York, Albany, and Boston. They are renowned retailers of garden seeds, brushes, farming utensils, &c. &c.

—James Fenimore Cooper, *Notions of the Americans,* 1828

GARDEN SEEDS

Can be obtained at all times fresh and of the best quality, at the "GENERAL SHAKER DEPOT," 96 John St. New York. Farmers and Gardeners wishing to obtain Seeds, can depend upon purchasing first rate Seeds, raised and prepared for market, in the most careful manner, by the Shakers. Orders addressed to T. R. HIBBARD, 96 John Street, will meet with prompt attention.

Also, always on hand, wholesale and retail, Herbs, Extracts, Brooms, Sieves, Diaper, Thread, Silk Gloves, old Cheese, and generally all articles raised and manufactured by the Shakers.

—*The American Agriculturalist,* vol. I, no. 1, April 1842

No Dutch town has a neater aspect, no Moravian hamlet a softer hush. The streets are quiet; for here you have no grog-shop, no beer-house, no lock-up, no pound; of the dozen edifices rising about you—workrooms, barns, tabernacle, stables, kitchens, schools, and dormitories—not one is either foul or noisy; and every building, whatever may be its use, has something of the air of a chapel. The paint is all fresh; the planks are all bright; the windows are all clean. A white sheen is on everything; a happy quiet reigns around. . . . Mount Lebanon strikes you as a place where it is always Sunday. The walls appear as though they had been built only yesterday; a perfume, as from many unguents, floats down the lane; and the curtains and window blinds are of spotless white. Everything in the hamlet looks and smells like household things which have long been laid up in lavender and roseleaves.

—Hepworth Dixon, *New America*, 1867

It was a Saturday evening. The weekly toil of the community had ceased, and a Sabbath stillness brooded over the populous town. Immense dwellings filled with men and women, and extensive workshops supplied with the choicest implements, lined the one broad street. Order and Neatness there held high court with a majesty I had never before seen. The very dust in the road seemed pure.

—Benson J. Lossing, "The Shakers," *Harper's New Monthly Magazine*, July 1857

The buildings are large and strong—constructed with a view of permanency. All resident houses in Ohio and Kentucky are built solid, and mostly of brick, and in the form of the letter T. Such houses in the Eastern States are of barn-like structure. . . . The Western houses have large

Twin staircases for the sisters and brethren in the 1824 Centre House at Shakertown at South Union, Kentucky. Separate doorways lead to the meeting room beyond. Photograph by Elmer R. Pearson.

hallways, with stairsteps on either side—the one side for the sisters and the other for the brethren.

—J. P. MacLean, *Shakers of Ohio*, 1907

In Cincinnati, Ohio, I met one day with a Shaking quaker. He wore a broad-brimmed hat, and shad-bellied coat of a bluish-gray homespun cloth, with his hair cropped short before and falling into the neck behind.... He gave me a friendly invitation to visit the Shaker village of Lebanon [Union Village, Ohio], twenty miles distant....

The domain of the Shakers was marked by striking peculiarities. The fences were higher and stronger than those on the adjacent farms; the woods were cleared of underbrush; the tillage was of extraordinary neatness; the horse, cattle, and sheep were of the best breeds, and in the best condition....

Simple utility is the only rule of architecture. There is not, in the whole village, one line of ornament. The brown paint is used only to protect the woodwork of the buildings. I did not see so much as an ornamental shrub or flower....

The women, old and young, ugly and pretty, dress in the same neat but unfashionable attire. There are no bright colours; no ruffles or flounces or frills; no embroidery or laces; no ribbons or ornaments of any kind. The hair is combed smoothly back under a plain cap; a three-cornered kerchief of sober brown covers the bosom, and the narrow gored skirt has no room for crinoline.

The rooms and furniture are as plain and homely as the external architecture. There is not a moulding nor any coloured paper; not a picture nor print adorns the walls, nor is there a vase or statue. The only books are a few of their own religious treatises, collections of hymns, and works of education, science, and utility.

But there is everywhere the perfection of order and neatness. The floors shine like mirrors. Every visible thing is bright and clean.... This order and neatness is carried out in the workshops, the yards, everywhere.

—Thomas Low Nichols, *Forty Years of American Life*, 1864. (Nichols was an all-round reformer, a one-time vegetarian, graham-flour advocate, promoter of women's rights and the water cure, and follower of Fourier and John Humphrey Noyes.)

Union Village, 4 miles w. of Lebanon, is a settlement of Shakers, or as they call themselves, "the United Society of Believers." They came

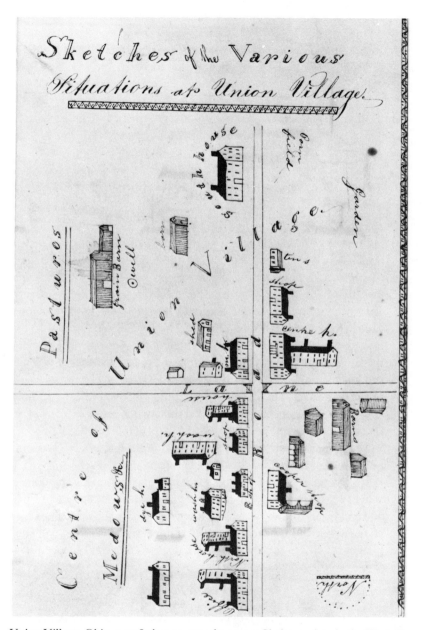

Union Village, Ohio, near Lebanon, was the parent Shaker society in the West. By the time this pen-and-ink drawing by George Kendall (from the original by Isaac N. Youngs), described it in 1835, the village had survived local "expeditions against the Shakers" and was settling into years of great prosperity. Courtesy of the Library of Congress.

here about the year 1805, and now number 400 souls. The village extends about a mile on one street. The houses and shops are very large, many of them brick, and all in a high degree neat and substantial. They are noted for the cleanliness and strict propriety of conduct characteristic of the sect elsewhere, and take no part in politics or military affairs, keeping themselves completely aloof from the world, only so far as is necessary to dispose of their garden seeds and other products of agriculture and articles of mechanical skill. They own here about 3000 acres of land, and hold all their property in common.

The community are divided into five families, each family having an eating-room and kitchen. A traveller thus describes their ceremonies at the table.

> Two long tables were covered on each side of the room, behind the tables were benches, and in the midst of the room was a cupboard. At a signal given with a horn, the brothers entered the door to the right, and the sisters the one to the left, marching two and two to the table. The sisters in waiting, to the number of six, came at the same time from the kitchen, and ranged themselves in one file opposite the table of the sisters; after which, they all fell on their knees, making a silent prayer, then arose, took hold of the benches behind them, sat down and took their meal in the greatest silence. I was told this manner was observed at all their daily meals. They eat bread, butter and cakes, and drank tea. Each member found his cup filled before him—the serving sisters filled them when required. One of the sisters was standing at the cupboard to pour out the tea—the meal was very short, the whole society rose at once, the benches were put back, they again fell on their knees, rose again, and wheeling to the right, left the room with a quick step. I remarked among the females some very pretty faces, but they were all, without exception, of a pale and sickly hue. They were disfigured by their ugly costume, which consists of a white starched bonnet. The men likewise had bad complexions.   —Henry Howe, *Historical Collections of Ohio,* 1847

Utopia Proved Possible

With their withdrawal from the world in 1787, the United Society of Believers became the first native American communitarians. The devel-

opment of the communal system under which the sisters and brethren lived in social and sexual equality, with united capital and labor, impressed the world's utopians.

Robert Owen, the Welsh reformer, was encouraged by the "first view of a Shaker village" to found his own ideal society in America. He bought a ready-made community in Indiana from the German sect of Rappites, who then followed their leader, Father Georg Rapp, back east to build a third prosperous communal village.

The economic success of the Rappites and the Shakers convinced Friedrich Engels, co-founder of Marxian socialism, that communism was practical. In an article published in 1845 in Germany he extolled both groups—sight unseen—and dismissed "the religious humbug" as unimportant.

The first people in America, and actually the world, to create a society on the basis of common property were the so-called Shakers. . . . Although their religious views and especially the prohibition of marriage frightened many away, they nevertheless found a following and now have ten large communities, each three to eight hundred members strong. Each of these communities is a handsome, symmetrically built village with houses, factories, workshops, meeting houses, and barns. . . . Their barns are always full of grain, their storerooms full of cloth, so that an English traveller who visited them said he could not understand why these people, who owned an abundance of everything, still worked; perhaps they worked only to pass the time of day. Among these people there are none who have to work against their will and none who search for work in vain.

Describing Pleasant Hill, Kentucky, he wrote:

They are free, rich and happy. . . . They breed cattle, practice agriculture and produce their own flax, wool and silk which they spin and weave in their own factories. What they cannot use is sold or exchanged with their neighbors. They usually work as long as there is light. . . . The community is divided into five families (sections) of forty to eighty members. Each family manages its own affairs and lives together in a large handsome house; each person receives as much as he needs from the general community storehouse without payment. . . .

They are happy and cheerful among themselves, there is no discord; on the contrary, friendship and love rule throughout their abode, and in all parts of the same there is order and regularity the likes of which do not exist.   —Friedrich Engels, "A Description of the Communistic Settlements That Were Formed in Recent Times and Still Exist," *Deutsches Burgerbuch*, 1845

The world as yet but slightingly appreciates the domestic and humane virtues of this recluse people; and we feel that in a record of associative attempts for the actualization of a better life, their designs and economics should not be omitted, especially as, during their first half century, a remarkable success has been theirs.

—Charles Lane, "A Day with the Shakers," *The Dial*, October 1843

The example of the Shakers has demonstrated not merely that successful Communism is subjectively possible, but that this nation is free enough to let it grow. Who can doubt that this demonstration was known and watched in Germany from the beginning; and that it helped the successive experiments and emigrations of the Rappites, the Zoarites and the Ebenezers? These experiments, we have seen were echoes of Shakerism. . . . Then the Shaker movement with its echoes were sounding also in England, when Robert Owen undertook to convert the world to Communism; and it is evident enough that he was really a far-off follower of the Rappites. France also had heard of Shakerism, before St. Simon or Fourier began to meditate and write Socialism. These men were nearly contemporaneous with Owen, and all three evidently obeyed a common impulse. That impulse was the sequel and certainly in part the effect of Shakerism. Thus it is no more than bare justice to say, that we are indebted to the Shakers more than to any or all other Social Architects of modern times. Their success has been the solid capital that has upheld all the paper theories, and counteracted the failures, of the French and English schools. It is very doubtful whether Owenism or Fourierism would have ever existed, or if they had, whether they would have ever moved the practical American nation, if the facts of Shakerism had not existed before them, and gone along with them.

But to do complete justice we must go a step further. . . . We must also acknowledge that the Shakers are the far-off echoes of the Primitive Christian Church.   —John Humphrey Noyes, *The History of American Socialisms*, 1870. (Noyes was the founder of the Oneida Community.)

The American Shakers

A Celibate, Religious Community

Coeval with the American Republic ; First Shaker Family formed at Watervliet, N. Y., 1776 ; First organized Shaker Community established at New Lebanon, N. Y., 1788 ; Fifteen Shaker Societies in seven States of the United States of America.

Beginnings.

Founder, ANN LEE, of Manchester, England, (1736-1784). In religious revival of 17th Century, arose the "Shaking Quakers," or "Shakers," 1754. Nine persons from Manchester and Bolton, emigrated, May 1774, for the purpose of founding a Shaker Church in America. Eight remained faithful. They were ANN LEE, William Lee, James Whittaker, John Hocknell, James Shepherd, James Partington, Mary Partington, Nancy Lee.

FROM ANN LEE'S TEACHINGS.

Basic Principles of the Shaker Order.

VIRGIN PURITY, PEACE, JUSTICE, LOVE.

expressed in CELIBATE LIFE, NON RESISTANCE, COMMUNITY OF GOODS, UNIVERSAL BROTHERHOOD-- held to be the Divine Order of Society.

Resultant Beliefs and Practices Held as Ideals
TO BE ATTAINED IN THE INDIVIDUAL AND SOCIETY.

Equality of the Sexes, in all departments of life,
Equality in Labor, all working for each, and each for all,
Equality in Property,--No rich, no poor, Industrial Freedom,
    Consecrated Labor, Dedicated Wealth, A United Inheritance,
    Each using according to need,
    Each enjoying according to capacity.
Freedom of Speech, Toleration in Thought and Religion. Often persecuted,
    Shakers have never been known to persecute.
Abolition of all Slavery.--Chattel, Wage, Habit, Passion, Poverty, Disease.
Temperance in all things.
Justice and Kindness to all living beings.
Practical Benevolence. Thou shalt love thy neighbor as thyself.
True Democracy, Real Fraternity, Practical Living of the Golden Rule.

Religious Ideals and Worship.

All life and activity animated by Christian Love is Worship. Shakers adore God as the Almighty Creator, Fountain of all Good, Life, Light, Truth and Love,--the One Eternal Father-Mother.

They recognize the Christ Spirit, the expression of Deity, manifested in fulness in Jesus of Nazareth, also in feminine manifestation through the personality of Ann Lee. Both, they regard as Divine Saviors, anointed Leaders in the New Creation. All in whom the Christ consciousness awakens are Sons and Daughters of God. Spiritual man has, as his divine prerogative and highest destiny, to live in clear conception of and in active harmony with the Highest Good. The Life of the Spirit not the form of expression is essential.

Practical Issues.

Beautiful, comfortable Community Homes, in each a Christ Family,
Daily manual labor for all, according to strength and ability. "Hands to work and hearts to God." (*Ann Lee*)
Opportunity for intellectual and artistic development, within the necessary limits prescribed by the common good.
Sanitation, Health, Longevity.
Simplicity in dress, speech and manner.
Purity in thought, speech and personal habits.
Freedom from debt, worry and competition.

Government.

No Government without God, No Body without a Head.
The Head of the Shaker Order is Christ. The Visible Human Representative is vested in a

DUAL ORDER OF LEADERS.

Spiritual Leaders, of both sexes, a Ministry over Societies, Elders over Families.
Temporal Leaders, of both sexes, Trustees, Deacons and Care-takers, in charge of Business and Industrial Interests.

The Inner Life,

according to the Shaker Faith, is twofold, embracing
Repentance--confessing and forsaking all sin :
Regeneration--the growth and unfoldment in the individual of the Christ Spirit, through living according to the teachings and practice of Jesus Christ. As opposed to the common life of human generation and selfish gratification, this is held to be the Resurrection Life.

Physical development, mental growth and spiritual unfoldment form the only rational basis for a harmonious and happy existence: self-denial the corner-stone of the structure. The truths inherent in Shakerism are the underlying truths of God-life in all ages and the mission of the Shaker is to unfold and demonstrate these truths.

A broadside of Shaker history and belief.

It is interesting to observe, that while [Charles] Fourier in France was speculating on the attainment of many advantages by union, these people have, at home, actually attained them. Fourier has the merit of beautiful words and theories; and their importation from a foreign land is made subject for exultation by a large and excellent portion of our public; but the Shakers have the superior merit of excellent actions and practices; unappreciated, perhaps, because they are not exotic.

—"The Millennial Church," *The Dial*, April 1844

They present the sublime and hope-inspiring spectacle of a community founded and built up on the conquest of the inexorable appetites: lust, avarice, ambition, revenge.... They have solved for us the problem of the possibility, the practicability, of a social condition from which the twin curses, pauperism and servitude, shall be utterly banished. They have shown how pleasant may be the labors, how abundant the comforts, of a community wherein no man aspires to be lord over his brethren, no man grasps for himself, but each is animated by a spirit of devotion to the common good.   —Horace Greeley, "Hints toward Reform," 1850; extracted in *The Shaker*, Oct. 1872

The temporary success of the Hernhutters, the Moravians, the Shakers, even the Rappites, have cleared away difficulties and solved problems of social science. It has been made plain that the material goods of life . . . are not to be sacrificed in doing fuller justice to the social principle. It has been proved, that with the same degree of labor, there is no way to compare that of working in a community, banded by some sufficient Idea to animate the will of the laborers. A greater quantity of wealth is procured with fewer hours of toil, and without any degradation of any laborer. All these communities have demonstrated what the practical Dr. Franklin said, that if everyone worked bodily three hours daily, there would be no necessity of any one's working more than three hours.

But one rock upon which the communities have split is, that this very ease of procuring wealth has developed the desire of wealth.... This is especially the case with the Shakers, whose fanaticism is made quite subservient to the passion for wealth, engendered by their triumphant success.

The great evil of Community, however, has been a spiritual one. The sacredness of the family, and personal individuality have been sacrificed. Each man became the slave of the organization of the whole. In becoming a Moravian, a Shaker, or whatever, men have ceased to be men in some degree.   —[Elizabeth Peabody] "A Glimpse of Christ's Idea of Society," *The Dial*, Oct. 1841

The most remarkable order of land-owners that I saw in the United States was that of the Shakers and the Rappites; both holding all their property in common, and both enforcing celibacy. The interest which would be felt by the whole of society in watching the results of a community of property is utterly destroyed by the presence of the other distinction; or rather of the ignorance and superstition of which it is the sign.

The moral and economic principles of these societies ought to be most carefully distinguished by the observer. This being done, I believe it will be found that whatever they have peculiarly good among them is owing to the soundness of their economic principles; whatever they have that excites compassion, is owing to the badness of their moral arrangements.

I visited two Shaker communities in Massachusetts. The first was at Hancock, consisting of three hundred persons, in the neighbourhood of another at Lebanon, consisting of seven hundred persons. There are fifteen Shaker establishments or "families" in the United States, and their total number is between five and six thousand. There is no question of their entire success, as far as wealth is concerned. A very moderate amount of labour has secured to them in perfection all the comforts of life that they know how to enjoy, and as much wealth besides as would command the intellectual luxuries of which they do not dream. The earth does not show more flourishing fields, gardens, and orchards, than theirs. The houses are spacious, and in all respects˙unexceptionable. The finish of every external thing testifies to their wealth, both of material and leisure. The floor of their place of worship, (the scene of their peculiar exercises,) the roofs of their houses, their stair-carpets, the feet of their chairs, the springs of their gates, and their spitting-boxes,—for even these neat people have spitting-boxes—show a nicety which is rare in America. Their table fare is of the very best quality.... If happiness lay in bread and butter, and such things, these people have attained the *summum bonum*. Their store shows what they can produce for sale. A great variety of simples, of which they sell large quantities to London; linen-drapery, knitted wares, sieves, baskets, boxes, and confectionary; palm and feather fans, pin-cushions, and other such trifles; all these may be had in some variety, and of the best quality. If such external provision, with a great amount of accumulated wealth besides, is the result of co-operation and community of property among an ignorant, conceited, inert society like this, what might not the same principles of association achieve among a more intelligent set of people, stimulated by education, and exhilarated by the enjoyment of all the blessings which Providence has placed within the reach of man? . . .

The co-operative methods of the Shakers and Rappites might be tried [in the Old World] without any adoption of their spiritual pride and cruel superstition. These are so far from telling against the system, that they prompt the observer to remark how much has been done in spite of such obstacles.

There must be something sound in the principles on which these people differ from the rest of the world, or they would not work at all; but the little that is vital is dreadfully encumbered with that which is dead. Like all religious persuasions from which one differs, that of the Shakers appears more reasonable in conversation, and in their daily actions, than on paper and at a distance. In actual life, the absurd and peculiar recedes before the true and universal; but, I own, I have never witnessed more visible absurdity than in the way of life of the Shakers. The sound part of their principle is the same as that which has sustained all devotees; and with it is joined a spirit of fellowship which makes them more in the right than the anchorites and friars of old. This is all. Their spiritual pride, their insane vanity, their intellectual torpor, their mental grossness, are melancholy to witness. Reading is discouraged among them. Their thoughts are full of the one subject of celibacy: with what effect, may be easily imagined. Their religious exercises are disgustingly full of it. It cannot be otherwise: for they have no other interesting subject of thought beyond their daily routine of business; no objects in life, no wants, no hopes, no novelty of experience whatever. Their life is all dull work and no play.

—Harriet Martineau, *Society in America*, 1837

The Shaker communities are the most rational, and probably the happiest of all conventual institutions. I should be glad if similar ones were found in all countries. People may say what they will, and do the best they can in the great community, but there will always exist the need of places where the shipwrecked in life, the wearied of life, the solitary and feeble, may escape as to a refuge, and where their good-will and their powers of labor may, under a wise and affectionate management, be turned to account; where the children of misfortune or misery may be brought up in purity and love; where men and women may meet and associate as brethren and sisters in good-will and friendship, laboring all for the benefit and advantage of each other. And this is the case here. The Shaker community is—admitting some small, narrowed peculiarities—

"Shaker houses, Enfield." From *Connecticut Historical Collections* by John Warner Barber, 1836.

one of the best small communities in the world, and one of the most useful in the great community.

This sect is, in general, misunderstood. People consider its dancing mode of worship to be the main principle, when, in fact, that might just as well be away, though I, for my part, would willingly retain it for its symbolic meaning.   —Fredrika Bremer, *The Homes of the New World: Impressions of America*, 1853

Political communitarians in England (from the early socialists in the 1820s to the anarchists in the 1890s) viewed the Shaker communities with mixed emotions—aware that the reasons for their success were in contradiction to their own ideals. The strict social system, which reduced many of the tensions that occurred in secular communities, was unacceptable to those who sought a humanist basis for freedom. The Shakers were driven by the depth of their millennial beliefs, convinced that the millennium had already begun, and thus freed from the insecurity of waiting for something that is always imminent but always beyond reach. The chiliasm of the Shakers set them apart from the rest of society and though undoubtedly successful in one sense, their communities were models which could not easily be adopted by secularists.

—Dennis Hardy, *Alternative Communities in Nineteenth-Century England*, 1979

In the middle of the nineteenth century Christianity was at a turning point, hesitating between a renewal of the church and a reform of society ... During this same period European communism was hesitating between the semireligious millenarianism of Cabet, Weitling, and even, in some respects, Owen, and a rigorous analysis of self-conscious class struggle. Where does the distant echo of Shakerism fit into this picture? Was it a vestige or rather a revival of early Christianity, which itself carried strains of the great Eurasian religions, as Leo Tolstoi has shown us? Was it a preview of modern socialism, and was it, unwittingly or unwillingly, an integral part of its gestation, as Engels thought?

The significance of the United Society of Believers seems to be that it was caught between two goals, and that it never evolved beyond the stage of this unsurmounted, if not unsurmountable, dilemma. The distant neo-Christianity of the Shakers remained a distant presocialism ... It ... might even be called a "missing link," since through it two such different trends or life styles seem to have, momentarily at least, come into rudimentary contact.   —Henri Desroche, *The American Shakers*, 1971

The Shaker experiment made both negative and positive contributions to the history of utopian societies. We may regard the restrictions upon personal liberty, the authoritarian government, and the unnatural suppression of sexual impulses as heavy sacrifices to make in the interests of a communal society that lasted for 150 years. Yet their positive contributions to the communal ideal were important. Almost alone among such communities, they produced skilled craftsmanship and a folk art of their own. Their insistence on absolute equality between men and women was revolutionary. So also was their tolerance of race and colour—for they were the only people of their time to include both Jews and Negroes in their settlements. They fought slavery, war, and the worst aspects of society at that time, not by pleading with a world in which their voices would have been lost, but by offering what they considered to be a model of the good life.   —Mark Holloway, *Heavens on Earth*, 1951

The excursion to Big Bone Lick, in Kentucky, and that to the Quaker village, were too fatiguing for females at such a season, but our gentlemen brought us home mammoth bones and shaking Quaker stories in abundance.

These singular people, the shaking Quakers of America, give undeniable proof that communities may exist and prosper, for they have continued for many years to adhere strictly to this manner of life, and have been constantly increasing in wealth. . . .

There must be some sound and wholesome principle at work in these establishments to cause their success in every undertaking, and this principle must be a powerful one, for it has to combat much that is absurd, and much that is mischievous.

The societies are generally composed of about an equal proportion of males and females, many of them being men and their wives; but they are all bound by their laws not to cohabit together. Their religious observances are wholly confined to singing and dancing of the most grotesque, and this is repeated so constantly as to occupy much time; yet these people become rich and powerful wherever they settle themselves. Whatever they manufacture, whatever their farms produce, is always in the highest repute, and brings the highest price in the market. They receive all strangers with great courtesy, and if they bring an introduction they are lodged and fed for any length of time they choose to stay; they are not asked to join in their labours, but are permitted to do so if they wish it.

—Mrs. Frances Trollope, *Domestic Manners of the Americans,* 1832

Women's Rights Gained

Was Mother Ann the first American feminist? Surely she was an activist in liberating the colonial woman. She saw women in a strong role as the spiritual equals of men. She promoted what she thought was a higher service for them than marriage, and she provided them with the good company of others with a like calling. She promised a great reward: salvation.

After her death, when the Believers drew together for security in community, dual government was established, in which the position of women was equal to that of men. This equality grew naturally from Shaker acceptance of the duality of the Christ spirit, with which Jesus and Ann were anointed, and of God. To Believers deity is not a Trinity or a Great Man. It is dual, male and female, Father and Mother.

Long ere this fleeting world began,
Or dust was fashion'd into man,
There *Power and Wisdom* we can view,
Names of the *Everlasting Two.*

The Father's high eternal throne
Was never fill'd by one alone:
There Wisdom holds the Mother's seat,
And is the Father's helper-meet.

This vast creation was not made
Without the fruitful Mother's aid;
For by the works of God we know
The fountain-head from which they flow.
                    —*Millennial Praises*, 1813

At a meeting of the Equal Rights Club of Hartford, Connecticut, on February 6, 1903, "The Motherhood of God" was the subject for discussion. The Old Testament statement, "And God said, 'Let us make man in our image, after our likeness,' " was featured as the dual, twofold principle in the animal, mineral, and vegetable kingdom. A press report of the meeting caught the eye of a Shaker eldress at Mount Lebanon, New York, who wrote a letter

To the Secretary and Members of the Equal Rights Club:
    The Hartford Daily Times of February ninth has just reached our quiet homes on the hillside, containing the utterances at the meeting of the Equal Rights Club on the Motherhood of God. Not since the days of Theodore Parker, who prayed in public to his Heavenly Father and Heavenly Mother, has anyone, to our knowledge, spoken in stronger and clearer terms upon this all important subject, so simple that the wise of this world overlook or do not understand the meaning of the word, "and God said let us make man in our image, after our likeness," showing as plainly as two and two are four that God is dual—Father and Mother. To us, the simple Shakers, this grand truth was revealed one hundred and thirty-three years ago. —Anna White, *The Motherhood of God*, 1904

    It is a very strange thing to the outside world, that the Shakers . . . should have hit upon the idea of the bi-sexuality of God, manifesting himself in the flesh, first in the male and then in the female—Jesus and Ann. . . . The Greek word, 'Theos,' God, is both masculine and feminine and conveys the idea of the Hindoo theology, the oldest on earth, that the sexes unite in the great First Cause.
    It may seem to strengthen this conception of the Divine Bi-Sexuality

when we contemplate the fact that the Shakers never got it from books. It seems to have been breathed upon them by the Spirit of God thru angels and glorified spirits. . . .

Mr. Darwin maintains that the human race was once androgynous; that is to say, the two sexes were united in the same person. . . . The finest human characters are those that blend the strength of the man with the purity and gentleness of the woman.

> —A. G. Bradford (ex-consul to China), "Bi-sexuality of God," *Shaker and Shakeress,* July 1873

The freedom for all women sought by Shakers was not militantly and negatively feminist, not something sought at the expense of the male principle. It was, as was the Shaker assertion of the masculine and feminine principles in the Godhead, essentially *androgynous.*

By the term "androgynous" I here mean what Carolyn Heilbrun has described as "a condition under which the characteristics of the sexes, and the human impulses expressed by men and women, are not rigidly assigned."

For me, and perhaps for most women, it has been necessary to progress from a sense of self as woman, as free person, to a recognition of the androgynous ideal. For me this recognition has also meant a far greater comprehension of the Shaker duality in Deity. . . .

Just as the Shaker saw in the equality and freedom of Shaker women a greater freedom too for men, a truly androgynous freedom, the Shaker also saw the emergence of an androgynous quality in the life of the world's people, the possibility of woman acting, not in competition, but in co-operation with man.

> —Virginia Weis, "Women in Shaker Life," from a paper delivered at the Bicentennial Conference at Sabbathday Lake, Maine, August 1974

The meeting in the evening at the City Hall was an immense crowd. . . . The aisles and lobbies of the great hall were filled, and many were turned away. There were probably 3000 people present. Several Shaker songs were sung, and addresses were delivered by Eldress Antoinette Doolittle, a very pleasing speaker, and by Elder Evans. Both touched upon political themes, and urged the necessity of trusting a share of the government to woman. Elder Evans said that there had been two revolutions needed in this country to free it from monarchy and slavery, and there are still in the constitution the elements of future revolutions. It was a pressing need that woman should have a voice in the government. If the Representatives are men, let the Senate be women, and whatever can receive the sanction of both houses will be likely to be right and safe.

—"The Shaker Meetings," *Transcript* (Portland), June 15, 1872

The increasing interest in, and agitation of the subject of women's rights, woman suffrage, &c. ... are a living prophecy progress will be made in that direction. But we believe that woman's true sphere can be fully comprehended only by those who recognize the fact that God is *mother* as well as *father*. The promulgation of correct views of Deity must ultimately result in the proper elevation of woman, and of a consequence, the race.   —C. E. S., *The Shaker*, Jan. 1871

If prophets predicted a Son should be giv'n,
And he to a Father should rise;
The prophets, the order of nature, & heav'n,
Declare there's a Mother likewise.

—*Hymns and Poems for the Use of Believers*, 1833

Is God a Woman?
Is Debated Here   —*The New York Times*, Feb. 10, 1974

Can we keep a proper reverence about this new androgynous concept of God?   —Harriet Van Horne, New York *Post*, Feb. 11, 1974

Visited the Shakers. I gain but little from their domestic or internal arrangements. There is a servitude somewhere, I have no doubt. There is a fat, sleek, comfortable look about the men, and among the women there is a stiff reserve that belongs to neither sublime resignation nor divine hope. Wherever I turn, I see the yoke on women in some form or other.

—(Abigail May Alcott, wife of Bronson Alcott) Odell Shepard, *Pedlar's Progress*, 1937

The Shaker ideal of equality for woman was *not* always achieved, as attested by the accounts of various Shaker sisters. Sometimes the inequality was apparently trivial, as in the unconscious male chauvinism of the brothers at table; sometimes, in the management of money, the economic consequences were rather serious. ... Infinitely more upsetting to [Sis-

The ironing room at Mount Lebanon, New York, from *Frank Leslie's Illustrated Newspaper*, September 1873. Joseph Becker was a staff artist who sketched a series of scenes of Shaker life.

ter] Aurelia [Mace] is the failure of the brothers to acknowledge the equality of their sisters in worship.

In her Journal account of the meeting house at Sabbathday Lake, Maine, she writes:

> Doors and walks were provided for both brethren and sisters,—until a great "He" Spirit entered. That was when this last new brick house [1883] was built. In that there was but one door and one walk across the road. It was laid out by that great and mighty "He," for the brethren to go out and over first and the Sisters to follow. Thus, as far as this Society was concerned, one of the great principles of the New Creation was over-ruled, the equality of the sexes.—The beauty was all destroyed, for the brethren would get into their ranks in the meeting house before the Sisters would enter.—The Sisters would be coming over behind the little boys.
>
> —Virginia Weis, "Women in Shaker Life," 1974

They hold strongly to the equality of women with men, look forward to the day when women shall, in the outer world as in their own societies, hold office as well as men. "Here we find the women just as able as men in all business affairs, and far more spiritual." "Suppose a woman wanted, in your family, to be a blacksmith, would you consent?" I asked; and [Elder Frederick Evans] replied, "No, because this would bring men and women into relations which we do not think wise." In fact, while they call men and women equally to the rulership, they very sensibly hold that in general life the woman's work is in the house, the man's out of doors; and there is no offer to confuse the two.

Moreover, being celibates, they use proper precautions in the intercourse of the sexes. Thus Shaker men and women do not shake hands with each other; their lives have almost no privacy, even to the elders, of whom two always room together; the sexes even eat apart; they visit each other only at stated intervals and according to a prescribed order; and in all things the sexes maintain a certain distance and reserve toward each other.   —Charles Nordhoff, *The Communistic Societies of the United States,* 1875

GOSPEL ORDERS CONCERNING INTERCOURSE BETWEEN THE SEXES

1st. The gospel of Christ's second appearing strictly forbids all private union between the two sexes.

2nd. One Brother and one Sister must not be together alone, except it be long enough to do a short and necessary errand, nor touch each other unnecessarily.

3rd. Brethen & Sisters must not work together, except on special occasions, and then it must be by the permission of the Elders.

4th. Brethren and Sisters are not allowed to make presents to each other in a private manner.

5th. It is contrary to good order for Brethren and Sisters to pass each other on the stairs.

6th. It is contrary to good order for members of the family to stop on broad stairs, or on the walks, or in the streets with those of our own order, or any other order, longer than to do some necessary errand or messages or to enquire after the wellfare of our friends &c. If any longer time be necessary to talk among ourselves, or with our neighbors we are taught to do it within some of our buildings.

7th. Brethren & Sisters must not go to each others apartments without a just and lawful occasion.

8th. Brethren & Sisters must not go into each others apartments after evening meeting; except on some needful occasion.

9th. When Brethren have occasion to go into Sisters apartments, or Sisters into the Brethrens apartments they must knock at the door & go in by liberty.

10th. The Brethren must all leave their rooms when the Sisters go in to make the beds or clean the room, unless prevented by sickness or infirmity.

11th. When Sisters walk out into the fields, or to the barns, or to the hen roosts, or even to the Brethrens' shops, there must be at least two in company; for it is considered unbecoming for one Sister to go alone on such occasions, unless by the special liberty of the Elders of their own sex.

—"The 'Millennial Laws' of 1821," ed. by Theodore E. Johnson, *Shaker Quarterly*, Summer 1967

In 1814, a disastrous storm at Mount Lebanon began one night in August. . . . Six inches of rain fell; the swollen brooks brought down from the mountains mud and stones, gullied the roads, gardens, door-yards and tan-yard. The dam broke and the rushing waters carried carding shop and fulling mill down stream to the valley below. Mother Lucy gave the people advice "for all to look pleasant, speak pleasant and labor to feel so." The advice did much good. All went zealously and cheerily to repair damages. On the day after the flood, Mother Lucy with the Elders, accompanied by the brethren and sisters, walked out over the tract of the washout and in the afternoon she "imparted to the sisters of both Orders a gift to go out and assist in the repairs." This gift, the logical outcome of Gospel sex equality, was accepted, and, accordingly, says the historian: "They came forth, leaving their spinning wheels for wheelbarrows, the needle for a shovel and their brooms for a hoe and rake; and encountering the huge mass of rubbish, like a band of strong men, with the assistance of a few brethren, the stone, gravel, wood, timber and slabs were removed, so that before night came on, our streets, lanes and yard appeared tolerably decent again."   —White and Taylor, *Shakerism*, 1904

women counted

hoed and shovelled
snow made the rules

One sister could turn
3 thousand times and
not get dizzy the

next morning dig as
many potatoes as a man
                    —Lyn Lifshin, *Shaker House Poems*, 1976

April 21, 1872. New Gloucester, Maine.

If the brethren in that family [Poland Hill] would manage as well as Sisters and be as enterprising, the family could sustain itself and pay its taxes.   —Sabbathday Lake, Maine, *Journals*

The women of the Shaker Societies claim to be fully emancipated—to have equal rights with the men in all respects. The Shaker government is dual in all its departments and offices. The women appear to have as much influence and voice as the men; a woman founded the organization, and a woman held its first office for twenty-five years during its greatest period of prosperity; women are as free as men to speak in their meetings; women are as free as men to write for their paper; women manage their own departments of industry independently of the men.

                    —William Alfred Hinds, *American Communities*, 1878

Although the Shakers have always recognized the most perfect equality of the sexes, yet in certain conditions, as for instance in worship, both cannot lead, and in this and similar cases the initiative was always conceded to the brethren. So also, as there was no divided financial interest, the brethren only were the trustees, the title of the Office Sisters being Office Deaconess. The brethren kept all the books of accounts, and in their names were made all deeds and titles to real estate.

                    —Nicholas A. Briggs, "Forty Years a Shaker," *The Granite Monthly*, December 1920

On March 14, 1818, the New York Legislature passed a special act dissolving the marriage of Eunice and James Chapman. In most states this would scarcely have been a memorable event, because legislative divorces were at that time commonplace. But New York was conservative in this matter, and Eunice's was the only divorce ever directly voted by the Legislature. To win it, a determined woman waged a three years' campaign that pitted her not only against her husband and his Shaker co-religionists, but also against the most determined forces of conservatism in the state. Yet the struggle for a divorce was only one campaign in Eunice's longer war to win custody of her own children. Historians have treated the Shaker arts and crafts with great respect, but have perhaps paid less attention than they should to the problems that occasionally arose out of the peculiar Shaker tenets on marriage and the family. . . .

Eunice Chapman finally obtained custody of her three children, whom the Shakers had hidden away from her.

As for the Shakers, they had, it is true, lost three promising little neophytes, but there were obvious compensations. No longer need they fear harassment from an implacable enemy, able to stir legislatures to action, to rally threatening mobs for support, and to disturb the slumber of the saints with the midnight roar of guns.

—Nelson M. Blake, "Eunice Against the Shakers," *New York History*, Oct. 1960

Any married person, being an inhabitant of this state, who shall hereafter attach him or herself to the society of Shakers in this state, shall be deemed and taken to be civilly dead, to all intents and purposes in the law, and his or her property may be disposed of in the same manner as if such person were really dead; and such person shall forever thereafter be incapable of taking any estate, real or personal, by inheritance.

—From An Act Concerning the Shakers, Legislature of New York, March 14, 1818

The New York State Legislature finally passed an act . . . which dissolved the Chapman marriage and granted parents the right to petition the court for the custody of children allegedly held by Shakers. The act also imposed penalties upon Shakers or anyone else secreting a child or carrying a child out of the state. The penalties were removed in 1896, but the basic legislation remained effective as Section 71 of the Domestic Relations Law until May 1975.

—Dorothy M. Filley, *Recapturing Wisdom's Valley*, 1975

The Democratic Study Group [an informal gathering of 33 New York State Assemblymen] . . . showed it could laugh at itself recently at a dinner when its counsel ... gravely read a list of supposed study-group priority bills. The measures included proposals to let teachers sell liquor to Indians, to let "Shakers detain children." ...

The measures have been on this year's agenda.

—*The New York Times*, June 17, 1975

It was customary for brethren and sisters to use separate doors and stairways, and to work apart in separate shops. The sexes did not mingle freely, never touched even when united in worship or attending "union" meetings.

Three evenings in the week are set apart for worship, and three for "union meetings." ... For the union meetings the brethren remain in their rooms, and the sisters, six, eight, or ten in number, enter and sit in a rank opposite to that of the brethren's, and converse simply, often facetiously, but rarely profoundly. In fact to say "agreeable things about nothing," when conversant with the other sex, is as common here as elsewhere. ... Nevertheless, an hour passes away very agreeably and even rapturously with those who there have chance to meet with an especial favorite; suc- ceeded soon however, when soft words and kind, concentrated looks be- come obvious to the jealous eye of a female espionage, by the agonies of a separation. For the tidings of such reciprocity, whether true or surmised, is sure before the lapse of many hours, to reach the ears of the elders; in which case the one or the other party would be subsequently summoned to another circle of colloquy and union. ...

No one is permitted to make mention of any thing said or done in any of these sittings, to those who attend another; for party spirit and mischief might be the result. Twenty minutes of the union hour may be devoted to the singing of sacred songs, if desired.

—Hervey Elkins, *Fifteen Years in the Senior Order of Shakers*, 1853

I have attended union meeting in all the rooms in the house once or more in a place. The brethren and sisters sit about six feet apart, and those that are hard of hearing appear as well contented as any that can hear all that is said.   —"Prudence Morrell's Account of a Journey to the West in the Year 1847," *Shaker Quarterly*, Fall 1968

The Shakers are nearly as far from limiting themselves to a Sunday meeting as the Oneida Communists. Nearly every evening in the week

"The Singing Meeting" by Joseph Becker. A wood engraving from *Frank Leslie's Illustrated Newspaper*, January 1873.

witnesses some gathering for conversation, singing or worship.

—William Alfred Hinds, *American Communities*, 1878

Every Sunday and Wednesday night, they have their union meeting, and the spiritual husband and wife sit opposite each other, though so near as to get fire from each other's pipes—they converse together in any little chit chat, as the people of the world do—the Elders have their Eldresses for their spiritual wives, and the Deacons have the Deaconesses; the Elders and Eldresses, sit at the head of the company forming a letter A. consequently they can have the shortest stems to their pipes; they also eat melons, apples and nuts, and drink cider, and sing their merry love songs, such as

> I love the brethren, the brethren love me,
> Oh! how happy, how happy I be,
> I love the sisters, the sisters love me,
> Oh! how happy, how happy I be.
> How pretty they look, how clever they feel,
> And this we will sing, when we love a good deal.

Then the spiritual husband each with his spiritual wife, withdraw to different apartments. The Elders and Eldresses, and Deacons and Deaconesses, have their separate union meeting, they feast on the richest dainties, with the best of spiritous liquors.

—Mary Dyer, *A Portraiture of Shakerism,* 1822. (Published by the author, who notes that "her only object in giving to the world this history, is, that the unsuspecting may not be entrapped by the apparent virtue and rectitude of the people called *Shakers.*")

Mary Dyer was an ex-Shaker who lost her husband and children to the Enfield, New Hampshire, Shaker society when she withdrew after four years. She devoted the rest of her life to loud accusations and unsuccessful lawsuits.

Even fruit of extra and rare properties is divided among elders, trustees, and common members, male and female, with rigorous exactness. "None, by reason of care and trust in them reposed, seek for anything more agreeable to eat, drink, or wear, then those have, to whom they stand

"The Shakers at Lebanon Enjoying a Sleigh-ride," a wood engraving from a sketch by Joseph Becker, *Frank Leslie's Illustrated Newspaper,* January 1873.

as leaders."   —Hervey Elkins, *Fifteen Years in the Senior Order of*
                              Shakers, 1853

Some people suppose that the opposite sexes among the Shakers never commune together; such are mistaken. While we live absolute virgin lives, there is much freedom in the social sense . . . but it is required to be free from all that would tend to carnal affections and actions. The power thus to live in purity and innocence, is found in the conviction that a spotless, virgin, angelic life is the order of the kingdom of Christ, and is higher, better, happier than a sensual, worldly life.

> —*Concise Statements Concerning the Life and Religious Views of the Shakers*, 1896

An Idle Person Tempts the Devil

Life among Believers was founded on union and love, and was not Spartan or joyless, despite strict guiding rules. Carefully kept daybooks and journals picture the way farm chores and household activities were shared among the thirty to one hundred members of each family. In the 1840s, for instance, records at Pleasant Hill, Kentucky, note: "Sisters went to the Shawney springs after boneset, a medicinal herb." "Brethren began to gather in the winter apples." On another day, "Sisters washed up all the counterpanes and gingham gowns."

Dec. 31st, 1847. Tabitha, Lucinda and Terrissa wove 32 yards of frock cloth. A very good days' work for these short days.

Oct. 27, 1842. All the Brethren and Sisters in the Center Family signed the article of agreement to quit the use of all strong drink and also the use of tea. Coffy and tobacco and the use of swines flesh in part.

Sept. 7, 1859. All who wished mounted in their carriages and buggies and went out to the new farm. Spent the day in pleasure.

Certainly, you have no menial service—none of your community think work is degrading; while in society at large, many men are ashamed of work, and, of course, ashamed of men (and women) who work, and make them ashamed of themselves. Now, the Shakers have completely done away with that evil, as it seems to me; that is one of their great merits and it is a very great one.

> —(Theodore Parker) John Weiss, *Life and Correspondence of Theodore Parker*, 1864

The Shakers are very diligent people, and yet seem always to have any desired leisure, as one notices in large, old-fashioned families where people do their own work.

—William Dean Howells, "A Shaker Village," *Atlantic Monthly*, June 1876

"Attractive Industry and Moral Harmony," on which Fourier dwells so promisingly, have long characterized the Shakers, whose plans have always in view the passing of each individual into his or her right position, and of providing suitable, pleasant, and profitable employment for every one.   —"The Millennial Church," *The Dial*, April 1844

Of the management of the homes, the people had devised the most complete system. Every department had its head or lead. The elder and eldress presided over the family: the trustees looked after the finances of the estate; the deaconesses provided the provisions; there was a deacon for the yard, another for the orchard, etc. etc. so that everything received the utmost care.   —J. P. MacLean, *Shakers of Ohio*, 1907

"Finishing Room," by Benson J. Lossing. *Harper's New Monthly Magazine*, July 1857.

In every department perfect order and neatness prevail. System is everywhere observed, and all operations are carried on with exact economy. Every man, woman, and child is kept busy. The ministry labor with their hands, like the laity, when not engaged in spiritual and official duties; and no idle hands are seen.

—Benson J. Lossing, "The Shakers," *Harper's New Monthly Magazine*, July 1857

Low, low! Low, low! In this pretty path I will go,
For here Mother leads me and I know it is right,
I will sweep as I go, I will sweep as I go,
For this Mother bids me and it is my delight.

—Enfield, New Hampshire, song

WINTER SHAKERS

"How do you manage with the lazy people?" I asked in many places; but there are no idlers in a commune. I conclude that men are not naturally idle. Even the "winter Shakers"—the shiftless fellows who, as cold weather approaches, take refuge in Shaker and other communes, professing a desire to become members; who come at the beginning of winter, as a Shaker elder said to me, "with empty stomachs and empty trunks, and go off with both full as soon as the roses begin to bloom"—even these poor creatures succumb to the systematic and orderly rules of the place, and do their share of work without shirking, until the mild spring sun tempts them to a freer life.   —Charles Nordhoff, *The Communistic Societies of the United States*, 1875

Little Band of Union

Contradictory as it may seem, family life was emphasized and cherished by the Shakers. The word family had, of course, a larger meaning for them than the usually accepted term. The world's use of the term seemed narrow and selfish to the Believers. To be brothers and sisters in a consecrated communion of the spirit was to be joined not only in human companionship with one another, but also in a spiritual relationship with Mother Ann and all Believers living and dead—a mystical relationship that reached back to the beginning of man's yearning toward God; and forward into Eternity. It was part of the mission of the Millennial Church

Many nineteenth-century prints of Shaker life usually seen separately appeared originally on pages like this. Joseph Becker was the artist who sketched the scenes for *Frank Leslie's Illustrated Newspaper* in the 1870s.

to make the Shaker communal life a practical demonstration of the earthly Utopia they preached. And since the family was a natural grouping of the human race, they continued in their growing communities the family division with which many of them had begun.

New Lebanon, largest of all the Shaker societies, numbered eight families at one time. . . . The average number of families in a society was three, and was likely to include a *Church* or *Center* family with the others designated by the direction in which they lay from the *Church*.

—Marguerite Fellows Melcher, *The Shaker Adventure*, 1941

Both simplicity and unity, in the Shaker experience, are very affirmative. It is others who have made them negative. To see Shaker furniture—and life—just as "stripped of ornament" and somehow barren of all human pleasure, is to fail to see the whole point of Shaker simplicity. To be truly simple is to know one's self honestly, yielding neither to pride nor to false humility. . . . Similarly, to equate unity with uniformity, . . . to reduce the whole concept to matters so external as uniformity in dress, is to mock it. For Shaker union is profoundly internal, not a superficial adherence to an external code. It is a coming together, and being one, in Christ. It is not primarily an act of obedience, but an experience of loving and being loved. . . . Neither simplicity nor unity, rightly understood, was ever meant to be a negation or denial of human nature. Rather, these were the qualities in which and by which one's human faculties to know and love might be most truly realized.

—Virginia Weis, "Every Good and Simple Gift," *Shaker Quarterly*, Spring 1974

UNION CAKE

A cupful of butter, two of sugar, one of sweet milk, three of flour, half a cupful of corn starch, four eggs, two teaspoonfuls of lemon flavor, one of cream of tartar, and half a teaspoonful of soda.

—*Mary Whitcher's Shaker House-Keeper*, 1882

Despite, or perhaps because of, the Pentecostal orientation of Shaker beliefs, they included elements which tended to make for greater liberality than did the orthodox theologies. Punishment of the wicked was not to be everlasting. Predestination and original sin were abandoned. Baptism, the

Communion, and concepts of the Trinity and the atonement, alike were discarded. Literal adherence to the Bible was supplanted by direct revelation. The chaste, honest, industrious, and saintly life a person led, rather than any sacrament or creed, was his chief claim to sanctification.

—Whitney R. Cross, *The Burned-Over District*, 1950

The most sacred and significant meeting of the year among the Believers was the "Christmas Gift" often called the "Yearly Sacrifice." This originated from an ancient Jewish custom which called for complete confession of sins and making restitution for such wrongs and thereby establishing peace and union among their fellow-men. The Shaking Quakers of England saw in this lovely ancient custom a suitable preparation for commemorating the birthday of our Lord. Mother Ann brought this custom to Niskayuna where it was faithfully kept; and when Father Joseph Meacham gathered the converts into Church Orders, he established this "Yearly Sacrifice" as an abiding ordinance in connection with Christmas which to the Shakers was a feast of love and fellowship.

—Caroline B. Piercy, *The Valley of God's Pleasure*, 1951

LOOK TO "THE LEAD"

The Church of Christ is a spiritual family; and as it is composed of visible members, there must be a visible head, to stand as the center of influence or leading power in that family. As the leading power of the visible church is vested in the Ministry, as the visible head; so in each separate family of the Society, which is considered as a branch of the church, the leading power is vested in the elders who are considered as the heads of their respective families. And so long as the visible head or leaders of any family conduct themselves in a manner worthy of this trust, it is necessary that they should be obeyed by all the members of the family. Without this obedience there can be no regulation, order nor harmony in the family.

—Green and Wells, *A Summary View*, 1823

It is rather difficult on the surviving evidence to determine how the society was so efficiently governed. All officials, administrators, business representatives, and religious leaders were appointed from the top. They were subject to a minimum of control by community meetings, more perhaps by "revelations." . . . So autocratic a system of government, espe-

Four able elders: from left to right, James S. Kaime, Canterbury, New Hampshire; Abraham Perkins, Enfield, New Hampshire; Benjamin H. Smith and Henry C. Blinn, Canterbury.

cially over small communities scattered from New Hampshire to Kentucky when much of the country was still wilderness, would be expected to result in factionalism and schism; yet in the case of the Shakers it did not. In both secular and religious governance the Society led an unusually untroubled life. . . .

One of the factors making for cohesion is cult. Medieval monasticism, with its continuous round of Mass, Divine Office—the chanting of psalms, hymns, canticles, and prayers every few hours throughout the day and night—and the continuously varying rites of the year, so involved the monk or nun that it was difficult even to think of breaking away. In America in the nineteenth century the Shakers undoubtedly had the most highly developed cult.—Kenneth Rexroth, *Communalism*, 1974

The question remains whether the Shaker system does not tend to produce too great distinctions between the governing and governed classes—whether even in a theocratic form of government, like that of the Shakers, it is not wisest to so conduct affairs that every one shall feel, not only that he is personally interested in the general prosperity, but that he contributes to it . . . —William Alfred Hinds, *American Communities and Co-Operative Colonies*, second revision, 1908

The office of an Elder is not to *govern*, in the ordinary sense of that term, but to *lead*. Elders are not to be *feared*, but *loved*. (They are to set others an example by *governing themselves*.) . . . The Elder's duty simply is, by *counsel*, *precept* and *example*, to aid others to govern themselves.

—Harvey L. Eads, *Shaker Sermons: Scripto-rational*, 1879

O what a great privilege I do enjoy!
  Good Elders to teach what is just,
And always a plenty of righteous employ,
  Sufficient to mortify lust:
So, how to find heaven I'm not at a loss,
  Nor how I'm to keep out of hell;
If I be obedient, and bear a full cross,
  No danger but I shall fare well.

—*Hymns and Poems for the Use of Believers*, 1833

When you feel conviction for any thing, tho' it may appear small to you—go to your Elders and there seek a privilege to confess it for if you allow yourself to keep it—wherever it may be, you will grow hardened and finally fall from the way of God.

—Unpublished manuscript, "A Short Account of a Gift of sweeping which Commenced in the North Family [New Lebanon, N.Y.] Dec 22nd 1841," in the New York Public Library

When you look up from the floor of the big room [at Mount Lebanon] where the Sabbath services were held, you see four slits in the rear wall that suggest some sort of primitive ventilation. Actually they are peepholes that were used by the ministry for looking down on the congregation. They are in twos, far apart on different horizontal levels. The two lower ones are slatted and more conspicuous than the upper ones, which are single slits like a slit in a letter box.

It is explained that the ministry did not go down to the floor of the church because they were too holy for that, and those who had the letter box slits were the holiest of all. Upstairs in the ell of the meetinghouse, the ministry were provided with chambers where they slept, but in 1875 they moved to a new dwelling erected for them.

—Clifton Johnson, "The Passing of the Shakers," *Old-Time New England*, July 1934

"Shaker Window," a photograph ca. 1935 by the noted artist Charles Sheeler of the Ministry's lookout in the meetinghouse at Mount Lebanon, New York. The window was eliminated when the meetinghouse was remodelled to be the library for the Darrow School, located in the former Shaker church headquarters. The photograph is in the collection of the William H. Lane Foundation.

A *true* Shaker ... seems almost a new being—a being who lives in the brightness, splendor, and beatitude of heaven. A zeal to do what he believes the will of God summons forth all the energies of the soul to forego any sacrifice.   —Hervy Elkins, *Fifteen Years in the Senior Order of Shakers*, 1853

If intensely imbued with *caritas* [charity], the Shakers were also one of the most disciplined and highly structured of Christian bodies. Early in their history they vested absolute spiritual and temporal authority in a central Ministry of two elders and two eldresses, trustees, and deacons. They evolved a code of "Holy Orders" which governed the behavior of the members even to the point of ruling on the eating of unripe fruit, sitting with their feet on the rounds of a chair, writing with red ink, or copying music. They "united," to use their significant phrase, in sacred dance and other rituals far more elaborate and disciplined than those used in any other American worship.

Thus Shakerism paradoxically conserved an intensely subjective emotionalism within the framework of extreme social control.

> —Daniel W. Patterson, "The Influence of Inspiration and Discipline upon the Development of the Shaker Spiritual," *Shaker Quarterly*, Fall 1966

The Shaker government, in many points, resembles that of the military. All shall look for counsel and guidance to those immediately before them, and shall receive nothing from, nor make application for anything, to those but their immediate advisers.

> —Hervey Elkins, *Fifteen Years in the Senior Order of Shakers*, 1843

Life With the Shakers

Life with the Shakers is very simple and uneventful.

The "brothers" and "sisters" of each "family" live in the same great four story "family house." The brethren have their rooms on one side of the wide, clean halls, and the sisters theirs on the other side. Two, three, four, or five brethren occupy one room with as many single beds. Two, three, four, or five sisters also share their room with one another, and each has her single bed.

The rising bell rings at five o'clock in summer and half-past five in winter. Upon rising the brethren take off their bed clothes, fold them neatly, and lay them across the backs of two chairs. They then go out and do the morning chores.

The sisters likewise, after properly caring for their rooms, attend to their morning chores.

An hour after the rising bell the breakfast bell rings, and all repair to the big dining-room, which they enter in two files, one composed of the brethren, from the oldest in regular gradation of age down to the youngest, and led by the elders, the other composed of the sisters, from the oldest down to the youngest, and led by the eldresses.

In this order they enter the dining-hall, and march down the long, spotlessly clean, but clothless table, the brethren on one side of the house and the sisters on the other. Arrived at their places, they all kneel for a moment in silent thanksgiving and prayer.

Then all seat themselves and eat the meal with speechless assiduity.

The table is completely furnished with food at intervals of four plates, and waiting sisters, who take monthly turns at this work, replenish the food-plates as fast as emptied. At the end of the meal all, at a signal from the elders and eldresses, kneel again, and thereafter pass quietly out in two files, but inverse order from that in which they entered.

Breakfast over, the work of the day follows. The brethren disperse over the farm and to the shops. The sisters go to the laundry, the ironing-room, the shops, or about the house work. Those sisters detailed for that work make the beds and arrange the rooms for the brethren. Others sweep the halls and polish them with their curiously hooded brooms.

Others work in the kitchen. All have work assigned for them to do. The endeavour is to give to each that which he or she can do best, and for the best good of all. It has been remarked of the Shakers that special talent is speedily recognised and appropriately utilised.

At half-past eleven all are summoned from work, and just at noon sit down to a silent but bountiful dinner. After dinner all work till their as-

"Dinner-time at Mount Lebanon" by A. Boyd Houghton, a wood engraving from the *Graphic* (London), May 1870.

signed task is done, or until summoned from work at five or half-past five. At six o'clock supper brings all silently together again, and a couple of hours quiet in their room for reading, writing, or study, prepares for bed at nine.

Sunday is preceded by a special service of song and silent prayer on Saturday evening. The great meeting of the day is in the afternoon, and consists of singing, marching, silent prayer, and exhortation. This meeting is held in the meeting-house or in the meeting-room of the family house of the "centre" or "church" family, and all are expected to attend, if not ill. A song and prayer service in the evening closes the quiet day.

> —*Manifesto*, reprinted in Frederick W. Evans, *Autobi-
> ography of a Shaker*, 1869

THOUGHTS ON LIVING IN A SHAKER HOUSE

This Shaker house is neat and low
And everything is made just so,
Its lineaments are straight and clean,
The household gods are epicene.

This house is full of pegs and sense,
A kind of grudging elegance
Informs each piece and artifact
Come down to us preserved intact:

Chairs and cabinets built for use
That never knew a child's abuse,
Household objects scarcely worn,
The makers dead, the heirs unborn.

One thinks of busy little souls
Bent over little wooden bowls,
Like bees in well-conducted hives,
Living their close peculiar lives,

Too occupied with sin and chairs
For ordinary griefs and cares,
Too much intent upon a vision
To see the saving imprecision.

Our rueful sense of lives ill-spent
Is, in the end, impertinent,
And does not in the least impair
The beauty of a Shaker chair.

    —Janet Malcolm, *The New Yorker*, Nov. 2, 1963

ORDER is the creation of beauty. It is heaven's first law, and the protection of souls.

Keep all things in order, as keeping the law of heaven; and keep the order of Zion, that heaven may protect you.

UNION is the cement wherewith souls are joined to the fountain of all good, and seals to the gospel of pure love.

CHARITY is a heavenly gift of God. As ye freely receive, so freely give. If ye have not this charity, ye are counted mean in the sight of God, and are as empty bubbles.

TO TRAVEL easy in the gospel, and make the swiftest possible progress toward the kingdom of righteousness and peace, is to keep a close union and joining to the body of the Church of God.

NEVER try to run on ahead, before the main body of good Believers, and above all, never fall back, but keep close up and be in the gift.

THE GREATEST TRAVEL, comfort and blessing a soul can gain, is to be found in being up and alive in every gift, feeling united in spirit, and thus the main body is strengthened, and Zion is built up and adorned.

    —*The Youth's Guide in Zion, and Holy Mother's Promises.* Given by inspiration at New Lebanon, N.Y., 1842

  Temperance and chastity, plainness and simplicity, neatness, industry and good economy, are among the virtuous principles which actuate the people of the United Society, in all their temporal concerns, and which tend greatly to promote the health and prosperity of the Society, and insure the blessings of Divine Providence upon all their labors. And it is found by many years experience, that this manner of life is more conducive to the general health of the body, than any other with which we are acquainted; and this experience has also proved, that fewer deaths have occurred in the Society, since its establishment, in proportion to the number of people, than is usual among those who live after the common course of the world.   —Green and Wells, *A Summary View*, 1823

SEPARATION FROM THE WORLD

We are not called to . . . be like the world; but to excel them in order, union and peace, and in good works—works that are truly virtuous and useful to man, in this life.

—Father Joseph Meacham

RULES TO BE OBSERVED IN GOING ABROAD & IN OUR INTERCOURSE WITH THE WORLD OF MANKIND

When any of the Brethren or Sisters go abroad it must be by permission of the Elders, & without such permission they ought not to go off the farm. From this order the Deacons at the office are exempt. . . .

No one is allowed for the sake of curiosity, to go into the world's meeting houses, prisons, or towers, nor to go on board of vessels, nor to see shoes, or any such things as are calculated to attract the mind and lead it away from the love & fear of God. . . .

Whenever any of the family go out and stay over night, or longer, when they return they must see the Elders before they take their places in the family; and give them an account of their journey as it respects their protection and prosperity while absent; then they may take their places in the family; but they must take their places behind all in the spiritual worship of God, until the Elders think proper to let them come into their ranks again. . . .

Believers, when walking or riding together, either at home or abroad, should not let an undercreature, whether human or unhuman get between them if they can consistently help it.

Father Joseph was very careful in this particular, he would while riding on the road, turn his horse to the opposite side of the way to prevent either man or beast from passing between him and his companion.

—Extracts from the *Millennial Laws, or Gospel Statutes, Adapted to the Day of Christ's Second Appearing; Given and Established in the Church, for the Protection Thereof: By the Ministry and Elders. New Lebanon August 7th, 1821. Shaker Quarterly*, Summer 1967

NOTICE.

IN consequence of the increasing amount of company to which we are at all times subject, it becomes necessary to adopt the following

RULES FOR VISITORS.

FIRST. We wish it to be understood that we do not keep a Public House, and wish to have our Rules attended to as much as any one would the rules of their own private dwelling.

SECOND. Those who call to see their Friends or Relatives, are to visit them at the Office, and not to go elsewhere, except by permission of those in care at the office.

THIRD. Those who live near and can call at their own convenience are not expected to stay more than a few hours ; but such as live at a great distance, or cannot come often, and have near relatives here, can stay from one to four days, according to circumstances. This we consider sufficient time, as a general rule.

FOURTH. All Visitors are requested to rise to take Breakfast at half past Six in the Summer, and half past Seven in the Winter.

FIFTH. At the Table we wish all to be as free as at home, but we dislike the wasteful habit of leaving food on the plate. No vice is with us the less ridiculous for being in fashion.

SIXTH. Married Persons tarrying with us over night, are respectfully notified that each sex occupy separate sleeping apartments while they remain. This rule will not be departed from under any circumstances.

SEVENTH. Strangers calling for meals or lodging are expected to pay if accommodated.

UNITED SOCIETY,

"Shaker costume," a wood engraving from a watercolor sketch at New Lebanon by Benson J. Lossing. *Harper's New Monthly Magazine*, July 1857.

All ought to dress in plain and modest apparel, but clean and decent according to their order and calling . . . neither too high nor too low, but in a just and temperate medium, suitable for an example to others.
—Father Joseph Meacham

THE MILLENNIAL LAWS

From chaos, first, came word
of time; and out of the jaws
of time came our good Lord
and the Millennial Laws.

He is our very cause.
And while, with the others here,
I shake and dance—it is
"contrary to order" for

Believers to rest the feet
on the rounds of chairs,
or, ascending, to put
the left foot first on stairs;

to offer the world greeting;
to have right and left shoes;
or, when going to meeting,
not to walk on toes;

to nickname; to mix any
seed with another seed;
to keep a beast for fancy,
or lie curled in bed.

Or own watches; in the halls
to go blinking or yawning;
to tell nonsensical tales.
And there is no returning.

> —Jonathan Aldrich, "Shaker Village," from *Croquet*
> *Lover at the Dinner Table,* 1977

OFF TO THE WORLD AND BACK

A friend of ours had a girl in her service, who had escaped from a Shaker family, after having been brought up in it from her early infancy. She had grown more and more weary of the insipid life, from which all books, amusements, and variety were excluded, when one Sunday she excused herself from church on the plea of illness. She saw from her window a pony grazing in the field; she could not resist the invitation to exercise and sport; got out of the window, jumped upon the pony's back, and galloped round and round the field. She went in before church was over; but she had been seen, and was reported. In the irritation of her mind she could not bear censure, and escaped. The service into which she entered for support was easy, and her mistress was like a mother to her; but her pride could not brook service; and, after a struggle of some months, she went back to the Shakers, not pretending that it was for any other purpose than the saving of her pride.

> —"The Shakers," *Penny Magazine,* London, Nov. 18,
> 1837. (The correspondent responsible for this article
> was Harriet Martineau, author of *Society in*
> *America,* also published in 1837.)

Sept. 29, 1849. Caroline Whittemore, the harlot of Harrodsburg, who had been brought from Lincoln County when a child and stayed till she was driven off in consequence of her wicked ways; came back here today with one or two of her associate prostitutes under the influence of liquor called to see Brother James. She, in violation of the order, sought and found him at the East Wash House where she grappled with him and bore him off, she carrying a large horse pistol in her hand and swearing vengeance to those who dared interfere. James made no resistance but walked willing along with her.

Lucy Lemon was kindly invited to go to the world. She went!
—*Journals*, Pleasant Hill, Kentucky

The Shakers have been celebrated as a peculiar people, separate from the world around them. Their furniture is cited as a testimony of their separateness. A reappraisal of Shaker habit, may, however, confute this assertion. Shaker separation was a psychic exercise: the believer sublimated himself in a religious scheme and so transcended the temporal. The familiar environment was translated into a spiritual conceit. Instructed by a vision of a heavenly sphere, the Shakers pared the superficial from the temporal and discovered an inner reality, a divine simplicity, in which they should live. However, although the premises of their belief circumscribed their habit, defection among the believers prevented the accomplishment of complete orthodoxy. The Shakers' rejection of the world was not so strict as reputed. Their furniture registers their disposition and so serves as an index of their attention to the mystic vision. . . .

Because the believer "put his hands to work and heart to God," this furniture has . . . been termed "religion in wood." . . .

But not all of the furniture called Shaker is religion in wood. Nor were all of the people called Shakers believers.
—Mary Lyn Ray, "A Reappraisal of Shaker Furniture and Society," *Winterthur Portfolio 8*, 1973

Set apart from the world by conviction, they seemed unworldly in character as individuals and as a sect, yet they became prosperous, and, as by clairvoyance, reflected major movements within the country, continually passing into new phases that mirrored dominant concerns—intellectual, emotional, social, practical—outside their own communities. Sometimes . . . they seemed an advance guard.
—Constance Rourke, *The Roots of American Culture*, 1942

When the Shakers spoke of their separation from "the World," they meant the world of the cultivated tradition—of Victorian ornament, academic painting, and aristocratic manners. In the world of the vernacular—of inventions, efficient business practices, factory methods, and democratic institutions—they moved with unconcerned ease and with conspicuous success. —Janet Malcolm, "The Modern Spirit in Shaker Design," *Shaker: Furniture and Objects from the Faith and Edward Deming Andrews Collections*, 1973

Trade with the World

It is the duty of the Deacons and Deaconesses, or Trustees, to see to the domestic concerns of the family in which they reside, and to perform all business transactions, either with the world, or with believers in other families or societies. All trade or traffic, buying and selling, changing and swapping, must be done by them or by their immediate knowledge and consent.

No new fashions, in manufacture, clothing, or wares of any kind, may be introduced into the Church of God, without the sanction of the Ministry, thro the medium of the Elders of each family thereof....

The Deacons or Trustees should keep all their accounts booked down, regular and exact, and as far as possible avoid controversies with the world.

Believers must not run in debt to the world....

Neither Trustees nor any one in their employ should be gone from home among the world, on trading business, more than four weeks at one and the same time.

Three brethren who shall be appointed by the Ministry, two of which if consistent, should be Deacons or Trustees, are sufficient to go to the great and wicked cities to trade for any one family.

Believers should have no connection in trade or barter with those who have turned their backs to the way of God....

When you resort to taverns, and public places, you shall not in any wise blend and gather with the wicked, by uniting in unnecessary conversation, jesting and joking, talking upon politics with them, or disputing or enquiring into things which will serve to draw your sense from the pure way of God.

All who go out among the world, should observe as far as possible,

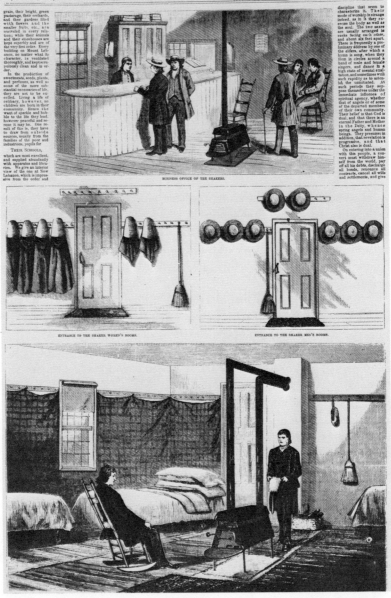

[SEPTEMBER 6, 1873.]   FRANK LESLIE'S ILLUSTRATED NEWSPAPER.   417

The Trustees' Office, where the Shakers dealt with the world's people, is pictured at the top of a page from *Frank Leslie's Illustrated Newspaper*, September 1873.

the order of kneeling, and should always kneel in prayer twice each day, if they have to do it by the road-side, or in the waggon while driving along.

—"The Order of Deacons or Trustees, and the Duties of Members thereunto," *Millennial Laws,* 1845, manuscript, Western Reserve Historical Society

NOT ECONOMIC SEPARATISTS

The role played by the communistic order of Shakers in the early industrial and social development of New York State, New England and the Kentucky-Ohio country is of such interest and importance that it seems strange that the subject has not hitherto been treated by the many observers who have written about this unusual sect. Although this religious society believed in separation from the world, so enlightened and forceful was its economic policy and so efficiently prosecuted were its complex industrial and agricultural activities that it influenced opinion and practice in many places and over a span of time reaching from the first formation of the American republic until well after the middle of the last century. . . .

The Shakers set an example of progressive business enterprise, on the plan of joint interest, that marks them as pioneers in this regard. Organized into closely knit communities as early as 1787, they should be numbered among the first to develop farming, gardening and manufacturing from a household scale to one marked by many of the essential factors in combination and mass production. Their numerous shops were equipped at an early date to produce on possibly an unprecedented plan, and the presence of large numbers undertaking communal life necessitated certain cooperative and inventive practices in which the Shakers were the leaders in America. Their pioneering contributions in such occupations as the growing and marketing of garden seeds, the manufacture of brooms and brushes, the growing, preparation and distribution of medicinal herbs and roots, the manufacture of chairs, etc., are especially deserving of recognition and record.

Not only did the Shakers thus initiate new methods and start new businesses, but so intimately related were these secular activities to the new religious idealism cherished by the members of the order that they early set a pattern for the most painstaking workmanship in all the productions of shop, garden and field. No organization in America held such an enviable reputation for honest dealing and dependable product. . . . The spirit with which the Shakers put their "hands to work and hearts to

God" is as significant as their actual achievements and early contributions to . . . the agricultural and mechanical arts.

—Edward Deming Andrews, *The Community Industries of the Shakers*, New York State Museum Handbook 15, 1932

The Shaker communities were a practical demonstration that competition is not necessarily the motivating force either of business success or of improved standards of living. Nothing they made was made primarily for profit. If they built up a good chair business at Mount Lebanon in the middle and latter part of the nineteenth century, if they found ready markets for the livestock raised in Ohio and Kentucky, the flannel manufactured in New Hampshire or the garden seeds and brooms put out by most of the societies, it was not because they had consciously striven for markets, or had produced for profit. Their first aim in any kind of production had been to supply their own needs—make themselves self-supporting and independent of "the world." That was why they had raised and manufactured so many different kinds of things.

Their second aim had been to achieve as nearly perfect an article as possible. They were building a kingdom of Heaven on earth and they could not defile it by inferior material furnishings. When they found themselves turning out a little more than they needed, they applied the same standard to everything they sold to "the world," lest the Shaker name be dishonored. This was the reason their products sold at a good price: the buyers knew they could depend on them. . . . The success, from a purely worldly point of view, of their outside business proves once again the truth of paradoxes, proves that a total disregard of the profit motive may, and does, build a profitable business. . . .

One of the intangible legacies the Shakers left to the world is their demonstration that it is possible for man to create the environment and the way of life he wants, *if he wants it enough.* Man *can* choose. In a world of defeatism, this is a cheering thought.

—Marguerite Fellows Melcher, *The Shaker Adventure*, 1941

HANDS TO WORK

We have a right to improve the inventions of man, so far as is useful and necessary, but not to vain glory, or anything superfluous.
—Father Joseph Meacham

In the early years the Believers worked hard to expand the kingdom of God for all who wanted to join it. The cry went out, "Make room for thousands!" But in later years the daily disciplined round of activities was less zealous. No one was overworked, though none were idle. Jobs were rotated, and because of the initial effort to be self-supporting, there was a wide variety of occupations. Shakers took pleasure in improving their skills and mastering several trades. Everyone made a contribution of labor, including the children raised among Believers. The ministry worked too in special shops.

From so much industry—so many hands to work—and so many needs—there was a flow of invention, an outpouring of mechanical gifts. The list of innovations and improvements is long: Shakers are the folk who gave us the flat broom, the common clothespin, cut nails, the metal pen, and the first garden seeds in small paper packets. Also, a tongue-and-groove machine, a screw propeller, a rotary harrow, a threshing machine, an improved washing machine, a pea sheller, an apple parer and corer, a revolving oven, and a notable wood-burning stove. They made water-repellent cloth, fabric that needed no ironing, and combination window sash. "Hair caps" were devised for brethren who were bald. And the legend persists that a Shaker sister invented the circular saw.

Sister Tabitha was gifted with rare inventive faculties, showing herself of kin to the noted Taunton goldsmith, the inventor of Babbittmetal. . . . She had noted that half of the motion of a reciprocating saw is useless for work, and while at her spinning the thought struck her that if there were teeth on the rim of her wheel it would cut continuously what was brought in contact with it. After making an experiment with a little tin disk fastened to the spindle, she was prepared to develop the idea of the buzz saw. . . . The idea of cutting nails and then heading them, instead of the slow process of hammering them one by one complete from the end of a nail rod, is sometimes credited to her, though also claimed by the Shakers of New Lebanon.

—Henry Stedman Nourse, *History of the Town of Harvard, Massachusetts*, 1894

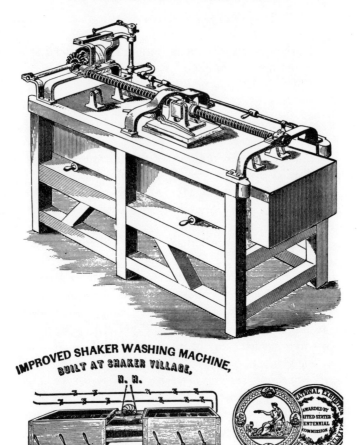

IMPROVED SHAKER WASHING MACHINE,
BUILT AT SHAKER VILLAGE,
N. H.

PATENTED July 28, 1877.

MANGLES, LAUNDRY APPARATUS.

CORN BROOMS & BRUSHES.

Address, J. S. Kaime, Trustee.

Hospitals, hotels, and commercial laundries were customers for the Shakers' improved washing machine, advertised here in *The Manifesto*, April 1884.

The Shakers had no fear of the machine. Their communities actually seem to have produced more mechanics and inventors per capita than most other towns and villages of comparable size. In the Shaker laundry and dairy at Canterbury, New Hampshire, at least as early as 1868 there was a stationary steam engine that did "all the work of lifting, lowering, turning, washing, ironing, drying, churning, etc."—which indicates a degree of mechanization not achieved in commercial laundries for some years thereafter. Indeed it is a noteworthy fact that the mechanical and inventive faculties which have so long been claimed as the peculiar virtue of rugged individualism turn out on inspection to have been a distinctive characteristic not only of the Shakers but of a number of other nineteenth-century socialist communities as well. . . . The severity and stripped quality of all Shaker objects (their furniture is never decorated with stencils or painted designs as are chairs and chests made in a true folk tradition like that of the Pennsylvania Dutch) was in perfect harmony with machine work. But its plain forms—though admired by "outsiders" for their utility—could scarcely have seemed beautiful to people who were accustomed to the ornamental design of the cultivated tradition. . . .

Shaker art was thus much more closely identified with the vernacular than with what the antiquaries call the folk arts. In its simplicity, lightness, linear clarity, and mechanical ingenuity it was sensitive to the technological environment, and its social aims were in harmony with equalitarian democracy. It had a share in molding the new tradition.

—John A. Kouwenhoven, *The Arts in Modern American Civilization*, 1948

Only a tentative explanation of Shaker innovativeness can be adduced, but it seems plausible that sexual repression, in combination with the hierarchical structure of the group and the anti-intellectualism of the Shaker elders, combined to direct the energies of many of the lower-ranking members toward practical concerns.

Junior members of the sect could move only very slowly upwards through its hierarchy; theological speculation was largely debarred by the authoritarianism of the elders and evangelism was the province of the most trusted senior members. In consequence, many of the younger members appear to have sublimated their sexual energies, and possibly their procreative desires, in the only way open to them—by developing high standards of craftsmanship and expending considerable energy and effort to improve the practical arrangements of the "earthly heavens."

—John McKelvie Whitworth, *God's Blueprints: A Sociological Study of Three Utopian Sects*, 1975

The Shakers at New Lebanon, Canterbury, and elsewhere made early use of the electric current for therapeutic purposes. . . . On April 2d

[1837] it is recorded that "Elder Sister . . . is not much better, but we keep her in and continue shocking her."

—Edward Deming Andrews, *The Community Industries of the Shakers*, 1932

It is a common charge against the Shaker system that it is unfavorable to individual development; but considering that, aside from the recruits brought them by revivals, the Shakers have had to depend for their new members largely upon the unfortunates who flock to them for homes when they find the struggle for existence too hard for them, and upon orphans and the children of poor people, glad to put their little ones where they will have enough to eat and wear, and be reared in habits of strict morality, the wonder is that so many capable men and women have developed in the Shaker societies; for they have had many persons who as thinkers, writers, speakers, and men of marked business capacity, would deservedly command respect for their ability in any circumstances; and they are credited with a long list of useful inventions.

—William Alfred Hinds, *American Communities and Co-Operative Colonies*, second revision, 1908

Few of the Shakers' inventions were ever patented. The families shared them, and outsiders were welcome to them. Gail Borden's invention of condensed milk was helped along the way by his use of a vacuum pan at Mount Lebanon.

The Believers' deep religious commitment to good craftsmanship

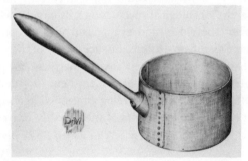

The initials D.M. on this wooden dipper are attributed to David Meacham, first deacon of the Church Family at New Lebanon, New York, who made or approved it. Courtesy of the Index of American Design, National Gallery of Art.

was expressed in the plain, everyday objects they used and sold, the practical buildings they constructed, and the functional furniture they designed. Although they were held to a strict goal of utility, a rare and lasting beauty came through in the careful work of their hands.

Let it be plain and simple, and of good and substantial quality which becomes your calling and profession, unembellished by any superfluities, which add nothing to its goodness or durability.

—A General Statement of the Holy Laws of Zion

The members of the church of God are forbidden to do any kind of work or to make any kind of tools or implements for the people of the world, the uses of which are disapproved in the church. They are also forbidden to make anything for Believers that will have a tendency to feed the pride and vanity of a fallen nature, or making anything for the world that cannot be justified among ourselves, or to purchase any of their manufactures to sell with ours for the sake of temporal gain.

—*Millennial Laws*, 1821

The Shaker communities, in the period of their greatest creative activity, have given us abundant evidence of their profound understanding of utilitarian design in their architecture and crafts. They understood and

Walk-in closets, built-in cupboards and dovetailed drawers line a room for storing clothing in the Dwellinghouse attic at Canterbury, New Hampshire. Drawing by June Sprigg, from *By Shaker Hands*, 1975. Courtesy of the artist.

convincingly demonstrated that rightness of proportion in a house or a table, with regard for efficiency in use, made embellishment superfluous. Ornament is often applied to forms to conceal uncertainty—and this applies to painting too. The Shakers would seem almost to have had a mathematical basis for their crafts, so knowingly and with such exactitude were their designs planned and realized. With knowledge of the tenets of their religion we are led to believe that beauty aside from utility was not desired. Their furniture and textiles and their tools of iron or wood represented conspicuous necessities, and so well were their plans for communal life formulated and practiced that they all but achieved a complete independence in agriculture and industry.

They recognized no justifiable difference to be made in the quality of workmanship for any object, no gradations in the importance of the task. All must be done equally well. Whether it was the laying of a stone floor in the cellar, the making of closet doors in the attic, or the building of a meetinghouse, the work required nothing less than all the skill of the workman.

It is interesting to note in some of their cabinet work the anticipation, by a hundred years or more, of the tendencies of some of our contemporary designers toward economy and what we call the functional in design. A combination of purposes was served within one unit in pieces of ordinary utility, as in a tall cabinet that has closet space with doors at the top and a number of drawers running the full width with smaller closets below made for special uses. The number of such adaptations and variations which the Shakers could create seemed almost infinite. One such tall cabinet has small drawers running all the way up to the top for apothecaries' remedies, another seems to have been made for seeds and for the labels and boxes which went with them—they sold their seeds, as they sold some of their crafts, to the "world."

It was also their custom to combine agreeably several kinds of wood in one piece of furniture, not for ornament but because one or another wood seemed to suit a particular place or function best. They could understand wood—that is, they well knew the medium in which they worked. They seemed to believe in a very simple way that there was a special life in material things. Read Hepworth Dixon's account of his talk with Elder Frederick Evans about the planting of an orchard and see if you know anything more beautiful.

—(Charles Sheeler) Constance Rourke, *Charles Sheeler: Artist in the American Tradition*, 1938

Multipurpose cupboard at the Darrow School, New Lebanon, New York. Photograph by Elmer R. Pearson.

This morning I have spent an hour with Frederick in the new orchard, listening to the story of how he planted it, as to a tale by some Arabian poet. "A tree has its wants and wishes," said the Elder; "and a man should study them as a teacher watches a child, to see what he can do. If you love the plant, and take heed of what it likes, you will be well repaid by it. I don't know if a tree ever comes to know you; and I think it may; but I am sure it feels when you care for it and tend it; as a child does, as a woman does. Now, when we planted this orchard, we first got the very best cuttings in our reach; we then built a house for every plant to live in, that is to say, we dug a deep hole for each; we drained it well; we laid down tiles and rubble, and then filled in a bed of suitable manure and mould; we put the plant into its nest gently, and pressed up the earth about it, and protected the infant tree by this metal fence." "You take a world of pains," I said. "Ah, Brother Hepworth," he rejoined, "thee sees we love our garden."

Thus, when a Shaker is put upon the soil, to beautify it by his tilth, the difference between his husbandry and that of a Gentile farmer, who is thinking solely of his profits, is likely to be great. While the Gentile is watching for his returns, the Shaker is intent upon his service. One tries for large profits, the other strives for good work. Is it strange that a celibate man, who puts his soul into the soil—who gives it all the affection which he would otherwise have lavished on wife and child—should excel a mere trading rival in the production of fruits and flowers?
—Hepworth Dixon, *New America*, 1867

Considering the homeliness of the buildings, which mostly have the appearance of mere factories or human hives, I asked Elder Frederick whether, if they were to build anew, they would not aim at some architectural effect, some beauty of design. He replied with great positiveness, "No, the beautiful, as you call it, is absurd and abnormal. It has no business with us. The divine man has no right to waste money upon what you would call beauty, in his house or daily life, while there are people living in misery." In building anew, he would take care to have more light, a more equable distribution of heat, and a more general care for protection and comfort, because these things tend to health and long life. But no beauty. He described to me amusingly the disgust he had experienced in a costly New York dwelling, where he saw carpets nailed down on the floor, "of course with piles of dust beneath, never swept away, and of which I had to breathe;" and with heavy picture-frames hung against the walls, also the receptacles of dust. "You people in the world are not clean according to our Shaker notions. And what is the use of pictures?" he added scornfully.   —Charles Nordhoff, *The Communistic Societies of the United States*, 1875

That there was nothing static in their beliefs must account in some measure for their productivity. Notably what they created was all of a piece; it was all social, all functional, all for use, chairs, tables, labor-saving devices, seeds, herbs. Perhaps their philosophy of change gave the Shakers still further creative strength, permitting flexible adaptations and a free flow of inherent creative powers.
—Constance Rourke, *The Roots of American Culture*, 1942

Everything which is made by the Shakers is substantial, but has something odd and devoid of taste in form and color.

—Frederika Bremer, *The Homes of the New World,* 1853

Seeing the Shaker meetinghouse at New Lebanon recently showed the difference in emotional response to the thing which is of one's own lineage from that which is not. It has a final assurance and is sufficient of itself to make one rejoice in having derived from the soil that brought it into being.

The building comprises a large and a small member, having the same axis, with a low arched roof over each. The larger member encloses the meeting hall, a room eighty by sixty-five feet, free of the usual obstructions of supporting columns. The arched ceiling is maintained in place by structural timbers between ceiling and roof. Rows of banked benches of simple and beautiful craftsmanship run the length of the longer walls, and above them are tall windows of fine proportions, placed at intervals in the wall spaces. Large double doors in these walls admitted those not of the faith. The entrance for the Shakers was through three doors at the end, opening from the smaller member of the building, the door on the left admitting men, the center the clergy, the one on the right admitting women. The smaller member of the building formed a cloak-room, with stairs leading to living accommodations for the ministry. The balance of vast space with that of more intimate proportions was achieved by the greatest economy of means.

"Interior of the Meeting House," by Benson J. Lossing, *Harper's New Monthly Magazine,* July 1857.

No embellishment meets the eye. Beauty of line and proportion through excellence of craftsmanship make the absence of ornament in no way an omission. The sense of light and spaciousness received upon entering the hall is indicative of similar spiritual qualities of the Shakers. Instinctively one takes a deep breath, as in the midst of some moving and exalted association with nature. There were no dark corners in those lives. Their religion thrived on light rather than the envelopment of a dark mystery—with the Shakers all was light, in their crafts and equally with their achitecture.

I don't like these things because they are old but in spite of it. I'd like them still better if they were made yesterday because then they would afford proof that the same kind of creative power is continuing.

—(Charles Sheeler) Constance Rourke, *Charles Sheeler: Artist in the American Tradition*, 1938

The simplicity of the buildings was impressive but not interesting.

—E. M. Forster, *Two Cheers for Democracy*, 1951

No theory of esthetic origins quite accounts for their crafts. Severe, tending to height, imperial even yet adapted to humble uses, their household and shop pieces seem to have been created out of their own way of life without reference to antecedents. Occasionally their furniture or textiles employed forms in use elsewhere, particularly in New England, but even these were usually given a distinctive stamp, and their typical chests and cupboards, tables and chairs were essentially their own. They are unmistakably Shaker. One of their sayings, "Every force has its form," seems to have proved itself in these wholly utilitarian objects.

—Constance Rourke, *Charles Sheeler*, 1938

The myth persists that anything Shaker is great, and that anything simple is Shaker. It is impressive that workers in Shaker communities sought to make things not as personal accomplishments but as God's expression through them; yet it does not necessarily follow that all their objects were endowed with quality. . . . Despite what is generally believed the Shakers did not—as a result of their retirement from the world and their focus on spiritual things—create a radically new concept of design contrary to their surrounding world. They were not the first . . . to get down to basic design. . . . Simple, plain, direct, and therefore inexpensive design had long been common. The men who went to Shaker communities and formed their taste in furniture selected one from the various approaches already existing. Their main aesthetic act was to choose this particular taste rather than some other. . . .

It is interesting that, according to tradition, their founder, Mother Ann, kept with her a chair with ring turnings on its posts. And, it should be noticed that such chairs do not, in fact, strip away all decoration: the back posts terminate in "useless" finials, the slats are arched, the front legs taper to the rockers, and . . . fancy-grained wood, such as tiger maple, is employed.   —John T. Kirk, *The Impecunious Collector's Guide to American Antiques*, 1975

Mother Ann . . . saw the devil and fought with him, and knew he was "a real being, real as a bear." The peculiar grace of a Shaker chair is due to the fact that it was made by someone capable of believing that an angel might come and sit on it.

—(Thomas Merton, Introduction) Edward Deming and Faith Andrews, *Religion in Wood*, 1966

An angel and a Shaker slat-back chair are details from a gift drawing, "An Emblem of the Heavenly Sphere," received January 1854 at Hancock, Massachusetts.

Armchair with five slats, in the collection of Charles F. Thompson. Photograph by Elmer R. Pearson.

To appreciate the straight chairs, one must know the whirling dances. To understand the rigid alignment of buildings, one must envision members marching through their orchards or rolling woodlands singing of a procession in their Heavenly City.

—Dolores Hayden, *Seven American Utopias*, 1975

Shaker's Chairs

We invite the attention of our customers and the public to the contents of this little pamphlet, which will give them, in a "concise form," a description and a representation of the different sizes of chairs and foot benches which we manufacture and sell. We would also call attention of the public to the fact that there is no other chair manufactory which is owned and operated by the Shakers except the one which is now in operation and owned and operated by the Society of Shakers, at Mount Lebanon, Columbia county, N.Y. We deem it a duty we owe to the public to enlighten them in this matter, owing to the fact that there are now several manufacturers of chairs who have made and introduced into market an imitation of our own styles of chairs, which they sell for Shakers' chairs, and which are unquestionably bought by the public generally under the impression that they are the real genuine article . . . Of all the imitations of our chairs which have come under our observation, there is none which we would be willing to accept as a specimen of our workmanship, nor would we be willing to stake our reputation on their merits.

The increasing demand for our chairs has prompted us to increase, also, the facilities for producing and improving them. We have spared no expense or labor in our endeavors to produce an article that cannot be surpassed in any respect and which combines all of the advantages of durability, simplicity and lightness. . . .

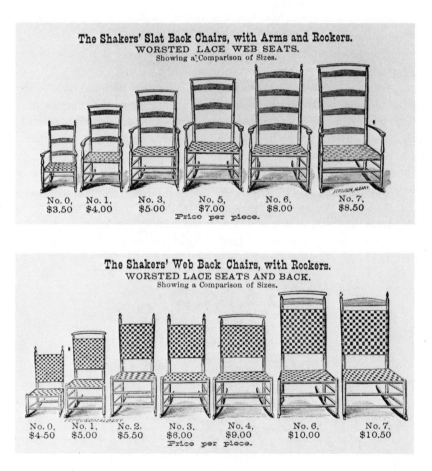

The Shakers' Slat Back Chairs, with Arms and Rockers.
WORSTED LACE WEB SEATS.
Showing a Comparison of Sizes.

No. 0,	No. 1,	No. 3,	No. 5,	No. 6,	No. 7,
$3.50	$4.00	$5.00	$7.00	$8.00	$8.50

Price per piece.

The Shakers' Web Back Chairs, with Rockers.
WORSTED LACE SEATS AND BACK.
Showing a Comparison of Sizes.

No. 0,	No. 1,	No. 2,	No. 3,	No. 4,	No. 6,	No. 7,
$4.50	$5.00	$5.50	$6.00	$9.00	$10.00	$10.50

Price per piece.

Many of our friends who see the Shakers' chairs for the first time may be led to suppose that the chair business is a new thing for the Shakers to engage in. This is not the fact, however, and may surprise even some of the oldest manufacturers to learn that the Shakers were pioneers in the business, and perhaps the very first to engage in the business after the establishment of the independence of the country.

The material with which we cushion our chairs is a specialty peculiarly our own. It is made of the best stock and woven on hand looms with much labor, and forms a heavy and durable article, much more so than anything which we are acquainted with. We have all the most desirable and pretty colors represented in our cushions, and they can be all one color, or have a different colored border or with different colored stripes running across the cushion.

We cushion the foot benches to match the cushioned chairs. They are twelve inches square on the top with an incline to favor one's feet while sitting in the chairs, and they are nicely adapted for the purpose of kneeling stools.

When any of our friends wish some of our chairs they can order them of us by mail, addressed to R. M. Wagan, Mt. Lebanon, Columbia Co., N.Y. Our chairs are all nicely wrapped in paper before shipping. It is advisable to ship the chairs by express when there are only a few of them. The expense will be more, but the risk will be less than by freight. We do not ship any goods at our own risk, but deliver them at the nearest or most accessible place of shipping, and there take a receipt for them, showing that they were received in good order, when our obligation ends . . .

Look for our trade-mark before purchasing—no chair is genuine without it. Our trade-mark is a gold transfer, and is designed to be ornamental. . . .

ALL CHAIRS OF OUR MAKE WILL HAVE A GOLD TRANSFER TRADE-
MARK ATTACHED TO THEM, AND NONE OTHERS ARE SHAKERS' CHAIRS.

>—*An Illustrated Catalogue and Price-List of the Shakers' Chairs. Manufactured by the Society of Shakers. R. M. Wagan, Mount Lebanon, N.Y.*

Wagan's chair catalogues listed eight basic, numbered models, rang-
ing from No. O, the smallest child's chair, to No. 7, the largest adult chair.
With the several variations of each type, there were in all 46 different
models, usually with a choice of seating. If to these 46 "canonical" models
we add the uncatalogued spindle-backs and bentwoods, we arrive at the
astonishing sum of 52 models (each of the spindle-backs is found in at
least two sizes, and the bentwoods in four). And occasional rare "sports"
are found, like the high chairs and double armchairs.

Aside from direct factory sales, outlets (frequently multiple) were
provided in many cities, such as Boston, New York, Pittsfield, Milwaukee
and many others; in 1888, indeed, efforts were made to establish sales
outlets in England and France, but nothing seems to have come of this
ambitious scheme. And since Mt. Lebanon produced by far the most
chairs for sale, and sold them most widely, people of today naturally tend
to think of chairs when they think of Shakers.

No statistics are available on the total production put out by the Second and South Families over the years, but the number certainly reached
into the tens of thousands of units. At the Philadelphia Centennial Expo-
sition of 1876, the Shakers had a display booth exhibiting chairs and foot-
stools, and sales boomed thereafter.

>—Robert F. W. Meader, *Illustrated Guide to Shaker Furniture,* 1972

Their designs were in their day modern and rooted in the late 18th-
and early 19th-century styles popular everywhere. The Sheraton Baluster
leg shows up on many chests. The Hepplewhite tables and the American
Empire desks are echoed in their products. As for chairs, the ladder-back
had evolved to a sparely framed design by the time the Shakers began to
refine it further—reshaping the bends, arms, finials and posts. Refine
them they did, transforming the rockers and virtually every other furniture form they touched into pieces that were always simpler and more
graceful, and frequently beautiful. Since the revival of interest in period
Shaker designs began in the 1950's, such accomplishments have found an
enthusiastic following.

Today's collectors of the Shaker style, developed by the United Society of Believers in the Second Appearing of Christ, invariably covet far more than the furniture. And no wonder. Candlesticks, brooms, kitchen utensils, seed and herb boxes, tools, labels, medicine bottles, jars, hangers, textiles, dresses, bonnets and bentwood boxes express the same ingenuity and refinement seen in the furniture. Many of these designs were much admired in their day and were mass-produced to sell to others.

> —Rita Reif, "Antiques: A Heyday for Shaker Enthusiasts," *The New York Times*, Sept. 9, 1979

Stoves

In this day of energy problems, the Shaker stove is as right as it was almost 200 years ago. . . . The style, use, and efficiency of the Shaker wood burning stoves have changed very little in their two century history.

Stoves were used very early in the Eastern Shaker communities. Although the Meeting Houses built by Moses Johnson at Mt. Lebanon, New York (1786), and Enfield, Connecticut (1791), had large chimneys to accommodate fireplaces, those of Canterbury, New Hampshire (1792), Shirley, Massachusetts (1793), and Sabbathday Lake, Maine (1794), were constructed to use the small stoves for heating. In the West, Pleasant Hill, Kentucky, replaced many fireplaces in the community with stoves in the 1820's while the Meeting House built at the beginning of that decade incorporated stoves from the beginning. The Meeting House at Union Village, Ohio, had fireplaces in use throughout its life. The consistent use of fireplaces and their wood fireplace doors are apparently unique to the Southwestern Ohio Shaker communities although many communities had fireplaces in shops and out buildings.

Eugene Dodd in "Functionalism in Shaker Crafts" (*Antiques*, October 1970) refers to an inventory of better than 200 variations in Shaker stoves. . . . Most were entirely of cast iron. Of these cast iron stoves, there are basically two styles: the box stove and the panelled.

The box or coffin stove was the most common form, having been produced at Mt. Lebanon and Hancock, Mass., and for the Kentucky settlements. It consisted of five parts: the body, cast in one piece; a plate upon which the body set; the legs to keep it off the wood floors; the door; and the small draft door to regulate the air supply. Many variations of this stove have been found. The shape of the legs varies from cast pegs to cabriole to wrought iron with penny feet. The intended purpose also dic-

Light crisscrosses shadow in this portrait of a stove on the third floor of the Meetinghouse at Sabbathday Lake, Maine. Photograph by John McKee, from *Hands to Work and Hearts to God: The Shaker Tradition in Maine*, Bowdoin College Museum of Art, 1969.

tated variations in design. Some had angled sides with a ridge to hold irons for the laundry room. Others were cast with a pan on top to act as a humidifier. Still others had a small unit on top which would provide more heating surface and, thus, more heat. This variation has been called a "super heater," "double decker," "double fire box," and a stove "with radiator."

The second basic style, the panelled stove, has the body consisting of five plates that are held together with long bolts. This style appears to have been designed, manufactured, and used primarily at Canterbury and is often referred to by the name of that community. While this stove is more ornate (some have cabriole legs with claw feet), it is also considered by modern day users to be more efficient.

Canterbury, like many of the communities including Mt. Lebanon, Hancock, and Enfield, Ct., had its own foundry and could have produced its own stoves. Canterbury did this until its later years when the stoves were cast by the Ford Foundry in nearby Concord from Shaker made patterns. Pleasant Hill, Ky. had its stoves made outside the community at commercial foundries in Western Kentucky, while stoves designed and used by South Union Shakers were manufactured in Cincinnati. Enfield, New Hampshire also had its stoves made outside the community. The following is quoted from the New Hampshire Historical Society's *True Gospel Simplicity: Shaker Furniture in New Hampshire.* It is a manuscript from Enfield to the Royal Blake ironworks in Brandon, Vermont, and dated 1855.

> About 10 days since I wrote you and ordered some cooking stoves but had not heard from you since. We have promised a number of the stoves and should like them sent forward so that we can supply our customers. We would also like a large box stove for warming our Mill. I think they are about 3 feet long with a hinge in the top of the stove so that a portion of the cover will swing up. Also we would like 3 small box stoves for warming chambers for sleeping rooms. Write by return of mail if you can not send them.

The letter is interesting not just from its insights into outside manufacturing but also because of the expression of the need to "supply our customers." . . . It can be readily concluded that stoves are to be included among the quality items that the Shakers produced for sale to the world . . . No doubt the corner grocery . . . found the Shaker stove as efficient and desirable as the energy saving collectors of our day do.

—Charles R. Muller, *The Shaker Way*, 1979

UP OR OUT

It was in 1847 that the Whitewater (Ohio) brethren started on a successful career of raising garden seeds for the markets. Trips for selling the seeds were made in different parts of the country. . . . This enterprise came to an end in 1873, because many firms began to put out garden and flower seeds in fancy colored papers and boxes, also in different size packages. "That our seeds did not take, as they were put up in a brown colored paper and a plain stained box, it was concluded we must keep up with the times or step down and out, which we did."

—J. P. MacLean, *Shakers of Ohio*, 1907

Minimal Victorian

To discount Victorian Shaker furniture is to withhold recognition from the climax of the Shaker experiment in New Hampshire. At a time when Shaker communities in Massachusetts and New York were going into a terminal decline after the Civil War, the communities in New Hampshire were enjoying a renewal of vigor. The energy of the 1840s had resulted from an effort to withdraw from the world. . . . The vitality of the Victorian period was generated by an eagerness to acknowledge the contemporary world while maintaining an allegiance to "gospel simplicity."

Just as they rephrased their beliefs of a hundred years in the mode of modern grammar, the Shakers also restyled their traditional furniture forms to meet new needs. Shaker Victorian is a minimal Victorian. . . .

During the Victorian period, much furniture was purchased from the world as well. The furniture trade established among the Shakers in earlier years had been set up not so much to turn out untainted furnishings for the dwellings of Zion but to equip the community's needs more economically than furniture could be purchased from the world. In the decades following the Civil War, as the number of males in the Society decreased sharply, many of the community industries were closed and the Shakers increasingly relied on the world to supply their needs. . . . After 1900 . . . little furniture was made by Believers.

To admonish Believers of the Victorian period for preferring furniture with "tasty" moldings and knobs "merely for fancy" is to forget that during the revival of the 1840s another generation of Believers were required to remove formerly-acceptable embellishments from furniture in use among them. It is in fact probable that the zeal of the reformers of the 1840s has severely distorted an accurate appraisal of the Shakers' attitude toward furniture. . . .

A survey of furniture attributed to the Canterbury and Enfield communities reveals distinct changes in form within the history of the Shaker experience in New Hampshire. But it should not be alarming that the garb of an idea was modified over two hundred years. What is remarkable is that the idea remained unchanged.

—Mary Lyn Ray, *True Gospel Simplicity: Shaker Furniture in New Hampshire*, 1974

WORSHIP IN SONG AND DANCE

Shaker feet were as nimble as Shaker hands. The spectacle of the Be-
lievers in their quaint costumes, dancing in their churches, drew the
world's people from near and far. They came with their horses and bug-
gies and on special excursion trains. And in the plain white meeting-
houses without spires (because Mother Ann called churches with spires
"the devil's steeplehouses") separate entrances were provided for visitors.
The Sabbath sermon was addressed to them, and the dancing justified by
Biblical examples. Did not King David leap and dance before the Lord?

The wild individual "laboring" that gave the Shakers their name
belonged to the past. In its place—and more to the taste of the world—
was a group ritual, introduced by Father Joseph Meacham after a dream
of angels dancing around the throne of God. Mother Lucy Wright fur-
ther refined the exercises, quickening the tempo in the East to match the
pace of the new recruits from the Kentucky Revival.

Shaker singing and dancing became a polished performance, re-
hearsed during the week. There were solemn marches and sober songs,
ring dances and rousing songs, quick dances, and "extra" songs for rest
periods. Gestures of the hands gathered in blessings, turned away evil,
shook away sin. To the Believers their worship was a divine and exhil-
arating experience. To the world's people it was a wonder.

Come old and young, come great and small,
Here's love and union free for all;
And every one that will obey,
Have now a right to dance and play;
For dancing is a sweet employ,
It fills the soul with heavenly joy,
It makes our love and union flow,
While round, and round, and round we go.
                              —*Millennial Praises*, 1813

Their mode of worship is strange indeed, as in it they exercise the
body as well as the soul. The two sexes are usually arranged in ranks facing each other, and about six feet apart. There is frequently a preliminary
address by one of the elders, after which a hymn is sung, when they form
in circles around a band of male and female singers, and dance in a high
state of mental exaltation, and sometimes with such rapidity as to as-

tonish the uninitiated. At such periods, they suppose themselves under the immediate influence of spiritual agency, whether that of angels or of some of the departed members of their own community.

—*Frank Leslie's Illustrated Newspaper*, Sept. 6, 1873

With respect to their dancing during religious worship, it may be thought a ludicrous appendage, but there is nothing in their dancing to excite levity; they indeed term it labouring, and many of the extravagances of an earlier period have been laid aside.

—W. S. Warder, "A Brief Sketch of the Religious Society of People Called Shakers," in *New View of Society*, published by Robert Owen, 1818

Come virgins in your marriage dress,
Your joy and gladness to express,
Come forth and dance in holiness,
On Zion's hill before him!

—*Millennial Praises*, 1813

No modern dance hall, with its tempestuous exhibitionism, its pigeonhips, snakehips, shags, and boogie-woogies, is any more electrified than was a Shaker dance-fest. The Shakers did not earn their name without exertion.   —V. F. Calverton, *Where Angels Dared to Tread*, 1941

Their family and church worship is to sing songs of their own composition (no form or appearance of prayer) in adoration to *Ann Lee*, in the most merry tunes, such as "Yankee Doodle," or "Over the river to Charley," &c &c. with the most ridiculous gestures, and motions and dance, and their appearance is so farcical, that it is difficult for spectators to tell whether they are in a Church or a Theatre!

—Mary Dyer, *A Portraiture of Shakerism*, 1822

The music was unlike any thing I had ever heard; beautiful, impressive, and deeply solemn. . . . Their songs and hymns breathe a pure and Christian spirit; and their music, unlike any to be heard elsewhere, captivates the ear because of its severe simplicity and perfect melody. . . . As I gazed upon that congregation of four or five hundred worshippers marching and countermarching in perfect time, I felt certain that, were it seen upon a stage as a theatrical exhibition, the involuntary exclamation of

"The Dance," as witnessed by Benson J. Lossing and recorded in *Harper's New Monthly Magazine*, July 1857.

even the hypercritical would be, "How beautiful!" The women, clad in white, and moving gracefully, appeared ethereal; and among them were a few very beautiful faces. All appeared happy, and upon each face rested the light of dignified serenity, which always gives power to the features of woman.   —Benson J. Lossing, "The Shakers," *Harper's New Monthly Magazine*, July 1857

Good evening, my friends,
And how are you tonight?
We'll see you in meeting
With pleasing delight;
We wish you all happy
With blessing and peace,
And ready to labor
For further increase;
And while we proceed
May the treasures of love,
Come flowing upon us
From heaven above;
May angels attend

Our devotions tonight,
And freely assist us
To worship aright.   —Old Harvard song, Clara Endicott Sears, *Gleanings
                         from Old Shaker Journals*, 1916

Sabbath, Feb. 7, 1840. Public meeting as usual. The meeting-house
was very much crowded with Believers and the world. It is judged there
were about 500 of the world attended one meeting to-day.
                         —Harvard, Massachusetts, *Journals*

THE FUTURE MRS. LONGFELLOW GOES TO MEETING

September 15, 1839
... Entered with a flock of other "females" the female door and left the
gents to seek their kind also, got a good seat in the middle of the side ap-
propriated for "world's people" and awaited the performances as at a theatre. Very gradually Shakeress after Shakeress opened noiselessly their
side door, glided on tiptoe noiselessly, across the beautiful floor, to their
respective pegs, hung thereon their white shawls, fichus, and straw bonnets (which resembled *en masse* huge hornets' nests), then sat down, as
jointed dolls do, upon the wall benches, handkerchief straight across lap
and hands folded over, turning not an eyelash to the right or left, like so
many draped sphinxes or corpses set on end. The little girls copying so
well the same rigid repose—so unlike the fidgetiness of youth—is a horrible sight, as if they were under a spell. The men came in later, but visitors
flocked in so fast that half their benches were civilly resigned to them by a
patriarch elder. After utter repose the men and women staring at each
other from their respective benches, rather dangerously if eyes are ammu-
nition to such sanctified shadows of humanity, they all rose, or rather stif-
fened up their joints like a machine, and putting back the benches began
to sing, one of the elders addressing them in unconnected, drawling scraps
of morality at one end of the aisle they formed, and then stepping tip-toe
to our gay ranks, held forth on the desirableness of proprietous behavior,
non-mounting of benches, as it would soil them, etc., pitying us for our
poor, lost condition, declaring *them* the favored of Heaven, the "salt of the
earth" (rather savorless I should think) and prophesying that one day we
should lament we were not Shakers! Confessed there was some virtue in
the world, though grossly obscured, but no *faith*—a dim belief in former
miracles but utter infidelity about those of the present day, which were

vouchsafed much more marvelously. An unhinged, stuttering discourse, as if the petrifaction extended over the man's body was reaching his brain. They then ploughed up and down (for it can't be called dancing), with their backs to us, and sang again very gay airs, terribly shrill under the large sounding board but sometimes sweeping through the gamut with great effect. I could only catch a few words: "Press on, press on to thy happy kingdom," etc. They then filed off into a double circle, one circle going one way, another two or three abreast, "laboring" round this large hall, knees bent, with a sort of galvanized hop, hands paddling like fins and voices chanting these wild airs, with a still smaller circle of elders and children in the center, stationary, giving the pitch of the songs, like so many old witches or enchanters, working over the caldron while the younger ones skipped through the force of their incantations. But no witch's sabbath, no bacchanal procession could be more unearthly, revolting, oppressive, and bewildering. The machinery of their stereotyped steps, plunging on in this way so long without rest, the constrained attitude forward, the spasmodic jumps and twists of the neck, and the ghastly visages of the women in their corpse-like caps, the waving of so many shrill voices, and the rigid expression of their faces combined to form a spectacle as piteous as disgusting, fit only for the dancing hall of the lower regions or the creation of a nightmare. There was one woman whose horrible contortions will haunt me forever. She wrenched her head nearly over her shoulder on one side and the other, and then jerked it nearly to her knee, with a regularity of manner for such an immense time that I thought I should have rushed out for relief, as my eye saw always this dreadful figure. I supposed at first it was St. Vitus dance, or a fit, but she stopped at the end and varied it by spinning like a dervish, twisting her arms round her head like snakes. Shrouded in such a dress, and carried to such a pitch, it was the most frightful human gesticulation ever perpetrated. Doubtless they regard her as a saint, for I saw a faint imitation of it in others. After interminable dancing, varied by changing of feet with great energy, we were relieved of this constant repassing of the same faces, mostly very disagreeable: one head like an idiot or a thief, one full of cunning and self conceit, with thin, prononcé features, and a lank of fringe of hair behind I shall never forget, and one youth, evidently wrought upon intensely by a devotional excitation leaping higher than the rest, with painful earnestness of expression, among the women all frightful but one tall girl with a fine profile, who seemed to curl her lip in some scorn at this insane mummery and waved her hands very languidly. There was a fat novice in worldly gear except the cap who presented an amusing contrast to her lank sisters. At one time they all knelt silently, like spectres rising from their graves, as awful a spectacle as the nuns in Robert le Diable, then sat waving their hands as if scattering cobwebs from their faces or spirits. The stupified elder at the end thanked us for our good behavior and right gladly we emerged into fresh air after the close heat and wearisome exhibition we had been forced to endure for so many hours. The concourse of visitors is extraordinary, for surely no mortal could wish to see this twice. I remember as a child being painfully impressed by it, but that was nothing to the shock the maturer judgment receives from such pitiful delusions; however, if this exercise excites in any one of them devotional feeling, doubtless God cares little by what means it is brought to light. . . . —(Fanny Appleton Longfellow), Edward Wagenknecht, ed., *Mrs. Longfellow: Selected Letters and Journals of Fanny Appleton Longfellow (1817–1861)*, 1956

There was a definite psychological purpose behind the Shaker marches, seldom explained, and rarely understood by the general Public. The perfect rhythmic body motions, of a worshipper, who combined this activity with a deep mental and religious fervor, developed within himself, a great spiritual inspiration, almost impossible to understand or describe, by one who has never witnessed or participated in this form of worship. But if one could have been present, as I was, and could have seen the perfect spiritual union, that was produced, when a soul combined the physical motions, the singing voice and the dedicated heart, in giving praise and thanks to God—I'm sure you would have agreed that the physical motions added a still greater dimension to the expression of Prayer. However, as years passed, and older members were unable to join in these marches, the exercises were discontinued, as it was considered necessary to maintain a perfect union among the members, a service in which all may participate as One. —Sister Lillian Phelps, *Shaker Music: A Brief History*, Canterbury, New Hampshire, 1960s

Curiously enough, while everything like art and beauty is ignored in the secular life of the Shakers, music and dancing make a part of their religious observances. But their singing is of the rudest character, and without any instrumental accompaniment. Their pious songs in praise of their Divine Mother who makes for them a fourth person in the godhead, are sung in rude choruses, which have little melody and no attempt at har-

mony. The dancing is as rude as the singing: it is merely a violent exercise, wholly destitute of corporeal grace, whatever may be its spiritual influences.
                         —Thomas Low Nichols, *Forty Years of American Life*, 1864. (His description is of Union Village, Ohio.)

   The public meetings were held on dry Sundays only, and no one was allowed to come when it was wet and muddy. The Shakers themselves did not cross the village streets to the meetinghouse on rainy days but held family services instead.
                         —Julia Neal, *By Their Fruits: The Story of Shakerism in South Union, Kentucky*, 1947

Sisters crossing the road from the Centre Family Dwelling house to the Meetinghouse at Pleasant Hill, Kentucky, ca. 1890. Photograph, courtesy of Shaker Village at Pleasant Hill.

Union Village, Ohio. June 6th, 1847. We attended public Meeting with the families at half past 10 A.M. Heard Brother Enoch and Charles Clapp speak to the world. The spectators occupied about half the room in the house besides a great company remained in the yard in time of meeting. The brethren spake very well. Brother Enoch, in the course of preaching to the world, compared their religion to an old man's prayer that he once heard of when he was a little boy. It was this:

O Lord, bless me and my wife. My son John and his wife; us four and no more.

This comparison he brought up to show to them their narrow contracted sense of salvation. The world behaved well, and paid good attention to the speaking. —"Prudence Morrell's Account of a Journey to the West in the Year 1847," *Shaker Quarterly*, Fall 1968

PAINFUL, TO HORACE GREELEY

Wilder and louder sweils the music; quicker and more intricate becomes the "labor." Now all are prancing about the room, in double file, to a melody as lively as Yankee Doodle; now they perform a series of dexterous but indescribable maneuvers; now they balance; now whirl one another around. . . . We hear of people crucifying their sinful affections, everywhere; it is here alone that we are permitted to observe the process. Here alone do we overlook the battle-ground of a war against all carnal impulses. . . .

When the "labor" commenced, the maidens of tender yet womanly years evidently felt a little of something like embarrassment at the presence, though accustomed, of so many strangers. Their conviction that they were doing God service was not shaken, yet there was evidently a feminine dread . . . that their worship would seem amusingly absurd to that mob of profane eyes and godless hearts: especially as they passed round in procession, within a breath of the masculine multitude, who formed a wall in close proximity to their path, you could mark the rising of a faint tinge of ruddier hue upon those else colorless and passionless features, evincing that their existence had not yet become all spiritual or vegetable. . . . As the exercises proceeded, and devotion became enthusiasm, all distinction was lost; and the young and fair were only remarkable among their elders by their excess of fervor, or perhaps of physical power. At length, what was a measured dance becomes a wild, discordant frenzy; all apparent design or regulation is lost; and grave manhood and gentler

The Shakers' zest in marching in concentric circles is captured by Joseph Becker in *Frank Leslie's Illustrated Newspaper,* November 1873.

girlhood are whirling round and round, two or three in company, then each for him or herself, in all the attitudes of a decapitated hen, or an expiring top. The scene and its interest grow painful. . . . The spell is dissolved; an elder proclaims that "the assembly is dismissed;" the multitude escape their merriment, and I to my meditation.

—Horace Greeley, "A Sabbath with the Shakers," *Knickerbocker; or, New York Monthly Mazazine,* June 1838

A THRILLING SIGHT, TO WILLIAM DEAN HOWELLS

We went regularly to the Shaker meeting. . . . The seats for spectators in the church were filled, and sometimes to overflowing, by people from the country and villages round about, as well as by summer boarders from the neighboring town of Lancaster, whose modish silks and millinery distinguished them from the rural congregation; but all were respectful and attentive to the worship which they had come to look at, and which, in its most fantastic phase, I should think could move only a silly person to laughter. . . .

The meetings opened with singing, and then Elder Wetherbee, of the

Church Family, briefly addressed the brethren and sisters in terms which were commonly a grateful recognition of the beauty of their "gospel relation" to each other, and of their safety from sin in a world of evil. . . . After the elder sat down, they sang again, and then the minister, John Whiteley, read a chapter of the Bible, and made a few remarks; then, with alternate singing and speaking (the speaking was mostly from the men, though now and then a sister rose and bore her testimony to her heartfelt happiness in Shakerism, or declared her intention to take up a cross against some or such a tendency of her nature), the services proceeded till the time for the marching came. Till this time the brothers and sisters had sat confronting each other on settees, which they now lifted and set out of the way against the wall. A group formed in an ellipse in the middle, with two lines of marchers outside of them, led by Elder Wetherbee. Some one struck into one of their stirring march tunes, and those in the ellipse began to rock back and forth on their feet, and to sway their bodies to the music, while the marchers with a sort of rising motion began their round, all beating time with a quick outward gesture of the arms and an upward gesture of the open palms. It was always a thrilling sight, fantastic, as I said, but not ludicrous, and it never failed to tempt the nerves to so much Shakerism at least as lay in the march. To the worshipers this part of their rite was evidently that sort of joy which, if physical, is next to spiritual transport. Their faces were enraptured, they rose and rose in their march with a glad exultation; suddenly the singing ceased, the march instantly ended, and the arms of each sank slowly down to the side. Some brother now spoke again, and when he closed, another song was raised, and the march resumed, till in the course of the singing and speaking those forming the central ellipse had been relieved and enabled to join the march. When it ended, the settees were drawn up again, and the brethren and sisters sat down as before. Generally, one or two of the younger sisters would at this point read some article or poem from the *Shaker and Shakeress*—the organ of the sect published at Mt. Lebanon, N.Y., and made up of contributions by members of the different families throughout the country. . . . When these were finished, Elder Fraser, of the North Family, came forward between the rows of Shakers, and addressed the world in the principal discourse of the day. . . .

I am not sure whether the different faces in the march had a greater or less fascination to us after we came to know their different owners personally. Each showed his or her transport in a different way, and each had some peculiarity of step or movement that took our idle minds and made us curious about their history and character. Among them, none was more

"The Religious Dance," by A. Boyd Houghton in the *Graphic* (London), May 1870.

striking than the nonagenarian, whose bent frame kept its place in the round, but whose nerveless hands beat time after a very fugitive and erratic fashion. Father Abraham is very deaf; and in the singing some final bit of belated melody always stuck in his throat, and came scratching and scrambling up after the others had ceased in a manner that was rather hard to bear. . . . At his great age he still works every day at basket-making, in which he is very skillful and conscientious. . . . He is rarely sick, and he takes part in all the details of the worship, as he did when he came, sixty years ago. He was then a young man, and it is said that he visited the community from idle curiosity, with his betrothed. Its life and faith made an instant impression upon him, and he proposed to the young girl that they should both become Shakers; but after due thought she refused. She said that she would not be a hindrance to his wish in the matter; if he was called to this belief, she gave him back his promise. . . . He has never regretted his course; she took another mate, saw her children about her knee, and died long ago, after a life that was no doubt as happy as most. But perhaps in an affair like that, a girl's heart had supreme claims. Perhaps there are some things that one ought not to do even with the hope of winning heaven.   —William Dean Howells, "A Shaker Village," *Atlantic Monthly,* June 1876

Howell's novel A Parting and a Meeting, *published in 1896, is based on the story of this old man.*

Howells' account of their worship is indeed the most satisfactory of any that I have read. It makes the reader feel in a degree how sincere and earnest these consecrated people are. I say in a degree; for it is impossible for one not in spiritual accord with them to fully depict in words the meetings of the Shakers. . . .

People inquire, "What holds the Shakers together?" I believe their meetings should have the principal credit. . . . They all have this peculiarity, that every member who is present takes some part in the exercises—if not in speaking, then in singing or marching; and all must feel in some degree their harmonizing, unifying power. Mere doctrines, however good, will not hold people together for a century; it requires an afflatus; and this is dependent for its effects upon the assembling of the members together. . . .

Only the Sunday meetings, in which all the Families of a Society take part, are open to the public; and that part of the public living within ten

"Shaker Evans at Home," a portrait of a Shaker meeting by A. Boyd Houghton, in the London *Graphic*, August 1871.

miles of this village [Canterbury, N.H.] fully appreciates its privilege in this respect. At the meeting here yesterday there were at least two hundred strangers and visitors present. I am informed that during the summer months this number is sometimes doubled, compelling most of the Shaker brothers and sisters to absent themselves; and that those who are present are often crowded into such close quarters that their "goings forth in the dance" are necessarily omitted. The meetings here are indeed wonderfully attractive. Thirty-seven carriages came yesterday from the towns near and distant, and many people on foot. Probably the greater number attend the meetings from mere curiosity; but some doubtless find in them spiritual nutriment.   —William Alfred Hinds, *American Communities,* 1878

Not many spectators were drawn by the show into the Shaker ranks. The elders' sermons often embarrassed them, in their fashionable clothes, with fancy carriages outside waiting to whisk them away from these exemplary, stripped-down lives.

Yesterday found us at the religious (?) services of the Shakers at Lebanon—a ghastly scene. A glass eyed preacher was holding forth like an escaped maniac. His sermon was a clumsy, impudent, disgusting affair, sufficiently so at times to have driven the ladies from the house. . . . The audience was very full of the city fashionables from Columbian Hall and it is said they have had some pretty strong doses lately from these Shaker expounders—The dance was long and protracted striking up afresh with new tunes, to the old saw filing, and some of them were profusely jolly. The handshaking accompaniment is ludicrous enough having the appearance of weighing some imaginary groceries in each hand.

> —(Evert Duyckinck) Luther Stearns Mansfield, "Glimpses of Herman Melville's Life in Pittsfield, 1850–1851: Some Unpublished Letters of Evert A. Duyckinck," reprinted from *American Literature,* March 1937. (Duyckinck was a literary friend of Melville and Hawthorne.)

SHAKERS.—A friend from New Lebanon informs us that on Sunday last several hundred "fashionables" from the springs attended the house of worship of the Shakers, many of whom behaved in the most disreputable and disgraceful manner. Many of the ladies, as well as gentlemen, indulged in ridiculing the members while worshiping in the dance, to such a degree as to interrupt the worship, and to break up the meeting. It is in

"The Final Procession" by A. Boyd Houghton, from the London *Graphic*, May 1870.

—*New York Express*, quoted in *The Washington Globe*, Aug. 22, 1838

the highest degree disreputable to interfere with any sect in the performance of their devotions, particularly so with the Shakers, who are proverbial for their peaceable, orderly, and quiet course of life.

The Shakers have excited much attention in our country, where they principally exist, and their peculiarities are the subject of much remark, especially among the visiters [*sic*] at Lebanon Springs, N.Y. For, although the waters are healthful in certain complaints, and the scenery beautiful beyond description, yet, the settlement of the Shakers, is, beyond all others, the great object of attraction. No visiter ever thinks of leaving the Springs without visiting the Shakers, and as their mode of worship is so singular and different from all other people, they generally contrive to remain till after Sunday, when they can have the opportunity of visiting their settlement and attending their meeting. Some visiters, it is true, feel a few qualms of conscience for spending the Sabbath in this way, nevertheless they generally endeavor to compose those matters amicably, and hie away to see the Shakers dance! I have been much amused at the remarks made upon the poor Shakers, by those who visit them. Some believe them a sincere but deluded people, while others pronounce them the most arrant hypocrites. Many will ridicule their grotesque and antique dress, their uncouth songs and ungainly dances; but all will bear testi-

A robust version of the popular Shaker "square order" print appeared in a French periodical, *L'Illustration*, about 1860. From the Bettmann Archive.

mony to their neatness, sobriety, and industry. And there is little doubt that this despised people are much more contented and happy, in their present condition, than many of the gay butterflies that fly to their settlement to ridicule and despise them.

> —(Barnabas Bates) *Peculiarities of the Shakers, Described in a Series of Letters from Lebanon Springs, in the Year 1832, Containing an Account of the Origin, Worship, and Doctrines of the Shakers' Society, by a Visiter,* 1832

    Mysterious Worshippers!
Are you indeed the things you seem to be,
Of earth—yet of its iron influence free
    From all that stirs
Our being's pulse, and gives to fleeting life
What well the Hun has termed, "the rapture of the strife?"

    Has not ambition's pean
Some power within your hearts to wake anew
To deeds of higher enterprise—worthier you,
    Ye monkish men,
Than may be reaped from fields? Do ye not rue
The drone-like course of life ye now pursue?

You, too! What early blight
Has withered your fond hopes, that ye thus stand
A group of sisters, 'mong this monkish band?
   Ye creatures bright!
Has sorrow scored your brows with demon hand,
Or o'er your hopes passes treachery's burning brand?

   Ye would have graced right well
The bridal scene, the banquet, or the bowers
Where mirth and revelry usurp the hours—
   Where, like a spell,
Beauty is sovereign—where man owns its powers,
And woman's tread is o'er a path of flowers.

   Yet seem ye not as those
Within whose bosoms memories vigils keep;
Beneath your drooping lids no passions sleep,
   And your pale brows
Bear not the tracery of emotion deep—
Ye seem too cold and passionless to weep! . . .

> —Charlotte Cushman, "Lines, Suggested by a Visit to
> the Shaker Settlement, near Albany, N. Y.," *Knick-
> erbocker*, Jan. 1837. (Ms. Cushman was a popular
> American actress.)

"Sisters in Everyday Costume" by Benson J. Lossing in *Harper's New Monthly
Magazine*, July 1857. Lossing's well-intended but bloodless characterization of
the Believers helped set the Shaker image in the nineteenth century.

ANSWER TO "LINES BY CHARLOTTE CUSHMAN"

We are, indeed, the things we seem to be,
Of earth, and from its iron influence free. . . .

We have outlived those day-dreams of the mind—
Those flattering phantoms which so many bind;
All man-made creeds, (your "faith's sustaining lever,")
We have forsaken, and left forever!

To plainly tell the truth, we do not rue
The sober, Godly course that we pursue;
But 'tis not we who live the dronish lives,
But those who have their husbands, or their wives!
But if by drones you mean they're lazy men,
Then, Charlotte Cushman, take it back again;
For one, with half an eye, or half a mind,
Can there see industry, and wealth, combined. . . .

The "bridal scenes," you say, "we'd grace right well!"
"Lang syne" there our first parents blindly fell!—
The bridal scene! Is this your end and aim?
And can you this pursue, "nor own your shame?"

Here, "Beauty's sovereign"—so say you—
A thing that in an hour may lose its hue,
It lies upon the surface of the skin—
Ay, Beauty's self was never worth a pin. . . .

But here, each other's virtues we partake
Where men and women all their ills forsake. . . .
And when the matter's rightly understood,
You'll find we labor for each other's good. . . .

Now if you would receive a modest hint,
You'd surely keep your name, at least, from print. . . .
As the great advocate of—(O, the name!)
Now can you think of this, "nor own your shame?"

But, Charlotte Cushman, learn to take a deeper view
Of what your neighbors say, or neighbors do.
And when some flattering knaves around you tread,
Just think of what a SHAKER GIRL has said.

> —From the Russellville (Kentucky) *Advertiser;* reprinted in Hervey Elkins, *Fifteen Years in the Senior Order of Shakers*, 1853, and in *The Shaker*, Jan. 1871

The author of this reply has been identified by Mary L. Richmond, in Shaker Literature: A Bibliography, *not as a Shaker girl but as Elder Harvey L. Eads, of South Union, Kentucky.*

Shakerism, as an actual fact in the domestic life of America . . . is far from being a mere folly, to be seen on a Sunday morning with a party of ladies, a diversion between the early dinner and the afternoon drive, to be wondered at, laughed over, and then forgotten as a thing of no serious consequence to the world. Mount Lebanon is the centre of a system which has a distinct genius, a strong organization, a perfect life of its own, through which it would appear to be helping to shape and guide, in no slight and unseen measure, the spiritual career of the United States. . . .

Of course, when they are measured against the thirty millions of Christian people living in the United States, some six or seven thousand celibate Shakers may appear of but small amount; and this would be the truth, if the strength of spiritual and moral forces could be told in figures, like that of a herd of cattle and a kiln of bricks. But if numbers are much, they are far from being all. One man with ideas may be worth a Parliament, an army,—nay, a whole nation without them. The Shakers may not be scholars and men of genius. In appearance they are often very simple; but they are men with ideas, men capable of sacrifice. Unlike the mass of mankind, who live to make money, the Shakers soar above the level of all common vices and temptations, and from the height of their unselfish virtue, offer to the worn and wearied spirit a gift of peace and a place of rest.

No one can look into the heart of American society without seeing that these Shaker unions have a power upon men beyond that of mere numbers. . . . Their influence on the course of American thought is out of all comparison with that of . . . minor sects. The Shakers have a genius, a faith, an organization; which are not only strange, but seductive; which have been tried in the fire of persecution, and which are hostile to society as it stands. A Shaker village is not only a new church, but a new nation. These people ... know nothing of New York, of the United States. They are not Americans; and have no part in the politics and quarrels so often raging around them. They vote for no President; they hold no meetings; they want nothing from the White House. The right to think, vote, speak, and travel, is to them but an idle dream. ... What need can such a people have for votings and palavers? God is their only right; obedience to His will their only freedom.

That such a community should be able to exist in the United States, is a sign; that it should have seized upon men's affections, that it should have become popular and prosperous, growing without effort, conquering without conflict, drawing toward itself many pure, unselfish persons from adjoining towns and states, is little less than a judgment on our churches. And such, in truth, the Shakers call it.

—Hepworth Dixon, *New America*, 1867

If he were summing up an account of the doctrine of Plato, or of St. Paul, and of its followers, Mr. Hepworth Dixon could not be more earnestly reverential. But the question is, Have personages like ... Elderess [*sic*] Polly, and Elderess [*sic*] Antoinette, and the rest of Mr. Hepworth Dixon's heroes and heroines, anything of the weight and significance for the best reason and spirit of man that Plato and St. Paul have? Evidently they, at present, have not; and a very small taste of them and their doctrines ought to have convinced Mr. Hepworth Dixon that they never could have. "But," says he, "the magnetic power which Shakerism is exercising on American thought would of itself compel us,"—and so on. Now, so far as real thought is concerned,—thought which affects the best reason and spirit of man, the scientific or the imaginative thought of the world, the only thought which deserves speaking of in this solemn way,—America has up to the present time been hardly more than a province of England, and even now would not herself claim to be more than abreast of England; and of this only real thought, English thought itself is not just now, as we must all admit, the most significant factor. Neither, then, can American thought be; and the magnetic power which Shakerism exercises on American thought is about as important, for the best reason and spirit of man, as the magnetic power which Mr. Murphy [a "Papist-baiting" contemporary] exercises on Birmingham Protestantism.

—Matthew Arnold, *Culture and Anarchy*, 1869

Since Mr. Dixon was a journalist of absolutely no distinction, one must take very seriously what he says because he only records the obvious.   —Gore Vidal, *Matters of Fact and of Fiction: Essays 1973–76*, 1977

THE SHAKERS AND THE SPIRIT WORLD

As natural to the Believers as their mode of worship—but bewildering to the world's people—was Shaker belief in communication from the spirit world. The Shakers were the first modern American spiritualists, although the Fox sisters of Rochester, New York, seized that title in 1848 with their notorious "spirit rappings."

Spiritualism brought forth Shakerism quite 100 years ago, and has abided with it ever since.

> —Harvey L. Eads, *Shaker Sermons: Scripto-rational,* 1879

They are all spiritualists, recognizing a succession of inspirations from the earliest times down to our own, when they claim to have been the first spiritual mediums. Five or six years ago before the spirits who have since animated so many table-legs, planchettes, phantom shapes, and what not began to knock at Rochester, the Shaker families in New York, Massachusetts, Ohio, and elsewhere were in full communion with the other world, and they were warned of the impending invasion of the world's parlor and dining-room sets. They feel by no means honored, however, by all the results. But they believe that the intercourse between the worlds can be rescued from the evil influences which have perverted it, and they have signs, they say, of an early renewal of the manifestations among themselves. In some way these have in fact never ceased. Many of the Shaker hymns, words and music, are directly inspirational, coming to this brother or that sister without regard to his or her special genius; they are sung and written down, and are then brought into general use. The poetry is like that which the other world usually furnishes its agents in this,—hardly up to our literary standards; but the music has always been something wild, sweet, and naive.

> —William Dean Howells, "A Shaker Village," *Atlantic Monthly,* June 1876

The gift of songs, has been earnestly sought, and liberally obtained by the People, whose name these Hymns and songs bear. They are, without exception, the product of Brethren and Sisters of the Order, who, having had but little scientific, musical education, have, in their arrangement—poetical and musical—chiefly relied upon the teachings of the Spirit. Conscious of their *scientific* imperfections, they go to the public for what they are—the simple offering, of a simple people.

We claim that the words and music, are not *all* of Earth, nor *all* of Heaven: simply inspirational gifts, appropriate to, and illustrative of, the life and testimony of Believers in Christ's First and Second Appearing, which find continued use in their sacred worship; wherein are seen Virgins rejoicing in the dance, both men and women together.

> —Preface to *Shaker Music: Original Inspirational Hymns and Songs Illustrative of the Resurrection, Life, and Testimony of the Shakers,* 1884

They live with angels, and are more familiar (as they tell me) with the dead than with the living. Sister Mary, who was sitting in my room not an hour ago, close to my hand, and leaning on this Bible, which then lay open at the Canticles, told me that the room was full of spirits; of beings as palpable, as audible to her, as my own figure and my own voice. The dreamy look, the wandering eye, the rapt expression, would have alarmed me for her state of health; only that I know with what sweet decorum she conducts her life, and with what subtle fingers she makes damson tarts.

> —Hepworth Dixon, *New America,* 1867

We do not, as a body, accept phenomenal spiritualism; but we seek to be spiritualists in the highest sense of the term. We believe that where Shakerism is in operation, there is realized the fulfillment of the Lord's prayer: "Thy kingdom come, Thy will be done, on earth, as it is in heaven." We do not view death as a separation from loved ones. Heaven here and heaven hereafter are, to us, very closely allied.

> —*The Story of Shakerism, by One Who Knows,* East Canterbury, New Hampshire, 1910

I was gravely told by the first Elder, that the inhabitants of the other world were Shakers, and that they lived in Community the same as we did, but that they were more perfect.

> —Quoted in John Humphrey Noyes, *History of American Socialisms,* 1870

The Era of Mother's Work

A unique spiritual revival occurred among the Believers during the late 1830s and lasted into the 1850s. It traveled throughout Shakerdom, east to west. Mystical rituals and unusual forms of worship, folk art, and music evolved. Thousands of "gift" songs, some in unknown tongues, came "by inspiration" to sensitive members called "instruments." Possessed by departed spirits, such "chosen ones" would swoon, hear divine music, declare messages from beyond, and record drawings that were often visions of heaven. New revelations of God's word were received. One of them, A Holy, Sacred and Divine Roll and Book from the Lord God of Heaven to the Inhabitants of Earth, *was published and five hundred copies were sent to foreign governments.*

It was a new high in spirit power, even for the Shakers, to whom spiritualism was nothing new. Their whole history was remarkable. The faith had begun with a vision in an English jail and reached America with the help of two angels at sea. Unusual powers had marked the missionary

"Mountain Meeting" first appeared in 1848 as the frontispiece in David R. Lamson's *Two Years' Experience among the Shakers*. The Believers are shown worshiping on Mount Sinai at Hancock, Massachusetts. In all day meetings they danced around the Fountain of Life.

work of foundress Mother Ann Lee and her few followers. Their strange wordless songs and dancing seemed part of an abundance of supernatural gifts and godsends.

And now among those who never knew her, there had come this remarkable increase in inspiration, which the central ministry solemnly declared to be "Mother Ann's work." And with it the four leading elders and eldresses saw a chance to purge the church of a certain worldliness and vanity that had crept in with material success. They told the Shakers in all the communes that Mother Ann wanted her children to return to the purity and plainness of her time.

And lo! there came divine commands for cleaning house and confessing sin and holding mysterious ceremonies on sacred ground. At night the Shakers were roused for prayer and marched through their buildings with imaginary spiritual brooms. By day they swept the floors with the actual flat broom they had invented. They scrubbed the brethren's, sisters' and children's workshops with sand, cleared every barn, pen, and field of litter and rubbish, until the communes renowned in America for their neatness were tidier than ever before.

—Flo Morse, *Yankee Communes: Another American Way*, 1971

In 1837 to 1844, there was an influx from the spirit world . . . extending throughout all the eighteen societies, making media by the dozen, whose various exercises, not to be suppressed even in their public meetings, rendered it imperatively necessary to close them all to the world during a period of seven years, in consequence of the then unprepared state of the people, to which the whole of the manifestations, and the meetings, too would have been as unadulterated "foolishness," or as inexplicable mysteries.

The spirits then declared, again and again, that when they had done their work among the inhabitants of Zion, they would do a work in the world, of such magnitude, that not a place nor hamlet upon earth should remain unvisited by them.

After their mission amongst us was finished, we supposed that the manifestations would immediately begin in the outside world; but we were much disappointed; for we had to wait four years before the work began, as it finally did, at Rochester, N.Y. But the rapidity of its course throughout the nations of the earth (as also the social standing and intellectual importance of the converts) has far exceeded the predictions.

> —Frederick W. Evans, *Autobiography of a Shaker*, 1869. (Elder Frederick was the Shaker best known to the world, although some Believers thought him too public and "conspicuous" a figure.)

The invaders only came . . . after asking permission, and at such intervals as did not interfere with the work of the community. The chief visitants were Red Indian spirits who came collectively as a tribe. "One or two elders might be in the room below, and there would be a knock at the door and the Indians would ask whether they might come in. Permission being given, a whole tribe of Indian spirits would troop into the house, and in a few minutes you would hear 'Whoop!' here and 'Whoop!' there all over the house." The whoops emanated, of course, from the vocal organs of the Shakers themselves, but while under the Indian control they would talk Indian among themselves, dance Indian dances, and in all ways show that they were really possessed by the Redskin spirits. . . .

The Shakers had among them a man of outstanding intelligence

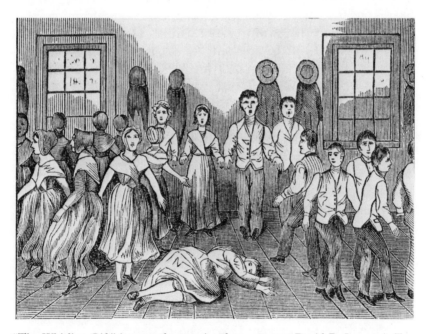

"The Whirling Gift" is a wood engraving from apostate David R. Lamson's *Two Years' Experience among the Shakers*, 1848.

named F. W. Evans, who gave a very clear and entertaining account of all this matter. . . . Mr. Evans and his associates after the first disturbance, physical and mental, caused by this spirit irruption, settled down to study what it really meant. They came to the . . . unexpected conclusion that the Indians were there not to teach but to be taught. They proselytised them, therefore, exactly as they would have done in life.

—Arthur Conan Doyle, *The History of Spiritualism,*
    1926

All who have died before hearing the Gospel, have the privilege of hearing it in the spirit land. When any great character enter and confess their sins, Mother Ann always sends word by the Visionest, to encourage the children of her earthly department. Alexander, Napoleon, Washington, Franklin:—together with the Patriarchs, Prophets, and Martyrs of the past, are said to have embraced the faith with great eagerness, and regret that it is not the gift for them to return to this world, and proclaim the faith in the body. Father Abraham and Sir Isaac Watts compose many songs, mostly in an unknown tongue: the visionests learn them of these good spirits. These are what are called laboring (dancing) songs,—here follows one from Father Abraham, which they dance with great zest.

> Father is a Leader,
>   Let us all be free that
> We may have a portion
> Of Mother's love and blessing—
>
> Vi al lo vi al le
> Vi al le a lando,
> Vi al lo vi al le
> Vi al le a lando.

This is called the round dance,—they run a measured step—the English, then stopping suddenly, face about, and shuffle the unknown tongue, repeating as long as the singers feel a gift.

A Visionest was asked by an Elder, if he saw anything of Sir William Pitt, he answered no, but he would ask after him. In a few moments he announced Sir Isaac, and was put in communication by the Elders, (here let it be understood the visionests are interpreters between the two worlds) when the following conversation ensued:—

Visionest,—Sir Isaac, our Elder wants to know—

Sir Isaac,—Don't call me Sir Isaac, but brother, plain brother Isaac.

Visionest,—Well then brother Isaac you hav'nt got so much pride as you used to have, have you.

Sir Isaac,—No, Mother Ann made me shake it all out of me, at the time I shook that old Devil Anti-Christ out.

Visionest,—The Elders want to know how you felt the first time you shook.

Sir Isaac,—(Laughing) Well, I had been wandering round all day after my arrival in the Spirit land, and could not find a soul I knew: I was so disappointed about heaven that I sat down on some old rubbish and began to cry, when a man came along, and we got into conversation, he asked me why I wept, and I told him, he said he felt so too when he first came, then he told me about Mother,—I wanted to see her, but it was no use, she would not see me till I believed, I could not believe without seeing her, so I groped along for three years; but at last I found I could not wander any longer, for I must be shut up in prison, then I received the Gospel, and Mother made me shake the most of the time for three months, to get rid of old Anti Christ:—he stuck to me like wax, the blood-sucker! (this recital created a great laughter) At this point brother Isaac began to shake.

The Visionest called upon the meeting to shake, when every one, old men and women, the middle aged and small children, commenced shaking and stamping in a violent manner, after which, the visionest sung with brother Isaac, the following characteristic song while all the family dance.

> Come life—Shaker life
>   Come life Eternal,
> Shake, shake, out of me
>   All that is carnal.
> I'll take nimble steps,
>   I'll be a David,
> I'll show Michael twice
>   How he behaved.   [I.Chron.xv.29]

Tecumseh has entered the Gospel, and is doing a great work among the Indians. He is stationed at that section of the spirit world, allotted to the different Indian tribes:—He has converted a chief of every tribe, and given them power to offer the gospel to their own people as soon as they die. These peculiar people are said to return and dance with the "inspired one's,"—singing songs in their own language.

—Anon., *Extract from an Unpublished Manuscript on Shaker History (By an Eye Witness) Giving an Accurate Description of Their Songs, Dances, Marches, Visions, Visits to the Spirit Land, &c.,* 1850

"The Gift of the Father and Son," from David R. Lamson's *Two Years' Experience among the Shakers*, pictures an extreme ceremony at Hancock, Massachusetts, during the spiritualist era of Mother's Work.

Sir Isaac Watts (1674–1748) was a dissenting English minister and writer of hymns. His style influenced the Shakers.

Tecumseh (1768?–1813) was a Shawnee Indian chief who wanted to reform the American Indians and save their lands from U.S. expansion in the West. He and his brother, a prophet and medicine man, tried to form a confederacy of all tribes. But their headquarters in Indiana was destroyed in 1811 in the Battle of Tippecanoe. Once, Tecumseh confronted the governor of the Indiana Territory, William Henry Harrison (the future ninth U.S. president), and expressed his difficulty in trusting white people. They did not recognize Jesus and killed him. "You have

Shakers among you," he said, "and you laugh and make light of their worship."

The Believers sent missions to the Shawnees in Ohio.

AN ABOLITIONIST FANTASY

Young sisters at North Union, Ohio, reported traveling in 1838 to the City of Delight in the "spirit land." There they saw slaveholders serving their former slaves. Another group of slaveholders, who had been unmerciful on earth, refused to serve their former slaves. They were cast out of the city and made to suffer until they repented. "God is just," the sisters said, "and all wrongs must be righted."

This fantasy reflects early Shaker concern about the institution of slavery. Although Mother Ann had seen in vision the "poor negroes" redeemed from their loss, with crowns on their heads, slavery presented a practical problem for the border-state Believers. They did not take an abolitionist stand, although slaveowners freed their slaves when they joined the Shaker societies. The ex-slaves at Pleasant Hill, Kentucky, lived as equals. But at South Union, Kentucky, which was more surrounded by slaveowning neighbors, blacks lived in a separate family and ate in a special dining room. Sometimes blacks were bought, converted, and given their freedom.

Today we purchased Jonas Crutcher a colored man who had been a believer about nineteen years. We kept him hired here while his owner retained him a slave. We have bought him to prevent his being sold South. He was accepted on equal terms.

—South Union, Kentucky, *Journals*

Black Shakers are pictured in some of the early prints showing the Believers dancing. They lived as equals in the northern communities. At various times during the 1840s to 1890s members of a black urban commune in Philadelphia, with ties to the Watervliet, New York, Shakers, worked in the city by day but otherwise lived in gospel order. Mother Rebecca Jackson, and later her adopted daughter, guided this black out-family in its special "travel."

The Tree of Life

City of Peace, Monday July 3rd, 1854. I received a draft of a beautiful Tree pencil'd on a large sheet of white paper bearing ripe fruit. I saw it plainly; it looked very singular and curious to me. I have since learned that this tree grows in the Spirit Land. Afterwards the spirit shew'd me plainly the branches, leaves and fruit, painted or drawn upon paper. The leaves were check'd or cross'd and the same colors you see here. I entreated Mother Ann to tell me the name of this tree: which she did Oct. 1st 4th hour P.M. by moving the hand of a medium to write twice over Your Tree is the Tree of Life.   —Seen and Painted by, Hannah Cohoon

BLESS HANNAH COHOON

who dwelt in the Shaker "City of Peace," Hancock, Massachusetts, where a spirit visited her, as frequently happened there, and gave her "a draft of a beautiful Tree pencil'd on a large sheet of white paper," which she copied out, not knowing till later, with assistance from the Beyond, that it was the Tree of Life; and who saw in another vision, which she likewise reproduced, the Elders of the community feasting on cakes at a table beneath mulberry trees; and who believed, according to the faith of the fol-

lowers of Mother Ann Lee, that Christ would return to earth in female
form.   —Stanley Kunitz, excerpt from "A Blessing of
                        Women," *New York Times*, Feb. 14, 1975; collected
                        in *The Poems of Stanley Kunitz 1928–1978*, 1979

*Sister Hannah's "Tree of Life" was pictured on a UNICEF Christmas
postcard in 1974.*

> Tree of Life. Arbre de vie
> Spirit Drawing / Oeuvre révélée
> Shaker Community Inc. (at / à
> Hancock Village) U.S.A.
> To benefit UNICEF. Au profit de l'UNICEF

Simple Gifts

*Besides "spirit drawings" like the Tree of Life, thousands of "gift
songs" were received, recorded, and learned by heart during this super-
spiritualist decade. One of the most popular songs was "Simple Gifts"
which came by inspiration about 1848 to Elder Joseph Brackett at Alfred,
Maine, to express the humility Believers were laboring for.*

'Tis the gift to be simple, 'tis the gift to be free,
'Tis the gift to come down where we ought to be,
And when we find ourselves in the place just right
'Twill be in the valley of love and delight

When true simplicity is gain'd
To bow and to bend we shan't be ashamed
To turn, turn will be our delight
Till by turning, turning we come round right

*Almost a hundred years later an American composer found a song
he liked in Edward Deming Andrews' book,* The Gift To Be Simple. *It
was the title song, "Simple Gifts." The composer, Aaron Copland, moved
to give the song new life, wove it into the score for a ballet by Martha
Graham, one of the founders of modern American dance. The ballet was*
Appalachian Spring, *and Miss Graham and her company first performed
it at the Library of Congress in Washington on October 30, 1944.*

The original scoring of the work called for a chamber orchestra of thirteen instruments, with the Shaker tune first played in its pristine form by the solo clarinet and then taken up in variations by the ensemble. Appalachian Spring, *with its inspired Shaker melody and flavor of Americana, received the Pulitzer Prize for music in 1945. The ballet, named by Miss Graham from a line in a Hart Crane poem, won the Music Critics' Circle award for the outstanding theatrical work of the 1944–45 season.*

Sister Hannah Cohoon's "Tree of Life" is as meaningful a guide to the Shaker doctrine of unity as Elder Joseph Brackett's "Simple Gifts" is to that of simplicity. The Tree of Life is a recurrent symbol in the Judaeo-Christian tradition from its first appearance in the Garden of Eden to Saint John Theologue's apocalyptic vision of it by the river of the water of life proceeding out of the throne of God and the Lamb. It is a recurrent Shaker symbol, too. We meet it first ... in Father James Whittaker's splendid vision in England of the Church in America, and a generation later it is for Elder Benjamin in *The Testimony of Christ's Second Appearing* a preeminent symbol for the Church. He writes, "the church is compared to a tree which hath many branches, united to the root; as every part of the tree is first formed under ground, so the church is first formed out of sight by the invisible operations of the word...." The tree, too, becomes in Shaker thought an excellent image for what we might call the vertical unity of the church, for to the Shaker the church is not of one time or place, but eternally omnipresent. It is not only the trunk representing the living church operative here on earth, but the deep, hidden roots, representative of the church to come, as well as the heaven-reaching branches, representative of the church triumphant, united for all eternity with the godhead. For Believers the symbolism of the tree served as a deeply beautiful reminder of the church in time. The tree provided, too, a particularly fitting example of the organic nature of the church and the organic unity of its members. The church like the tree was alive, ever-changing, ever-growing, ever-adjusting to new life demands. ...

The second of our fundamental theological concepts is simplicity. It is in Saint Paul's words, "not thinking of ourselves more highly than we ought to think." It involves that most awful of all confrontations—the confrontation with self. True simplicity may be gained only when in Elder Joseph's words, "we come down where we ought to be." It is only through that simplicity that grows from self-understanding that the Be-

"The City of Peace," is one of the few inspired drawings set down by a Shaker brother. Elder Joseph Wicker of Hancock, Massachusetts, was the first to celebrate the symbolism of the tree. Circles representing the Christian virtues are linked like Mother Lucy's chain above the black tree, and writing in unknown language covers the background in geometric forms. Elder Joseph, swept up in the spiritual manifestations at Hancock, received this vision in 1844. Photograph, courtesy of the Western Reserve Historical Society.

liever may truly realize the sense of being part of that holy fellowship which is the church united in Christ's body. It is only through this simplicity that he may realize that basic Christian right and responsibility of self-fulfillment. Shakerism values human fulfillment highly and believes that man fulfills himself by being nothing more nor less than himself. It teaches that love in the Christ spirit is a love beyond disillusionment, for we cannot be disillusioned with people being themselves.

> —Theodore E. Johnson, "Life in the Christ Spirit: Observations on Shaker Theology, Being in Substance Remarks Delivered at the Shaker Conference, Hancock, Massachusetts, September 7, 1968," *Shaker Quarterly*, Fall 1968

Be what you seem to be, and seem to be what you really are, and don't carry two faces under one hood.

> —Father James Whittaker

SOME LITERARY VISITORS

No Admittance—and No Exception for Charles Dickens

Excitement smoldered under the outward calm of the Shaker villages during the era called "Mother's Work." Because of the unpredictable nature of the "visitations," the world's people were no longer welcome on the Sabbath. Who had time for the courteous reception of outsiders when the great of all ages were dropping in? Noah, Napoleon, George Washington, Queen Esther, and many others (mostly men) were visualized by the Shakers. Even Jesus was reported to be "at home" at North Union, Ohio.

In 1842, Charles Dickens, on the last lap of his first American tour, journeyed to New Lebanon, New York, to see the famous Shaker worship. He was turned away. The dashing young English novelist, having been lionized all over the rest of the country, was indignant, and he recorded in American Notes for General Circulation *his distaste for what little of Shakerism he had seen.*

We walked into a grim room, where several grim hats were hanging on grim pegs, and the time was grimly told by a grim clock, which uttered every tick with a kind of struggle, as if it broke the grim silence reluctantly, and under protest. Ranged against the wall were six or eight stiff high-backed chairs, and they partook so strongly of the general grimness, that one would much rather have sat on the floor than incurred the smallest obligation to any of them.

Presently, there stalked into this apartment, a grim old Shaker, with eyes as hard, and dull, and cold, as the great round metal buttons on his coat and waistcoat: a sort of calm goblin. Being informed of our desire, he produced a newspaper wherein the body of elders, whereof he was a member, had advertised but a few days before, that in consequence of certain unseemly interruptions which their worship had received from strangers, their chapel was closed to the public for the space of one year.

Charles Dickens paced up and down the streets of the New York Shaker village, looking at the buildings barred to him. The place of worship seemed "a cool clean edifice of wood ... like a spacious summer house." Other many-storied buildings reminded him of English factories. When he stepped into the Shaker store, he found it "presided over by something alive in a russet case." The elder, he said, told him it was a

The effect is said to be unspeakably absurd: and if I may judge from a print of this ceremony which I have in my possession, and which I am informed by those who have visited the chapel is perfectly accurate, it must be infinitely grotesque. (Charles Dickens)

woman, "and I suppose it was *a woman," wrote Dickens tartly, "though I should not have suspected it."*

He described the Shakers from hearsay.

These people are called Shakers from their peculiar form of adoration, which consists of a dance, performed by the men and women of all ages, who arranged themselves for that purpose in opposite parties; the men first divesting themselves of their hats and coats, which they gravely hang against the wall before they begin; and tying a ribbon round their shirt-sleeves, as though they were going to be bled. They accompany themselves with a droning, humming noise, and dance until they are quite exhausted, alternately advancing and retiring in a preposterous sort of trot. The effect is said to be unspeakably absurd: and if I may judge from a print of this ceremony which I have in my possession, and which I am informed by those who have visited the chapel is perfectly accurate, it must be infinitely grotesque.

They are governed by a woman, and her rule is understood to be absolute, though she has the assistance of a council of elders. She lives, it is said, in strict seclusion, in certain rooms above the chapel, and is never shown to profane eyes. If she at all resembles the lady who presided over the store, it is a great charity to keep her as close as possible. . . .

All the possessions and revenues of the settlement are thrown into a common stock, which is managed by the elders. As they have made converts among people who were well to do in the world, and are frugal and thrifty, it is understood that this fund prospers: the more especially as they have made large purchases of land. . . .

They eat and drink together, after the Spartan model, at a great public table. There is no union of the sexes, and every Shaker, male and female, is devoted to a life of celibacy. Rumor has been busy upon this theme, but here again I must refer to the lady of the store, and say, that if many of the sister Shakers resemble her, I treat all such slander as bearing on its face the strongest marks of wild improbability. But that they take as proselytes, persons so young that they cannot know their own minds, and cannot possess much sense of resolution in this or any other aspect, I can assert from my own observations of the extreme juvenality of certain youthful Shakers whom I saw at work . . . on the road.

They are said to be good drivers of bargains, but to be honest and just in their transactions. . . . In all matters they hold their own course quietly, live in their gloomy silent commonwealth, and show little desire to interfere with other people.

This is well enough, but nevertheless I cannot, I confess, incline toward the Shakers. . . . I so abhor, and from my soul detest that bad spirit . . . which would strip life of its healthful graces, rob youth of its innocent pleasures, pluck from maturity and age their pleasant adornments, and make existence but a narrow path towards the grave. . . . In these very broad-brimmed hats and very sombre coats—in stiff-necked solemn-visaged piety, in short no matter what its garb, whether it have cropped hair as in a Shaker village, or long nails as in a Hindoo temple—I recognize the worst among the enemies of Heaven and Earth, who turn the marriage feasts of this poor world, not into wine but gall.

> —Charles Dickens, *American Notes for General Circulation,* 1842

Dickens left the Shaker village "with a hearty dislike of the old Shakers, and a hearty pity for the young ones," whom he did not blame for running away when they grew older and wiser.

The hostility with which Americans met Charles Dickens's *American Notes for General Circulation* (1842) is a matter of record. The American press even indulged in name-calling; the New York *Herald,* for example, charged "that famous penny-a-liner" with having "the most coarse, vulgar, impudent, and superficial" mind ever to record observations of "this original and remarkable country." Americans, insecure about their adolescent nation's status, were certainly over-sensitive to criticism of virtually any sort, especially that which would achieve such wide currency as anything published by Dickens. Yet Dickens himself was hardly free from fault. . . .

Why did he imply that he had spent two days visiting the Shakers? . . . He admits to having little information about the sect.

> —Duncan A. Carter and Laurence W. Mazzeno, "Dickens's Account of the Shakers and West Point: Rhetoric or Reality?," *The Dickensian,* London, Sept. 1976

Yesterday I read Dickens' *American Notes* . . . a readable book, nothing more. Truth is not his object for a single minute, but merely to make good points in a lively sequence. . . . As an account of America . . . it is too short, and too narrow, too superficial, and too ignorant, too slight, and too fabulous, and the man totally unequal to the work. . . . As a picture of American manners nothing could be falser.

—Ralph Waldo Emerson, *Journals*, Nov. 25, 1842

Ralph Waldo Emerson

A few months before entering the above comment in his journal, Emerson visited the Shakers at Harvard, Massachusetts, with Nathaniel Hawthorne. It was not his first visit to a Shaker community. Many years earlier, in the late 1820s, he had called on the Canterbury, New Hampshire, Shakers and described them in letters to his brother. Emerson often referred to the Shakers in his essays and lectures, after first musing about them in his journals, which were the source of his literary work.

But while he was more cordial toward the Believers than Charles Dickens and Hawthorne were, Emerson did not admire communal living and the popular idea of "association" that flowered in the 1840s in America. Instead of covenants like the Shakers', he favored "inward union."

Of the Shakers, Emerson, in assorted places, wrote:

In the Shakers, so-called, I find one piece of belief, in the doctrine which they faithfully hold that encourages them to open their doors to every wayfaring man who proposes to come among them, for, they say, the Spirit will presently manifest to the man himself and to the society what manner of person he is, and whether he belongs among them. They do not receive him, they do not reject him. And not in vain have they worn their clay coat, and drudged in their fields, and shuffled in their Bruin dance, from year to year, if they have truly learned this much wisdom.   —Essay on Worship, 1860

The fiery reformer embodies his aspiration in some rite or covenant, and he and his friends cleave to the form and lose the aspiration. The Quaker has established Quakerism, the Shaker has established his monastery and his dance; and although each prates of spirit, there is no spirit, but repetition, which is anti-spiritual.

—"Goethe; or, The Writer," 1860

Of the Shaker society it was formerly a sort of proverb in the country that they always sent the devil to market.

—Essay on Power, 1860

Men as naturally make a state, or a church, as caterpillars a web. If they were more refined, it would be less formal, it would be nervous, like that of the Shakers, who, from long habit of thinking and feeling together it is said are affected in the same way, at the same time, to work and to play: and as they go with perfect sympathy to their tasks in the field or shop, so are they inclined for a ride or a journey at the same instant, and the horses come up with the family carriage unbespoken to the door.

—Essay on Worship, 1860

I am going if the day be fair tomorrow to the Shaker Society, at Canterbury with a sleighing party, & perhaps I will put on the drab cowl. Among the earliest institutions to be invented, if I read the stars right, is a protestant monastery, a place of elegant seclusion where melancholy gentlemen & ladies may go to spend the advanced season of single life in drinking milk, walking the woods & reading the Bible and the poets. I have a treatise on this subject in preparation.

—Letter to Charles Chauncey Emerson, Concord, New Hampshire, Jan. 1, 1828, from *The Letters of Ralph Waldo Emerson*, edited by Ralph L. Rusk, 1939

At the Shaker's house in Harvard I found a spirit level on the windowseat, a very good emblem for the society; but, unfortunately, neither the table, nor the shelf, nor the windowseat were plumb.

—*Journals*, Oct. [8], 1842

Here I am quietly seated at Deacon Winkleys table among the brothers and sisters of Shaking faith. . . . Ellen and I came hither in a chaise this morning, an easy ride of 12 miles from Concord. . . . Mother Winkley or Sister Winkley hath given Ellen & I a long & earnest sermon on the "beauty of virginity" and striven to dissuade us from our sinful purpose of "living after the way of mankind and womankind in the earth" but I parried her persuasion & her denunciation as best I might & insisted we were yoked together by Heaven to provoke each other to good works so long as we lived—This society is divided into three families & own about 2000 acres of land, and excepting a shrewd handful of male & female oligarchs are a set of clean, well disposed, dull, & incapable animals. One man I have talked with was very well read in the bible & talked very logically from the Scriptures literally taken, but was strangely ignorant for a Yankee about every thing beyond his daily & weekly errands in the country round.   —Letter to Charles Chauncey Emerson, Canterbury, New Hampshire, Aug. 7, 1829, from *The Letters of Ralph Waldo Emerson*, edited by Ralph L. Rusk, 1939

A WALK WITH HAWTHORNE

September 30, 1842

September 27 was a fine day, and Hawthorne and I set forth on a walk. . . .

Our walk had no incidents. It needed none, for we were in excellent spirits, had much conversation, for we were both old collectors who had never had the opportunity before to show each other our cabinets, so that we could have filled with matter much longer days. . . . After noon we reached Stow, and dined, and then continued our journey towards Harvard, making our day's walk, according to our best computation, about twenty miles. . . .

Next morning we began our walk at 6:30 o'clock for the Shaker Village, distant three and a half miles. Whilst the good Sisters were getting ready our breakfast, we had a conversation with Seth Blanchard and Cloutman of the Brethren, who gave an honest account, by yea and by nay, of their faith and practice. They were not stupid, like some I have seen of their society, and not worldly like others. The conversation on both parts was frank enough; with the downright I will be downright, thought I, and Seth showed some humor. I doubt not we should have had our own way with them to a good extent . . . if we could have stayed twenty-four hours; although my powers of persuasion were crippled by a disgraceful barking cold, and Hawthorne inclined to play Jove more than Mercurius. After breakfast Cloutman showed us the farm, vineyard, orchard, barn, herb room, pressing-room, etc. The vineyard contained two noble arcades of grapes, both white and Isabella, full of fruit; the orchard, fine varieties of pears and peaches and apples.

They have fifteen acres here, a tract of woodland in Ashburnham, and a sheep pasture somewhere else, enough to supply the wants of the two hundred souls in this family. They are in many ways an interesting society, but at present have an additional importance as an experiment of socialism which so falls in with the temper of the times. What improvement is made is made forever; this capitalist is old and never dies, his subsistence was long ago secured and he has gone on now for long scores of years in adding easily compound interest to his stock. Moreover, this settlement is of great value in the heart of the country as a model-farm. . . . Here are improvements invented, or adopted from other Shaker communities, which the neighboring farmers see and copy. From the Shaker Village we came to Littleton and thence to Acton, still in the same redundance of splendor. . . . And from Acton we sauntered leisurely homeward, to finish the nineteen miles of our second day before four in the afternoon.

—*Journals*

Nathaniel Hawthorne

Monday, October 10th, 1842.— . . . A week or two ago (September 27 and 28) I went on a pedestrian excursion with Mr. Emerson, and was gone two days and one night, it being the first and only night that I have spent away from home. We were that night at the village of Harvard, and the next morning walked three miles farther, to the Shaker village, where we breakfasted. Mr. Emerson had a theological discussion with two of the Shaker brethren; but the particulars of it have faded from my memory. . . . I recollect nothing so well as the aspect of some fringed gentians, which we saw growing by the roadside, and which were so beautiful that I longed to turn back and pluck them.

—Nathaniel Hawthorne, *Passages From The American Note-Books*, 1868

Hawthorne was of two minds about the Shakers. As a young man of twenty-seven, he may have half seriously considered joining them, after a visit to the society at Canterbury, New Hampshire.

I walked to the Shaker village yesterday, and was shown over the establishment, and dined there with a squire and a doctor, also of the world's people. On my arrival, the first thing I saw was a jolly old Shaker carrying an immense decanter of their superb cider; and as soon as I told him my business, he turned out a tumblerful and gave me. Our dining-room was well furnished, the dinner excellent, and the table attended by a middle-aged Shaker lady, good looking and cheerful.... This establishment is immensely rich. Their land extends two or three miles along the road, and there are streets of great houses painted yellow and tipt with red.... On the whole, they lead a good and comfortable life, and, if it were not for their ridiculous ceremonies, a man could not do a wiser thing than to join them. Those whom I conversed with were intelligent, and appeared happy. I spoke to them about becoming a member of their society, but have come to no decision on that point.

—(Nathaniel Hawthorne) Hyatt H. Waggoner, *Hawthorne: A Critical Study*, 1963

Later Hawthorne joined Brook Farm, an intellectual utopian community located outside of Boston. He based his novel The Blithedale Romance *on his actual experience at Brook Farm, but two melancholy tales about the Shakers seem to have emerged from the dark side of his imagination. There is no hint of his early friendliness in "The Canterbury Pilgrims" and "A Shaker Bridal." His final opinion was a harsh one.*

August 8th. Friday. (1851) ... Between eleven and twelve, came Herman Melville, and the two Duyckincks, in a barouche and pair. Melville had spoken, when he was here, of bringing these two expected guests of his to call on me.... They proposed a ride and a pic-nic, to which I readily consented.... We set out, taking Julian, of course.... We took the road over the mountain toward Hudson, and by and by came to a pleasant grove, where we alighted and arranged matters for our pic-nic....

After talk about literature and other things, we set forth again, and resolved to go and visit the Shaker establishment at Hancock, which was but two or three miles off. I don't know what Julian expected to see— some strange sort of quadruped or other, I suppose—at any rate, the term Shakers was evidently a subject of great puzzlement with him; and probably he was a little disappointed when I pointed out an old man in a gown and a gray, broad-brimmed hat, as a Shaker. This old man was one of the fathers and rulers of the village; and under his guidance, we visited the principal dwelling-house in the village. It was a large brick edifice, with admirably convenient arrangements, and floors and walls of polished wood, and plaster as smooth as marble, and everything so neat that it was a pain and constraint to look at it; especially as it did not imply any real delicacy or moral purity in the occupants of the house. There were spit-

"Shaker village in Hancock, Massachusetts," from *Historical Collections . . . of Every Town in Massachusetts*, by John Warner Barber, 1841.

boxes (bearing no appearance of ever being used, it is true) at equal distances up and down the long and broad entries. The sleeping apartments of the two sexes had an entry between them, on one side of which hung the hats of the men, on the other the bonnets of the women. In each chamber were two particularly narrow beds, hardly wide enough for one sleeper, but in each of which, the old elder told us, two people slept. There were no bathing or washing conveniences in the chambers; but in the entry there was a sink and wash-bowl, where all their attempts at purification were to be performed. The fact shows that all their miserable pretence of cleanliness and neatness is the thinnest superficiality; and that the Shakers are and must needs be a filthy set. And then their utter and systematic lack of privacy; the close function of man with man, and supervision of one man over another—it is hateful and disgusting to think of; and the sooner the sect is extinct the better—a consummation which, I am happy to hear, is thought to be not a great many years distant.

In the great house, we saw an old woman—a round, fat, cheerful little old sister—and two girls, from nine to twelve years old; these looked at us and at Julian with great curiosity, though slily and with side glances. At the doors of other dwellings, we saw women sewing or otherwise at work; and there seemed to be a kind of comfort among them, but of no higher kind than is enjoyed by their beasts of burden. Also, the women looked pale, and none of the men had a jolly aspect. They are certainly the most singular and bedevilled set of people that ever existed in a civilized land; and one of these days, when their sect and system shall have passed away, a History of the Shakers will be a very curious book.

—Nathaniel Hawthorne, *American Notebooks*, ed. by Randall Stewart, 1932

Hawthorne's literary friend, Evert Duyckinck, from New York, offers another description of their visit with Herman Melville in August 1851 to the Hancock, Massachusetts, Shakers. In a letter to his wife he mentioned "the fine mountain drive" to the community:

We met them mowing their carefully groomed fields and at the Hancock settlement met again old Father Hilliard and trod the neat quiet avenues whose stillness might be felt. Here is the great circular barn where the winter cattle feed with their heads all to the huge hay mow in the centre.... I ... induced venerable Father Hilliard to open to us the big house. Its oiled and polished pine floors were elegant in spite of Shakerdom. The glazed finish of the white walls were as pure as yesterday's work, though they have been there these twenty years. You see no flowers in the sisters' rooms but a volume of unreadable theology (of its kind) with a pair of crossed spectacles by its side on a small table.

The editor of the Literary World *had visited the Shakers the summer before, and had written to his wife, "I have seen no 'jumping quakers' yet but will look out." He had also quipped, "On Sunday I meditate a walk or drive to the Shakers who are then at their spasms." He described a tour of Mount Lebanon and Hancock with the Melvilles, when some "snug little boxes and baskets" were bought.*

An old Shakeress with a dry Yankee twist in her voice took us to the bedroom &c and explained to us a curious camel's hump raised in the middle of the bed, lengthwise, a kind of imitation Berkshire mountain range where two sisters slept together—that they should not roll on one another. Old Shakeresses speak plain Saxon. Herman M saw a long handled brush at a bed head & asked its object. "Why I guess it's for him to scratch himself with when he itches." This was at Lebanon. We passed on among the 7000 Shaker acres by the immaculate yellow houses, glazed like a pail, the red barns and the bricky natives, by well cultivated fields to the Hancock village where we saw the huge barn. . . . An extraordinary splendid day it is & we are off at eight, calling on Hawthorne at Lenox.

> —(Evert A. Duyckinck) Luther Stearns Mansfield,
> "Glimpses of Herman Melville's Life in Pittsfield,
> 1850–1851: Some Unpublished Letters of Evert A.
> Duyckinck"

THE CANTERBURY PILGRIMS

The summer moon, which shines in so many a tale was beaming over a broad extent of uneven country. Some of its brightest rays were flung over a spring of water, where no traveller, toiling, as the writer has, up the hilly road beside which it gushes, ever failed to quench his thirst. The work of neat hands and considerate art was visible about this blessed fountain. . . .

While the moon was hanging almost perpendicularly over this spot, two figures appeared on the summit of the hill, and came with noiseless footsteps toward the spring. They were then in the first freshness of youth . . . and yet they wore a strange, old-fashioned garb. One, a young man with ruddy cheeks, walked beneath the canopy of a broad-brimmed gray hat; he seemed to have inherited his great-grandsire's square-skirted coat, and a waistcoat that extended its immense flaps to his knees; his brown locks, also, hung down behind, in a mode unknown to our times. By his side was a sweet young damsel, her fair features sheltered by a prim little bonnet, within which the vestal muslin of a cap; her close, long-waisted gown, and indeed her whole attire, might have been worn by some rustic beauty who had faded half a century before. . . .

"Thee and I will rest here a moment, Miriam," said the young man, as they drew near the stone cistern, "for there is no fear that the elders know what we have done; and this may be the last we shall ever taste this water."

Thus speaking, with a little sadness in his face, which was also visible in that of his companion, he made her sit down on a stone, and was about to place himself very close to her side; she, however, repelled him, though not unkindly.

"Nay, Josiah," said she, giving him a timid push with her maiden hand, "thee must sit further off, on that other stone, with the spring between us. What would the sisters say, if thee were to sit so close to me?"

"But we are of the world's people now, Miriam," answered Josiah.

The girl persisted in her prudery, nor did the youth, in fact, seem altogether free from a similar sort of shyness; so they sat apart from each other, gazing up the hill, where the moonlight discovered the tops of a group of buildings. While their attention was thus occupied, a party of travellers, who had come wearily up the long ascent, made a halt to refresh themselves at the spring. There were three men, a woman, and a little girl and boy. . . . They all looked woe-begone, as if the cares and sorrows of the world had made their steps heavier as they climbed the hill. . . .

"Good-evening to you, young folks," was the salutation of the travellers. . . .

"Is that white building the Shaker meeting-house. . . . And are those the red roofs of the Shaker village?"

"Friends, it is the Shaker village," answered Josiah, after some hesitation.

The travellers, who, from the first, had looked suspiciously at the garb of these young people, now taxed them with an attention which all the circumstances, indeed, rendered too obvious to be mistaken.

"It is true, friends," replied the young man, summoning up his courage. "Miriam and I have a gift to love each other, and we are going among the world's people, to live after their fashion. And ye know that we do not transgress the law of the land; and neither ye, nor the elders themselves, have a right to hinder us."

"Yet you think it expedient to depart without leave-taking," remarked one of the travellers.

"Yea, ye-a," said Josiah, reluctantly, "because Father Job is a very awful man to speak with; and being aged himself, he has but little charity for what he calls the iniquities of the flesh."

"Well," said the stranger, "we will neither use force to bring you back to the village, nor will we betray you to the elders. But sit you here a while, and when you have heard what we shall tell you of the world which we have left, and into which you are going, perhaps you will turn back with us of your own accord." . . .

The whole party stationed themselves round the stone cistern; the two children being very weary, fell asleep upon the damp earth, and the pretty Shaker girl, whose feelings were those of a nun or a Turkish lady, crept as close as possible to the female traveller, and as far as she well could from the unknown men. . . . The chief spokesman now stood up, waving his hat in his hand, and suffered the moonlight to fall full upon his front.

"In me," said he, with a certain majesty of utterance, "in me, you behold a poet."

"A poet!" repeated the young Shaker, a little puzzled how to understand such a designation, seldom heard in the utilitarian community where he had spent his life. "O, ay, Miriam, he means a varse-maker, thee must know."

This remark jarred upon the susceptible nerves of the poet, nor could he help wondering what strange facility had put into this young man's mouth an epithet, which ill-natured people had affirmed to be more proper to his merit than the one assumed by himself. . . .

A long harangue by the poet on the failure of his muse confused the young Shakers.

"I thank thee, friend," rejoined the youth, "but I do not mean to be a poet, nor, Heaven be praised! do I think Miriam ever made a varse in her life. So we need not fear thy disappointments. But, Miriam," he added, with real concern, "thee knowest that the elders admit nobody that has not a gift to be useful. Now, what under the sun can they do with this poor varse-maker?"

"Nay, Josiah, do not thee discourage the poor man," said the girl, in all simplicity and kindness. "Our hymns are very rough, and perhaps they may trust him to smooth them." . . .

Without noting this hint of professional employment, the poet turned away, and gave himself up to a sort of vague reveries, which he called thought. . . . He listened to that most ethereal of all sounds, the song of crickets, coming in full choir upon the wind, and fancied that, if moonlight could be heard, it would sound just like that. Finally, he took a draught at the Shaker spring, and, as if it were the true Castalia, was forthwith moved to compose a lyric: A Farewell to his Harp, which he swore should be its closing strain, the last verse that an ungrateful world should have from him. This effusion, with two or three other little pieces, subsequently written, he took the first opportunity to send, by one of the Shaker brethren, to Concord, where they were published in the New Hampshire Patriot.

Meantime, another of the Canterbury pilgrims, one so different from the poet that the delicate fancy of the latter could hardly have conceived of him, began to relate his sad experience. He was a small man, of quick and unquiet gestures, about fifty years old. . . . He held in his hand a pencil, and a card of some commission-merchant in foreign parts, on the back of which . . . he seemed ready to figure out a calculation.

"Young man," said he, abruptly, "what quantity of land do the Shakers own here, in Canterbury?"

"That is more than I can tell thee, friend," answered Josiah, "but it is a very rich establishment, and for a long way by the roadside thee may guess the land to be ours, by the neatness of the fences."

"And what may be the value of the whole?" continued the stranger. . . .

"O, a monstrous sum,—more than I can reckon," replied the young Shaker.

"Well, sir," said the pilgrim, "there was a day . . . when I stood at my counting-room window, and watched the signal flags from three of my own ships entering the harbor, from the East Indies, from Liverpool, and from up the Straits. . . . I could have put more value on a little piece of paper, no bigger than the palm of your hand, than all these solid acres of grain, grass and pasture-land, would sell for."

"I won't dispute it, friend," answered Josiah, "but I know I had rather have fifty acres of this good land than a whole sheet of thy paper."

"You may say so now," said the ruined merchant, bitterly, "for my name would not be worth the paper I should write it on. . . . You see me here on the road to the Shaker village, where, doubtless (for the Shakers are a shrewd sect), they will have a due respect for my experience, and give me the management of the trading part of the concern, in which case, I think I can pledge myself to double their capital in four or five years." . . .

The third pilgrim now took up the conversation. He was a sunburnt countryman, of tall frame and bony strength, on whose ruddy and manly face there appeared a darker, more sullen and obstinate despondency, than on those of either the poet or the merchant. . . .

"When I was about of your years, I married me a wife,—just such a neat and pretty young woman as Miriam, if that's her name,—and all I asked of Providence was an ordinary blessing on the sweat of my brow. . . . We had no very great prospects before us; but I never wanted to be idle, and I thought it a matter of course that the Lord would help me, because I was willing to help myself. . . .

"I have labored hard for years; and my means have been growing narrower, and my living poorer, and my heart colder and heavier, all the time; till at last I could bear it no longer. I set myself down to calculate whether I had best go on the Oregon expedition, or come here to the Shaker village . . . to make my story short, here I am. And now, youngsters, take my advice, and turn back." . . .

The yeoman's misfortunes won more sympathy from the young fugitives than the failure of the poet and the merchant. They could identify with him.

"But thy wife, friend?" exclaimed the young man. . . .

The female pilgrim had been leaning over the spring wherein latterly a tear or two might have been seen to fall. . . . "I am his wife," said she. . . . "These poor little things, asleep on the ground, are two of our children. We had two more, but God has provided better for them than we could . . . by taking them to himself."

"And what would thee advise Josiah and me to do?" asked Miriam, this being the first question which she had put to either of the strangers. . . .

"Though my husband told you some of our troubles, he didn't mention the greatest, and that which makes all the rest so hard to bear. If you and your sweetheart marry, you'll be kind and pleasant to each other for a year or two . . . but, by and by, he'll grow gloomy, rough, and hard to please, and you'll be peevish . . . so your love will wear away by little and little, and leave you miserable at last. It has been so with us; and yet my husband and I were true lovers, once, if ever two young folks were. . . ."

For a brief moment the husband and wife felt a return of their old affection. But the moment passed, and the children awoke and began to wail.

The varied narratives of the strangers had arranged themselves into a parable; they seemed not mere instances of woeful fate that had befallen others, but shadowy omens of disappointed hope, and unavailing toil, domestic grief, and estranged affection, that would cloud the onward path of these poor fugitives. But after one instant's hesitation, they opened their arms, and sealed their resolve with as pure and fond an embrace as ever youthful love had hallowed.

"We will not go back," said they. "The world can never be dark to us, for we will always love one another."

Then the Canterbury pilgrims went up the hill, while the poet chanted a drear and desperate stanza of the Farewell to his Harp, fitting music for that melancholy band. They sought a home where all former ties of nature or society would be sundered, and all old distinctions levelled, and a cold and passionless security be substituted for mortal hope and fear, as in that other refuge of the world's weary outcasts, the grave. The lovers drank at the Shaker spring, and then, with chastened hopes, but more confiding affections, went on to mingle in an untried life.

> —Nathaniel Hawthorne, from *The Token and Atlantic Souvenir*, 1833; collected in *The Snow Image and Other Twice-Told Tales*, 1851

May 6th, 1850.—. . . Took my way through the sloppy streets to the Athenaeum, and found two of my old stories ("Peter Goldthwaite" and the "Shaker Bridal") published as original in the last "London Metropolitan!" The English are much more unscrupulous and dishonest pirates than ourselves. However, if they are poor enough to perk themselves in such false feathers as these, Heaven help them! I glanced over the stories, and they seemed painfully cold and dull.

> —Nathaniel Hawthorne, *Passages from The American Note-Books*, 1868

Herman Melville

When Melville was polishing his great novel, Moby-Dick, *he lived at Pittsfield, Massachusetts, near two Shaker villages. In July 1850 he visited the Hancock Shakers and bought a copy of the Shaker history* A Summary View of the Millennial Church. *But his summer reading also included Timothy Dwight's* Travels in New-England and New-York, *with its unsympathetic comments on the Shakers. Both works may have influenced the development of a character in* Moby-Dick, *a seaman named Gabriel who shipped out of Nantucket on the whaling boat* Jeroboam. *Gabriel is described as a short, yellow-haired, freckle-faced man, clad in a long brown coat and showing a "deep fanatic delirium" in his eyes.*

He had originally been nurtured among the crazy society of Neskyeuna Shakers, where he had been a great prophet; in their cracked, secret meetings having several times descended from heaven by the way of a trap-door, announcing the speedy opening of the seventh vial, which he carried in his vest-pocket; but, which, instead of containing gunpowder, was supposed to be charged with laudanum. A strange, apostolic whim having seized him, he had left Neskyeuna for Nantucket, where, with that cunning peculiar to craziness, he assumed a steady, common sense exterior, and offered himself as a green-hand candidate for the Jeroboam's whaling voyage. They engaged him; but straightway upon the ship's getting out of sight of land, his insanity broke out in a freshet. He announced himself as the archangel Gabriel, and commanded the captain to jump overboard.

The captain and the ignorant crew feared the self-styled prophet, and his power over them was great. He warned them against attacking the White Whale,

in his gibbering insanity, pronouncing the White Whale to be no less a being than the Shaker God incarnated; the Shakers receiving the Bible.

A year or two later, when the White Whale, Moby-Dick, was sighted, the chief mate disregarded Gabriel's warning, attacked the whale, and lost his life.

Artemus Ward

This popular nineteenth-century American humorist cashed in on the comic aspects of his countrymen. In his typical style of misspelled words, he satirized the Shakers in an account of a stay among them.

ARTEMUS WARD ON THE SHAKERS

The Shakers is the strangest religious sex I ever met. I'd hearn tell of 'em and I'd seen 'em, with their broad brim'd hats and long wastid coats; but I'd never cum into immejit contack with 'em, and I'd sot 'em down as lackin intelleck, as I'd never seen 'em to my Show—leastways, if they cum they was disgised in white peple's close, so I didn't know 'em.

But in the Spring of 18–, I got swampt in the exterior of New York State, one dark and stormy night, when the winds Blue pityusly, and I was forced to tie up with the Shakers.

I was toilin threw the mud, when in the dim vister of the futer I obsarved the gleams of a taller candle. Tiein a hornet's nest to my off hoss's tail to kinder encourage him, I soon reached the place. I knockt at the door, which it was opened unto me by a tall, slick-faced, solum lookin individooal, who turn'd out to be a Elder.

"Mr. Shaker," sed I, "you see before you a Babe in the woods, so to speak, and he axes shelter of you."

"Yay," sed the Shaker, and he led the way into the house, another Shaker bein sent to put my hosses and waggin under kiver.

A solum female, lookin sumwhat like a last year's beanpole stuck into a long meal bag, cum in and axed me was I a thurst and did I hunger? to which I urbanely anserd "a few." She went orf and I endeverd to open a conversashun with the old man.

"Elder, I spect?" sed I.

"Yay," he said.

"Helth's good, I reckon?"

"Yay."

"What's the wages of a Elder, when he understans his bisness—or do you devote your sarvices gratooitus?"

"Yay."

"Stormy night, sir."

"Yay."

"If the storm continners there'll be a mess underfoot, hay?"

"Yay."

"It's onpleasant when there's a mess underfoot?"

"Yay."

"If I may be so bold, kind sir, what's the price of that pecooler kind of weskit you wear, incloodin trimmins?"

"Yay!"

I pawsd a minit, and then, thinkin I'd be faseshus with him and see how that would go, I slapt him on the shoulder, bust into a harty larf, and told him that as a *yayer* he had no livin ekal.

He jumpt up as if Bilin water had bin squirted into his ears, groaned, rolled his eyes up tords the sealin and sed: "You're a man of sin!" He then walkt out of the room.

Jest then the female in the meal bag stuck her hed into the room and statid that refreshments awaited the weary travler, and I sed if it was vittles she ment the weary travler was agreeable, and I follored her into the next room.

I sot down to the table and the female in the meal bag pored out sum tea. She sed nothin, and for five minutes the only live thing in that room was a old wooden clock, which tickt in a subdood and bashful manner in the corner. This dethly stillness made me oneasy, and I determined to talk to the female or bust. So sez I, "marrige is agin your rules, I bleeve, marm?"

"Yay."

"The sexes liv strickly apart, I spect?"

"Yay."

"It's kinder singler," sez I, puttin on my most sweetest look and speakin in a winnin voice, "that so fair a made as thow never got hitched to some likely feller." [N.B.—She was upwards of 40 and homely as a stump fence, but I thawt I'd tickil her.]

"I don't like men!" she sed, very short.

"Wall, I dunno," sez I, "they're a rayther important part of the populashun. I don't scacely see how we could git along without 'em."

"Us poor wimin folks would git along a grate deal better if there was no men!"

"You'll excoos me, marm, but I don't think that air would work. It wouldn't be regler."

"I'm fraid of men!" she sed.

"That's onnecessary, marm. *You* ain't in no danger. Don't fret yourself on that pint."

"Here we're shot out from the sinful world. Here all is peas. Here we air brothers and sisters. We don't marry and consekently we hav no domestic difficulties. Husbans don't abooze their wives—wives don't worrit their husbans. There's no children here to worrit us. Nothin to worrit us here. No wicked matrimony here. Would thow like to be a Shaker?"

"No," sez I, "it ain't my stile."

I had now histed in as big a load of pervishuns as I could carry comfortable, and, leanin back in my cheer, commenst pickin my teeth with a fork. The female went out, leavin me all alone with the clock. I hadn't sot thar long before the Elder poked his hed in at the door. "You're a man of sin!" he sed, and groaned and went away.

Directly thar cum in two young Shakeresses, as putty and slick lookin gals as I ever met. It is troo they was drest in meal bags like the old one I'd met previsly, and their shiny, silky har was hid from sight by long white caps, sich as I spose female Josts wear; but their eyes sparkled like diminds, their cheeks was like roses, and they was charmin enuff to make a man throw stuns at his granmother if they axed him to. They comenst clearin away the dishes, castin shy glances at me all the time. I got excited. I forgot Betsy Jane in my rapter, and sez I, "my pretty dears, how air you?"

"We air well," they solumly sed.

"Whar's the old man?" sed I, in a soft voice.

"Of whom dost thow speak—Brother Uriah?"

"I mean the gay and festiv cuss who calls me a man of sin. Shouldn't wonder if his name was Uriah."

"He has retired."

"Wall, my pretty dears," sez I, "let's have sum fun. Let's play puss in the corner. What say?"

"Air you a Shaker, sir?" they axed.

"Wall my pretty dears, I haven't arrayed my proud form in a long weskit yit, but if they was all like you perhaps I'd jine 'em. As it is, I'm a Shaker pro-temporary."

They was full of fun. I seed that at fust, only they was a lettle skeery. I tawt 'em Puss in the corner and sich like plase, and we had a nice time, keepin quiet of course so the old man shouldn't hear. When we broke up, sez I, "my pretty dears, ear I go you hav no objections, hav you, to a innersent kiss at partin?"

"Yay," they sed, and I *yay'd*.

I went up stairs to bed. I spose I'd bin snoozin half an hour when I was woke up by a noise at the door. I sot up in bed, leanin on my elbers and rubbin my eyes, and I saw the follerin picter: The Elder stood in the doorway, with a taller candle in his hand. He hadn't no wearin appeerel on except his night close, which flutterd in the breeze like a Seseshun flag. He sed, "You're a man of sin!" then groaned and went away.

I went to sleep agin, and drempt of runnin orf with the pretty little Shakeresses mounted on my Californy Bar. I thawt the Bar insisted on steerin strate for my dooryard in Baldinsville and that Betsy Jane cum out and giv us a warm recepshun with a panfull of Bilin water. I was woke up arly by the Elder. He sed refreshments was reddy for me down stairs. Then sayin I was a man of sin, he went groanin away.

As I was goin threw the entry to the room where the vittles was, I cum across the Elder and the old female I'd met the night before, and what d'ye spose they was up to? Huggin and kissin like young lovers in their gushingist state. Sez I, "my Shaker frends, I reckon you'd better suspend the rules and git married."

"You must excoos Brother Uriah," sed the female; "he's subjeck to fits and hain't got no command over hisself when he's into 'em."

"Sartinly," sez I, "I've bin took that way myself frequent."

"You're a man of sin!" sed the Elder.

Arter breakfast my little Shaker frends cum in agin to clear away the dishes.

"My pretty dears," sez I, "shall we *yay* agin?"

Artemus among the Shakers. "Yay," they sed, and I *yay'd*. Illustration, *Artemus Ward, His Book* (Charles Farrar Browne), 1862.

"Nay," they sed, and I *nay'd*.

The Shakers axed me to go to their meetin, as they was to hav sarvices that mornin, so I put on a clean biled rag and went. The meetin house was as neat as a pin. The floor was white as chalk and smooth as glass. The Shakers was all on hand, in clean weskits and meal bags, ranged on the floor like milingtery companies, the mails on one side of the room and the females on tother. They commenst clappin their hands and singin and dancin. They danced kinder slow at fust, but as they got warmed up they shaved it down very brisk, I tell you. Elder Uriah, in particler, exhiberted a right smart chance of spryness in his legs, considerin his time of life, and as he cum a dubble shuffle near where I sot, I rewarded him with a approvin smile and sed: "Hunky boy! Go it, my gay and festiv cuss!"

"You're a man of sin!" he sed, continnerin his shuffle.

The Sperret, as they called it, then moved a short fat Shaker to say a few remarks. He sed they was Shakers and all was ekal. They was the purest and Seleckest peple on the yearth. Other peple was sinful as they could be, but Shakers was all right. Shakers was all goin kerslap to the Promist Land, and nobody want goin to stand at the gate to bar 'em out, if they did they'd git run over.

The Shakers then danced and sung agin, and arter they was threw, one of 'em axed me what I thawt of it.

Sez I, "What duz it siggerfy?"

"What?" sez he.

"Why this jumpin up and singin? This long weskit bizniss, and this anty-matrimony idee? My frends, you air neat and tidy. Your lands is flowin with milk and honey. Your brooms is fine, and your apple sass is honest. When a man buys a keg of apple sass of you he don't find a grate many shavins under a few layers of sass—a little Game I'm sorry to say sum of my New Englan ancesters used to practiss. Your garding seeds is fine, and if I should sow 'em on the rock of Gibralter probly I should raise a good mess of garding sass. You air honest in your dealins. You air quiet and don't distarb nobody. For all this I givs you credit. But your religion is small pertaters, I must say. You mope away your lives here in single retchidness, and as you air all by yourselves nothing ever conflicks with your pecooler idees, except when Human Nater busts out among you, as I understan she sumtimes do. [I giv Uriah a sly wink here, which made the old feller squirm like a speared Eel.] You wear long weskits and long faces, and lead a gloomy life indeed. No children's prattle is ever hearn around your harthstuns—you air in a dreary fog all the time, and you treat the jolly sunshine of life as tho' it was a thief, drivin it from your doors by them weskits, and meal bags, and pecooler noshuns of yourn. The gals among you, sum of which air as slick pieces of caliker as I ever sot eyes on, air syin to place their heds agin weskits which kiver honest, manly harts, while you old heds fool yerselves with the idee that they air fulfillin their mishun here, and air contented. Here you air all pend up by yerselves, talkin about the sins of a world you don't know nothin of. Meanwhile said world continners to resolve round on her own axeltree onct in every 24 hours, subjeck to the Constitution of the United States, and is a very plesant place of residence. It's a unnatral, onreasonable and dismal life you're leadin here. So it strikes me. My Shaker frends, I now bid you a welcome adoo. You hav treated me exceedin well. Thank you kindly, one and all."

"A base exhibiter of depraved monkeys and onprincipled wax works!" sed Uriah.

"Hello, Uriah," sez I, "I'd most forgot you. Wall, look out for them fits of yourn, and don't catch cold and die in the flour of your youth and beauty."

And I resoomed my jerney.

> —Artemus Ward [Charles Farrar Browne], *Vanity Fair*, Feb. 23, 1861

THE SHAKER CONCERTS.—We supposed that there can be little doubt that the performers at the Apollo Saloon, last evening, have been Shakers, albeit they do not now profess much love to that community. It is probable that this absence of affection is mutual. We scarcely know what to say about the exhibition. As a portion of the industrial community the Shakers have won golden opinions from all sorts of men. And this may be said of their peculiar notions, which can scarcely be said of any other of the numerous *ism* tribes, that they do not offensively thrust their peculiarities before the community. To the indulgence and, if the term be applicable, the enjoyment of their odd customs, on their own grounds, they have indisputable right. . . .

So far we should object to any caricature of their thinkings and doings. But there is an inherent curiosity in the minds of men, who "want to know" something more than the accredited members of the community are willing to disclose, and such will attend these concerts, where certainly they will see and hear things that will astonish them. Nor do we think the performers can be justly charged with unfairness; bating a little pardon-

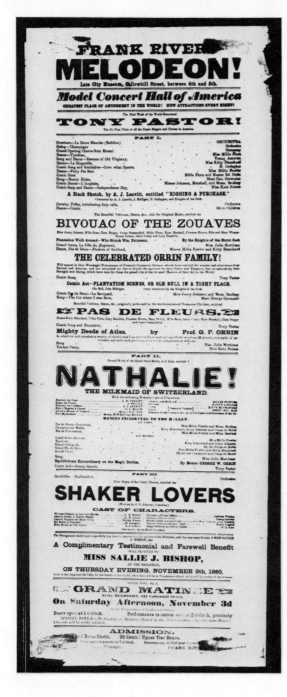

A broadside for Frank Rivers' Melodeon in Philadelphia in the 1860s advertises *The Shaker Lovers*, by S. D. Johnson. It was adapted from the tale of the same name by Daniel Pierce Thompson, published in 1848.

able wit at the expense of the customs and tenets of the sect,—perhaps partly in retaliation for some exercise of discipline—there does not appear on the part of the exhibitors any vindictive or hostile spirit. As to the wonderful power of one of the females to "whirl about," it really passes belief. . . . The advertisements say she turns round 1500 times—if she did not do the thing "to a turn" last night, it was we verily believe because she over did it.   —New York *Commercial Advertiser*, Sept. 1, 1846

July 23rd 1847. We still keep hearing from Tripure & Company [Canterbury, New Hampshire, apostates]. The people in the county do not appear to have any fellowship with their conduct. The Cincinnatians say they hope the Ohio turnoffs will never act in this manner. And moreover there is a piece of rebuke respecting them in nearly all of the newsprints of late about here. . . . I will copy one piece in my daybook out of one of these prints.

SECEEDING SHAKERS

There is a severity in the following communication; but it is so richly that we will not abate one syllable of its terms.

Mr. Editor. I perceive that a number of Seceeding Shakers, male and female, have been engaged by the managers of the Athenaeum to give public exhibitions of the mode of divine worship practiced by the sect to which they belonged. Will such things be countenanced or supported by the community? Will the press suffer to go unrebuked the efforts of a lazy set of men and shameless women to ridicule the religion of a peaceable, orderly, hardworking, & strictly honest community as the Shakers are known to be? Can there be found in Cincinnati an audience who could so far forget themselves as to encourage by their presence a set of sturdy lubberly felons, who for pay will consent to tickle the ears and gratify the sight of the groundlings, with the same sounds and the same actions, which scarcely a year ago they offered to their maker as holiest incense? If we know the tastes of the people, and we think we do, their reception will be such as they richly merit.   —"Prudence Morrell's Account of a Journey to the West in the Year 1847," *Shaker Quarterly*, Summer 1968

THE WICKED DANCE---As viewed by our City Divines.

From *Judge*, June 30, 1883. Courtesy of the New York State Library.

CIVIL WAR

The long roller-coasting history of the Shakers dipped down in the second half of the nineteenth century. The unique religious quickening called Mother Ann's Work had come to an end, although inspiration has always remained a Shaker gift. It was a meaningful internal development, but did little to spread the faith. There were periodic revivals and excitements that brought in members, like the Millerites, who had expected the world to end in the 1840s. But these special events and opportunities for expansion grew rare as the country suffered a Civil War and underwent an industrial revolution. Americans became more materialistic and less religious. Their crises were more economic than emotional. It grew harder and harder to rally converts around the sacred standard of Mother Ann.

The Civil War placed a heavy burden on the Shaker communes in Kentucky, drained their strength, destroyed their markets, and distracted them from their religious goals. They were the victims of their own charity, unable to deny food, supplies, and lodging to the insistent and ruthless soldiers of both the Union and Confederate armies.

Eldress Nancy Moore of South Union, Kentucky, expressed in a wartime diary the anxiety of these border-state Believers. "We have a feeling to record," she began, "some of the important items or incidents, concerning this unnatural war, which has brought, and is now bringing so much destruction, distress and desolation over our once free and happy land."

Aug 15 [1861].   The Rebel Colonel Forest with a company of Cavalry eighty six in number, passed thro' our village from above; they had several small secesh flags flying at their horses ears (we supposed to plainly show who and what they were). They passed on very civilly and encamped at the head of our Mill pond.

We accomodated them with supper and breakfast, also furnished them with plenty of fruit, Apples, Peaches &c.; without charge. . . .

Janry 22nd 1862.   There were ninety wagons belonging to the Secesh army passed thro' our village. . . . About 200 artillery horses with their horsemen stopped here. They drove into the Lot facing the Office, and there struck their tents and built camp fires. This company burned some new fence rails from around the Fowl yard and robbed two Bee hives. . . . Also the same evening Colonel Scott's regiment of Cavalry nearly one thousand strong called and wished to remain with us a day or two. . . . Just as the family was retiring at nine o'clock; an order came from the Officers to the Sisters for six hundred pounds of bread. The Sisters without murmuring set to work to fill the order. The Soldiers occupied the ground from the Office to the West lot, having their camp fires all over the lots.

As we look out of our windows, we see the Western portion of our little village, to all appearance a Barrack for soldiers. The fires blazing, the sparks flying in high winds, their shouting and cheering contrast strongly with the peaceful and quiet appearance which has always characterized this place.

We counted one hundred and fourteen baggage wagons as they passed thro' our village. They were immediately followed by another company of Cavalry; Thinking all the wagons had passed I retired and quit counting. More wagons came on, and kept passing until about midnight. One of the Officers stated to the Brethren, that there were no less than 1200, twelve hundred soldiers camped on our premises that night.

Feb 11 1862.   Two horses were stolen from the East Family last night. About two o'clock, thirty one Cavalry stopped fronting the Center house . . . wished to know if they could get dinner. . . . We carried a table out and placed it under the Cedar Trees in the Office lot, while we were preparing for them, they sat quietly on their horses, & were very civil. When all was ready, the Captain spoke in a low voice, and said, these are religious orderly people, and you must be very quiet and orderly while here. They obeyed. . . .

Feb 13th.   Early in the Morning 36 Rebel Cavalry called at the East family for a drink of milk; they were supplied, and passed on through our village, to the Depot. They soon shewed themselves to be a band of robbers, by pressing all the horses they could lay their hands on. We had previously learned from some of our friendly neighbors if the Army was obliged to leave B [Bowling Green] they would steal all the horses and Negroes they could catch, and especially the free Negroes; with this warning the brethren took most of our horses to the woods & hid them. . . . About four o'clock in the afternoon, seven heavily armed robbers came dashing up into our village from the East. . . . They rushed down the North Lane, and into the horse lot . . . then came to the public street near the center house. . . . Well said they—We wish to get some of your fine riding horses— (Ans) We have none; you have taken most of our best horses some time since. . . .

Rebels. Well, come and go with us and we will give you a receipt for your horses, we wish to get some cloth of you.

Bror. Urban. We have none for sale.

R. We know you have, & we will have it. . . .

They went on to the Office. . . . Eldress Betsy soon had a company of Sisters collected, who got to the Office in time to get possession of the steps and the yard around them, while the brethren decoyed them into the Post Office. They soon became satisfied that, that was not the house to break into.—

The Sisters still occupied the steps, and a considerable space around them; when they found the doors were locked, they said, they cared not for locks, they intended to be into that house, and would see into every room in it. . . . They enquired of the Sisters if we had any cloth for sale, they were told we had none, we had sold it all as fast as we could make it.— But said they, we know you have it, we have been told so by your neighbours. . . . Eldress Betsy said you are more gentlemen than to rob poor helpless women & children of their hard earnings that which they have worked for with their own hands. To which one replied we know your resources, we know you have plenty of money. . . . He took hold of Sister Nancy's shawl with his fingers, & said to her, you bought that did you not? we replied, we did some years ago, but we make most of our clothing. He said you wear silk, and do you not buy that, pointing to her neckerchief—Nay, she replied: we make all our own silk, we raise the worms, spin and weave the silk. . . .

We asked them if they would have some dinner to which they gruffly replied no, we have had dinner. Finally by exercising every means ingenuity could devise, we got them off the steps, and engaged them in conversation till they appeared to be more calm. By this time, the fine warm loaf of bread, a bucket of milk, some pie and stewed peaches, were brought over from the Center. . . . After they had partaken of our hospitality, their feelings were quite softened down. The Sisters gathered around them and gave them some good advice, and after a lengthy conversation & they had done eating, the foreman said I declare you are mighty friendly any how, and mounting his horse said, you must have the cloth ready for us when we return tonight, and we will get it; and *then* we will give you a receipt for your horses.—They dashed off in a hurry. . . .

Most of the Brethren and Sisters were up all night, the brethren watching out of doors, the Sisters in doors. The most intense excitement prevailed through out; for, we had heard that B. Green was fired, and our own place was threatened. . . .

We knelt together in humble prayer to God for his divine assistance to guard and protect us from the ravages of the enemy, by fire, or any other depradation, that this rebellious band of robbers could inflict upon us.... Our daily prayer was and had been, for wisdom to direct and protect us, thro' all these trying scenes, and that we might be ennabled to keep the Gospel in its purity, and stick together unitedly....

On the night of the 13th we carried almost every valuable article out of the Office, such as shirting, prints, Gray & brown cloth, spool thread, blankets &c; and stored them away in different places where we thought they would be most secure from fire....

24th.   All our hand labor is pretty much suspended, and the greater number of us are engaged in service for the army. The Brethren are actively engaged in hauling wood, and attending to the various calls for the soldiers. The Sisters are cooking baking &c; trying to keep the house in some degree of order and decency....

February 1st Sabbath (1863) ... At this time our minds are so much carried off with wars and rumors of war that it seems our spiritual travel is greatly impeded....

Eldress Nancy E. Moore, who kept the Civil War diary (right end, front row) and Elder Harvey L. Eads, a notable Western leader (third brother from the right) in a photograph of the Church Family at South Union, Kentucky, about 1883. Courtesy of Shakertown at South Union.

31st [August 1864].   Wednesday . . . The soldiers left at day light without any demands for breakfast. This afternoon we visited the sisters in the Gathering order.

A little after three oclock this morning, I seemed to hear a voice say distinctly. I've been to see Lincoln, and you may depend he give me a real dressing. It may do some good, for he is a man of God and a Prophet. This spirit seemed in a degree humbled or subdued.

—Mary Julia Neal, *The Journal of Eldress Nancy,* 1963

WAR ORPHANS ADOPTED BY SOUTH UNION

There are many records in Shaker annals of money donated for charity among the "world's people." As early as 1820, Enfield and Canterbury, New Hampshire, sent $500 to Troy, New York, to help relieve the suffering from a great fire. In 1847, when all Ireland was suffering from a serious famine, many of the Shaker societies sent help. Union Village, Ohio, gave one thousand bushels of corn; Pleasant Hill, Kentucky, gave 254 bushels of corn and ten bushels of beans. After the Civil War the South Union Shakers adopted twenty orphans from Tennessee. In 1878 the Pleasant Hill society contributed $50 for the yellow fever sufferers in New Orleans. In addition to these donations to non-Shakers, the different societies were always generous with each other when the need arose, as in the case of fire or property loss from some other cause. Pleasant Hill gave $500 to New Gloucester, Maine, in 1867 to help them meet a deficit that came from careless stewardship. But never were the Shakers known to ask or accept aid from any of the "world's people." They took care of themselves and of their own, and all they asked from the world was tolerance and fair treatment.   —Marguerite Fellows Melcher, *The Shaker Adventure,* 1941

THE SHAKER

For the last thirty years of the nineteenth century, The Shaker *was the voice of Shakerism, its missionary to the world. The monthly journal changed its name three times: in 1873 to* Shaker and Shakeress, *later to* The Shaker Manifesto, *and finally to* The Manifesto. *Although it re-*

THE SHAKER.

"I WILL SHAKE ALL NATIONS, AND THE DESIRE OF ALL NATIONS SHALL COME; AND I WILL FILL THIS HOUSE WITH GLORY, SAITH THE LORD."

Published Monthly, by, and under the direction of the Mt. Lebanon Bishopric.

VOL. I.   SHAKERS, ALBANY, N. Y., JANUARY, 1871.   No. 1.

Salutatory.

To the Public:—Knowing it to be duty, to do all the good we can to our fellow travelers on the journey of life, withholding the knowledge of no good thing—impressed with the conviction, that there lies within our power the possibility of doing more good than heretofore; and being urged continually, by friends of reform, to communicate to the world of mind our ideas of life and happiness as viewed from the Shaker platform, are the reasons for our taking the bold step of appearing before you, as solicitors of your attention to the columns of THE SHAKER.

Claiming no distinction on the grounds of erudition, but, bowing beneath the rebuke of learned criticisms, we mean to tell you from our humble position, where, in our understanding, lies "the pearl of great price,"—Christ, or the kingdom of heaven on earth; thus explaining the peculiar testimony and life of the people, called *Shakers.* The policy of THE SHAKER will be, to treat of a more excellent way of life, than is the ordinary practice of the multitudes. It will be devoted to the cause of religious truths; devoid of speculative theories of a theological nature. It will aim to illustrate life, in accordance with God's pleasure; and in conformity with the operation of that "quickening spirit," that resurrects souls above the plane of earthly selfishness, where the spirit of *mine* is cast out, and the Pentecostal system of community of goods is in full exercise. It will be the aim of THE SHAKER to keep before the public mind the necessary distinction between life on the earthly plane, however proper, and the heavenly, or angelic life, however humble. It will not fail to contend that the celibacy of the Angel plane, is a necessary component of eternal life, and practiced with propriety *on the earth,* by those who love to think of its reality in the heavens; while admitting the propriety of marriage and procreation by those who have not risen sufficiently in love with the Christ life. It will advocate peace; deprecating, and expressing disbelief in the necessity of wars, whether of households or of nations —Christians never did, never can fight.

THE SHAKER will ever meet correspondents, in its various communications upon "Does Christianity admit of private property?" with a negative answer, from the most advanced reasons of a spiritual life. Its freedom from the arena of political parties will conserve the righteous idea of those whose name it bears. It will sketch, biographically, the founders and early communicants of the Society; and illustrate life, as it is enjoyed by the Society at present. The poetical sentiments of society will find an exponent in THE SHAKER; while "Answers to Correspondents" will receive due attention. It will advocate temperance in all things; and urge reformation and resurrection from the earthly, sensual life, to a life, "eternal in the heavens." Friends of reform— lovers of wisdom—servants of God—aid us; bless our efforts to do good. Extend the cause of Christ to the notice of your neighbors; and let us all seek to walk "the way," learn "the truth" and live "the life "—being imitators of the beautiful Jesus — Christ.   •

Who are the Shakers?

Historically and derivatively considered, the Shakers have their rise from the French prophets, a class of Divinely inspired senters from the Catholic and Protestant church of the seventeenth and eighteenth centuries, as the legitimate fruit of the Reformation. They were religious revivalists of a very remarkable character, called fanatics, and are to be prominently numbered among the few witnesses of the true Christ church during the gloomy reign of Antichrist.

In future pages of our paper a more full history of them may be properly given. Their testimony, in substance, was " *The end of the world* " in all followers of Christ; and they were the harbingers to declare *the near approach of the kingdom of God; the establishment of new heavens and a new earth; the kingdom of the Messiah; the marriage of the Lamb; the first resurrection from the dead;* the planting of the New Jerusalem. About 1706, some of these spiritual new lights and prophets went from France to England. About 1747, a small number of these witnesses,

in the neighborhood of Manchester, England, were led, by Divine, spirit influence, to form themselves into a society for mutual support, physically and spiritually, under the ministration of James and Jane Wardly; and the first pioneers of the Shaker Church were distinguished members of this Society, among whom Ann Lee became the acknowledged, divinely inspired leader, and a *spiritual mother,* and the Eldress of this infant Church. The *name* of this Church, "SHAKERS," was given them in derision, by the world, as descriptive of the religious exercises of body by which the members of this Church were affected during the seasons of their devotion to God, as the fruit of that spiritual baptism, under the influence of which they were bearing a testimony of God's truth, which was shaking the foundations of Antichrist's kingdom. So that the title, "SHAKERS," though given in derision and persecution, was appropriate, and as providentially applied as was the title, "KING OF THE JEWS," given to Jesus by the persecuting Jews.

Ann Lee became the acknowledged Eldress of the Shaker Church in the year 1770, while in England, so that it now has survived a century. A more extended history of the Shakers' rise and progress to the present day, may, perhaps, appropriately form the subject of future notices in our periodical.

WHAT ARE THE SHAKERS?

As national citizens, they are observers of the counsel of Paul, and recognize civil magistrates as powers of God, for the government of worldly citizens; hence, *Shakers* are law-observing and law-abiding.

As politicians they are nondescripts, and, in fact, not to be found; they are, truly, non-essentials!

As socialists, or, relative to society arrangements, they are Christian Communists; the property of a Community is common to *all,* and *each,* of the members forming that Community, but not common to all the communities belonging to the household of faith in the same town, county, State, or country, *except* in a moral, charitable and religious sense, in which sense all property dedicated to the Com-

flected self-confidence and union under all four banners, it also solicited inquiries from readers interested in sharing the Shaker faith.

The Shaker, a neat eight page paper, full of excellent sentiments and breathing a progressive spirit gives evidence of an awakening among them, and kindles the hope that this community will ere long change its customs and clothes, and annex itself to modern civilization.

—Utica *Daily Bee*, April 1871

From **The Shaker**

Most radically religious monthly in the world. Organ of the societies of the people called Shakers. Teaches thorough Christianity, unbiased by man-made creeds. Proclaims self-denial to be the efficacious remedy for sin. Declares that Jesus was baptized CHRIST, and thence became the pattern for all who name the name of Christ, to follow. Gives information of Shaker life, habits, economy, success; theology, prophecy, inspirations, revelation and expectations. Deprecates war, either in the nation or in the household. Demands of all Christians, lives devoted to communion of interests. Certifies that celibacy is the order of heaven, and that marriage belongs to the earth only, and is not practiced by Christians. Testifies against all intemperance, lusts of the flesh, and worldly pride. Inculcates true love; separation from worldly customs, politics, etc. Claims God as Father and Mother of all souls—a duality, and therefore teaches the equal rights of their children, regardless of sex, color, race, education, circumstances, or custom. Is a radical exponent of true Spiritualism—Shakers are Spiritualists. Objects to riches; poverty; slavery of either mind or body. Establishes the only true system of dietetics, and is a preserver of health. Guarantees salvation to all who will live as our great exemplar, Jesus, lived. Believes all can be baptized by the same Christ Spirit, and thus become saviours to the lost or fallen, first being saved themselves. Is just the thing for the uneasy infidel, and bigoted sectarian. Loves all, means all shall be saved; teaches the way. Every individual expecting the re-appearance of Christ, should read THE SHAKER, and learn that the SHAKERS believe Christ's life puts an "end to the world."

Price fifty cents per annum; costs, and is worth one dollar. Address G. A. LOMAS, Editor, Shakers, N.Y.

SHAKERS WANTED. 100,000 Shakers wanted, soon as convenient. None need apply, who cannot shake, or learn to shake themselves free from all prejudice, all wrong, all sin.

"Why do Shakers appear to have so little respect for their deceased members? Why do they neglect to furnish them monuments, and bedeck their graves with flowers, shrubbery, etc.?" I answer: . . . Virtues are more enduring than granite. . . . We believe in decently interring the mortality of those who are happily released from the troubles of the earth. A plain slab, with name and age, marks the spot. Mother Ann Lee's grave differs not at all from those of her surrounding children. We advise that the various appropriations now uselessly spent on cemeteries, should be used for the elevation of the downcast, homes for the destitute, and for charitable and religious purposes generally.

—Otis Sawyer, June 1872

Was Jesus a Shaker? . . . We believe in the multiplicity of Christs; are individually aiming to be Christs; and have full faith in the possibility of becoming as good as Jesus was. . . . We call ourselves Christians . . . because we have chosen as our pattern, the principles that made Jesus, the Christ.

The Phrenological Journal for June, contained an article entitled "Have the Shakers Made a Mistake?" and followed this question by an argument seeking to prove that Ann Lee never taught celibacy, but merely chastity in marriage. . . . Is it common for a class of individuals to become more radical than the founder of that class, particularly upon a point so adverse to natural inclination, yet so conjoined to angel nature as an entire abnegation of sexual coition? Ann Lee was the leader of Shaker societies in her day, but is not now. Yet, having improved upon some of the themes and practices of her day, we are only as strong on *this*, as she was. You give her large credit as a sensible woman; too much so, you think, to inaugurate a system so unnatural as existing Shakerism. . . . The Shakers admit the large good in marriage, when properly conducted—but claim that there is no "kingdom of heaven" on earth, in marriage.

THE SHAKER WOMAN'S RIGHTS. There is much written and spoken in these days with regard to "Woman's Rights," though we do not remember to have seen any article treating upon this subject with the qualifying word *Shaker* prefixed to the title. We, therefore, propose to say something about a class of women who have already obtained their rights ... the only women, we believe, whose rights of body, soul and spirit, are truly respected ... the only persons in the civilized world who have equal rights with their brothers in the daily struggles of an earthly career.

NATIONAL SINS.—The constant use of superfine flour bread by the American people, is a prolific source of trouble in the flesh, and also in the bones, of the American nation. ... Give children and youth bone-making material—bran-bread, milk and oat meal, with plenty of good vegetables and abundance of fruit.

Our Society is not a public establishment—a free hotel, or boarding house, for curiosity-seekers. Nor for city people, seeking "an out in the country," at little expense to themselves. It is our home.

EXCERPTS FROM LETTERS.—Please change my P.O. address from ——— to ——; my husband don't like *The Shaker*, while I do, and will have it.

My son is greatly interested in the Shakers. As I cannot let him go to them, it will be a pacification for him to have *The Shaker*.

The greatest thing the Shakers have ever done for the world is the publication of *The Shaker*. (J. M. Peebles)

☞ Any one desirous of circulating a few copies of THE SHAKER, may obtain a select parcel, on application to this office.

DO GOOD

There are many societies established for the improvement and happiness of humanity. We wish in these few words to give a hearty "God bless" to the "Societies for the Prevention of Cruelty to Animals." They are doing a noble work, and are worthy the sympathy and active aid of every humane member of society, capable of feeling sympathy and able to lend a helping hand. Our Bro. R. M. Wagan, Mt. Lebanon, N.Y., has some beautifully printed cards, with border, which aim to aid the good work. The cards contain a poem, beginning with, "The man of kindness to his beast is kind." Send for a dozen, fifty cents.

—*The Shaker*, Nov. 1872

SPECIAL NOTICE

With the beginning of next volume of THE SHAKER the management changes. The present editor retires to the position of Publisher; and the present, able head of the Novitiate Orders of Shakers—Elder F. W. Evans— becomes its Editor, AND TO WHOM ALL SUBSCRIPTIONS SHOULD BE ADDRESSED. This is a consummation long and devoutly wished for. Let the subscriptions be sent to him "fast and numerous."

—*The Shaker*, Dec. 1872

In January 1873, when Elder Frederick W. Evans became editor of the Shaker newspaper, its name was changed to Shaker and Shakeress. *Eldress Antoinette Doolittle was editress.*

1861–1892. This thirty-year period inaugurated by the shock of the Civil War was dominated by the great figure of Elder Frederick W. Evans. It is through him that reporters like Charles Nordhoff and Elie Reclus

Elder Frederick William Evans (1808–1893).

came to know and write about the Shakers. A onetime disciple of Owen, after his conversion to Shakerism he carved himself a prominent niche in the history of the United Society. Along with Joseph Meacham and Richard McNemar, but less than Ann Lee, he remains one of the foremost personalities of the movement. Unlike so many of the society's uncultured or narrow-minded members, Evans had read, traveled, and absorbed vast blocks of modern culture from the eighteenth and nineteenth centuries. He liked to announce his loyalty to Voltaire and Paine. Realizing the element of myth and nonsense in the notion of a sudden worldwide conversion to Shakerism, he tried to resolve their problem by a reflective conversion of Shakerism to the world. He was the Shaker humanist. He talked firmly and loudly, and his voice carried far.

> —Henri Desroche, *The American Shakers*, 1955, ed. and trans. by John K. Savacool, 1971

More from The Shaker *and* Shaker and Shakeress

Elder H. L. E. writes: I sought to have a neighbor subscribe. He replied: "Do you think I am fool enough to create a disturbance in my family by subscribing for *The Shaker?*"

If there were not so much cross and self-denial I should almost be persuaded to become a Shaker!

"Do the Shakers want accessions?" However this may be, we do not, nor ever will want accessions badly enough to recede from any principles in life, maintained by our great exemplar—Christ. Should we admit any, who would not confess and depart their sins—then there would be a humiliating spectacle—the Shakers joining the world.

PUBLICATIONS

Christ's First and Second Appearing	$1.25
Dunlavy's Manifesto	1.25
Millennial Church	1.00

Tracts free, where postage is paid.

Who feels interested in the approaching centennial anniversary of Shakerism in America? How shall the 6th of August 1874 be celebrated?

WOMAN'S SPHERE— ... Must all educated, intelligent women perform household service, to be crowned with the plaudit: "She has labored in her sphere?" . . . Woman is a slave . . . cradled in folly, dandled on the knee of fashion, taught to esteem personal charms above moral excellence. . . . Woman's sphere, as well as man's, should be working in humanity's cause, each bearing part in public service.

SOCIETY RECORD

MT. LEBANON.—The South Family have been improving the appearance of the village by clapboarding their laundry building. . . . Second Family have slated the roof of the office-barn. The Church Family have put on 150 squares of slate this season. We do *not* like the black paint on their beautiful new fence. . . . Canaan Families are looking beautifully; paint, with hard labor, have made a wonderful transformation!

WATERVLIET.—Company of visitors started for Mt. L. on the 8th. South Family have repainted several buildings, and improved dooryard considerably. This Society donated $800 to Groveland—a brotherly offering.

A stereograph view of the Shaker village at Watervliet, New York (formerly Niskayuna) by James Irving, about 1875. Courtesy of the New York State Museum.

GROVELAND.—The ground, blackened by the late fire, is already improved by better buildings than those burned. No one wishes Groveland a streak of good luck, more than *The Shaker.*

ENFIELD, CONN.—Church Family have built a new barn, 50 × 60, and are improving their grass considerably. "Our Second Family are building a large Sisters' Shop and wash-house. Good health here."

SHAKER COMMUNITIES. *Are they Charitable Institutions for the Body, or for the Soul?*

So long as Shakers were known to the religious world as a band of superstitious fanatics, who condemned marriage *per se,* and danced on the Sabbath, it treated them with ridicule as law-breakers, or with silent contempt.

When influential and highly educated men and women . . . and not a small company of priests . . . founded societies in different States, they ascended above contempt and a great persecution arose. At first, this took the form of personal abuse, and often destruction of property. . . . Impossible crimes were laid to the charge of Ann Lee, and the leadership generally. All manner of evil was said, and often sworn to as truth, until the powers of the Judiciary were evoked to prove these imaginary crimes. . . . Lawsuits were instituted to prevent the holding of property "in common," and thus break up these society-deranging establishments.

In process of time these Shakers having become reputedly rich, are considered also to have become respectable, and are voted a place among the Christian sects. . . . A new danger besets them; that of popularity, and the "friendship of the world."

Living necessarily in large houses, to accommodate large numbers, the wondering public, not considering how many families reside and have their *homes* in one of these great unitary dwellings which to them look so grand and so much like some individual rich man's mansion, speak to one another: "Are not these Shakers always neat and clean? Is there not even the glow of contentment upon their countenance, indicative of well-supplied physical wants, and comfortable social conditions? Do they ever run in debt? or do any of their members ever end their days in a poor-house? Certainly they must be rich. . . ."

"And now that we, the discriminating public, have ridiculed, contemned, calumniated, lawsuited—*persecuted*—these Shakers into an American institution—and now that they have become an object of general curiosity to the political economist, the socialist, the cooperative people; to the moralist, with his 'social evil' problems; to the advocates of Woman's Rights, who desire a mixed government of male and female elements, and that taxation and representation should be united; to physiologists . . . to Spiritualists and theologians generally, and to religionists in particular, who behold with awe and reverence the re-incarnation of the Christ Spirit—a veritable Primitive Church—furnishing to the European tourists much of the staple of their books of travel in the United States of America;—the momentous question arises, what are these Shakers for? and to what *use* can *we* put their successful industrial establishments?"

And the answer comes back spontaneously from all people who "have the poor always with them,"—turn them into eleemosynary institutions!! they will, as such, exactly meet the wants of the age in which we live. The aged and the infirm; the merchant who has failed in business, and lost hope in the struggle for pre-eminence; the lone widow, the orphan children, and poor relatives, generally, who are a burden to their friends; how convenient it will be to have them taken into these charitable public institutions where they will receive more than parental and filial care from the religious, the good, the Christian people called Shakers. . . .

This is not, as many suppose, an eleemosynary institution for the relief of physical, human suffering. . . . This is strictly a *religious* order; a home for the souls of seekers after righteousness, those who are not and cannot be satisfied with the righteousness of worldly Christians, who "marry and give in marriage," hold private property, and "fight" about it and their *husbands* and *wives*.

We seek the best physiologically the world can produce—those who are compelled by the wants of their souls to come, with the intent and hope of making them better. We can take a limited number of children of good parentage.   —(Frederick W. Evans)

CHARLES NORDHOFF has been engaged in collecting the materials for a detailed account of the Communistic Societies now existing in the United States. He has been visiting and personally examining all of these societies—no slight undertaking. . . . The subject is novel and attractive, and the facts collected by him will be so presented as to be not only of interest to the reader for amusement, but of value to the student of social science, for their practical bearing and illustration of the possibilities and difficulties of a community of goods, a subject which is now widely agitated among some workingmen here and in Europe.

—*The Shaker*, July 1874

Nordhoff, a journalist who wrote for the New York Herald, *devoted nearly a quarter of his book to the Shakers.*

The Shakers have the oldest existing communistic societies on this continent. They are also the most thoroughly organized, and in some respects the most successful and flourishing.

Mount Lebanon, the parent society, and still the thriftiest, was established in 1792, eighty-two years ago.

The Shakers have eighteen societies, scattered over seven states; but each of these societies contains several families: and as each "family" is practically, and for all pecuniary and property ends, a distinct commune, there are in fact fifty-eight Shaker communities, which I have found to be in a more or less prosperous condition. These fifty-eight families contain an aggregate population of 2415 souls, and own real estate amounting to one hundred thousand acres, of which nearly fifty thousand are in their own home. . . .

The Shakers are a celibate order, composed of men and women living together in what they call "families," and having agriculture as the base of their industry, though most of them united with this one or more other avocations. They have a uniform style of dress; call each other by their first names; say yea and nay, but not thee and thou; and their social habits have led them to a generally similar style of house architecture, whose peculiarity is that it seeks only the useful, and cares nothing for grace or beauty, and carefully avoids ornament. . . .

They assert that the second appearance of Christ upon earth has been; and that they are the only true Church, "in which revelation, spiritualism, celibacy, oral confession, community, non-resistance, peace, the gift of healing, miracles, physical health, and separation from the world are the foundations of the new heavens."

In practical life they are industrious, peaceful, honest, highly ingenious, patient of toil, and extraordinarily cleanly.

—Charles Nordhoff, *The Communistic Societies of the United States,* 1875

APRIL.

THE

MANIFESTO.

PUBLISHED BY THE UNITED SOCIETIES.

HARVARD MASS.

"Blessed are those that hear the word of God and keep it."

SHAKER VILLAGE, N. H.

1884.

The Manifesto spoke for the Shakers from 1883 to the end of the nineteenth century.

We met Charles Nordhoff in the lobby at seven o'clock. I confess that at first I was somewhat intimidated by this stern Prussian-born man of forty whose profession it is to write about Washington politics for the *Herald*. . . . Nordhoff is a thick-set man with . . . a "nautical swagger"; at least, he walks with a peculiar lurching gait, memorial to his many years at sea. . . . Nordhoff worked for Bryant at the *Post* until he was sacked because—everyone but Bryant says—of his attacks on the Tweed Ring. . . . Last year Nordhoff found time to write a most interesting book which I have read called *Communistic Societies of the United States*. This subject proved our bond.   —Gore Vidal, *1876* (a novel), 1976

MOUNT LEBANON, N.Y., 5th August.—Frederick W. Evans, Elder in the Order of Shakers, and his companion, Dr. J. M. Peebles, have returned from their missionary tour in Great Britain, which was undertaken some months ago with a view to establishing there the doctrines of the Order. They speak with hearty satisfaction of their experience abroad. Their reception was most cordial, and they believe that their work will result in a great revival of interest in Shaker doctrine and practice in England and Scotland.   —New York *Tribune*, Aug. 8, 1887

I am not a Shaker, believing there is a better way, and am quite ready to see the Shakers' faults . . . but for all that I will speak of the good I find. It has taken a century to live down the lies that have been told about them, and a good omen for Socialism is that they are likely to have fairer play the next hundred years. Howells' article in the June 1876 *Atlantic* gives them a good send-off. It by no means tells the entire truth; but it does proclaim to a vast audience that this people, once so despised, persecuted and belied, are worthy examples in many respects to the whole Christian world.   —William Alfred Hinds, *American Communities*, 1878. (Hinds was a member of the Oneida Community.)

WILLIAM DEAN HOWELLS: CHRONICLE OF A DECLINE

A SHAKER VILLAGE

It was our fortune to spend six weeks of last summer in the neighborhood of a community of the people called Shakers—who are chiefly known to the world-outside by their apple-sauce, by their garden seeds so

SHAKER APPLE SAUCE

Address **D. C. BRAINARD**, MT. LEBANON, COL., CO., N.Y. ·····• PACKED AT •·····

punctual in coming up when planted, by their brooms so well made that they sweep clean long after the ordinary new broom of proverb has retired upon its reputation, by the quaintness of their dress, and by the fame of their religious dances. It is well to have one's name such a synonym for honesty that anything called by it may be bought and sold with perfect confidence, and it is surely no harm to be noted for dressing out of the present fashion, or for dancing before the Lord. But when our summer had come to an end, and we had learned to know the Shakers for so many other qualities, we grew almost to resent their superficial renown among men. We saw in them a sect simple, sincere, and fervently persuaded of the truth of their doctrine, striving for the realization of a heavenly ideal upon earth. . . .

Mainly, their faith is their life; a life of charity, of labor, of celibacy, which they call the angelic life. . . .

The editor of the Atlantic, *however, saw the quiet country homes of these angels mostly as refuges for the poor, the bruised, the hopeless.*

As I recall their plain, quaint village at Shirley, a sense of its exceeding peace fills me; I see its long, straight street, with the severely simple edifices on either hand; the gardens up-hill on one side and down-hill on the other; its fragrant orchards and its levels of clovery meadow-land stretching away to buckwheat fields . . . and it seems to me that one whom the world could flatter no more, one broken in hope, or health, or fortune, could not do better than come hither and meekly ask to be taken into that quiet fold, and kept forever from his sorrows and himself. . . .

I could not encourage Elder Fraser to indulge great hopes, when one day in a burst of zeal for Shakerism he said, "We want cultivated people—half the subscribers to the *Atlantic Monthly*—to come and fill up our vacant ranks. . . ." These were not the people, I said, among whom to make converts; the disappointed, the poor, the destitute, were the field from which to reap. . . .

The proportion of those reared in Shakerism whom the Shakers expect to keep is small; they count quite as much for their increase upon accessions of mature men and women from outside, whom the Shaker life and doctrine persuade. These they invite now, as always, very cordially to join them, and they look forward to a time when their dwindling communities shall be restored to more than their old numbers.

One bad effect of the present decrease, which all thoughtful Shakers deplore, is the employment of hired labor. This, as communists, they feel to be wrong; but they are loath either to alienate their land or to let it lie idle.

There are several reasons for the present decrease, besides that decrease of the whole rural population. . . . The impulse of the age is towards a scientific, a sensuous, an aesthetic life. Men no longer remain on the lonely farms, or in the little towns where they were born, brooking upon the ways of God to man; if they think of God, it is too often to despair of knowing him; while the age calls upon them to learn this, that, and the other, to get gain and live at ease, to buy pianos and pictures, and take books out of the circulating library. . . .

The Shakers used to spin and weave all the stuff they wore, but to do this now would be a waste of time; they buy the alpaca and linen which both sexes wear in summer, and their substantial woolens for the winter.

There are no longer carpenters, blacksmiths, and shoemakers among the Shakers at Shirley, because their work can be more cheaply peformed by the world-outside, and the shops once devoted to these trades now stand empty.

I should be sorry to give the notion of a gloomy asceticism in the Shaker life. I saw nothing of this, though I saw self-restraint, discipline, quiet, and heard sober, considered, conscientious speech. They had their jesting, also; and those brothers and sisters who were of a humorous mind seemed all the better liked for their gift of laughing and making laugh.

The sum of Shaker asceticism is this: they neither marry nor give in marriage; but this is a good deal.

—*Atlantic Monthly,* June 1876

"What do you think," Boynton asked . . . "of our Shaker friends? Does their life strike you as the solution of the great difficulty?"

"No," said Ford; "it strikes me as begging the question."

"Yes, so it is," assented Boynton; "so it is, in some views. It is a life for women rather than men."

An indefinable pang seized Ford. "I don't quite understand you. Do you think it is a happy life for a woman?"

"There is *no* happy life for a woman—except as she is happy in suffering for those she loves, and in sacrificing herself to their pleasure, their pride and ambition. The advantage that the world offers her—and it does not always offer that—is her choice in self-sacrifice; the Shakers prescribe it for her." . . .

"Don't you think the possible power of choice is a great advantage? I don't know that as a man I expect to be happy; but I like to make my ventures in unhappiness. It saves me from the folly of accusing fate. If I surrendered myself to Shakerism, I should feel myself a prisoner; I should not run the risk of wounds, but I should have no chance of escape."

"A woman doesn't like to fight," replied Boynton. "Besides, there are no irrevocable vows in Shakerism. When you do not like it you leave it. It is no bad fate for a woman. For most women it would be a beneficent fate."

An image of Egeria in the Shaker garb, with her soft young throat hidden to the chin, and the tight gauze cap imprisoning her beautiful hair, rose in the young man's thought, and would not pass at his willing. It was with something like the relief of waking from an odious dream that he saw the girl enter the room in her usual dress.

—William Dean Howells, *The Undiscovered Country,* 1896

In The Undiscovered Country, *Howells explores nineteenth-century American spiritualism, with its cheap and commercial aspects as well as its pure adherents, including the Shakers. A notable Maine Shaker, Eldress Aurelia Mace, commented on the novel.*

We have been brought before the public in *The Undiscovered Country* by W. D. Howells. To my understanding he leaves the country undiscovered, or the world in doubt of its existence. The work shows that the Shakers felt sure of a future life of happiness, but also a chance that they were mistaken. Of the child that had died, the outside man said: "If it knows anything." But the Shaker said: "We are sure that it knows." Friend Howells is very fair and correct in what he says about the angel life; but hardly gives credit to our people for the intelligence which belongs to them. In our ranks are found men with a collegiate education, and women learned and cultured.

—Aurelia G. Mace, *The Aletheia,* 1899

TOLSTOY FINDS THE SHAKERS

In the final decade of the nineteenth century Shaker principles still had the power to affect the work of a great writer and Christian reformer. In 1889 in Russia Count Leo Tolstoy received some books and tracts from Shaker leaders. He wrote excitedly in his diary.

"I read the Shakers. Excellent. Complete sexual restraint. How strange it is that just now, when I'm concerned with these questions, I should receive this." —Ernest Joseph Simmons, *Leo Tolstoy,* 1946

Tolstoy began to correspond with Elders Frederick William Evans and Alonzo G. Hollister of the North and Church Families at Mount Lebanon, New York.

Anapura, Oct. 19, 1889

Last year I began a new work about marriage and thinking more and more on the topic I came nearly to the same conclusions as the Shakers. My idea to put it shortly is this: The ideal of a Christian must be complete chastity, marriage is the state of men and women who striving to attain that ideal could not reach it and if the ideal is chastity the marriage will be moral. But in our society the ideal of men and women is marriage, and therefore our marriage is unmoral. You can think how welcome to me were your books and tracts. I agree with you in all your views of sexual relation... and got much profit in perusing your speeches and sermons.

The work was the controversial The Kreutzer Sonata, *published in 1889. In one version of the story Tolstoy mentioned the Shakers' example in his hero's argument for celibacy. But the reference was deleted in the final manuscript.*

Toula. Yasnaya Poliana.
Febr. 3/15. 1891.

Dear Friend and Brother,
I received your long
letter, and have read it
with interest; but I
must confess that all
your argument taken
from John 's revelation
do not convince me. I
do not consider that book
as a moral guide. I think
that God 's revelation
must be simple and able
to be understood by the
simpest soul. In general
as I told you before,
dear Friend, I agree com-
pletely with your prac-

A letter "in brotherly love" from Tolstoy. From the collection of the Western Reserve Historical Society.

Anapura, Mar. 5, 1890

I thank you heartily for your letter; I expected it. I knew that my ideas about marriage would be approved by your community. Your books and tracts, especially "What would become of the world if all were Shakers" corroborated my views and helped me very much to a clear understanding of the question. I am very much astonished how a Christian can not approve of your and my view of marriage. I admire very much your explanation of the comparison of the Kingdom of Heaven to a net, and the conclusion that the fishes taken in the net can/will not depopulate the sea, and that if they do it will be after the will of God. . . .

But pardon me in brotherly love and spirit, I must tell you the truth: it was very painful for me to read in your letter the account of the influx of spirits from heaven and so on. It is painful for me because not only your faith (excepting Anna Lee and the manifestation of spirits) and your practice of life, as far as I know it is a true Christian faith, corroborated by your way of life—and it should have attracted to you all the people who crave for a true Christian life, but your peculiarities—manifestations, of spirits—repel them.

Tolstoy disagreed with the Shakers' expectation of new truths and revelation.

God's truth has been known always in the old times, the same as now. The true progress, the establishing of the kingdom of God on earth consist not in producing new truths, but in sifting the truths that are known to us, by putting aside the lies and superstition with which they are intermingled.—You have put aside a great quantity of lies and superstitions of the external world, but I am afraid you have accepted new ones.—Put them aside. Analyze them. Don't keep to beliefs only because they have been beliefs a long time and are old. Put them away and your Shaker faith with your chaste and spiritual life, with your humility, charity, with your principle of moderation and manual work will conquer the world. Please pardon me if I have offended you. I have written this only because I think and feel it and because I love God, I try to love Him, and through Him to love you my brethren.

All that you say about the time fast approaching in which the Divine light will be spread over all the world and darkness dispelled is quite true. I feel it, and therefore write thus to you.

—Yours in brotherly love,
LEO TOLSTOY

Elder Alonzo Hollister responded (Nov. 22, 1889):

The revelation of Ann Lee may not come to you in this world, but I think you will not be long in receiving it, & perceiving its beauty and power, after you escape from this mortal shell . . . the parting with which, is as truly a birth, as our coming into it, and a great advance for those who have made a proper use of their opportunities here. That Ann Lee had a revelation of exalted quality & power, I think is proved by the existence of Shakers 100 years after her translation, and by their manner of life, so contrary to the pride & selfishness of human nature.

Tolstoy later inquired:

Toula. Yasnaya Poliana
Feb. 15, 1891

You are, as I know, nonresistants. How do you manage to keep communial but nevertheless—property? Do you acknowledge the possibility for a christian to defend property from usurpators? I ask this question because I think that the principle of non-resistance is the chief unit of true

Christianity and the greatest difficulty in our times is to be true to it. How do you manage to do so in your community?

Elder Frederick answered (Mar. 6, 1891):

We, the Shakers, hold and defend our communal property under the civil laws of "the new earth"; but in no case, or under any circumstances, should we injure a fellow being. You see that our civil government is the voice of the people, *"vox populi vox Dei,"* and the people, who are the rulers are more progressed than are the rulers of Russia, or of any Church-and-State government on the face of the earth. Consequently, we, the Shakers, can under the American secular government, carry out the abstract principles taught by the Christ-Spirit's revelation, more perfectly than has, hitherto, ever been done by mortal men and women. Just as we do carry out sexual purity, notwithstanding that the sexes are brought face to face, in every day life, yet living without bolts or bars, in the same household of faith.

Dear friend, come and see what God hath wrought. Come to Lebanon, and find your joining to the Church of Christ's Second Appearing. Then, return, and found the order in Russia, with consent of the Government, which the Shaker Order can and will obtain for you.

Calvin Green, one of our prophets, many years ago, predicted a glorious spiritual work in Russia. A Russian minister visited Lebanon and was very friendly: he invited the order to Russia. Has not the time arrived; and art not "thou the man?"

When you can see seventeen communities of people whose every right is secured to them, whose every rational want is supplied, does it not demonstrate that all mankind may be made happy in this world?

Our sisterhood are redeemed. The Rights of woman are theirs, the rights of property we enjoy. Capital and Labor are at peace. Hygience is religion with us.

On December 6, 1890, three years before he died, Evans told Tolstoy:

A poor, illiterate, uneducated factory woman has confounded the wisdom of all *men*—reformers, legislators, & scholars, who have come to nothing, as promoters of human happiness. Their systems have ended, in Christendom, as you now see it.... The end has come! & Tolstoy & Shakerism remain, as the last hope of mankind.

Of the future of Shakerism and the question as to whether they will exist as a body to pass the two hundredth mile-stone of their years, is a matter for speculation. Great and stirring events are crowding fast upon us as a nation. What will be our fate when the year 1976 shall have been reached is hard for us to foretell. . . .

—Charles Edson Robinson, *A Concise History of the United Society of Believers Called Shakers*, 1893

PART

III

IN THE
TWENTIETH
CENTURY

•

To the End of the World

We will all go home with you
Home to worlds of glory
Where an eternal interview
Awaits the pure and holy
Bless this soul-connecting bond
Which the cross ensureth
We may never meet in time
But our love endureth

—Song of farewell,
Canterbury, 1862

To the End of the World

THE SHAKERS

The conviction that our work is dear to God, and cannot be spared, defends and sustains us.

—"Solid Extracts of Truth," nineteenth-century broadside

THE WORLD'S PEOPLE

Brook Farm, and Fruitlands . . . and all the centres where the spirit moved were silent; all had gone except the Shakers, and they, in peaceful quietude, retreated more and more from the world's inspection, leading still their busy and industrious lives, but now devoid of exaltation.

—Clara Endicott Sears, *Gleanings from Old Shaker Journals*, 1916

THE SHAKERS

A new age of spirituality is at hand, and the conditions now existing in embryonic form in the old-time Shaker communities will develop in a manner perhaps as startling to the Shakers as to the world . . . Conditions suited to the needs of the age will develop . . . The Shaker faith and the Shaker life will from their elastic nature, be ready to receive the impress of newly revealed truth and expand in new forms.

—Anna White and Leila S. Taylor, *Shakerism*, 1904

THE WORLD'S PEOPLE

Though it may be many years yet before the last Believer leaves the last surviving community, the contributions of "the children of the free woman" to the religious folk art of America long ago came to a close.

—Edward Deming Andrews, *The Gift to Be Simple*, 1940

THE SHAKERS

I don't want to be remembered as a piece of furniture! (I guess I will be remembered for that statement.)

> —Sister Mildred Barker, Sabbathday Lake, Maine, 1974

THE WORLD'S PEOPLE

Renewed public interest tracks down every fragment of information about outward Shaker accomplishments—pioneer dairy methods, seed culture, herb gardening, broom making, to say nothing of the remarkable inventions and much-admired furniture—but the seekers most rewarded are those who search into the secrets of the inner life which inspired such outward gifts.

> —Wallace Winchell, "The Poetry of the Shakers," *Religion in Life*, Winter 1970

THE SHAKERS

Zion is the working hands of God in the world.

> —Elder Giles B. Avery

THE WORLD'S PEOPLE

Theirs was a spirit of which we can take some heed. *The simple spirit*—the concept conjures an aura of religious serenity and utilitarian design, an attitude of a believing people needing a disciplined pace and tranquil refuge to exercise their thrift and faith.

> —Samuel W. and James C. Thomas, *The Simple Spirit: A Pictorial Study of the Shaker Community at Pleasant Hill, Kentucky*, 1973

THE SHAKERS

Our mission now seems to be to present knowledge of our faith to many young seekers. Having been given much may we in turn help others to choose wisely as we show by example the beauty of true Shaker living.

> —Sister Bertha Lindsay, Correspondent, "Home Notes from Canterbury, New Hampshire," *Shaker Quarterly*, Summer 1967

THE WORLD'S PEOPLE

Once we explore Shakerism, even superficially, we discover that it is far more than a historical phenomenon or religious oddity. It is a force within Christian history which, even in its present-day ebbing, brings to us some unique and indelible lessons. Traditional values of community, celibacy, equality and peace take on added power and dimension in the context of a people who somehow translated them into daily reality. Shakers offer new appreciation of simplicity, order, work, worship, ministry and witness.   —Pam Robbins and Robley Whitson, "Gift from the Shakers," *Sign*, Nov. 1979

THE SHAKERS

The problem is—we're not history yet.
                        —Sister Frances Carr, Sabbathday Lake, Maine, 1975

STORYBOOK SHAKERS

Illustration by N. C. Wyeth from *Susanna and Sue* by Kate Douglas Wiggin, 1909.

"More love, Elder Gray!" called Issachar, on his way to the toolhouse.
"More love, Brother Issachar!"
"More love! Brother Ansel!"
"More love! Brother Calvin!"

"More love!" "More love!" "More love!"
So the quaint not uncommon Shaker greeting passed from Brother to
Brother; and as Tabitha and Rosetta met on their way to dairy and laundry and seed-house, they, too, hearing the salutation, took up the refrain,
and Susanna and Sue heard again from the women's voices that beautiful
morning wish, "More love!" "More love!" "More love!" speeding from
heart to heart and from lip to lip.

        —Kate Douglas Wiggin, *Susanna and Sue*, 1909

I suddenly felt like writing a tale of life among the Shakers. As a child
I had been taken to attend the religious services and visit the brethren and
sisters in Alfred, Maine; and I had seldom let a year go without renewing
my acquaintance with those still living in the settlement. The number has
sadly dwindled now, masculine converts being especially few and far between. What wonder when "open confession," "celibacy," and "holding
of goods in common" are the foundation-stones of the Shaker creed as laid
down by Mother Ann Lee, founder and patron saint of the sect?

When the book was nearly finished, I wrote to Elder Green and Sister Lucinda . . . outlining my story, and asking if I might come over and
stay a few days in the Women's Community House.

A glad welcome came by return post, and . . . with my manuscript on
the seat beside me, I drove along the sixteen miles of country road between "Quillcote" and the Shaker Village.

The background of *Susanna and Sue* stands out more vividly than
that of most of my books, because it is a thing apart, so unique, so hidden
away, and of such heavenly tranquillity. Busy, indeed, and thrifty are the
Shaker brethren in the fields, with their tilling or sowing or harvesting or
gathering the hay into the great barns. No less busy are the sisters at their
household tasks, their bottling and preserving and pickling, their wonderful basket-weaving and fancy-work, their gathering and putting-up of
garden seeds for the market, and other labors well known throughout
New England as good, honest, sound and profitable.

She imagined herself as Susanna.

I ate my plain meals in a little dining-room that shone with cleanliness; then hurried back to my equally spotless bedroom, with its white
floor, its iron bedstead, its lavender-scented cotton sheets, its straight-
backed, rush-bottomed chairs, and pine tables. It was a beautiful place in
which to write, and a more beautiful place in which to be still, and think,

surrounded as one was by such unworldly examples of cheerful self-denial, temperance, and devotion to an ideal that required all these qualities in a true Believer. After supper I used to play the cabinet organ and sing Shaker hymns with Elder Green and some of the sisters. I really forgot my own personality and always imagined myself as "Susanna" during my entire visit. On two mornings I read to the children of the Community, many of them orphans, or motherless; some of them waifs and strays cared for and taught with the ardent hope that they might upbuild the Shaker faith. I had told the sisters and Elder Green the plan of my story, but it was with some embarrassment that I read it aloud for their criticism, although I had such respect for the unassuming virtues of their lives that I knew I had treated their creed with deference and understanding. As for the two young lovers in my book, who tried hard to believe in celibacy, but failed, and ran away from the Settlement to be married and live what the Shakers call "life on the plane of Adam"—that tragedy they knew, as well as I, had been of not infrequent occurrence in the otherwise tranquil procession of the years.

[There was a startled moment of recognition, a tremulous approach, almost an embrace, of regard; each sent an electric current across the protective separating space, the two pairs of eyes met and said, "I love you," in such clear tones that Nathan and Hetty marveled that the Elder did not hear them. (—*Susanna and Sue*)]

The Shakers have an affection for *Susanna and Sue*, their "own book," as they call it—written as it was by a dear, though religiously misguided friend and a copy of it lies on the cabinet organ in the sitting-room, just under a photograph of the author.

—Kate Douglas Wiggin, *My Garden of Memory*, 1933

Peacemakers

The Shakers still had a storybook quality at the beginning of the twentieth century. But they were no longer picture perfect. They had not lived for decades in the utter simplicity time has chosen to cast them in forever. Much of the world's clutter had crept into their rooms, and many causes beyond their own attracted their interest.

"Our chief aim has been purity," Eldress Anna White told the Universal Peace Meeting at Mystic, Connecticut, in 1899, "and yet in God's great family how various and how varied is the work to which our hearts

and hands must turn. There are no longer cowardly places in which we may hide complacently to contemplate by our farthing candles our farthing virtues: nay, we realize profoundly our duty to be zealous in all that makes for righteousness."

Thus Shaker leaders worked for the rights of women, the rights of labor, the protection of animals, temperance, peace. On August 31, 1905, they gathered delegates from the world into the meetinghouse at Mount Lebanon, New York, for a peace convention. A Shaker elder presided over orderly meetings, and the addresses were interspersed with Shaker singing. Resolutions called for reduced armaments, an international police force, international arbitration, a strengthened world court, and the neutrality of "the great waterways of commerce."

Resolved, That in disarmament, and the consequent reduction of taxes which now falls so heavily on the producing classes, would be found a remedy for many of the industrial disturbances which are menacing our whole social system.

Eldress Anna and Sister Sarah Burger later carried the peace resolutions to Washington in a blizzard. The two women were received warmly by President Theodore Roosevelt, who welcomed the spirit of the resolutions but regretted their impracticality "under existing circumstances among nations." The resolutions were introduced in Congress.

Who in this country's past first spoke out for conscientious objection to all war and for refusal, under any terms, "to support the cause of war and bloodshed"? The Shakers, a little-known sect . . . now reduced to a remnant of old people, even remembered incompletely. A recent article . . . summed up the Shakers as "a celibate, communistic, separatistic, millennialistic sect," and then reviewed their great contribution to the "vernacular" crafts of America, their domestic and architectural innovations, without once mentioning what is, to my mind, their most notable contribution to the life of this nation, their early, impregnable pacifism. . . .

Under the leadership of a tough-minded woman named Ann Lee . . . they refused to join the colonial cause despite their sympathy for it. For this they were imprisoned.

Eighty years later, while maintaining their theoretical abolitionism, the Shakers would not fight for the Union in support of their views, and so became the first group in this country to be granted the official status of conscientious objectors. . . .

Almost unnoticed in the histories of pacifistic documents is the Shakers' pamphlet published in Albany, N.Y., in 1815 . . . a *Declaration of the Society of People, Shewing Their Reasons for Refusing to Aid or Abet the Cause of War and Bloodshed, by Bearing Arms, Paying Fines, Hiring Substitutes or Rendering Any Equivalent for Military Services.*

> —Doris Grumbach, "American Peaceniks, 150 Years Ago," *Commonweal*, Nov. 13, 1970

Gather the Saints Together

But for all its bold intervention in universal concerns, the ministry at Mount Lebanon spoke for little more than a thousand Shakers. And the number declined as the century progressed. Urbanized, industrialized America produced few believers to whom a rural religious way of life appealed. Eighty percent of the orphans and other children raised among Believers went off with their Christian virtues to the cities, or else succumbed to "the flesh."

You must take care of the rising generation: for if they are protected, the time will come when they will be the flower of the people of God.

> —Father James Whittaker, 1787

Shaker boys with their caretaker at Watervliet, New York, ca. 1875. Stereograph view, courtesy of the New York State Museum.

The Essenians for several ages subsisted by adoption: we shall see if the Shakers continue so long.

—Samuel Taylor Coleridge, *Letters, Conversations, and Recollections of S. T. Coleridge*, 1836

Eldress Anna White and Eldress Leila S. Taylor, who proposed many of the peace resolutions, inherited the optimism and oratory of Elder Frederick Evans.

Is Shakerism dying? Nay! not unless God and Christ and eternal verities are dying.

In a brave impassioned book they tried to "gather the saints together."

Fifteen societies, separate, each from each, families within each society forming still smaller integrate particles, can no longer hold their own in domestic, business and spiritual efficiency. For the future of this noble inheritance . . . we should unite our forces.

Has not the day arrived when that grand, divinely ordained theocracy, which united the spiritual man of earth to the heavens and to God, may, without endangering the structure, readjust its temporal relations? When the method of theocratic control in all the details of life . . . may give place to the broader freedom that belongs to men and women who have attained intellectual maturity? . . . The man and woman of today . . . cannot be bound and shackled in swaddling clothes. . . .

Give to . . . the faithful, covenant-keeping members, a voice in all the affairs of financial and temporal import. Grant them the intellectual freedom their development requires. Fit Shakerism to humanity today, as the Fathers and Mothers of the past fitted it to their age and time. . . .

Let Shakers keep their birthright of leadership, in the van of human progress. Let Truth and Steadfastness, those two bright "angels by the mast," guide the Gospel Ship safely to the port of opportunity and world-wide service. Let Shakers . . . go forth to seek the quickened spirits in the outer realm. . . . Through consolidation and consecration alone can . . . Shakerism restore the depleted ranks.

—White and Taylor, *Shakerism*, 1904

Gospel kindred, how I love you, tongue or pen cannot portray
The deep feelings of affection growing stronger day by day

Eldress Anna White (1831–1910).

Bind these sacred ties together, sealed with friendship ever true
Show to all that Christ the Savior is creating things anew

> —Anna White, song for a slow march, Mount Lebanon, 1865

If the same persistency had been continued by the later Shakers as was manifested by the original leaders, this sect would not have been on the wane as so clearly demonstrated at this time. . . . At this day it is wholly wanting in missionary enterprise. At Union Village there are but two men under fifty years of age. The Society has all the appearance of being doomed to extinction when the present members pass away. Still, we do not know. No man knoweth what another hour may bring forth.

> —J. P. MacLean, *Shakers of Ohio*, 1907

Important changes have . . . taken place in the internal character of Shakerism; its leaders are more liberal and tolerant than they were a half century ago; more ready to see good in other systems, and less prompt to condemn what does not accord with their own. It is also obvious that there is a growing party of progressives among the Shakers—men and women who, while firmly adhering to all the essentials of Shakerism, demand that non-essentials shall not stand in the way of genuine progress and culture. One of their Elders (G. Albert Lomas) wrote to the author some years ago: "The stringency of our rules can be attributed to Elder Joseph Meacham—in many of which he fairly copied the blue laws of Connecticut." Still it is natural that the more conservative should question the policy of the progressives. "I do not think," says one of their ablest thinkers and writers, in a recent letter, "we have gained anything by relaxing discipline, or letting down from the cross."

—William A. Hinds, *American Communities*, revised
edition, 1902

The Shakers owned too much land in proportion to their numbers. Fifty thousand acres, not counting distant property, Nordhoff estimated in 1875, a century after the Shakers arrived in America. Now that sisters

Young sisters at Enfield, New Hampshire, in 1906 pose for a picture while hooking a rug. Photograph, courtesy of the United Society of Shakers, Sabbathday Lake, Maine.

outnumbered brethren, thousand of acres and home farms reverted to forest and timber. Farmland was tilled by "hirelings," rented, or sold off as the population of able-bodied men plunged down. Eventually the handwork in which the sisters were skilled—the stitching of cloaks and shirts, the lining of boxes, even the putting together of chairs, and, of course, the output of their kitchens—became the mainstay of Shaker economic life.

The ascetic life has not made the women of the order unmindful of creature comforts, and a sense of beauty in apparel, for the famous "Shaker preserves" fetch the highest prices, while the long lines of the Shaker mantles known as the "Dorothy-cloak" are among the most popular of the styles for evening wraps for city belles.

—Pauline Carrington Bouve, "The Shaker Society: An Experiment in Socialism," *New England Magazine*, July 1910

A LETTER TO ELDER HENRY GREEN AT ALFRED

Boston, January 28, 1900

Dear Elder Henry:

I enclose a check for $15, for which will you please ask Eldress Fanny to send this week a selection of pretty things about like those that were sent before. Perhaps there might be a few wooden things added, the work-boxes with handles and a closed box or two.... I am much interested in a fair here for good objects, and my friends were much pleased with the idea of my getting a box from Alfred.

With kind love to all my Shaker friends, I am ever,

Yours sincerely,

S. O. JEWETT

[Sarah Orne Jewett]

Shaker, Box, Oval 9 In 95.00
Shaker, Box, Carrying, Oval 11 In .. 125.00

—*The Kovels' Complete Antiques Price List*, 1978–79

The Maine storyteller Sarah Orne Jewett, author of the American classic, The Country of the Pointed Firs, *never wrote about her Shaker friends at Alfred and Poland Spring, Maine. (She did bring to Alfred a Frenchwoman, Mme. Blanc-Bentzon, who described her observations in a magazine article published in France. The Shaker cloak Mme. Blanc purchased on her 1897 visit was said to be the talk of Paris.)*

But other novelists continued to find romance in the picturesque decline of the old Shaker homes.

Romantic Views

Mr. Osborne was about to take [Martha] up to Vermont and board her . . . but he decided instead, to place her with the Shaker Sisterhood at Harvard, Mass. This is called the "North family of Shakers." Mr. Osborne having made the acquaintance of some of the Brethren, had the highest respect for them as honest, God fearing people. Mr. Osborne did not sign away his right to reclaim her at any time, but they received Martha all the same, with love and kindness, and it was not long before the bleeding tendrils of the child's heart, found strength to rise and twine around these new friends who opened their doors and took her in.

It *did* seem as if upon this whole earth, no safer, purer, happier home could be found for a homeless little child, than among these gentle, sweet-faced people, of whom the world apparently knows so little. Strict in discipline, it is *true*, but God fearing and holy, and so absolutely just to all, that Martha soon gave her whole childish heart to them.

When in later years, by force of circumstances, she was obliged to turn away from this safe Harbor of Refuge, she experienced some such feeling, as I think Eve must have felt, when she departed from Eden, and the gates closed behind her.

> —Marietta Holden, *The Story of Martha; or, Love's Ordeal*, 1909; originally published in 1904 as *Uncovered Ears and Opened Vision*, by "The Princess."

FINDING THE WAY

At the foot of the hill the road widened into a grassy street, on both sides of which, under the elms and maples, were the community houses, big and substantial, but gauntly plain; their yellow paint, flaking and peeling here and there, shone clean and fresh in the sparkle of the morning. . . . The settlement, steeped in sunshine, showed no sign of life. There was a strange remoteness from time about the place; a sort of emptiness, and a silence that silenced even Athalia.

"Where *is* everybody?" she said, in a lowered voice; as she spoke, a child in a blue apron came from an open doorway and tugged a basket across the street.

"Are there children here?" Lewis asked, surprised; and their guide said, sadly:

"Not as many as there ought to be. The new school laws have made a great difference. We've only got two. Folks used to send 'em to us to bring up; oftentimes they stayed on after they were of age. . . ."

They had come to the open door of a great, weather-beaten building, from whose open windows an aromatic breath wandered out into the summer air. As they crossed the worn threshold, Athalia stopped and caught her breath in the overpowering scent of the drying herbs; then they followed Brother Nathan up a shaky flight of steps to the loft. Here some elderly women, sitting on low benches, were sorting over great piles of herbs in silence—the silence, apparently, of peace and meditation. Two of them were dressed like world's people, but the others wore small gray shoulder-capes buttoned to their chins, and little caps of white net stretched smoothly over wire frames; the narrow shirrings inside the frames fitted so close to their peaceful, wrinkled foreheads that no hair could be seen.

"I wish I could sit and sort herbs!" Athalia said, under her breath.

Brother Nathan chuckled. "For how long?"

The two visitors followed Brother Nathan down the room between piles of sorted herbs, and out into the sunshine again. Athalia drew a breath of ecstasy.

"It's all so beautifully tranquil!" she whispered, looking about her with blue, excited eyes. . . .

But as they went along the grassy street this sense of tranquillity closed about them like a palpable peace. Now and then they stopped and spoke to some one—always an elderly person; and in each old face the experiences that life writes in unerasable lines about eyes and lips were hidden by a veil of calmness that was curiously unhuman. . . .

Athalia asked many questions of Eldress Hannah, who had taken them in charge, and once or twice she burst into impetuous appreciation of the idea of brotherhood, and even of certain theological principles— which last diverted her husband very much. Eldress Hannah showed them the dairy, and the work-room, and all there was to see, with a patient hospitality that kept them at an infinite distance. She answered Lewis' questions about the community with a sad directness.

"Yee; there are not many of us now. The world's people say we're dying out. But the Lord will preserve the remnant to redeem the world, young man. Yee, when they come in from the world they cast their possessions into the whole; we own nothing, for ourselves. Nay; we don't have many come. Brother William was the last. Why did he come?" She looked coldly at Athalia. . . . Because he saw the way to peace. He'd had strife enough in the world." . . .

Later Athalia's husband, Lewis, admitted that there was more to it than he had supposed. "They've studied the Prophecies; that's evident," he said. "And they're not narrow in their belief. They're really Unitarians."

"Narrow?" said Athalia,—"they are as wide as heaven itself! And, oh, the peace of it!"

Athalia left Lewis and joined the Shakers as a novice. Lewis came to visit her, and eventually was given lodgings in a little cabin nearby. He had long, profound conversations with Brother Nathan.

Sometimes they talked of work that must be done, and sometimes they touched on more unpractical things—those spiritual manifestations which at rare intervals centred in Brother William and were the hope of the whole community.

In a year's time Athalia grew restless, as was her nature. She emerged from her infatuation with the Shakers. By now, however, Lewis was drawn toward them. He continued to study their doctrines. Just as he was convinced of becoming a Shaker, Athalia approached and begged him to take her home. It was too late. This time she left him with the Believers. Ten years later word came that she was dying and wanted to see her husband. It was agreed that he should go to her. Athalia begged Lewis to be forgiven. "I have nothing to forgive," said the contented old man.
—Margaret Deland, *The Way to Peace*, 1910

A POSTHUMOUS NOVEL BY HOWELLS

A late novel by William Dean Howells was published after he died in 1920. It described a university professor's summer rental of a twenty-five-room Shaker dwelling.

One day [Kelwyn] received a very odd visit.

This visit was paid him by a quaintly dressed old man, who said he was an Elder of the people called Shakers, and that he had come to Kelwyn because of some account he had read of the kind of work he was doing in the university, and had thought he would be pleased, in his quality of lecturer on Historical Sociology, to know something of the social experiment of the Shakers. It presently appeared that he had counted so much upon Kelwyn's interest in it as to believe that he might make it the theme of a lecture, and he had come with a little printed tract on the Shaker life and doctrine which he had written himself, and which he now gave Kelwyn with the hope, very politely expressed, that it might be useful to him in the preparation of his lectures. The whole affair was to Kelwyn's mind so full of a sweet innocence that he felt it invited the most delicate handling on his part. . . . Inwardly he was filled with amusement at the notion of his august science stooping to inquire into such a lowly experiment as that of those rustic communists; but outwardly he treated it with grave deference. . . . He was curious enough to ask some questions about the Family to which his visitor belonged, and then about the general conditions of Shakerism. It amused him again when his visitor answered, from a steadfast faith in its doctrine, that his sect was everywhere in decay, and that his own Family was now a community of aging men and women, and must soon die out unless it was recruited from the world-outside. He seemed to feel that he had a mission to the gentler phases of this world, and he did not conceal that he had come with some hope that if the character of Shakerism could be truly set forth to such cultivated youth as must attend Kelwyn's lectures, considerable accessions from their number might follow. The worst thing in the present condition of Shakerism, he said, was that the community was obliged to violate the very law of its social being, for the brethren were too feeble to work in the fields themselves, and were forced to employ hireling labor. Kelwyn learned from his willing avowals that they had some thousands of acres which they could only let grow up in forests for the crops of timber they would finally yield, and that it was not easy always to find tenants for the farms they had to let. He spoke of one farm which would be given, with one of the Family dwellings, to a suitable tenant at a rent so ridiculously low that Kelwyn said, with a laugh, if the Shakers would furnish the house, though twenty-five rooms were rather more than his family needed, he did not know but he might take the farm himself for the summer.　　　—William Dean Howells, *The Vacation of the Kelwyns: An Idyll of the Middle Seventies*, 1920

Bookplate for the Wallace H. Cathcart Shaker Collection at the Western Reserve Historical Society in Cleveland. Photograph, courtesy of the Western Reserve Historical Society.

Realistic Views

While new books were being written about the Shakers, the fine old books by the Shakers were being collected. Two Ohio residents, a bookseller named John Patterson MacLean, and Wallace H. Cathcart, director of the Western Reserve Historical Society, competed with each other for old books and manuscripts still in the hands of the Believers. History-conscious Shaker leaders, notably Elder Alonzo Hollister and Eldress Catherine Allen of Mount Lebanon, were convinced of their "bounden duty" to help the two men preserve Shaker history in the nation's libraries.

In 1905, MacLean compiled A Bibliography of Shaker Literature, *containing 523 items. By 1911, Cathcart had secured most of the items in the bibliography and many more. By 1920, his efforts made the Western Reserve Historical Society in Cleveland the world's leading repository of Shaker books and manuscripts.*

Bibliographer MacLean also wrote about the western Shakers. Early in the twentieth century he reported

a marked change in the order. . . . Many a fiction has been laid aside, so that at the present time, there is absolutely no more discipline exerted than is found to be absolutely necessary.

If the Shakers are not a happy people, he said, it is certainly their own fault,

for they are surrounded by all the comforts of life, and no restraint is placed on their opinions. They have no creed and the widest latitude is given for religious belief. Mr. Moore S. Mason, a Believer, volunteered to conduct me through all the buildings at Union Village [Ohio]. From garret to cellar, I was all through the dwellings. Everywhere there was cleanliness and order. The cellar was filled with useful stores. The gardens surpassed all those I had ever entered before. So far as I could see the members were happy and contented. By invitation of Eldress Clymena Miner I sat down with the family to a bountiful repast. No conversation, save that which was necessary, was indulged in. Each retired quietly when sufficed, without any ceremony. On retiring I asked my guide: "Do you live that well all the time?" He replied, "That is a sample of our usual meals." When I see the distress and hardship endured by so many deserving people who are and have been unfortunate, I can but wonder why they do not seek a retreat that presents so many advantages as afforded by the Shakers. . . .

Do not think [they] always wear somber faces. I have heard them roar with laughter, and I have engaged in the most lively conversation with them. They are of the same flesh and blood as other people—only their discipline is of a different stamp. Nor must it be surmised that communism keeps down all ambition, or dwarfs the intellect. The Shakers have published quite a list of inventions made by their membership. Among these Elder John Martin of Union Village in 1847 invented a machine to knead dough. The journal, under various names, published from 1871 to 1899, shows the Shakers of Ohio to have been possessed of literary taste and a poetic genius of no mean ability.

—J. P. MacLean, *Shakers of Ohio*, 1907

MAKING A SHAKER

There was a young man living in the family of our next neighbor. His name was William Dumont, nineteen years of age. Though of a lively disposition, he was of a thoughtful turn of mind. Our aged Elder Joseph Brackett said one day, "William Dumont would make a good Shaker, and I will get him if I can." Brother Granville made answer: "I have thought the same thing and will do all I can to help draw him out from the sea." He then began with prayers and spiritual labors whenever an opportunity presented itself. He was very persistent, and the work soon began to have an effect.

After a while our young brother acknowledged hearing the call to a higher life. Then the struggle commenced, for he had been promised a vessel and was to be the captain. He had many misgivings and finally came to the conclusion that he could live the higher life outside and not bind himself to this community.

When Granville found where he stood he gave him a searching look and said, "They that are not for us are against us, and they that gather not with us scatter abroad."

Thus our young brother found every weapon taken from his hands, and made up his mind to a full consecration. In this he has remained faithful to this day, and is now the leading elder of the Societies in Maine.

—Aurelia G. Mace, *The Aletheia: Spirit of Truth*, second edition, 1907

NOTES FROM MOUNT LEBANON

—Eldress Anna's 80th birthday passed with some kind remembrance messages from friends both within and without our order, which are warmly appreciated by all within the home.

—The children are watching the skies with eager eyes, looking for a snow storm which shall bear promise of a possible sleighride. Their usual pre-Christmas sleighride failing them, the Pittsfield measles epidemic having alarmed their caretakers, they feel as though the winter had not yet been half fair to them.

—Sister Florence Kemp, after a three weeks' absence among old friends in Provincetown and Boston, Mass., returned on Friday. She spent the last two days of her visit with our Harvard kindred from whom she brought a good report of health and prosperity, with the usual supply of good Shaker love and affection. . . .

—Monday's sunshine was improved by a party of sisters in a trip to Pittsfield, under the care of Elder Daniel Offord. Stores and banks were on the bill of fare and a pleasant but cold ride was among the features of interest and enjoyment. Few rides are more delightful, even in winter, on a sunny, quiet day, than the ride over Lebanon mountain and return.
—Pittsfield *Eagle*, Jan. 20, 1911

In 1900, Charles Tiffany, president of Tiffany and Company in New York City, was a guest at the famous Poland Spring House, a resort near the Shaker village at Sabbathday Lake, Maine. One day he took a hike and lost his way. After wandering about in his dusty clothes, he stopped at the Shaker community and was mistaken for a tramp by Eldress Aurelia Mace. She fed him, dusted off his coat, and sent him on his way. Only later did she learn his identity. In gratitude Mr. Tiffany is said to have sent the Shakers a silver service.

TAKE THE MILK CART FROM HARVARD VILLAGE

Life in the Shaker community is a very industrious but a very peaceful existence. On the faces of those living in these communities there is the imprint of peace and purity. Weaving, preserving, teaching the young people who are taken under their charge, caring for the poultry and keeping the "family" homes scrupulously neat are the duties of the sisters. Farming, sheep-raising, the concoction of healing potions, among which witch hazel has attained worldwide celebrity, wood-sawing and carpentry are the avocations of the brothers and elders, and on a summer afternoon, elders, sisters, and the children, may be seen gathering apples or sitting on the doorstep chatting together very much as any ordinary family of ordinary farmer folk. . . .

At Harvard, Massachusetts, the visitor who cares to see the life of a Community may get an interesting glimpse of the daily routine followed by these worthy but very singular people. The temporary guest sometimes finds the milk cart from the village the only means of conveyance to the Community but the journey is not unpleasant.

Once within the shadow of the ungainly, ugly buildings, he falls under the spell of a certain sort of picturesqueness. The Elderesses and Sisters, in their tight-fitting caps and their prim capes or kerchiefs are usually sweet-faced elderly women, who are really under the influence of their own belief in the "Spirit."

A portrait of a Harvard, Massachusetts, sister by John H. Tarbell is crisply captioned "A Shaker Type" in *New England Magazine*, July 1910.

Many of the Communities have been forced to coalesce, because their numbers are insufficient to till the soil and keep the settlement self-supporting. The eyes of the young generation are turned worldward, and the serene-faced women and grave-eyed men who hold the remaining Communities feel that "Ichabod" is written over the portals of their doorways.

The reason for this is that the force which made the Communal system successful under their shrewd and provident management,—the religious idea—is dying. The socialism that is expressed by segregated groups of people dividing their property equally is a failure. The spiritual life and teaching of these people have been a good influence in American life. The Shakers have handed down to us an ideal, strained and impracticable, perhaps, but still an ideal of purity, and having done this, their mission is ended.   —Pauline Carrington Bouve, "The Shaker Society: An Experiment in Socialism," *New England Magazine,* July 1910

The Harvard community, northwest of Boston, was two miles north of the town center . . . hidden in the woodlands. . . .

The last of the diminishing Shaker residents migrated to other colonies about fifteen years ago, and the property now belongs to aliens. Most of this wide realm of the Believers has reverted to woodland and only stone walls in the forest show where the old fields and pastures were. Some hay and apples are still salvaged, and there are patches of land cultivated by tenants. Several buildings have burned and the process of deterioration continues. The summer is enlivened more or less by vacation folks who rent rooms in the old living-quarters of the big houses.

The most imposing of surviving structures is a great stone barn with one end abutting a hillside so that loads of hay can be driven in at an upper story. This barn was built with money realized in selling Shaker-made turkey-feather fans, except the shingles, which were a gift from the New Hampshire Shakers floated down the Merrimac River on a raft to Lowell.

More interesting than all else is the cemetery, an expanse of about two acres on a gentle grassy slope where some ancient pines cast their shadows. A massive stone wall has been built around it. . . . The graves are in serried ranks all facing the same way, and each with an inscribed marker of iron painted white. . . . The cemetery at Harvard was the one spot in all the old Shaker territory at Harvard that showed no trace of neglect.

In some of the cemeteries, as for example at Mount Lebanon, Enfield, Connecticut, and Canterbury, New Hampshire, all the old flat stones that marked the individual graves have been removed, and there is substituted in the center of the cemetery a fair-sized but unostentatious monument.

—Clifton Johnson, "The Passing of the Shakers," *Old-Time New England*, Oct. 1934

ANOTHER MOTHER CHURCH

It is curious to find so many points of similarity between this rapidly disappearing religious body and that recent sect which is daily augmenting its numbers—Christian Science.

—Pauline Carrington Bouve, "The Shaker Society," *New England Magazine*, July 1910

When she was on the staff of McClure's Magazine, *Willa Cather edited a series of articles on Mary Baker Eddy and the history of Christian Science. The articles appeared in 1907–08, and later were published in a controversial book that was attributed for many years to Willa Cather.*

An influence ... which had an effect upon [Mary Baker's] later career, may be traced to the sect known as Shakers, which had sprung up in that section of New Hampshire. Their main community was at East Canterbury, N.H., five miles from Tilton, and Mary Baker was familiar with their appearance, their peculiar costume, and their community life. She knew their religious doctrines and spiritual exaltations, and was acquainted with their habits of industry and thrift. In her girlhood there were still living in the neighbourhood people who remembered Ann Lee, the founder of the sect. All through Mary's youth the Shakers were much in the courts because of the scandalous charges brought against them, and on one occasion they were defended by Franklin Pierce, in whose office Albert Baker studied law. Laws directed against their community were constantly presented to the Legislature, and complaints against them were frequently heard. A famous "exposure" of Shaker methods, written by Mary Dyer, who had been a member of the [Enfield] community, was published in Concord in 1847; and the Shakers and their doings formed one of the exciting topics of the times.

That these happenings made a profound impression on Mary Baker and became irrevocably a part of her susceptible nature is evident; for we find her reverting to and making use of certain phases of Shakerism when, later, she had established a religious system of her own.

The Appendix to the book adds:

There is no fundamental similarity between Christian Science and Shakerism, but there are significant resemblances. Ann Lee's main contribution to religious theories or pretensions, was the idea that God is both masculine and feminine. She, herself, claimed to be the "female principle of God." . . . Mrs. Eddy also teaches the femininity of God, and Christian Scientists have claimed that she is the "feminine principle of Deity." . . . The Shakers prayed always to "Our Father and Mother which are in Heaven," while Mrs. Eddy has "spiritually interpreted" the Lord's Prayer, making it read: "Our Father-Mother God." The Shakers proclaimed Ann Lee to be the woman of the Apocalypse, calling her the "God-anointed Woman," and the "Holy Comforter." In *Science and Health*, Mrs. Eddy has called the attention of her followers to the significance of the chapter in Revelation on the woman of the Apocalypse and its "relation to the present age," suggesting that the woman represents the founder of Christian Science. In the original Mother Church in Boston is a stained-glass window, showing the woman of the Apocalypse clothed in the sun and crowned with twelve stars. It is titled "The Woman God Crowned," and above it is a representation of the book *Science and Health*. Shakers always called Ann Lee "Mother"; Christian Scientists formerly thus addressed Mrs. Eddy. Mother Ann, like Mother Eddy, declared that she had the gift of healing. She also believed that she took upon herself the sins and sufferings of others; in the early days, Mrs. Eddy had the same idea. The Shakers believed that Mother Ann had spiritual illumination—the mind that saw things as they were; that the rest of the world was deceived; that the evidence of the senses, used against her, might mislead; this is a prevailing idea in regard to Mrs. Eddy among Christian Scientists. . . . The Shakers called their establishment "The Church of Christ"; Mrs. Eddy used the same name, adding the word "Scientist." They called the original foundation the "Mother Church"; Mrs. Eddy so designated her first Boston building. Ann Lee forbade audible prayer, teaching that it "exposed the desires"; Mrs. Eddy opposes audible prayer, which may "utter desires which are not real." Finally, Ann Lee enjoined celibacy. Mrs. Eddy teaches that celibacy is a more spiritual state than marriage; she permits the marriage relation merely as "expedient,"—"suffer it to be so now."

—Georgine Milmine, *The Life of Mary Baker Eddy and the History of Christian Science*, 1909

With its emphasis on the spiritual healing that Mother Ann and the early Shakers practiced, Christian Science won the devotion of Eldress Anna White and other Believers.

FROM HIDDEN CUPBOARDS

It has been my great privilege to be counted as a friend among the Shakers in the old township of Harvard, in Massachusetts, which crowns the uplands overlooking the broad valley of the Nashua. A little band of loyal souls still keep the candle of their faith burning in their secluded village, far removed from the outside world, like a shrine in a sanctuary of hilly woodlands . . .

I was permitted to pore over cherished records of the past, and worn-out journals, and touching books of verse . . . These are kept in hidden cupboards where the curious cannot find them.

And while I read the faded pages, odd fantasies would seize me. . . . Out of the past I seemed to hear the shouts of triumph and the songs of praise of the "Believers"; and hurrying footsteps creaked the floors—the place was peopled with a host of brethren and sisters whirling in the ecstasy of their strange worship.

And then another sound would reach me—ominous and threatening. Oaths and curses rent the air—the mob had come; had reached the door, mad with antagonism and venom. Stones and missiles shot through the window panes, and cries and imprecations followed them. But high above the tumult rang the songs of Zion, challenging and triumphant. Out through the woods and over the fertile meadows echoed the hymns of Glory. And then a veil would cover the Past again with its mysterious folds; silence returned—heavier than before.

"Eldress," said I [to one whose vital mind still reaches to far horizons], "where has the fervor gone, and all the ardor and enthusiasm, and all the spiritual fire that swayed these men and women? . . ."

"Yea, oh, yea," she replied musingly, ". . . Times have changed . . . .

And life is looked at from a different angle. But nothing that has gone before is lost. The Spirit has its periods of moving beneath the surface, and after generations pass, it sweeps through the world again and burns the chaff and stubble."

"And who would dream in passing through these country roads," I said, "that every inch could tell its tale of thrilling history?—persecution and suffering first, and then the years of great prosperity; and finally a handful left to close the chapter! As years went by, Eldress, the people grew to love the Shakers."

"They were good men and good women," she answered simply.

—Clara Endicott Sears, *Gleanings From Old Shaker Journals*, 1916

Clara Endicott Sears was one of the first writers to publish insights on the Shakers from their own unpublished records. Gleanings From Old Shaker Journals *personalizes the story of Mother Ann's missionary journey and the way the Believers lived, worked and worshipped in the Harvard area.*

Gleanings *was followed in 1922 by a novel with an air of mystery and a Shaker twist. One of the charms of* The Romance of Fiddler's Green *is a recipe for a Shaker garden:*

Brother Simeon seated himself upon an old tree-stump and opened a large unbleached cotton umbrella to protect his eyes from the sun's rays. His round, florid face and kindly expression bespoke a life of honest labor and calm contentment.

"Go dig up young cedar trees from the hill yonder," he suggested, pointing to them, "and plant them as a hedge around the garden like the wall o' flesh imprisoning thy soul. Now, plant lilies in and out of the larkspur and thee'll have white for purity and blue for wisdom—the two are linked together. See to it that thee plant a circle in the center o' golden marigolds, for yellow is the color of the sun and gives thee health, and the circle means Eternity—no end and no beginning. And put the roses by themselves, John, for they breathe out love, and naught should mar their perfume, for there's none to equal it."

Brother Simeon paused a moment and looked about him for further inspiration.

"Now, there should be a plant or two o' rue and rosemary and the climbing eglantine, and here and there a bunch o' bleeding-heart. And sow white poppy seeds for sleep, and purple pansies for a sign o' thoughts; and over yonder plant sweet lavender and heliotrope and the modest mignonette—they'll fill the breeze with incense when the sun basks on 'em."

John was growing confused, but, quite unconscious of it, Brother Simeon continued his directions, thoroughly enjoying sitting in the spring sunshine and weaving a web of fancies for the making of the garden.

"Now, John," he said, continuing, "on the edges o' the little brook should grow the stately iris that are straight like temple pillars, and here is where the border o' forget-me-nots will please the eyes; the blue and violet combined spells Wisdom o' the Spirit. Thee should try to learn the language o' colors if thee plans a garden. Green, the color o' grass, means sympathy, so circle all the flower beds with even, close-trimmed borders that the gracious gift may bind the whole together. When thee has done thy planting thus, John, thee will have thy garden o' delight."

PRESERVING THE SHAKER HERITAGE

The First Shaker Museum

In 1920 a former Trustees' Office was carefully moved from the vacated Shaker village in Harvard to Prospect Hill, a few miles away. From the new location the building looked out over the Nashua Valley all the way to and beyond the former Shaker "twin" community at Shirley, Massachusetts.

This "Shaker House" became the first Shaker museum. It was founded by Clara Endicott Sears, a pioneer in appreciating and preserving Shaker architecture, furniture, tools and objects of everyday life. It was, and still is, part of Fruitlands, a group of museums on her estate.

These turnings of delight,
roped off, extend a will
to see a versatile
cure for the world's blight

in singleness: to see
in a spare and alien
order, even
here, variety.   —Jonathan Aldrich, "Shaker Village," *Croquet Lover*
                          at the Dinner Table, 1977

FRUITLANDS

Blankets and Comfortables should be of a modest color, not checked, striped, or flowered. . . . One rocking chair in a room is sufficient. . . . Believers should not keep any beast that needs an extravagant portion of whipping or beating, but such had better be sold to the children of this world, or killed.   —From the *Millennial Laws*, 1821

"So when a Shaker died," our guide
explains, "they put him in a pine
unpainted coffin, sometimes with
only initials, age and date
on a small marker facing west,
in simple rows. . . ."
                        A room brightened
as if by skylight—somehow a faint
pinwheel attraction floating over
us. And how to move in this?
No people left, no animal
or mouse, nothing alive at all!
And if they never wanted babies,
why that little cradle there?
How long since the last gathering
in song and dance we hear about,
meetings when a whole community
went shaking into the small hours?
Many questions I don't ask.
The light swallows jangle outside
to the day's undoing, as we go round
and round the inventions of an old
order—a circular saw, the first
flat brooms and metal pens, a palm-
leaf bonnet loom, and common clothespin,
left to the children of this world.
                —Jonathan Aldrich, *Croquet Lover at the Dinner
                Table*, 1977

Collecting

ONE COOL SEPTEMBER AFTERNOON IN 1923 . . .

After a day in the countryside looking for old furniture, glass, china and pewter, we were driving home in our Model T along the route which . . . passed by the old Hancock Shaker village. We had heard about the delicious Shaker bread. We decided to stop to inquire if it could be bought, and when the basement door in the large brick dwelling was opened to us, we were greeted by the aroma of fresh-baked loaves.

A soft-voiced Shaker sister welcomed us warmly. We bought two loaves of bread. And in the long clean "cook-room" we saw much besides: a trestle table, benches, rocking chairs, built-in cupboards, cooking arches, all beautiful in their simplicity. Later, eating the bread, we knew that our appetite would not be satisfied with bread alone.

The acquisition of our first chair was a memorable experience. Though born and raised within a few miles of the Hancock Shakers, neither of us knew much more about them than the current gossip that they were a "peculiar" sect. We had never heard that they made their own furniture. No one had ever collected it. No one knew the history of their chair industry, nor when or by whom the furnishings of the community dwellings and shops were produced. The Shakers themselves took their craftsmanship for granted. Yet here, we came to discover, was a distinct school of joinery and industry about which nothing had been written. When we purchased those loaves of bread and that simple three-slat side chair with its woven seat, we did not know that we were taking the first steps in a work which would open up vast avenues of research. We did not know that as time went on we would become deeply involved in the attempt to preserve, in words as in objects, a richly productive strain in American history. It was to become a lifework.

—Edward Deming and Faith Andrews, *Fruits of the Shaker Tree of Life*, 1975

The Magazine ANTIQUES *in 1928 published the first article on Shaker furniture by Edward Deming Andrews. Eight books and more than fifty articles, essays, and pamphlets later, this collector-scholar and his wife Faith have had a broad influence on appreciation and study of the Shakers. He died in 1964.*

Charles Sheeler: Around 1927 ...

Shaker furniture and crafts were taking an important place in Sheeler's considerations as an artist, similar to that of the buildings and crafts of Bucks County [Pennsylvania]. They belong to the same general order of communal expression, even though the Shakers were more closely united than any of the groups of settlers in Pennsylvania who gave their practical arts distinctive forms. . . .

Several years after he first came to know them well, around 1927, Shaker pieces began to appear in Sheeler's paintings: the favorite long table and benches are used, with Shaker boxes and a little music stand: it is characteristic of Sheeler's approaches that they did not appear immediately. They were not primarily objects.

—Constance Rourke, *Charles Sheeler: Artist in the American Tradition*, 1938

On a Shaker Theme by American artist Charles Sheeler, who painted or photographed twenty-three works with Shaker themes or objects. This 1956 oil on canvas measures 31-3/4 × 26 inches. The Stephen and Sybil Stone Foundation. Courtesy of the Museum of Fine Arts, Boston.

As with the limited number of items from his Shaker collection which appear in his interiors, Sheeler used only a few structures to exemplify Shaker architectural design.

The Shaker building that most attracted him was the laundry and machine shop at Hancock [Massachusetts], which appeared four times over about a twenty-five year period. Its unique shape was the result of several renovations of the original three and one-half story structure built in 1790. . . . Beyond its aesthetic appeal, Sheeler may have been interested in this building because, serving as a washhouse, machine house, herb and seed room, and woodshed, it exemplified the Shaker principle of maximum utility and because it was, in part, an early American factory.

On a Shaker Theme . . . is not a detailed description of a particular building, but a variation on the shape of the structure. Characteristic of Sheeler's late style, the actual forms are reduced further than ever before to abstract geometric shapes, and different views are combined within one work. Beginning about 1946 he carefully composed overprintings from several photographic negatives or the same negative printed several times and used these as studies for paintings. To create the composition of *On a Shaker Theme*, Sheeler superimposed two images, one slightly smaller and in reverse, of the portion of the laundry depicted in an earlier painting, *Shaker Detail*. In overlapping, the two images of the central window and two images of the small door on the wall of the tallest story intersect. A greater portion of the west side of the building is visible at the extreme left than in *Shaker Detail*. The windows, doors, and walls have been radically reduced to their geometric equivalents; the clapboards and window frames are no longer defined. . . . The Hancock laundry . . . is . . . finally abstracted into geometric shapes which are rearranged in a way only vaguely resembling the actual structure.

—Mary Jane Jacob, "The Impact of Shaker Design on the Work of Charles Sheeler," unpublished M.A. thesis, 1976

In 1962 the artist gave fifteen pieces of Shaker furniture from his small choice collection to the new museum-restoration of Hancock Shaker Village in Pittsfield, Massachusetts. Although most of the pieces had come from Hancock, he did not buy them directly from members of the declining community. The old village founded in 1790 was rescued in 1960 from a tawdry commercial future by a dedicated local group headed by Mrs. Lawrence K. Miller. Today Hancock Shaker Village is an

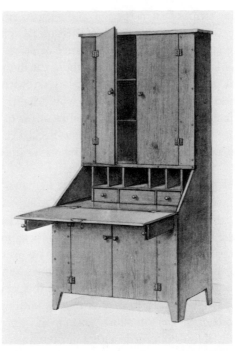

A butternut secretary made at Hancock was a gift from Charles Sheeler to the restored Shaker village of Hancock in Pittsfield, Massachusetts. Drawing by Howard Weld, Index of American Design, National Gallery of Art.

energetic indoor and outdoor museum-complex in the cultural center of the Berkshires.

There was a Shaker settlement near the city where we used to live, and it was a pleasure to visit there, so hospitable were the kindly aged folk, and amid such an aroma of sweetness did they lead their celibate lives.

We wondered at times, finding them so gently cordial to us, when we knew that the cold text of their religion taught them to be distrustful of people of the outside world and to hold but necessary communication with them, whether they hoped to draw us in as proselytes for their community, so sorely in need of younger blood; but if they ever cherished the hope that we should find inward and spiritual grace among them they assuredly gave no outward and visible sign that such was their thought. They were hospitable, in a simple, old-fashioned way, and we were welcome to enter their doors, to walk through their halls, with polished floors, covered with long strips of rag carpeting, and with everywhere an odor of herbs and of sanctity; we were welcome at their meals of bread and butter, and fried chicken, and jelly of apple and sauce of pear, when, in silence, the men ate at a long table at one side of the great dining-room and the women, as silent, at the other. Back to back they sat, with the broad space between; and one standing in the middle would have seen, on the one hand, a line of men's heads, bent over the table, a row of blue coats, with tails carefully parted on either side of the low-backed chairs, and, on the other side, a row of little muslin caps, and the plain tippets and dresses of calico. . . .

One of the oldest of the Sisters gave us her own particular chair which had been made specially for her, in her youth, when she taught sewing to the children whom they then had in their school.

It is a slender narrow rocker, with slim, high back; impossible to rock, indeed, for the dear old lady had found it liable to tip over backward, or to threaten to tip, and so had had one of the Brothers saw off the rockers short and fasten on the stubby ends prohibitive bits of cork. The chair, charmingly proportioned, with low-set arms, has nothing about it that is elaborate; the code of Shakerism allows nothing of display; but it is most carefully made, is splint-bottomed, with a curious variety of Roman-key design, and the ends of the arms and the tops of the side pieces end in delicately ovaled knobs. —Robert and Elizabeth Shackleton, *The Quest of the Colonial*, 1907

If you own a Shaker chair, preserve it with great care, for it will soon be considered an antique, and a rare one at that. These chairs are still being manufactured to a very limited extent at Mount Lebanon, New York, but their day is rapidly passing. Fifty years ago these simple and useful chairs were common enough, but the Shakers found it difficult to compete with cheap machine-made products, and to-day most people would not know a Shaker chair if they saw one. . . .

There is as yet no established market value on old Shaker furniture. Modern chairs may still be bought for a few dollars apiece, and I have seen older chairs purchased in Mount Lebanon for $10 or $15. On the other hand, collectors have recently paid as high as $75 for trestle tables and writing desks of unquestioned age. The market values will undoubtedly increase as Shaker furniture becomes more scarce and more collectors become interested in it. For that reason, if for no other, now is the time to secure any pieces obtainable.

There is a charm about genuine Shaker furniture that cannot be put into words. It is stoutly made and lovingly fashioned. In character it seems somehow to reflect the honesty and simplicity of the unique and admirable people who made it.

> —Walter A. Dyer, "The Furniture of the Shakers: A Plea for Its Preservation as Part of Our National Inheritance," *House Beautiful*, May 1929

> Soaring Demand
> For Shaker Designs

> —Rita Reif, "Antiques," *New York Times*, Jan. 21, 1979

ON REVERING SHAKER FURNITURE

Is there a Shaker aesthetic? Is this a valid question to ask of a people whose vision was focused on a millennial conceit and so might be expected to be more concerned with obtaining entrance to heaven than with what sort of chairs or carpets heaven was furnished with?

We should be able to begin this inquiry by simply looking at a Shaker chair and assessing what we see. But it is difficult to look at a chair as for the first time again because we have been shown and reshown Shaker furniture in an iconography that has very much influenced our perceptions.

Fundamental to the iconography of Shaker furniture is a mystique, or mystery, of mysticism for which Thomas Merton provided a caption in suggesting that "the peculiar grace of a Shaker chair was due to the fact that it was made by someone capable of believing that an angel might come and sit on it."

Another element of this iconography has been an asceticism, or circumspection, emphasized in 19th century graphics by a linearness of posture, of placement and form, reinforced by an attributed sternness that Dickens called "grim" and Nordhoff "homely."

Perhaps most influential, though, have been the photographs of William Winter published in the Andrews' first book of *Shaker Furniture*. These photographs visibly ascribe a reverence and awe to Shaker furniture and experience; but in these photographs interiors are not shown as found but as composed, by Winters and by the Andrews. This sort of composition and lighting is what has been replicated by curators and col-

"Shaker Harmony," a print reproduced from a 1973 painting by Pennsylvania artist Constantine Kermes. Known for iconlike portrayal of "American saints," this artist's work exemplifies "the Shaker image."

lectors since and so has contributed very significantly to the sense of reverence we feel toward Shaker furniture.

> —Mary Lyn Ray, from a talk, "Is There a Shaker Aesthetic?" presented at the Shaker Seminar of the Museum of American Folk Art, New York, September 1979

Shaker Perfection Prized

By the 1930s the special quality of Shaker arts and craftsmanship was well-appreciated. Furniture and objects were being collected, exalted and exhibited. The New York State Museum in Albany, directed by Dr. Charles Adams, formed an early and impressive collection with the aid of Edward Deming Andrews, photographer William F. Winter Jr., and William Lassiter. Their opportunity lay in the county's acquisition of the Church Family property at Watervliet, the Shakers' first communal home in America.

Two future founders of museums soon began their gathering. John S. Williams was drawn to the technology of Shaker enterprise. He sought the machinery and tools once ahead of their times that became the basis

In the summer of 1930 William F. Winter, noted for his portraits of Shaker furniture, photographed a guest room furnished in Victorian style at the South Family in Watervliet, New York. Photograph, courtesy of the New York State Museum.

for the abundant display at the Shaker Museum at Old Chatham, New York, founded in 1950. Mrs. Curry Churchill Hall first lodged a western Shaker collection in an old church in Auburn, Kentucky. When the 1824 Centre House at nearby South Union was purchased, the collection was moved there, and restoration began at Shakertown at South Union, which opened in 1971.

Dance of the Chosen

Shaker dancing and marching was also recognized as an art. Doris Humphrey, a pioneer in modern American dance, saw Shaker worship as an emotionally and psychologically charged ritual. After some study she gave her interpretation the fluid form of a work for thirteen dancers, and she named it Dance of the Chosen. *Later it was called simply* The Shakers. *Miss Humphrey danced the role of The Eldress.*

The dance was first performed in 1930 at the McMillan Theatre of Columbia University in New York City. In February 1931 it was presented downtown at the Craig Theatre. The Shakers *has often been revived, with variations on the Humphrey choreography and its accompaniment by drum, accordion and voice. Its presence in American dance repertory reflects another artistic influence of the Shakers.*

Did we, as the "original" Shakers, sense the "immortality" of Doris Humphrey's inspired work when we started rehearsals? I only remember that we approached the *Dance of the Chosen* (as it was first billed) with the same spirit of dedication that we felt to all of our director's choreographic concepts. The historical fact that the Shaker clan would gather in their immaculate Meeting Houses to pray together and then to dance out their creed "Ye shall be saved when ye are shaken free of sin," was as stimulating to us as it was to Miss Humphrey. Our costumes were to be the traditional Shaker dress: full-skirted brown burlap garments with white collars and bonnets for the women, long black robes and wide-brimmed black hats for the men.

Kneeling, our hands clasped in prayer, we formed an open square, the sisters on one side, the brethren on the other. Down the center between the sexes was an invisible line, which no sister or brother crossed, no matter how fervent their dancing would become. Together with the Eldress (danced by Doris Humphrey), who was seated upstage on a small bench, we started swaying to the sound of a woman's voice accompanied by an accordion.

Doris Humphrey as the Eldress in the finale of *The Shakers* performed in 1938 by the Humphrey-Weidman Group. Charles Weidman is the center brother in this photograph by Barbara Morgan.

As the music swelled, hymn-like, one by one the dancers rose, each man and woman tensely turning to face one another across the self-imposed barrier. Drawing back abruptly, they travel together upstage, tilting obliquely away from each other. Almost imperceptibly the tempo increases. Formations, always exact in geometrical patterns, change constantly. Gradually, the shaking rhythm begins . . . a loose, thrusting motion of the hands downward from the wrists, and a light hopping first on one foot, then on the other. A single dancer breaks loose. Letting the pulsating rhythm surge through his body, he traverses his half of the stage in an impassioned run. Stopping short of the invisible line, he wheels around and rushes back to his starting point, only to repeat the movement with mounting excitement. Others, men and women, begin to join him, each one tearing across at a different moment in the same frenzied run, a run in which they drop forward sharply, turn, fall forward again and recover with hands clasped to chest.

Now the stage seethes with bodies beating against the invisible wall in an excess of sexual frustrations and religious fervor. Suddenly, the Eldress breaks into an ecstatic "speaking in tongues": words indistinguishable for meaning, but vibrant with feeling. Dropping on their knees to face her in galvanized silence, the dancers hold their breath, and then, compulsively, begin their final ritual of self-purification: a wild thrusting of bodies towards and from the floor. This increases in intensity until all the dancers are jumping straight upwards with arms flung sideways into the air. At the height of their transport come the healing chords of "Amen" sung offstage, and the enraptured dancers fall on their knees, the Eldress alone erect, all trembling with the certitude of redemption.

Structured with the same simplicity of design that marks the superb Shaker craftsmanship of daily objects—boxes, tools, furniture of classic functional lines—Doris Humphrey's "The Shakers" achieves the ultimate in choreography.   —Ernestine Stodelle, "Flesh and Spirit at War," New Haven *Register*, March 23, 1975

The Shaker song "Simple Gifts" was one of the "musical nuggets" that inspired Aaron Copland's score for *Appalachian Spring*, a modern ballet of the 1940s by Martha Graham. The lilt of the music is captured here in the dancing of Martha Graham and Erick Hawkins. Photograph by Arnold Eagle.

In this heavenly vision a small male angel rides in a flying machine labelled "Freedom." The gift drawing in ink and watercolor on pale blue paper was "A Present from Mother Ann to Mary H. Nov. 29th 1848" at New Lebanon, New York. It is preserved at the Abby Aldrich Rockefeller Folk Art Center, Williamsburg, Virginia.

Gift Drawings Brought to Light

A major exhibition of Shaker furniture and art was featured in 1935 at the Whitney Museum of American Art in New York.

Here for the first time, will be shown a number of pictures that reveal a hitherto almost unknown and unrecognized phase of Shaker life and activity. These are the so-called inspirational drawings, dating for the most part from the 1840's and 1850's, when, it would appear, the sect was responsive to influences that may perhaps be characterized as occult. During this period were held ceremonies that could hardly have been seriously enacted except by participants elevated to ecstasy by some form of hypnosis. Such group upliftings were reflected in individual experience. Super-terrestrial voices spoke messages attuned to ethereal vibrations, and holy symbols were disclosed to eyes aware of the unseen. The urge to capture such symbols and record their form and meanings for the benefit of the faithful became so strong as to overcome the prevailing injunctions against pictorial representation of any kind. . . .

That a gift long denied release should at one leap reach so high a level of decorative and technical mastery as we discover in these drawings becomes comprehensible only when we accept some part of the doctrine of inspiration. . . . These works of art are worthy of study as independent phenomena, whose resemblance to other primitive creations is not due to any process of imitation but instead is the evidence of a kinship of the subconscious so deeply . . . implanted in humankind as to be almost unaffected . . . by discrepancies of time.

> —H. E. K. [Homer Eaton Keyes], "The Coming Shaker Exhibition in Manhattan: A Gallery Note," *The Magazine ANTIQUES*, Nov. 1935

CHANGING FORTUNES

As the Shakers at Mount Lebanon have decreased in numbers, farm labor has been taken over more and more by hired men, and smaller quantities of fruit and vegetables have been available for market. Some work in cloak-making, in poplar-weaving for fancy baskets, in the lining of oval boxes and baskets, etc. is still done at the Church family, and fancy work of various kinds is also carried on by the North family. The Center family has been absorbed by the Church family. At the Second family, chairs, foot rests and oval boxes are still made in the tradition of 75 years ago. The chairs are finished, seated and sold at the chair shop in the South family. The braids, listing or webbing used by Eldress Sarah Collins in the seating of the frames are no longer woven by the Shakers themselves, but the occupation retains much of its old time leisurely charm, and is the oldest continuous industry of any importance in the settlement.

> —Edward Deming Andrews, *The Community Industries of the Shakers*, 1932

Brother Charles Greaves (1828–1916) was an elder of the North Family at Mount Lebanon, New York. Carpentry was one of his several skills. Photograph, courtesy of Hancock Shaker Village.

The Selling of Mount Lebanon

Mount Lebanon (New Lebanon until 1861) was the most important Shaker society in the United States. It was the model for all communities of Believers, and the most populous with at one time six hundred members and eight families engaged in twenty-five industries. Only Union Village, Ohio, the parent society in the West, had that many members.

Mount Lebanon laid down the law—the famous Millenial Laws, in the moderate and extreme versions of 1821 and later revisions. The central ministry of the entire body of Believers lived and served at Mount Lebanon. Therefore it was a momentous decision in 1930 to sell forty of the most historic buildings and 300 acres of the Church and Center Families to the Lebanon School for Boys.

It was Sister Emma Neale's idea. A former teacher better known for conducting the cloak business, she decided that a school would make good use of the empty village. The Shakers were "going out," she said, and they had to provide for the future.

With their blessing a new school was established, to preserve something of the Shaker tradition. Later the name of the school was changed to Darrow after early New Lebanon Believers. David Darrow served as elder at New Lebanon until 1805 when he became the first elder of the Western societies. The second meetinghouse at New Lebanon, now remodelled as the school library (but carefully preserving the original walls of the building), was built on the site of George Darrow's house.

The few New York Shakers lived on in a great six-story dwelling until 1947. Seven years before she died at the age of 97, Sister Emma and her younger sister Sadie received a visit from Carl Carmer, a writer interested in York State folk.

The late-winter sun was promising the spring when I turned off the Pittsfield road east of Albany and saw before me, along the upward slope of a mountain, a confusion of white patches of snow and patches of a more dazzling whiteness which were Shaker houses. I drove onward and upward—past the meetinghouse with its famous curved roof—and stopped at a tall three-story frame residence.

I must have waited several minutes after I had rung the bell before the door slowly opened. I remember my surprise at seeing that the old lady with her hand on the knob was wearing the gray dress and shawl-like kerchief that have long been the Shaker sisters' costume; and my impatience with myself for being surprised.

"I hope you'll forgive a stranger's coming to call on Sunday afternoon," I said, "but I have been wanting to see you and talk to you about the Shakers for a long time." . . .

"Sunday afternoon," she said in a clear voice, "is a good time to talk. Won't you come in and climb the stairs? My sister and I are sitting in the sunlight that comes through the windows of our room on the top floor. You go first, for it will take me longer to get there than you."

I walked up the two long flights slowly. At the top stood an erect, white-haired, pink-cheeked little figure. The kerchief about her shoulders met in a fold just above her tiny waist and her gray skirt spread out voluminously below it.

"He has come to talk with us about the Shakers, Sister Emma," said the woman behind me. "I think he wants to write about us."

"Will you come in and sit down?" said the little lady. "There aren't very many Shakers left to write about."

I entered a room flooded with sunshine, a big room so clean that it smelled clean. It was simply furnished with a few slat-backed Shaker chairs, a simple desk, a straight-lined table. We all sat down and I looked at my most recent acquaintance closely. She was undoubtedly the older of the two and yet when she spoke there was a humor about the mouth, a sparkle in the eye that made her seem younger.

"There are just a few left at Watervliet," she continued, "and here we keep only a few houses open. This one is for the Church Family. They took in the members of the old Center Family years ago. And the house beyond us is where the South Family lives. They took in the Second Family. There were four others here—the Upper and Lower Canaan Families, the North and the East. They have all died out just as we are dying out now."

"You see," said the younger sister, "we used to add to our members by adopting orphan children. But when state and denominational orphan asylums became more numerous, the children who were offered to us frequently turned out to be more suited to reform schools than to our way of life."

"And now," said Sister Emma, "we take no more children and I am ninety-two and my sister is in her late eighties. But you came here to ask us questions. I suppose you want us to tell you about Shakerism."

"Very much," I said.

She paused for a moment and a reminiscent smile came to her face.

"It was a noisy religion," she said. "We used to dance in the Square Order Manner—and then there was the Quick Manner. I'm sorry that I am too old to illustrate that for you."

"Perhaps I—" began the younger sister.

"Nay," said Sister Emma with gentle emphasis and a sharp glance. "You are too old to try it again." Then she turned to me. "But if you will excuse my moving slowly I will show you how our Square Order Manner went. It was not different from your waltz in some ways." She rose and lifted the many folds of her wide-spreading gray skirt until I could see the little black-clad feet beneath them. I shall not forget how straight she was nor with what grace her tiny figure advanced and turned.

"You see," she said, smiling, "toe to heel and the other heel raised—like this."

"Yes," I said, "I see.". . .

Just as I thought it best to be leaving, Sister Emma said: "If you are going to write about us, you must surely mention Norwood's Tincture of Veratrum Viride. As you know, it is made from American hellebore and it is still one of the very best of heart remedies. We should sell much more of it than we do."

"I will surely mention it," I said. "And now I'd like to take a picture of you two with my Kodak if I may."

"I am sorry to have to refuse you," said Sister Emma. "I suppose it's all right but our religion never approved of the singling out of any members. What work we did, we did for the whole Family and no one ever claimed individual credit. I feel that a picture might be considered vanity."

"There is a little shop across the hall," said her sister. "Perhaps you would be interested in seeing some of the things the Shakers still make?"

"I would, indeed," I said.

"Then we will say good-bye to each other now," said Sister Emma, taking my hand. "I suppose it's really all right but I never enter the shop on Sunday."

From the collection of dolls in Shaker costume, brooms, needlework and furniture I finally purchased a sturdy, rush-bottomed stool. And after I paid for it I saw Sister Emma standing on the threshold but not entering. . . .

The sun was already behind the hills when I reached the main road

"Shaker Buildings in New Lebanon," from *Historical Collections of the State of New York*, by John W. Barber and Henry Howe, 1841.

again. A deep violet shadow had invaded Mount Lebanon and in it the white Shaker houses seemed to be growing luminous.

—Carl Carmer, *Listen for a Lonesome Drum*, 1936

P. T. Barnum used to buy woolen horse blankets for his circus from the Mount Lebanon Shakers.

—Clifton Johnson, "The Passing of the Shakers," *Old-Time New England*, Oct. 1934

They grew poppies, and for a time made most of the opium used in America. —Ulysses Prentiss Hedrick, *A History of Agriculture in New York State*, 1933

In 1947, Jerome Count, a lawyer, and Sybil A. Count, bought the South and West Families' buildings and property at Mount Lebanon, including the old chair factory. They founded the Shaker Village Work Group, a summer educational project for teenagers. This Shaker-oriented youth camp closed in 1969.

E. M. FORSTER CALLS AT MOUNT LEBANON

E. M. Forster, English author of A Passage to India, *got his facts mixed and his spelling wrong in this amusing but savage account of a visit to Mount Lebanon in 1947. Later, the last residents of the community moved over the mountain to Hancock Shaker village in Massachusetts.*

Two hundred years ago, Anne Lee, a Quaker of Manchester, England, went to New England and became a Shaker. She founded a sect. The early records of the Shakers are curious and show fantastic elements which have disappeared. There was an attempt to rectify Christianity in the interests of the female—an attempt also made by Mariolatry in the Middle Ages. Mother Anne made a half-hearted bid for equality with Christ, and there are hymns—not sung today—in which homage is paid to them both as the co-regents of the universe, and Adam celebrated as bisexual. This had to be dropped. The sect did not take the intransigent route of Mormonism, it dug up no plates of gold, and commended itself to its neighbours by hard work, good if dull craftsmanship, satisfactory bank-balances, honesty, and celibacy—recruiting its ranks from orphanages. It became a quiet community of men and women—simple folk who liked to feel a little different: even the simplest have this weakness. Meetings were held where sometimes they were seized by the Spirit and shook: otherwise nothing remarkable occurred.

The sect has almost died out, for its industry has been superseded by industrialism, and orphans have something better to do. But a few settlements of aged people survive or recently survived, and the friends with whom I was stopping in Massachusetts in 1947 were in touch with the most considerable of these settlements: Mount Lebanon, where Mother Anne herself had once dwelt. It was arranged that we should call at Mount Lebanon. We had with us a pleasant journalist from the *New Yorker* who had been commissioned to write the Shakers up, though I never saw his article—only what he wrote up on me. It was a twelve hours' expedition. The month was April but the weather wintry and myriads of birch trees were bare and sharp against the sky. We ascended to a broad pass with a view over sub-Alpine scenery, half covered with snow. The settlement was down hill, below the high-raised modern road. Life had shrunk into one enormous house, a huge wooden box measuring a hundred and eighty feet long and fifty feet thick, and it was five or six storeys high. We knocked at the door and an old lady peeped out and greeted us in a dazed fashion. This was Elderess Theresa. Further down the box another door opened and another old lady peeped out. This was Sister Susan and she was bidden to retire. They seemed a bit dishevelled, and it was agreed we should go away for lunch and come back again: they wished they could have entertained us. My friends were in great excitement. The experience was more romantic for them than it was for me, and the idea of home-made chairs hanging from pegs on a wall filled them with nostalgia. It was part of the "dream that got bogged," the dream of an America which should be in direct touch with the elemental and the simple. America has chosen the power that comes through machinery but she never forgets her dream. . . . Having had our lunch at a drug store, we returned.

They had smartened themselves up no end. Elderess Theresa wore a dove-coloured cape and Sister Susan's hair had been combed. Sisters Ellen, Ada, Maimie and Ruth also appeared—the first-named sensible and companionable and evidently running the place. Each had plenty of room in the vast building since the community had shrunk: it was like an almshouse where the inmates are not crowded and need not quarrel, and they seemed happy. I had a touching talk with the Elderess, now ninety-one, who had come from England. . . . She did not regret the days when Mount Lebanon had eighty inmates. "It is much better like this," she said. Her room was full of mess and mementos, all of which she misdescribed as Shaker-made. It was nothing to the mess in the apartment of Sisters Ada and Maimie, who kept kneeling without obvious reason on the carpet and crackling toilet paper at the parrot to make him dance. On their wall ticked a clock which had the face of a cat, and a cat's tail for pendulum. Up and down the enormous passages Sister Susan stalked, her raven locks flying, and gesticulating with approval on the presence of so many men. We saw the dining-room, where a place was laid, a little humorously, for Christ. We saw the communal meeting-room. Did they—er—shake ever? No—nobody shook now. Did they—er—meet here for prayer? No, said the Elderess complacently. We used to meet once a month. Now we never meet. They were in fact bone idle and did not even know it. . . .

While the New Yorker questioned them, I went out and looked at the five or six other houses which completed the original Mount Lebanon colony (Shaker houses are always in little colonies). They were empty except for ponderous wooden machinery. The ground still sloped into a view, and bright streams and pools of water twinkled at every corner. The sun shone, the snow melted, the planks steamed. The simplicity of the buildings was impressive but not interesting. I went back into the main building to meet Brother Curtis. For the sisters above described only occupied half the huge house. On each floor in the longitudinal central passage was a door, which was locked or supposed to be locked, and beyond the doors, all alone in the other half, dwelt the enigmatical Brother Curtis. He could also be reached by walking along outside. He was a healthy elderly man in overalls, very stupid from the New Yorker point of view, though probably not from his own. Much time was spent in trying to make him say something characteristic: he was understood to have different ideas on carrying in logs from the Sisters' ideas, but since he carried in the logs his ideas prevailed. Perhaps he had been interviewed before. He had a roguish twinkle. Then we took our leave. One of our party found a tin dust-pan in the attic, and was allowed to purchase it; and I myself became an object of envy because the Elderess presented me with a ruler. It is an ordinary wooden ruler, it is eighteen inches long, it rules, but little more can be said of it. We waved goodbye—Sister Susan again bursting out of her special door—and that is the last I saw of these gentle harmless people, though the New Yorker returned on the following day to consolidate his investigations. My companions were moved by them to a degree which I could not share; they were a symbol of something which America supposes herself to have missed, they were the dream that got bogged. Mount Lebanon has, I believe, now been closed down.

—E. M. Forster, "Mount Lebanon," Two Cheers for Democracy, 1951

SISTER JENNIE DEFENDS EIGHTY-ONE ROOMS

The New Yorker *writer who called on the Shakers at Mount Lebanon in 1947 in the distracting company of E. M. Forster returned the next day and had a talk with Sister Jennie Wells. She was seventy years old, sprightly, sharp-witted, and sharp-tongued. The "New Yorker," as Forster called him, knew little about Shakerism. Sister Jennie filled him in.*

"I'm trying to think where to begin," she said. "Most of our visitors these days are antique collectors, and all they're interested in is buying up what little fine old handmade Shaker furniture we have left. Why, those people would grab the chairs right out from under us if we'd let them. Our furniture is very fashionable all of a sudden, you know. I understand it's called modernistic. . . ."

Sister Jennie took him on a tour.

"I want you to see the rest of the place. Then we'll come back to the dwelling house. . . . There are only seven of us left in the North Family, and our house has eighty-one rooms. . . . The men lived in the left half and the women in the right. My stars, I hope you didn't think that we actually *lived* together!"

They started up the road.

The Great Stone Barn of the North Family, Mount Lebanon, New York (1859–1972). Photograph, courtesy of the New York State Museum.

"I'm sure there's no need to point out our barn. You couldn't very well miss it, could you? . . . It's the biggest stone barn in the whole United States. . . . The Shakers always built for permanence. We say that Shakerism can't be told: it must be lived. Still, you can learn a lot about it just from that barn.

"We're a very practical people. There's no foolishness about anything we do. Our barn was made the length it is for good reason. The men wanted to have room enough for a dozen or more loaded wagons on the floor at the road level, in case a sudden storm came up during haying. That doesn't mean much now, of course. We don't raise much hay. Our stock is down to ten milch cows and four horses. . . . The North Family farm was good-sized once—nearly a thousand acres—but now it's not much more than two hundred, including pasture and wood lots, and we have to hire two men to do the work. . . . Another thing about that barn is that it's wide enough for a big team and wagon to turn around in. The reason it's built on a slope is so hay can be hauled in at the top floor and pitched *down* to the mows. Then it's pitched *down* from there to the stock stalls below. In most barns, you know, hay has to be pitched *up*. A good many Shaker barns are built like this. Shakers have never seen any sense in fighting against gravity."

As they walked down the path, bordered by knee-high grass, the writer asked Sister Jennie how long she had been a Shaker. Practically all her life, she told him. Her mother thought she'd be better off with the Shakers than with a cruel stepfather. She grew up from the age of four with the Shakers at Groveland, the third Shaker community to "go under," and then moved to Watervliet, New York. She moved to Mount Lebanon in 1930, eight years before the Watervliet village where Mother Ann made her home was given up. The community at Mount Lebanon needed someone young and active. She gave him a challenging look.

"I might as well admit I do most of the work here—the marketing, the meal planning, the cooking, and in the winter I even tend the furnace. The truth is, I'm about the only one who can. That's in addition, of course, to making all my own clothing. Most of the others buy their clothes, which is contrary to order, but they are no longer able to make their own, so it can't be helped. Also, I keep my eye on things in general, except for finances. What little money we've accumulated over the years, mostly from the sale of property but partly from selling the things we've made, is handled by a more business-minded member, over at Hancock."

They passed six buildings that looked to the "New Yorker" big, gaunt, and empty. They made him feel uncomfortable and did not seem quite real in the setting. Sister Jennie looked up admiringly and said:

"If this were the old days, we wouldn't even be able to hear ourselves think. These buildings were about the busiest workshops you ever saw. I couldn't begin to tell you how many different trades were carried on in these shops. The North Family did weaving, dyeing, tailoring, hatmaking, shoemaking, broommaking, soapmaking, blacksmithing, metalwork, carpentry, woodworking, seed drying, and goodness knows what else. Practically every family did a lot of different things. And, of course, all the families did a good deal more than just take care of their own needs. The different families in a village used to make things for each other. They all made things to sell to the world, too.... The North Family's specialties were brooms and packaged seeds. I'll tell you something that you probably don't know. The Shakers here at Mount Lebanon were the first people in the United States to sell seeds in little packages."

As they were passing one of the former shops, a white-haired man in overalls suddenly came around the corner. He stopped, looking startled and uneasy. Sister Jennie greeted him with kindly warmth.

"This is Brother Curtis White.... He keeps me supplied with

stovewood, and he's wonderful with the chickens. Brother Curtis is sixty years old, and he's the youngest of the family."

Brother Curtis cleared his throat.

"Place was alive forty years ago. . . . You liked to work here then. I came here as an orphan when I was eleven. Started out sickly, but work made me well. Used to be I'd milk twenty cows and cut a cord of wood every day. I'd cut a cord in three hours—times I've done it in two. Been cutting wood over forty years and I've lost only two toes."

He nodded and walked away. They wandered back to the dwelling. On the way Sister Jennie described the Shaker meetinghouse, which she said was more like a ballroom or a gym.

"We had our last meeting here in Mount Lebanon in 1933, just before we sold the meetinghouse. . . . We're all too old now to march any more."

At the dwelling the writer met Sister Sarah Collins, now senile, who kept saying, "I like a new face." Eldress Rosetta Stephens told him she had come from England when she was eleven years old with Elder Frederick Evans, after his mission to England. Sister Jennie showed him her room. It was crowded with furniture, and some chairs hung from pegs on the wall. She said happily:

"There isn't a thing in this room that I'd let one of those greedy antique collectors lay a finger on, except over my dead body."

—Berton Roueché, "A Small Family of Seven," *New Yorker,* Aug. 23, 1947

The Best-preserved Home

The charming expanse of water that this Maine commune [Sabbathday Lake] borders lies some twenty miles north of Portland, where its name was derived from the habit a hunting party had of meeting Sundays on the lakeshore. In 1793 the conversion of a local dweller to Ann Lee's gospel gave the Shakers a foothold here. Within a fortnight the neighboring families were gathered in, a few months later a society had been organized.

At present the buildings and environment rank it among the best preserved Shaker homes in New England. Its ancient meetinghouse is

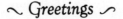

ᴖ Greetings ᴖ

To YOU, from the Society of American Shakers, who, though living among you for more than a century and a half (1774-1937) and claiming the distinction of existing longer than any other Communistic order, are yet little known and less understood.

Communism,* though as old as history itself, seems never to have gained a foothold in any community except when identified with some religious creed, hence, the Shakers credit their long existence to the religious principles of their order:-

Virgin Purity — Peace — Justice and Love, expressed in a
Celibate Life, United Inheritance, and Universal Brotherhood.

The first to recognize Sex Equality, Freedom of Thought and Religious Tolerance, the Shakers have found that "Peace that Passeth Understanding" in their Brother and Sister Relationship, realizing the while that Their's is the field for the few rather than the many, though open to all sincerely-minded persons.

Their motto, "Hands to work and Hearts to God" demands a life of Service, which finds fulfillment in the care and education of needy children (which may or may not remain with the Society when becoming of age) wholly by their own efforts, without any reimbursement by the State.

These children are early taught the art of handwork and the results of their efforts, when well done, are placed on sale to help in their support. Your patronage or contribution thus helps those who cannot care for themselves.

Let us ask you to sum up the Shakers life effort in the words of the well known poem:-

Do all the good you can,
In all the ways you can,
To all the people you can,
In every place you can,
At all the times you can,
As long as ever you can.

*Please do not confuse with Soviet Communism.

A broadside in behalf of needy children raised among Believers at Sabbathday Lake, Maine, 1935. (By Sister R. Mildred Barker)

now a fascinating museum of Shaker relics. But the most comprehensive collection of such relics, is that of the State of New York at Albany.

—Clifton Johnson, "The Passing of the Shakers," *Old-Time New England,* Oct. 1934

The Shakers are looked upon, ofttimes, as a wealthy people, this impression being given because they are obliged to keep their premises in good condition, as well as whatever comes into their possession. Economy is one of the strictest rules, and no Shaker is supposed to mar or deface any thing belonging to them or to anyone else. They have always been thrifty and find a way to earn their living. There have been, and are today, fine mechanics among the brothers, who aid in repair work or whatever they can do to keep our homes in good condition. . . .

Worldly ideas are not practiced in dress, the simplicity of our dress bringing much respect to us from the world outside our home, and we appreciate the way we meet kindness and courtesy wherever we go. . . .

Another fact to be made plain is the confession of sin. It does not bring harm to anyone to admit wrong doing, or correct human imperfections, or talk over problems that bother mentally, discouragements, etc. Everyone expects children to admit the truth in childish misdemeanors. The Shakers believe that we are all children of God, and, to be pure in heart, we must keep our hearts free from all that God can not own and bless. —Sister Gennie Coolbroth, *Facts about the Shakers, 1794–1933*, Sabbathday Lake, Maine, 1933

Recalling Shakertown at Pleasant Hill, Kentucky

The Society had among its members men and women from all walks and callings in life. There was no particular need that could not be filled within the Society by men and women skilled in their line of endeavor when they "lived in the world." Then too, the Shakers would especially train in college such youth in the colony as showed particular aptitude in the arts and sciences.

Wm. Pennebaker was the physician, while his brother, Frank Pennebaker, was the dentist. William refused to wear the Shaker garb.

The steamboat Blue Wing, plied between Louisville and the Shaker wharf at the ferry. This gave them an outlet to the markets on the Ohio and Mississippi rivers. In 1843 the Steamer Ocean served them.

When the Shakers fared forth it was a rule they went in threes. No reason is assigned for this custom, though there was probably a good one.

The Shakers owned prize winning cattle. Henry Clay was a friend of the Shakers and when he imported livestock he included in his importation an order for the Society. Their Shorthorns were famous. They had what was known as the "Wild Eyed" strain. At the Mercer County Fairs over 60 years ago the Shakers were contenders in the Shorthorn rings . . . [and] carried off their share of the honors.

Dr. Francis Pennebaker with a group of sisters on the stoop of the West Family house at Pleasant Hill. Style of dress appears optional, with a symbolic casting off of a bonnet on the windowsill. Photograph, courtesy of Shaker Village of Pleasant Hill.

It is an interesting fact that they never raised mules or used them. They claimed that the mule was not one of God's natural creatures, but a man-created animal. Their religious scruples seemed also to cause them not to breed horses, yet they used stallions as beasts of burden. The Pennebaker family never seemed, at least in later years, to observe this rule.

Old newspaper files reveal that in the spring they offered the services of their inbred stallions and jacks to the public.

An interesting feature in connection with the construction of the Shaker residence houses is that the doors are locked only from the inside. The circumstances of no one being out of the house at night made it unnecessary to unlock the door from without. Bars were provided for extra strength in fastening doors. All the residence houses have two front doors and two side doors. Women entered the right door and ascended the stairs on the right. The men used the left door and stairs.

Marcus Gregory, Elder of the shoe shop, received his orders to have his workers make summer and winter shoes to the number and of sizes necessary. The women wore cloth shoes very largely in the house.

High up on either side of the church room are small rooms where the monitors took position and looked out through a louver. A brother in one and a sister in the other. They would observe their sex and note any irregularity of conduct. Some means of punishment or admonition was sure to follow a slip in conduct.

In 1817 the little stone cottage was turned into a tavern and Family Deacon Tyler Baldwin was appointed its keeper. It ran as an inn until 1836 when the Society declared that conducting an inn for pay was not in accordance with their principles and it was discontinued. However, in the '70's they again received approved guests and about 1890 to 1910 their entertainment was proverbial for its good qualities.

Elder Micajah Burnett was a man of education, an architect and civil engineer. The stately office building was designed by him. He planned and laid out the spiral stairways. In woodwork it is as outstanding in its ingenious trussing as the stone stairway at the Old Capitol building at Frankfort. Here we let the records speak what the Scribe set down: "January 10, 1879—Micajah Burnett demised this day. He was an accomplished civil engineer, a master mathematician, a competent surveyor, a mechanic and machinist of the First Order and good millwright, and withal, a firmly established, honest hearted christian Shaker, beloved, respected and honored by all."

The West Lot . . . was occupied by Swedes with Andrew Bloomberg as Elder; Odie Olston, Farm Deacon; and Eric Larixson, as Live Stock Deacon. There was, no doubt, two or three female officers.

Looking down the well of one of a pair of circular stairways in the Trustees' Office at Pleasant Hill, Kentucky. Photograph, courtesy of Shaker Village of Pleasant Hill.

THE END COMES

Unluckily, and one might say inevitably, the passage of the years brought changes inimical to the welfare of the organization. . . . The end was near, and the survivors, realizing this, induced one of their number, Dr. W. F. Pennebaker, a prominent member of the Society, to deed their remaining land, some 1,800 acres, to Mr. George Bohon of Harrodsburg,

One of the last sisters at Pleasant Hill gazes from the east door of the Centre Family house. The high arched doorways are typical of western Shaker architecture. Photograph, courtesy of Shaker Village of Pleasant Hill.

on condition that he would provide for them in every way during their respective lives. Mr. Bohon undertook the trust, but later reconveyed to Dr. Pennebaker 650 acres of land for the maintenance of himself and his family. The latter, when he came to make a will, left this land in trust for the founding of the Pennebaker Home for Girls.

The dissolution of the Society took place in Sept. 1910 and later with the passing of Dr. Pennebaker and Mary Settles, a well known Elderess and teacher in the Society, the doings of the Shakers passed into the realm of forgotten things. Upon the dissolution of the Society all of the eleven members signed the agreement.

—Daniel M. Hutton, *Old Shakertown and the Shakers: The Sacred "Yea" and "Nay" of Their Gentle Voices Are Silent,* 1936

After its dissolution in 1910, Shakertown at Pleasant Hill languished for half a century until two men and a government agency set out to re-

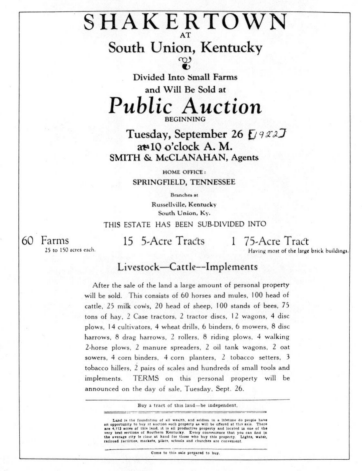

SHAKERTOWN

AT

South Union, Kentucky

Divided Into Small Farms
and Will Be Sold at

Public Auction

BEGINNING

Tuesday, September 26 [1922]
at 10 o'clock A. M.
SMITH & McCLANAHAN, Agents

HOME OFFICE:
SPRINGFIELD, TENNESSEE

Branches at
Russellville, Kentucky
South Union, Ky.

THIS ESTATE HAS BEEN SUB-DIVIDED INTO

60 Farms   15 5-Acre Tracts   1 75-Acre Tract
25 to 150 acres each.   Having most of the large brick buildings.

Livestock—Cattle—Implements

After the sale of the land a large amount of personal property will be sold. This consists of 60 horses and mules, 100 head of cattle, 25 milk cows, 20 head of sheep, 100 stands of bees, 75 tons of hay, 2 Case tractors, 2 tractor discs, 12 wagons, 4 disc plows, 14 cultivators, 4 wheat drills, 6 binders, 6 mowers, 8 disc harrows, 8 drag harrows, 2 rollers, 8 riding plows, 4 walking 2-horse plows, 2 manure spreaders, 2 oil tank wagons, 2 oat sowers, 4 corn binders, 4 corn planters, 2 tobacco setters, 3 tobacco hillers, 2 pairs of scales and hundreds of small tools and implements. TERMS on this personal property will be announced on the day of sale, Tuesday, Sept. 26.

Buy a tract of this land—be independent.

Land is the foundation of all wealth, and seldom in a lifetime do people have an opportunity to buy at auction such property as will be offered at this sale. There are 4,113 acres of this land, it is all productive property and located in one of the very best sections of Southern Kentucky. Every convenience that you can find in the average city is close at hand for those who buy this property. Lights, water, railroad facilities, markets, pikes, schools and churches are convenient.

Come to this sale prepared to buy.

This great public auction in 1922 was preceded a few years earlier by an auction of Shaker furniture.

store it. Earl Wallace and James L. Cogar, first curator at Colonial Williamsburg in Virginia, formed a nonprofit educational corporation that raised funds to buy the property back from ten owners. Long term aid from the Area Redevelopment Administration allowed the gradual replacement of the modern aspect of the old village—the paved roads, utility poles, gas pumps, signs. The restoration was opened to the public in 1968, and today is a National Historic Landmark, open the year round, with exhibition areas, a conference center, dining room, crafts shops, and guest quarters in old Shaker rooms.

FACTS AND FICTION

The First Modern History

What to make of a diminished thing, muses Marguerite Fellows Melcher as she launches into the first modern history of the Shakers, published in 1941. This descendant of a Shaker great-aunt and a Shaker great-uncle takes a sympathetic view of what she calls The Shaker Adventure.

In 1949 The Shaker Adventure *was the only book listed under* Shaker *in the Standard Catalog for Public Libraries.*

By 1953 when a supplement was issued, The People Called Shakers *by Edward Deming Andrews was included, having been published that year. A more objective and comprehensive history than Melcher's and enriched by the author's collection of primary materials, Andrews' book gained authority in the field.*

Both pioneering works were joined two years later by an analytical account published in France by a sociologist and former monk, Henri Desroche. Like Friedrich Engels, Desroche had never visited a Shaker community. His book became available in English in 1971 as The American Shakers: From Neo-Christianity to Presocialism, *translated and edited by Williams College Professor John K. Savacool.*

A Master Bibliography

A steadily growing interest in the Shakers and their way of life has increased the production of printed materials to such an extent that a comprehensive bibliography has become imperative.

Thus a new Shaker bibliography in two volumes was announced and published in 1977. Compiler Mary L. Richmond devoted many years to searching for obscure material, checking uncertain information, and concisely annotating works from the eighteenth century to the 1970s. Legends and errors were corrected in the long scholarly labor that resulted in a listing of 4,000 items in Shaker Literature: A Bibliography. *The first Shaker bibliography published in 1905 by J. P. MacLean contained 523 entries.*

Pages from Shaker Novels

A REFUGE FOR KATE

In the Sabbath hush before the ten o'clock service in the large white meeting-house, city folk began to arrive at the Shaker village [Mount Lebanon] from Lebanon Springs, famous for its gayest of summer colonists. They came on horseback, in every kind of stylish conveyance, and afoot; for the noted resort of wealth and fashion was less than three miles away.

A clear blue sky, and a cool morning breeze from the mountains in the north, brought a larger Sunday crowd than usual to see the Shakers at their strange service of worship.

But this day, no dust-cloud settled over the village with the coming of the worldly throng. Brother Jethro had made a sprinkling device for a water cart which the wagon makers, with Elder Joseph's consent, had worked until midnight to finish; and for the first time, the rose-bowered lane had been sprinkled from end to end.

But from end to end, the lane took on for the Shakers the festive air of a place of ungodliness. Rambling along it with other vehicles came a coach and four, followed closely by another, and presently by a stage, to turn noisily in the dooryard of the Second Family's overflow community known as the South Branch, and to rumble back to wait at the church.

Everywhere carriages stopped; and men and women in colorful dress got out to chatter and exclaim, and to peer in at windows, even the windows of the dwellings. Here and there the more adventurous prowled through the idle shops, which were never locked; and before time for service, several girls had filled their arms with roses gathered from the bushes at the roadside.

The Believers appeared and walked sedately to meeting in their Sunday best; the men in plain straw hats, drab coats, blue vests, white cotton stocks and blue-and-white-striped trousers; the women in their brown dresses and their bonnets of palm leaf covered with reddish brown silk. They were trailed by visitors who laughed at them and made offensive comments, to which neither the Brothers nor the Sisters gave the slightest heed.

In the absence of all four members of the Ministry, each of whom had gone on a mission to some other community of Believers, Elder Joseph had sent an aged Brother, and Eldress Hannah an old Sister, to wait in the church behind locked doors to guard the sacred place against any danger of vandalism.

All the Shakers who were free to attend service, all the novitiates and indentured children, timed their departure from the dwellings so that each family's groups could take their places in the line of churchgoers, the Brothers falling in behind Brothers and the Sisters behind Sisters.

The men, who led the way, had begun to press quietly through the crowd waiting at the meeting-house, and the women were turning in from the lane with Eldress Hannah at their head, when a youth surrounded by girls with roses in their arms caught sight of Kate and began to bow and scrape, and to sing to her softly: "Pretty Mistress Polly Perkins, Howdy-do! Howdy-do!" A few other visitors took up the popular song in a merry mood, as a way was cleared to the Sisters' entrance door; and the singing caused an outburst of laughter.

Kate could not repress a smile at the fun-making youth, until she saw John Talbot among the visitors. Then she moved on to the meeting-house with head bowed and eyes downcast, in as devout an attitude as any of the other Sisters. But attention had been called to her by the incident, and another visitor exclaimed, as he pointed a finger at her:

"Cheeks painted, by God!"

Janet Hathaway, the indentured girl, who was walking directly behind her, turned to him boldly; and in a loud, defiant voice answered:

"Yea, and by God only!"

More laughter greeted the quick retort; and Kate's flushed cheeks grew rosier still as her embarrassment increased. Many of the older Sisters cast sternly reproving glances at the pert, comely Janet; and a few of the younger ones seemed to be trying to keep their faces straight.

John Talbot, who had come to wait at the church, stood laughing among the visitors until he saw that the girl singled out and made conspicuous by the two gay youths was Kate. . . . A moment before he had felt contempt for the Shakers and their pious airs, and had rather enjoyed seeing them baited and laughed at. Now he thrust himself in among the girls with the roses until he and the man who was still singing were face to face.

"What church are you and your friends here members of?" he asked.

"What's that to you?" the young fellow sent back flippantly.

"I'm curious!" Talbot answered. "I'd like to know what brand of faith has bred you men and women and sent you here to insult these worshippers of another faith on their way to religious service!"

There was a sudden hush; and Kate glanced toward John anxiously. She saw the man to whom he had spoken glare menacingly and grow very red, while the girls about Talbot stared at him shocked and sober-faced. But they all turned and moved away. Kate was amazed by the number of visitors. Fully a hundred must be already waiting, she thought, to push in behind the Believers; and a hundred more, who had been rambling about the village, were hurrying now to join the others.

At both doors, after the Sisters had gone in at one and the Brothers at the other, the men and women from out in the world were allowed to enter together. For them there were long benches in tiers close against the east wall; but no seats were provided for the worshippers, who stood on the bare floor, the men facing the women across a considerable unobstructed space.   —Robert W. McCullough, *Me and Thee,* 1937

SHAKER BOY

"The fascinating life of the Shakers has been little used by novelists," said the dust jacket of Dancing Saints *when the novel was published in 1943. It tells the story of a boy, divided from his sisters and brothers, who is placed in a declining Shaker family.*

Orville felt very manly on his first march to the Sisters' retiring room, in his new Sabbath clothes and linen collar fastened with a bone stud. Even the Sisters' room had a second door. When he crossed the threshold, he saw the Sisters standing behind their chairs, facing the door. "Good evening," they welcomed the small procession. . . .

Facing the Sisters was a row of chairs for the Brothers, a five-foot space between the rows. They all sat and drew large white handkerchiefs from their pockets to spread on their knees. . . .

Eben faced Hannah; Caleb, Eunice; and the others filled the rows according to executive position. Orville in an end chair found himself looking straight at Thankful, but now that she was in the Sisters' retiring room she was wearing a cap, not quite like the Believers' caps, but white and sheer. Maybe he couldn't see her ears, but they hadn't covered her hands. . . .

Mark started a hymn. They beat time on their handkerchiefs and sang heartily. . . .

Then came conversation which was supposed to be agreeable but needn't be instructive. Thankful, quite at ease, offered the information that measles were prevalent in Hadonsfield and were dangerous to the eyes. . . .

[She] said that Albert had been in Cedarsville that morning and seen a house burned down. Not a thing was saved.

Finally to his hesitant tongue came a question he could ask her. What was the most members to live at The Cedars?

She replied promptly. In 1847 a great revival swept through this region and in six months four hundred and three souls were ingathered, making a total in Church, East, West, and South Families of five hundred and twelve. One hundred and eighty-four lived in the Church Family. Then there were two dwellings, the novitiates' house was full, and the guesthouse often crowded. The Ministry lived over the big meetinghouse room, the Elders and Eldresses in the brick house, and the Trustees in rooms over the store as they did now. Deacons and Deaconesses had had rooms near the departments of which they'd charge. There used to be a bishop over two or three communities, but for a long time there hadn't been enough members to need a bishop, and for nearly twenty years there'd been no Cedars Ministry. . . .

[Thankful] understood that Orville's present task was making some new beds for the infirmary. Wasn't Amos a wonderful doctor? Orville said that he was, and did she know of the new ointment Amos had made for burns? She hadn't heard of it. He went into details of its healing powers and the Family's decision to sell it in the store, proud that he could tell her something she hadn't known.

Altogether it was a pleasant evening, and he began on Monday to think of things to tell Thankful the next Sunday. But he found that at each "invitation meeting" the Brothers moved down a chair, and the next Sabbath, Hannah being away, he sat opposite Eunice. Raymond talked with Thankful, and her pretty smile came and went almost continuously.

—Ann George Leslie, *Dancing Saints*, 1943

THE BELIEVERS

A Turbulent Saga of the American Frontier
and the Love That Defied Age-Old Beliefs
Against Unendurable Odds

OUTCASTS!

"I only know for certain that there was no one else for me, and that I had only to look upon him to feel tender and soft and loving toward him, bending near him with a yearning to touch him, always."

Rebecca Fowler had always loved Richard Cooper. She could not remember a time when she had not loved and trusted him and followed where he led. And when, with marriage, she followed him to the land of The Believers—an agonizing world where husbands and wives lived apart—she trusted her love to see them through their bizarre, heartless ordeal. For only one hope lay open—if she dared to betray a vow she held sacred.

—Janice Holt Giles, *The Believers*, cover, paperback
edition, 1976 (first published 1957)

The time of our gathering was in September. My Journals begin in that month. I do not know why I was minded to keep one. It may have been to ease my troubled heart. Or it may have been because journal-keeping was so common among the Believers I caught the infection. I have forgotten the reason, and it does not much matter now. But here they are, old, brown-backed, and here is the date of the first entry, September 10, 1811. It says:

We were this day gathered into order. Richard and I are assigned to Brother Rankin's old home with the others of the Novitiate. Already we are called the East Family because the house lies east of the Church Family Dwelling.

With us in this house are Permilla and Thomas, Henry and Lacey

Akins, Robert and Annie Jewett, William and Amanda Steel, John and Viney Parks, and others. Set over us as spiritual leaders we have Samuel Shannon and Priscilla Stewart. Richard is appointed a deacon to have charge of the men. No deaconess is appointed. Sister Priscilla will have charge of the work of the women herself. I suppose they do not think any of us worthy yet. I am appointed to the washhouse for my first duty. This is the hardest duty we have, and I think it is to chasten my unbelieving spirit. It does not matter. I am able and stout to work and what Sister Priscilla does not know is that washing has ever been a pleasure to me.

Sent to us to be over the entire village along with Brother Benjamin are Joseph Allen and the sisters, Molly Goodrich and Mercy Pickett. They are all from the East. They appear to be godly and trustworthy.

Our home is to be torn down so that the lumber may be used in the village. The land remains in our name, but its use is given to the Society. We have been required to hand in an inventory of everything brought with us and given to the Society, so that should we ever decide to leave, what is rightfully ours may be given back to us. We were not required to sign the Covenant, since we are not yet admitted to full membership, but we did sign an agreement that we came willingly and donated both ourselves and our property to the further use of the Believers. We had also to sign that we had paid in full all debts and obligations and that there was no call upon us by the world.

Our furnishings have been distributed where they were needed. The bed in which I am to sleep is not my own. I have nothing of my own any longer, except the clothing which I wear, and except for a change even that has been taken for use with others who had less. We are allowed two dresses each, two shifts, two caps and two bonnets.

Permilla, Lacey, Amanda, Annie Jewett and poor old Viney Parks are in the room with me. A wall was torn out between two rooms to make this large bedroom which we share. There is another, larger bedroom which houses eight women. Across the hall is a similar arrangement for the men. . . . It all seems very strange to me. . . .

I had long since resigned myself, as best I could, for resignation does not come easy to me. But no one can know until the time comes how he is going to feel when parted from all that is familair to him, when he goes into a life so new that there is nothing about it known or apprehended. It is a desolate feeling. It would be desolate enough to go hand in hand with one's husband, but there would at least be the comfort of knowing he stood beside you. Instead of that comfort, there was the certain knowledge that never again would Richard stand beside me . . . that so long as we lived he was no longer my husband. He was a man of the Shakers, and my thoughts were supposed never to linger on him, nor my ways to be joined with his. . . .

Cassie, Sampson and Jency went with us. Richard called them into the house the night before the removal. He had made out papers of manumission to give to them. He explained to them what we were going to do. "But you need not go with us," he told them. "Those papers I have just given you set you free. You can go where you will—or you can come with us if you'd rather."

Cassie folded her paper. "I ain't aimin' to go nowhurs. I goin' with Miss Becky. I been give to her, an' I s'pose to tend her. An' that's whut I aims to do. Sampson, you aims to do the same."

Then Richard explained that they would never work for us again, that their work would be assigned to them in the village. "Don't make no difference to me," Cassie said firmly, "I goin' whur Miss Becky is at."

Richard gave up and offered to keep the papers for them. "But remember," he said, "if you ever want to leave, all you have to do is ask for your paper and you can go."

In great relief Cassie and Sampson handed back their papers, sighing to be rid of them. Jency held on to hers, however. "Hit's mine," she said.

"It's yours," Richard told her, "but not to play with. This is a legal paper, and someday you may want it very badly."

Cassie, Sampson, and Jency went to live in the Black Family.

In our part of the country Brother Benjamin thought we would do well to raise purebred cattle, to make a good quality of whiskey, to make straw hats for sale, and especially he thought it would be profitable for us to develop a seed industry. Those were his plans for us.

Most of us were hand-minded; that is, we had no talent for leadership, but since our leadership came from the East, that was nothing to worry about. . . .

As we passed from the meeting room in orderly file, I saw Annie Jewett, who walked ahead of me, brush softly against Robert, who somehow was near her, saw her hand touch his and saw him jerk as if a coal of fire had touched him, draw away. I did not blame her, though I would not have dared touch Richard so. But I knew what had made her touch him. We were supposed to report any such breaking of rules. I would have cut out my tongue before reporting it. Let them see for themselves what went on under their noses! . . .

Brother Samuel rose to lead us forth in the dance, but before he had had time to signal us, Richard stood. "There is one among us," he said, "who has need for humiliation. I accuse Sister Rebecca of pride and arrogance of spirit, of lack of faith and zeal." He paused, and I thought he would go on and accuse me of tempting him. But, white-faced and suddenly wavering on his feet, as if ill, he stopped and sat down.

Every eye was turned on me and in Sister Priscilla's there was a triumphant gleam. Brother Samuel asked me to stand. "In what way, Brother Richard, has Sister Rebecca been guilty of pride and arrogance?"

Richard's eyes, also, were fixed on me, stonily. "In steadfastly refusing to entreat for full membership, for complete dedication. In holding material things more important than the salvation of her soul."

It was Prissy who cried "Woe," first, but it was taken up by many others within a few moments, and the cries of "Woe, woe, woe" echoed round and round the room. If you have not stood in the center of a ring, ringed about by people who have suddenly become your judges, and listened to their cries of shame and contempt, there is no way you can know the feeling. It is a shriveling experience, all the more shriveling for me because my own husband had brought it about. I would not have believed he could do it, that he so wanted to become a full member that he would take this way of forcing it. . . . The cries, at first piercing me and hurting, slowly became simply a sound, a concert of sound, which beat on my ears, but no longer entered my soul. I stood, alone, through it all, knowing that now I was truly guilty of pride and arrogance. For it was pride which came to my rescue. . . .

Brother Samuel was kind. He called for the cries to cease, and said, "We are all equally guilty. Let us kneel and pray." Then he led us forth in the dance, and Richard was the most abandoned of all, whirling time and again into a single dance, leaving the circle, spinning, as if under some spell. . . . At the end he was as white and shaken as when he had accused me, and only sorrow showed on his face.

—Janice Holt Giles, *The Believers*, 1957

In the original version of The Believers, *Mrs. Giles's editor recalls, Richard died in a fire or accident. The author changed the ending when she learned that a divorce was possible at that time if a husband or wife joined the Shakers. Rebecca left the community and married the teacher who had been the leader of the School Group, although he was not a Believer. Mrs. Giles died in 1979.*

A Shaker Hoax

Peck, Robert Newton. *A Day No Pigs Would Die.* New York: Alfred A. Knopf, 1972. 150 pp.

A charming and earthy story laid in rural Vermont. The young boy's father is supposed to be a Shaker, although married and living with his wife. There was no Shaker community in Vermont; reference to a Shaker meeting in Learning, Vermont, is purely fictitious as are some other Shaker references. The reader is assured that the author "was raised in the Shaker way."   —Mary L. Richmond, *Shaker Literature: A Bibliography,* Vol. II, No. 2561

Don't take this book for gospel. Certainly not for Shaker Gospel. Confronted with Shaker fact, Mr. Peck recently confessed to this reviewer that the "Shaker Way" described in his best-selling novel about his Vermont boyhood is fiction. The Shaker part, he says, is "only incidental." Yet there are at least thirty references to things Shaker in the 150-page book. And Shaker background is plugged on the dust jacket and in a note about the author stating that he was "raised in the Shaker tradition like many Vermont folk." This is news to many Vermont folk as well as to the State Historical Society, where there is evidence of Vermont Pilgrims, Dorrilites, Millerites and other sects, but not of Vermont Shakers. . . .

All this invention in an otherwise wholesome story caricatures Believers and the true Shaker way. . . . Shakers have no monopoly on good, but not all good people are Shakers or have the right to that hallowed name. . . . It is too bad that *A Day No Pigs Would Die* has been promoted as a book about personal experience in a Shaker family. Most "world's people" . . . know too little about genuine Shakerism to recognize the errors and opportunism in Mr. Peck's bold characterization of his family as Shakers.   —Flo Morse, review of *A Day No Pigs Would Die,* *Shaker Quarterly,* Winter 1972

Acting Like Shakers

FOUR PLAYS

Old journals of the North Union, Ohio, society provided the incidents for a three-act play with songs and dances, More Love, Brother, *by Miriam Ann Cramer, produced at Cain Park in Cleveland in the summer of 1945. In her foreword, the playwright says she was intrigued by one diary's disclosure that once the Covenant was usurped and returned only after a compromise.*

A local minister disapproved of her interpretation.

It was an attempt to portray the practices and principles of the Shaker movement which flourished around these Shaker Lakes for almost a century. The play was, of course, fictitious, having no historical basis except perhaps a clash of personalities and a struggle for power which took place in one of the societies in the south of this state . . . there was also a love element. . . . But all in all the play seemed such a caricature of Shakerism that I was impelled to look a little more closely at the history of this religious sect. From the play one would get the impression that these Shakers were not only queer and fanatical, but perhaps demented. Such, however, was not the case. . . . These Shakers lived calmly, serenely, unpretentiously, industriously, while at the same time possessing a keen sense of moral reponsibility for their acts.

> —The Reverend John Schott, from a sermon preached at Fairmount Presbyterian Church, Cleveland, Feb. 24, 1946

Rose in the Wilderness, *a play by Marguerite F. Melcher, author of* The Shaker Adventure, *was well received when it was produced in January 1949 by the Abbe Practical Workshop at the Master Institute in New York City. The play inspects the fading fortunes and failing spirituality of a Shaker community in the 1860s. Its Prologue and Epilogue, in which "An Artist" appears, are based on the actual sale in 1902 to an artist of the old Enfield, New Hampshire, Shaker meetinghouse. In her book Mrs. Melcher notes that the purchaser was Augustus Saint-Gaudens. But it was his brother and assistant, Louis, and his sculptor-wife Annetta, who moved the 1793 meetinghouse to a hilltop in Cornish, New Hampshire. (See Robert P. Emlen,* Historic New Hampshire, *Fall, 1975.)*

For this play Doris Humphrey provided a vivid dance.

> *SIMPLE GIFTS*, Shaker ceremonies,
> songs, dances, dir. by Kenneth Ca-
> vander, on Thurs-Sun to Mar 18 at
> 8. Thtr. of the Open Eye, 316 E
> 88th, 534-6363.

The tale [*Simple Gifts*] centers around Eli, a worldly man with an apparently bad marriage, who along with his wife, joins the Shakers after coming to see one of the services. Eli is not a skeptic—he really wishes to see a better world—but he is a backslider. Sex is not something he can easily give up, nor can he make himself see visions, the "gifts" from the other world incorporated into Shaker services after Mother Ann's death.

Eli's presence gives Cavander a chance to discuss the quiet question that always arises when people get past the Shakers' achievements: How much cheating and how did they cope? It also gives him a chance to be remarkably unsentimental about the society. Most of *Simple Gifts* is concerned with the social control used to keep believers together, to prevent backsliding, and to harness sex. . . .

His primary interest in psychology has totally obscured the social context. . . . The Shakers were as much a social movement as a religion. They reached their height just as proximate New England communities became mill towns, and the contrast between Shaker industry and industrialization embodied the philosophical differences that drove people to separate themselves from the world. Cavander doesn't see this and so misses the basic integrity of Shaker works. He doesn't seem to understand the relationship between Shaker belief and Shaker products.

> —Terry Curtis Fox, "Simplified Gifts," *Village Voice*,
> March 19, 1979

Sedate and austere as was this sect, Shakertown [at Pleasant Hill, Kentucky] was not entirely devoid of romance. Occasionally the sly young god, Cupid, crept into the realms of Shakerism and played havoc with its tenants.

Some years ago two gifted young men of Harrodsburg took advantage of this fact and wrote a charming little musical comedy called *Amor; or, The Pretty Shakeress*.

The composer of the music was L. C. Walter, a pupil of the Royal Conservatory of Music at Leipsic, Germany; the author of the libretto was Henry Cleveland Wood, who has written for many of the leading magazines. . . .

In this production are preserved many of the quaint customs, hymns, religious dances, and the system of supervision of the older Shakers over the younger and less serious minded ones. It very strikingly brings out the struggle between the spiritual marriage to the Lamb and the carnal marriage to the flesh.   —Daniel M. Hutton, *Old Shakertown and the Shakers: The Sacred "Yea" and "Nay" of Their Gentle Voices Are Silenced*, 1936

SHAKER HOMES

In 1949 Life *went to a Shaker community.*

On a well-kept hill near East Canterbury, N.H. is a rambling cluster of big frame buildings. One hundred years ago this was the home of 150 members of the United Society of Believers, called Shakers by their neighbors because of their energetic form of worship—a kind of frenetic marching which often inspired them to leap, jerk, and roll on the floor for hours. At their peak the Shakers numbered about 6,000 members and operated 18 colonies. Today Canterbury is one of three tiny settlements still holding out, with a total U.S. population of less than 50. (Others are at Pittsfield, Mass., and Sabbathday Lake, Maine.) Canterbury's farm has shrunk from 3,500 acres to 1,500. Its last male member died 10 years ago

Shaker Village at Canterbury, New Hampshire, 1979. Photograph, courtesy of John E. Auchmoody.

and only 16 women live there now. Shy and old (average age: about 60), they scatter out, one or two to a house, in summertime to give the place an illusion of its former bustle. Too old for shaking, they still wear their reverent garb and practice their famous habits of neatness and practicality, which once made them one of the strangest but most noble and prosperous religious sects in the U.S....

But with the coming of the industrial revolution, they found that their kind of "perfect" society was not good enough. As industrialism grew, the Shakers crumbled. For some reason the men died first, leaving their women to carry on.

> —"The Shakers: A Strict and Utopian Way of Life Has Almost Vanished," LIFE, March 21, 1949

A sympathetic public is prone to pity us and deplore the passing of the Shaker homes as a proof that Shakerism has failed. We are not depressed. It is all in the process of evolution. Shakerism was founded on revelation and truth and is progressive. The material homes may fail but ... the good lives on forever.

In the early days the knowledge of Shakerism was confined to its boundaries, but today it is broadcast through the world. The light and truth of its revelation is a working factor of many religious movements. The principles are preached in the pulpits, broadcast through the news columns, become a part of the technique of the industrial combines and weave themselves into the philanthropic care of the aged, and into the charitable homes for boys and girls.

We have been well compensated in the gratitude expressed by the boys and girls for whom we have cared, to whom we gave a good grammar school education, training in household and farm industries and gently instilling into their young lives a code of Christian morals and manners. The early impressions of training, kindness and love have followed them through life. The seed was sown and is bearing fruit. One sows, another reaps.

> —Eldress Emma B. King, *A Shaker's Viewpoint*, East Canterbury, New Hampshire, 1956

Our Shaker homes have been like caskets of priceless jewels where precious human souls were dedicated to a life of unselfish and unstinting service—each giving of his heart and hand—loving not with a selfish love but with a universal love, consecrating and re-consecrating his life and his soul, dedicated to making the Kingdom of Heaven a living, personal reality.

> —Eldress Marguerite Frost, *The Shaker Story*, Canterbury, New Hampshire, 1963

Sister R. (for Ruth) Mildred Barker in Cleveland, 1960. Photograph, courtesy of the United Society of Shakers, Sabbathday Lake, Maine.

Revival Due When Down to Five

When Sister Mildred Barker, Co-Trustee of the Shaker colony at Sabbathday Lake, Maine, visited the Shaker Historical Society in October, 1960, she commented on the Shaker membership. "We have fourteen members at Sabbathday Lake, eleven members at the East Canterbury, New Hampshire colony, and two members at the Hancock, Massachusetts, colony. Although the Hancock colony was recently sold for use as a Shaker Museum, the two members are being maintained in that town for the present time. Of the fourteen members at Sabbathday Lake, two are in their thirties and we have a young girl who may be permitted to sign the Covenant—if she so chooses—when she is twenty-one."

In accordance with Shaker principles, life at the colonies is simple but active. While most of the land at Sabbathday Lake is rented out, the one remaining Brother, eighty-eight year old Delmer Wilson, manages the farming operations. Sister Mildred, who is sixty-three, drives one of the two late model cars owned by the colony into the nearby town to do the necessary shopping. In addition to their household duties, the Sisters make candy, aprons and other items to be sold in the shops that are maintained at both colonies. . . .

Sister Mildred, always serene and tranquil, was alert and well-informed. There are four television sets at Sabbathday Lake and each member has a radio. The kitchen is equipped with all modern appliances and in the laundry the old washing machine, devised by the Shakers, stands idle, and automatic washers and driers are now used.

And what of the future? The Shakers are not inclined to make conjectures concerning their future but perhaps some of the members believe as Brother Maxwell Macklin believed when he wrote: "Soon the time will come when we may see whether Mother Ann's prediction of a revival when the numbers are down to five, proves correct. I am not aware of any errors thus far in any of her predictions." But Sister Mildred, during her unusual visit, observed only that past estimates of the end of Shakerism have been proven wrong.

"The principles and ideals which the Shakers were first to expound have gone out into the world and, like a pebble dropped into the water, we cannot measure the distance of the influence they have borne. First in so many things we now take for granted—sex equality, religious tolerance, and so forth—Shakerism is not dying out, nor is it a failure."

—Mary Lou Conlin, *The North Union Story*, 1961

> The Shaker life
> is dying, but
> its gifts endure
> —*US* magazine, Sept. 1978

The Last of the Old Brethren

In 1961, Elder Delmer Wilson died at the age of eighty-eight at Sabbathday Lake, Maine. This last of the old Shaker brethren was a one-

Elder Delmer Wilson with a good season's work: 1,083 carriers, shaped under
steam around oval forms. Photograph, courtesy of the United Society of Shakers, Sabbathday Lake, Maine.

*man-band of a Believer who kept the faith for almost a lifetime, having
been brought to the community with his brother at the age of nine. Until
his final illness he wrote in the diary he kept for seventy-five years, su-
perintended the farm and orchard, and made the famous oval boxes. He
was also a photographer and painter. His many contributions to the
Maine Shaker Village he loved included building a water tower and a
small garage for the community's first car, a 1910 Selden. This was the
last building constructed by a Shaker brother.*

A New Shaker Publication

Shaker Quarterly, Vol. I, No. 1, Spring, 1961–to date. Sabbathday Lake,
Poland Spring, Me.: Published by the United Society [Portland, Me.,
Anthoensen Press], 1961–date. 22cm illus. ports.

NOVITIATE ORDER, POLAND HILL.

"Shaker Village, View from the North West, West Gloucester, Maine." Lithograph by Everts and Peck, from a drawing by Phares Goist, in *A History of Cumberland County*, Maine, 1880.

It is recognized in the first issue of this Shaker periodical that "many changes have been wrought both in the Society and in the world," since publication of the last issue of *The Manifesto* in 1899. "Despite the vicissitudes which time has worked upon us the divine truths upon which Shakerism has rested for nearly two hundred years are unchanged and unchangeable. It is the desire to serve these same truths that has resulted in the 'wave of enthusiasm' which Elder Henry C. Blinn long ago hoped would some day once again draw Believers into the world of periodical literature." The new *Quarterly* is devoted to all historical aspects of Shaker interest and contemporary interpretations of Shaker theology including original articles by Shakers and non-Shakers, historical articles on former communities and industries, music, biographical sketches of Shakers, book reviews, and Shaker writings heretofore available only in manuscript. "News and Notes," a regular feature, provides news of the two remaining Shaker communities at Sabbathday Lake, Me., and Canterbury, N.H. Edited by Theodore E. Johnson.

—Mary L. Richmond, *Shaker Literature: A Bibliography*, Vol. I, 1977, No. 1299

THE SHAKER QUARTERLY

| Volume I | Spring 1961 | No. 1 |

OUR STILL SMALL VOICE

It is with deep humility that we send *The Shaker Quarterly* forth into the world. During the sixty-one years that have passed since the United Society regretfully stopped the publication of the beloved *Manifesto*, many changes have been wrought both in the Society and in the world. Despite the vicissitudes which time has worked upon us the divine truths upon which Shakerism has rested for nearly two hundred years are unchanged and unchangeable. It is a desire to serve these same truths that has resulted in the "wave of enthusiasm" which Elder Henry C. Blinn long ago hoped would some day once again draw Believers into the world of periodical literature.

We have been, quite naturally, both amused and concerned at the efforts of a generation of researchers to sound our death knell. Shakerism is not dead, nor will it soon be. We believe confidently that neither truth nor good can ever die. Since even our critics seem still to find something of these virtues in the movement, we feel that the end for which many have waited so long is not yet at hand. We are, however, quite ready to give over the movement itself as well as this, our latest venture in faith, into God's hands. Fully confident of His mercy and justice we shall, through this new medium, strive humbly to serve both Him and His truth. It is in this spirit that we raise this our still small voice.

Facing Page: From an old print of Shaker Village, Sabbathday Lake, circa 1875.

Page one of the first *Shaker Quarterly*, Spring 1961.

HISTORY ON RECORD

A highly valuable collection of Shaker historical materials has just been issued in a limited edition by Bill Randle of Cleveland Broadcasting's WERE. Each set, consisting of nine LP records, contains the complete text of the five seminars given by the Canterbury Shakers in the summer and fall of 1960, as well as thirty-seven Shaker hymns and songs recorded by the Sabbathday Lake Shakers. The recording closes with Eldress Emma B. King of the Parent Ministry reading her now well-loved "A Shaker's Viewpoint." The records are contained in an attractive slipcase with designs in the Shaker tradition executed by Cleveland artist Tom Wilson. WERE plans wide distribution of the records to educational and historical institutions.

—"News and Notes," *Shaker Quarterly*, Spring 1961

In 1967 Life *took another dim view:*

Serene in their faith, the aged women sit in silent communion. They are Shakers, stalwarts of an all but extinct sect whose members only a few decades ago were numerous enough to fill their meeting halls . . . Today just two active communities exist with a total membership of 18, all women: the one at Sabbathday Lake, Maine, and another at Canterbury, N.H. . . .

As in the early days of the sect, religion is still something that infuses everyday living, but in modern-day Shakerism there is also room, within certain limits, for individual interpretation.

For Eldress Marguerite [Frost], Heaven is all around us. . . . You don't have to sprinkle yourself with water or get down on your knees to pray, or dance and sing like the early Shakers—religion is what you feel. It's what you are, not what you put on. We like color in our costumes now; that doesn't take away from our spiritual life. . . . Christ is in all of us.   —David Martin, "The Shakers: Serene Twilight of a Once-Sturdy Sect," LIFE, Mar. 17, 1967

From Sabbathday Lake, Sister R. Mildred Barker protested Life's *grim portrait. She wrote to the magazine:*

You missed the Brightness and Light which is Shakerism, the light, joy and vitality that is the product of Shakerism. Regardless of our numbers or our age, we have what the world is seeking and it will yet come into its own. What God has made alive will not stay buried.

The Canterbury sisters had no objection to the Life *article. After its publication they received many requests for membership. Mostly from men, said Sister Lillian Phelps, aged ninety-one. "We were not in a position to receive them," she said. "We can't teach them."*

Three Barns, Two Fires

The famous Round Barn at the museum community, Hancock Shaker Village, at Pittsfield, Massachusetts, was opened after complete restoration in 1968. (The opening was the occasion for a pioneering Conference on the Cultural Heritage of an American Communal Sect.)

A feature of the [Hancock] village which has always been regarded as a curiosity is a round stone barn with a circumference of two hundred and seventy feet. This rises from a rocky eminence, and its widespreading massiveness is suggestive of a grim medieval castle. In the primitive times when it was built the cost was eight hundred dollars, which seemed a big

The 1829 Round Barn at Hancock, Massachusetts. A painting of the Shaker landmark by Michigan naïve painter Kathy Jakobsen, 1978. Oil on canvas, 24″ × 36″. Courtesy of Dr. Robert Bishop.

price to pay then. About fifty years ago, after the barn had been gutted by a fire that started from an overturned lantern, the masons charged considerably more than that just for repointing the stone work.

—Clifton Johnson, "The Passing of the Shakers," *Old-Time New England,* July 1934

Two other Shaker landmarks were not so lucky.

In 1972 the Great Stone Barn at Mount Lebanon, New York, measuring 296 by 50 feet, was completely destroyed by fire except for the stonework. Completed in 1859 for the use of the North Family, the slate-roofed barn had five floors. Three could be entered by doors opening directly onto ground levels on the steep hillside into which the barn was built. The building had not been used since the 1930s. In 1979 the Darrow School purchased the ruins of the barn and surrounding property.

In 1973 the huge two-and-a-half-story cow barn at Canterbury Shaker Village burned to the ground. It was the largest barn in New Hampshire. U-shaped, it measured 255 feet on the longest section. The barn, built in 1856, contained valuable old Shaker tools and the only machine in existence for making the window sash that Shakers invented. The barn was on the edge of a cluster of eighteen buildings.

"All Things Anew"

When Charles Nordhoff visited Sabbathday Lake in 1874 he found little that would have led him to predict a long life for those who had long been known as "the least of Mother's Children in the East." He was struck by the fact that the buildings showed "signs of neglect" and was prompted to comment that this society seemed "less prosperous than most of the others." It has been this very lack of prosperity in the material realm combined with the challenge of wresting a living from our somewhat grudging Maine soil that has contributed to the long life of Shakerism here at Sabbathday Lake.

Those things which God may have withheld in terms of earthly treasure have been more than compensated for by an over-abundance of spiritual gifts. Through the marvelous working of Divine Providence we find ourselves entering the twentieth decade of Believers' testimony here at Sabbathday Lake. The light that kindled in that first meeting in Gowen Wilson's farmhouse has not yet been extinguished. We pray God that it may never be. Although it may not seem to burn as brightly as it once did it is still alive. It has the latent power to kindle within human hearts the warmth of divine love and peace. It has the power to bring light into the minds of all those seekers who are open to divine truth and understanding.

For some years it has been fashionable in some quarters to look upon Shakerism as dead. Let this serve as our assurance that it is not. Our Blessed Mother taught that salvation unto souls comes by generations and that so long as one person in a generation had the saving inner knowledge of the Gospel the work would go on. Although few in number it is our resolution that we be caught up more and more in the blessed work of God. We pray that with heavenly Guidance we may so make ourselves instruments of divine truth and light that the way of Believers may once again appear to the children of God as a meaningful, vital and challenging way of life. We solemnly commit ourselves to the task of so fanning the flame of Mother's Gospel that as this new decade which is now opening draws to its close we may see that Christ our Saviour is indeed creating all things anew and that the Testimony shines forth more brightly than at any other time in this century.

THE SABBATHDAY LAKE SHAKERS
—Shaker Quarterly, Winter 1972

SHAKER BICENTENNIAL: 1774–1974

Conference at Sabbathday Lake Described in a Letter to Jennifer

Chosen Land
August 6, 1974

My dear Jennifer,

Many years ago, wonderful things happened among the people called Shakers which would not be known of today if a Shaker sister or brother had not written of them in a diary or a letter, as I am writing to you. . . .

Today we have observed the 200th anniversary of the arrival in America of Mother Ann Lee. Right now this name probably does not seem too important to you, even though . . . you sing songs about her, but years from now, perhaps you will realize how much this one person gave to the world and how her life affected the lives of so many others. It is very late as I write this but I want to write while I am still filled with the fullness of Spirit that all of us here at Shaker Village share as Tuesday, August 6, 1974, comes to an end.

The last four days have been very important ones in the history of the Shaker Church. . . . I will try to tell you about a few of the things that were particularly special to me. . . . All the talks, meetings, and services, everything except meals, our trip to the former Shaker communities at Alfred and Gorham, the picnic at lovely Sabbathday Lake, and our special exhibition [An American Inspiration: Danish Modern and Shaker Design], took place at the Meeting House. . . . It was there that all of us, teachers, students, people from all walks of life, together with the members of the community and our closest friends would meet each day. Each session would be announced by the sounding of the old bell which hangs behind the Meeting House, and it was impressive to see everyone coming together.

One of the pictures vivid in my mind is the sight of all those people in the break between lectures, all around the Meeting House lawn and lined up along the white picket fence. It was a lovely sight: happy people, yet hushed in almost a reverent sort of way. Seeing the Meeting House itself packed to the walls was very inspiring. Often I would leave a little early as things were breaking up just so I could look over and see the people. During the Sunday meeting, a little boy of about twelve who has been with us for the summer started the song, "Simple Gifts." It is not easy for a boy of that age to do this, so it was especially meaningful. Then Sister Mildred spoke, reminding us how Mother Ann loved children, and I thought of you, Jennifer, and the many other children who have known the Shaker way, and it made me happy.

I remember especially how Sister Mildred looked each morning as she sat herself on the front bench ready to partake of the spiritual food with which she has nourished herself throughout her life. How wonderful it is, Jennie, that you have known Sister Mildred, that she has hugged you and loved you because some day she will be known in the world for all the good she has done. She is a saint on earth, although as a simple and humble person, she does not see herself that way and would not want me to say so. She feels happy and well satisfied with all that took place. . . .

Oh, there are so many things that we will all remember for as long as we have the power, the singing in which somehow everyone took part even though they did not know the songs, the way so many of our friends rose to speak so personally in meeting. . . .

We had all waited for Brother Ted to talk about Mother Ann. . . . One thing that he emphasized was Mother's happiness, something which I had never given much thought to. Of course Mother was happy and of course she laughed, because Mother was love, and love, regardless of the form it takes, is joy. . . . I will always think of Mother Ann as a happy person, knowing that when one suffers a great deal as she did, the times of happiness are all the more exquisite and then it is good to laugh.

Jennie, as you grow up, you may find many in the world to be cynical. To many people, there is no such thing as a miracle, but because of the last four days, I know that miracles do happen. I know because I have seen them, experienced them, and the memory of them will be with me always. . . . My prayer is that all of us who were a part of this wondrous experience will keep the feeling of love, no matter what the future brings.

Good night, Jennifer.

SISTER FRANCES [CARR]

Service on the Lawn at Canterbury

On August 11, a Service of Commemoration of the two hundredth anniversary of Shakers in America was celebrated at the Shaker Village in Canterbury, New Hampshire. About 150 invited guests attended the

Eldress Bertha Lindsay, the late Sister Miriam Wall, and Eldress Gertrude Soule face invited guests at a quiet outdoor Bicentennial ceremony. Photograph by Elmer R. Pearson.

ceremony which featured short addresses by the remaining sisters, Eldresses Bertha Lindsay and Gertrude Soule, and Sister Miriam Wall,
along with the Reverend Robley Whitson. The Concord Chorale provided
hymns for the occasion. Staged out on a huge lawn, totally shaded by
stately maples, overlooking the countryside, one could not help but be inspired and reflect on the great achievements of this communal sect.

—*Antiques Gazette*, Sept. 1, 1974

There are several dates in Shaker history which could serve well as
the bases for centennial celebrations: 1747, the first gathering at Manchester; 1770, the awakening to Christ come again; 1780, the opening of the
Gospel in America. Or there is Mother Ann's day of birth or day of death.
Or there is the founding of the first Shaker home at Niskeyuna but a few
weeks after America's Declaration of Independence. But we, as others before us, celebrate the date of the journey, the best symbol in Shaker history for what it means to be a Believer: one who travels in the Gospel,
travels along the Gospel road which has no hitching posts, no place to stop
and call a halt. Travel in the Gospel is a limitless progression, for Faith is
not a possession, not a static "thing" to be kept, but the opening into
Christ-Life. . . .

Eldress Catherine Allen of the Mt. Lebanon ministry reminded
Shakers why they celebrated Mother Ann's voyage:

The date of our writing is the 123rd anniversary of the arrival in
America of Mother Ann Lee and her eight companions, and marks an
epoch in history which we believe will be much more widely and
clearly appreciated in future years than at present. It seems a fitting
time for all Believers who realize the value to mankind of the Gospel
testimony, to recount the accomplishment of the past, consider the
means of success and the causes of failure, distinguish between customs and principles, understand whether certain habits and rules had
their origin in consideration of principles or the necessities of the
times, and while comparing present conditions of society with those
which existed more than a century since let us adjust ourselves for
present duty and future advancement [1897].

—Robley Edward Whitson, "The Shaker Vision," Address, Service of Commemoration, 200th Anniversary of the Shakers in America, Shaker Village,
Canterbury, New Hampshire, Aug. 11, 1974

September 1974

Smithsonian

Remaining Shakers (p.40)
observe 200th year;
Sister Mildred, 77,
plays and sings 'Progress'

Sister Mildred sings on the *Smithsonian* cover, September 1974. Photograph ©
Alfred Eisenstaedt/Time Inc.

BLOWUP

*In the summer of 1974 a giant poster of a Shaker sister was plastered
on billboards in New York and Chicago railroad stations, commuter
trains, and buses. The poster was a blowup of the cover of the* Smithson-

ian *magazine for September 1974, which carried a story on the Bicenten-nial of the American Shakers.*

Sister Mildred disliked the cover portrait by distinguished photogra-pher Alfred Eisenstaedt because it showed her with her mouth open, as she played the organ in the music room at Sabbathday Lake, Maine, and sang a favorite Shaker hymn called "Progress" ("I must live, must have my being; faith and conscience must be free ...").

Printed at the top of some of the posters displayed as advertising sales promotion was the improbable question: "Isn't it curious that a maga-zine which doesn't rely on sex, politics or gossip is the second fastest growing magazine in America?"

Celebration in Ohio

In Cleveland next month, scholars and friends of Shakerism will gather at the Shaker Bicentennial Convention, thus beating by more than a year the celebrations of the nation's own Bicentennial. It will be a 200th-birthday observance for the remarkably tenacious little religious sect that, in America, started out with nine members, reached a peak of about 6,000 and is now down to its last dozen. The convention, jointly sponsored by the Shaker Historical Society and the Western Reserve His-torical Society, will hear from authorities on Shaker architecture and in-vention, Shaker cooking and herbs, Shaker manuscripts and music, and Shaker theology.

The meeting promises to be well attended because of reviving public interest in The United Society of Believers in Christ's Second Appearing, as the order was originally known. However, few of the 12 surviving Shakers ... all female and all resident in the two remaining villages of the society, are likely to show up, although privately both villages will have their own ceremonies. Most of them already have made one rather tiring Bicentennial-year trip from New England into the world outside, visiting an exhibition of the Edward Deming and Faith Andrews collection of Shaker furniture and implements at the Smithsonian's Renwick Gallery in Washington last winter. ...

What is being commemorated at Western Reserve is the Shakers' own discovery of America.

—Richard L. Williams, "The Shakers, now only 12, observe their 200th year," *Smithsonian,* Sept. 1974

An auction launched the Shaker Bicentennial Convention in Cleve-
land in October 1974. The Shaker sisters flown in from Canterbury
smiled at the poplar boxes that had once sold for 35 cents going for $35.

The three elderly Shaker ladies who are belles of the Shaker Bicentennial Convention here were a little exhausted yesterday.

They arose at 6 A.M. and ventured out with their velvet bonnets tied
snugly under their chins and, after a full morning of meetings at the Western Reserve Historical Society Eldress Bertha Lindsay, Eldress Gertrude
Soule and Sister Miriam Wall had grown weary of the quick-paced life a
conventioneer must lead.

"They aren't used to all the excitement, especially the TV and flash
cameras," said Bert Phillips, caretaker for the ladies at their home in Canterbury, N.H.   —Cleveland *Plain Dealer*, Oct. 12, 1974

Never before has the Shaker story received more attention than in
the last decade. Four Shaker villages have become historical shrines.
Shaker furniture, arts, and crafts have received both national and international attention. Numerous books have been published; articles have appeared in papers and in periodicals; and a number of documentary films
have been made. So the movement that was only a glowing ember has
been fanned anew; the United Society of Believers in Christ's First and
Second Appearing have again become an influence in American utopian
thought.   —The Canterbury Shakers, Foreword to the 1974
                   Canterbury edition of Charles Edson Robinson, *The*
                   Shakers and Their Homes, 1893

Eldress Bertha [Lindsay] said that Shakers are more honored now
than ever, and I said they were not.
                   —Sister R. Mildred Barker

TWO STRONGHOLDS

Both of the surviving communities, at Canterbury and at Sabbathday
Lake, are lovely, well-ordered agrarian villages where brick dwellings, the
product of Shaker kilns, and immaculate white clapboard barns and shop
buildings nestle among rolling orchards and pastures. Both depend on
male and female civilians to keep them going, for four sisters in one village
and eight in another could not possibly maintain the real estate and enter-

prises the society owns. At both villages, the sisters' dresses—prints, checks, even solid scarlet—are "caped" with a fore-and-aft rounded bib that masks the bosom. The two remnant communities do, however, differ on minor details. The sisters in Maine still say "yea" and "nay"; those in New Hampshire say yes and no. The only sister at Sabbathday Lake who customarily wears the traditional starched lawn cap is Sister Mildred; all the sisters at Canterbury wear it and speak of having "put on the cap" in their teens in preparation for "signing the covenant" at 21. . . . More important, some years ago the parent church at Canterbury decided that in all realism, Shaker membership had to be closed. Some members of the village at Sabbathday Lake feel that the ruling was unwise and would prefer that, in theory at least, new members, male or female, be admitted.

Both outposts contain Shaker museums—and at both the sisters resent being categorized as museum pieces, gawked at and Polaroided in the tourist season, because they feel very much alive.

> —Richard L. Williams, "The Shakers, Now Only 12, Observe Their 200th Year," *Smithsonian,* Sept. 1974

"Shaker Christmas," an Associated Press laserphoto, 1978. World Wide Photos.

Newspapers across the country published a picture of Eldress Bertha Lindsay and Eldress Gertrude Soule on Christmas Eve, December 24, 1978. The sisters were shown decorating the Christmas tree at Shaker Village, Canterbury, New Hampshire. The caption called them "two of the remaining nine members of the dying Shaker religion, known for its superb craftsmanship and straight-line furniture."

Faith, Not Furniture

The modern Shaker looks with respect on the handiwork of forebears in the Faith, but declares, "I don't want to be remembered as a stick of furniture!"

It is to the *consecrated life* that the Shaker has always given allegiance, not to its by-product. The Believers therefore prize more deeply the Shaker heritage of song. The songs are the immediate voice of their faith and aspiration. In worship they serve for prayer and testimony. They bridge the two extremes of Shaker experience, for they originated in private gifts of inspiration but are used to gather the feelings of the group into union.

The Shakers were of course but one of many bands of Evangelical Protestants who between the Revolution and the Civil War drew on traditional music to create an enormous body of new spiritual folk songs. Blacks and whites contributed to the repertory, Germans and Scotch-Irish, town dweller and frontiersman, Baptist and Adventist. But the Shakers were probably the group most prolific in song. Though few in numbers, the Shakers left a written record of some ten thousand songs— and this was only a portion of their total repertory. Several hundred of these are still alive in Shaker oral tradition. The present recording offers a sampling of 19th-century Shaker spirituals sung in traditional unaccompanied style by sisters of the United Society of Shakers at Sabbathday Lake, Maine. —Daniel W. Patterson, notes accompanying *Early Shaker Spirituals*, recorded 1976

Music pervaded the Shakers' whole lives, Dr. Patterson wrote in the first Shaker Quarterly *(Spring 1961). "They sang in worship, they sang at work, they welcomed visitors with song, they sang for recreation. Sometimes they even dreamed songs."*

He encouraged a retention of song at Sabbathday Lake. With his help Sister Mildred Barker has recorded many of the hundreds of songs she learned as a child among Believers at Alfred, Maine. The sisters have learned songs from him, too, favorites from eight hundred surviving songbooks that have been his special study. These manuscripts are an important American heritage. A compendium of Shaker songs and folklore by Dr. Patterson, The Shaker Spiritual, *was published in 1979.*

Music from an old Shaker "tune book." Courtesy of the Library of Congress.

SINGING IN THE IRONING ROOM

As a child I loved to sing, and I would sing almost anything I heard. And when I was hearing these old Shaker songs, they attracted me. Probably the easy rhythm and words were a great attraction too. And then I tried to learn every one that I heard—it would be sort of a passion with me to see how many I could learn. And I learned a great many from Eldress Harriet Coolbroth, and also as I grew older, we used to learn quite a number from Sister Lucinda Taylor. At the laundry, we used to get her into the ironing room and get her up on one of the big ironing tables. When she got older, she was about eighty-five, eighty-six years old then, we'd ask her to sing songs to us. She was kind of shy. She'd say, "Oh, you don't want me to sing to you." We'd say, "We do, we do! We want to learn a song." And then we'd get her to show us some of the early dances, which we never saw, and one special tune which was most beautiful was "The Heavenly Father's March," which she could do. She was so graceful, and she had a voice just like a bird. A beautiful voice, even at that extreme age. So she really enjoyed the singing, the little singing periods, as much as we did. From then on I went on to learn every song that I could. I couldn't learn them from the books because I didn't understand the letteral notation which was the Shakers' way of noting the songs in the manuscripts, and so we just learned them from hearing other people sing them.

> —Recollections of Sister R. Mildred Barker, from Side 19 of *The Shaker Heritage,* a set of 10 recordings edited by William Randle, Cleveland, 1961. This account and the following one also appear in notes accompanying *Early Shaker Spirituals,* a recording of songs at Sabbathday Lake, Maine, 1976

MOTHER HAS COME WITH HER BEAUTIFUL SONG

When I was a little child, there was an older sister named Paulina Springer. Sister Paulina was very very dear to me. I loved her. She was ninety years old, and she used to ask if I could be the one to come and help her do her chores every morning, make her bed, and clean up her room. It was my greatest delight to do it because I thought she was just an angel. . . . I think perhaps it was two years I served her. And she was taken ill very suddenly. She didn't have a sickness and linger. She just sort of faded away. And when she was dying, the last day she lived—everyone knew she wouldn't live past noon—she asked if the children could come in and see her. She was fully conscious. So I was one, and I happened to be the last one in the line to come in and see her. So she spoke to each one as they passed through. When I came up to her bed, she took my hand and said, "Mildred, I want you to promise me something." At that point in my life I'd have promised her anything in the world, I didn't care *what* it was! Oh, I certainly would, I'd promise her anything. She said, "Promise me that you'll be a Shaker." Of course I promised her, but it took me a great many years to fulfill the promise and to really come to the point where I knew what that promise meant. But it's always followed me—and as I've gone through life, this little song that she sang, not especially at that time, but some years before, she had had the gift of this little song. But after she talked with us, we left, and she said to the sisters in the room, "I'm not going to be here much longer." She said, "There's two angels standing over by the cupboard door waiting for me." About twelve o'clock she just passed away. So this is the song:

> Mother has come with her beautiful song—ho ho talla me ho
> She's come to bless her children dear—ho ho talla me ho
> And Christ your Savior will be near—ho ho talla me ho

She told us that she learned that from a little bird.

—Recollections of Sister R. Mildred Barker, from Side 19 of *The Shaker Heritage*

It is not expected that the people of God will ever be confined, in their mode of worship, to any particular set of hymns, or any other regular system of words—for words are but the signs of our ideas, and of course, must vary as the ideas increase with the increasing work of God.

—Preface, *Millennial Praises*, 1813

Another Musical Tradition

From the first, a special gift of harmony has seemed to rest upon the Canterbury society and many of the most refined and soul thrilling of the Shaker hymns have emanated from here.

> —Anna White and Leila S. Taylor, *Shakerism: Its Meaning and Message*, 1904

At Shaker Village at Canterbury, New Hampshire, the folk melodies have given way to the hymns and anthems in the Shaker Hymnal *published by the society in 1908. This preference reflects the gradual change in musical taste as well as in the worship service to a more traditional style. "Our church service is quiet and more formal," wrote the late Sister Lillian Phelps in 1960, "resembling perhaps the prayer meetings held in many of the churches of other denominations." As in other churches, singing in harmony was popular.*

Eldress Bertha Lindsay, now in her eighties and one of two members of the Parent Ministry, remembers singing in a group who entertained the Merrimack [County] Farmers' Exchange in 1917. In a picture taken on the steps of the meetinghouse, she is the fifth sister from the right. One of her favorite songs, composed at Canterbury, is this hymn:

There are notes of joy and beauty
In my psalm of praise today;
There are chords of peace and blessing,
Sweetly blending all the way.
I will add no strain of discord,
But attune my voice to prayer,
Giving heart and hand in service,
Sing my psalm with trust and care.

Eldress Gertrude Soule, formerly of Sabbathday Lake, and the second member of the Parent Ministry, has no preference among the many songs and hymns she knows by heart. "Each one answers your need," she says.

A recording, Shaker Songs, *was made in the chapel at Canterbury in 1977. While the sisters helped to select the music, the singer is soprano Nancy Thompson, wife of the curator, Charles Thompson, accompanied by organist Richard Crooks.*

Beyond the Shaker Image: Canterbury Revisited

A long-term historical survey and planning project at Canterbury is determined to "get beyond the reverence" and the "Shaker image" to the real facts about Shaker community life.

Accomplishments of the first two phases were reported in 1979 in a 268-page volume to the sponsor, the New Hampshire State Historical Preservation Office.

Citing the lack of a thorough study of any remaining Shaker settlement, the report challenged existing Shaker studies as mostly imitative and superficial, content to confirm what everyone assumes to be true about the Shakers. Unwilling to accept as typical of every community the pattern established by a portrait of Mount Lebanon, summer research teams of archaeologists, architects, and historians are exploring, mapping, and documenting the incorporated New Hampshire village.

The work is a prelude to a plan of action to preserve, develop, and maintain the twenty-two remaining buildings on 617 acres left after the rapid sale of Shaker property in the twentieth century. The largest portion of the village has either burned down or been dismantled, including a great number of mills.

An associated course in American Studies at Boston University in 1978 produced a set of provocative articles on the social history of the community. Published in the report, it challenges current assumptions and raises questions like these:

1. In what ways did Canterbury exemplify variation within the Shaker movement? Are existing studies of New (Mount) Lebanon adequate for describing Shaker practices and beliefs everywhere else or did Canterbury demonstrate considerable autonomy from the ruling ministry?

2. What evidence is present for growing secularization within the Shaker movement during the nineteenth and twentieth centuries? In what ways did the revival of the 1840s manifest itself? What changes were evidenced in Canterbury society once the ruling ministry transferred from Lebanon to here?

3. What factors led to the introduction of the crafts and industries practiced in Canterbury? How were these industries modified by influences from the outside world, and how were they merchandised to the world? To what extent did they simply imitate the vernacular crafts of the world around them?

4. What was the impact of the Shakers upon the outside world? In what ways did they modify the land? How were they perceived by their local contemporaries and by local people of today? What legacy have they left for modern day New Hampshire?

With the generous cooperation of the Shaker sisters and of John E. Auchmoody, then executive director of Shaker Village, Inc., Professors David Starbuck and Margaret Supplee Smith, both formerly of Boston University and now with the University of New Hampshire, have managed the first two years of research. According to Starbuck, an archaeologist, personnel will change according to the demands of the project.

Eldress Bertha Lindsay has shared with the researchers fourteen tapes on which she has recorded memories of her long Shaker life. "Eldress Bertha signed the Covenant shortly after her twenty-first birthday, as did most signers who grew up in the society," says an article in the 1978 report on "The Shaker Covenant: 1795–1957." "She related that candidates studied the Covenant and heard it read before signing it in the presence of witnesses. For Eldress Bertha signing the Covenant meant a

or their respective positions, except perhaps to note that its basis is the very question being discussed here. Two of the Shakers residing in Canterbury are surviving members of the Society's Parent Ministry; on the advice of counsel, they have chosen to extend the decision taken at Canterbury to Sabbathday Lake. Pointing to the provisions of the Covenant, which states that "the door must be kept open for the admission of new members into the Church," the Sabbathday Lake Shakers have challenged their authority to do so. The issue is complex and it has resulted in a breakdown in relations which is deeply distressing to both sides.

While they work quietly for the resolution of these problems, the Sabbathday Lake Shakers continue to order their community life in the time-honored traditions of the Maine Shakers. The bell at the top of the Village's 1883 Central Brick Dwelling may be heard announcing the time for changes in the day's activities, members still take three-week "terms" in the kitchen, much of the customary hand labor is done, and the spirit of community may be experienced.

But there is more. Young people have been permitted to enter the family, either as provisional members or to volunteer service, and they have helped bring new inspiration to Shaker life. The crafts tradition is beginning to see a rebirth. . . .

Worship services today are more exuberant. No longer held privately in the family chapel of the Brick Dwelling, Shaker meeting is open again to the public. Visitors from the World are present every week and participate freely in the service, many having learned some of the Shaker songs from the community's well-received recording. Frequently they include members of other Christian religious communities with which the Shakers have established close relations in recent years. The liturgical practices, for example, of the well-known Benedictine community at Weston, Vermont, have been influenced by the monks' visits to Sabbathday Lake, and the Shakers are able again to experience a sense of belonging to a wider fellowship. The religious testimony of the Church is no longer withdrawn from the world. Through an active program of community outreach, the Sabbathday Lake Shakers have conducted worship services as far away from home as Ohio and in such diverse places as the Divinity School of Yale University and the Chapel of St. Elizabeth of Hungary at the Ann Lee Home in Colonie, New York, originally the meetinghouse of the Watervliet Shakers.

There is also an impressive educational program. Utilizing the rich archival resources of the Shaker Library, the Institute of Shaker Studies was established at Sabbathday Lake about four years ago. Since then, it annually has offered courses, seminars, workshops, and lectures on almost every aspect of the Shaker experience. In conjunction with the University of Southern Maine, it provides facilities for the earning of college credits in Shaker studies. Part of these concerns are also expressed in the Society's publishing and printing endeavors. . . .

And of course, there is the herb industry. Until the old Herb House itself is restored, the packaging of herbs grown in the Society's gardens must be done in the spacious Ironing Room of the community's Laundry or Sisters' Shop. Community members and their young helpers often work late into the night to fill orders from customers, and the attendant chores of bookkeeping, purchasing supplies, packing and shipping, not to mention cultivation, gathering, harvesting, drying, and processing herbs, now touch the life of almost every member of the community. . . .

Shaker life is not intended to be static. There can be no doubt that continuity is bringing change with it, but the Sabbathday Lake Shakers welcome changes grounded in their faith, nourished by their tradition, and expressing the spirituality of their way. . . . True to the best of their

---

---

great heritage, [they] intend to remain open to the moving of the Spirit. It may be too early to predict the outcome of their efforts, but if there is to be no future for the United Society, it will not be for want of trying.

> —Gerard C. Wertkin, " 'The Flame is Never Ceasing . . .' Continuity in Shaker Life at Sabbathday Lake," *The Clarion*, published by the Museum of American Folk Art, Fall 1979

Anyone Can Be a Shaker

"I've had letters from people in California and Iowa who wished to start a Shaker community and were very enthusiastic about it. We sent them information they sought.

"And a lot of students come here through the year to talk to me and ask questions. So I am hopeful."

But not that the Shaker faith will endure in the same form she [Eldress Bertha Lindsay] knew when she came to Canterbury 73 years ago from Everett, Mass. as an orphan obeying one of the last wishes of her mother. . . .

As for the beliefs . . . they do not need out-of-the-way communes or settlements to endure, Eldress Bertha said. Nor do they need any of the outward trappings of the religion she has loved for a lifetime.

"Anyone," she said, "can live as a Shaker, because it means living by the teachings of Jesus." —"Celibate Shaker Sect Is Last of Dying Creed," *Boston Herald American*, May 14, 1978

If All the World Became Shakers

By now you would like to ask, "What would happen if all the world became Shakers?" This question has been asked down through the years. The answer is very simple. There is no more likelihood that this will happen than that all people will be of one opinion on any one subject. We have never felt our faith to be a proselyting one since the early days. Jesus said, "Strait is the gate and narrow is the way that leadeth unto life, and few there be that find it." This does not mean that the inner Christ is not for all, the high, the low, the favored and the down-trodden, but that few will make the effort involved to find this condition. One must become a spiritual specialist and we expected small numbers.

Were the Shakers expecting to develop a Utopia? Not at all. Something far more important. Their aim, as I see it, was not to do something for social betterment only (though that came about) but what they sought was to bring about a climate in which souls could become fully developed spiritually. The word they heard within was, "Be ye therefore perfect."

When we consider the diminution of the Shakers it will be well not to stop at celibacy as though that is the one important factor of the decline. . . . The little group of nine people who came from England grew to be at least six thousand and carried on successfully for many years with no way of gaining membership but from the outside. . . . The effect that war had upon them, though they took no part in it themselves, the extension of national manufacturing which largely took away their industries, and within themselves an aging membership (with fewer young people coming among them) made it difficult to keep alive the same religious enthusiasm.

As for us, the handful of living members of the two remaining Shaker communities, we will still walk our daily path believing that the greatest force in the universe is the love of God which fills all immensity and the second greatest power is interior prayer whereby man finds his union with God.   —Eldress Marguerite Frost, *The Shaker Story*, Canterbury, New Hampshire, 1963

Jonestown

Jonestown had many precedents, said the New York Times *on November 26, 1978. The newspaper published an artist's rendering of the horror of the mass suicide in Guyana, South America, that included an adaptation of an 1848 print of the Shakers. The accompanying article said, "America has had a long history of similar religious cults. Among the better known of these were the Shakers, the Mennonites, the Amish, Jehovah's Witnesses, Father Divine's Peace Mission, and Aimee Semple McPherson's Church of the Foursquare Gospel."*

This linking of Believers to the People's Temple of the Reverend Jim Jones provoked an indignant letter to the editor:

Chosen Land
30 November 1978

Sir:

Although we find much of interest in Boyce Rensberger's *Jonestown Has Many Precedents* (November 26, 1978), we must raise strong objections to Shakers having been in any way a precedent for such groups as The People's Temple. Indeed, we find that Mr. Rensberger has chosen rather unlikely company for us. To be sure, we certainly recognize a common heritage shared with the Mennonites and Amish, but find virtually no points of similarity between ourselves and Jehovah's Witnesses and the followers of Father Divine and Aimee Semple McPherson. I fear too that we must take umbrage at being classed as a "religious cult." We consider ourselves rather to be part of the one holy and catholic church founded and still directed by the Christ. François Colos' adaptation of "the whirling gift" which originally appeared in David R. Lamson's *Two Years Experience Among the Shakers* does not represent our past any

Jonestown Has · Many Precedents

An 1848 print of the Shakers (see page 175 for "The Whirling Gift") became part of an illustration by Francois Colos for *The New York Times*. © 1978 by The New York Times Company.

better than it did when it first appeared in 1848. It is, in fact, merely the misconception of a disgruntled apostate who after many attempts found no community to suit him.

Sincerely,
THE SABBATHDAY LAKE SHAKERS

A New York Times *editor replied that the writer did not intend to suggest similarity between the Shakers and other groups mentioned, and meant no offense in calling Shakers a "religious cult."*

The Shaker Connection

USES OF THE PAST

THE NEW SUFI: Like the Sufi of the Middle East, they use dance ("dervishing") to help achieve the *kairos* [ecstasy] ... in the Third Great Awakening. The Shakers did it with dance in the Second Great Awakening.   —Tom Wolfe, "The Me Decade," *New York*, Aug. 23, 1976

A religious group of Sufi lives and worships in the South Family buildings at Mount Lebanon, one of a variety of uses that the old Shaker communities now serve. All have become, wholly or in part, museums, religious institutions and retreats, schools, correctional facilities, retirement or nursing homes, private property, or airfields. The Albany airport borders the Shaker cemetery where Mother Ann and the first Shakers are buried.

While Canterbury is still the home of Believers, it has joined the ranks of three other nonprofit museum-communities as Shaker Village, Inc. The others are Shaker Village at Pleasant Hill, Kentucky; Shakertown at South Union, Kentucky; and Hancock Shaker Village at Pittsfield, Massachusetts. The restored villages offer nineteenth-century serenity and a glimpse of Shaker perfection. They also generate interest in the history and heritage of the Shakers by festivals, pageants, and "world's people's dinners."

At Canterbury, visitors who tour the village have an opportunity to meet the Parent Ministry of the United Society of Believers. Eldress Bertha Lindsay and Eldress Gertrude Soule take turns in greeting visitors. (A third sister, Ethel Hudson, is more retiring.)

At Sabbathday Lake, where a museum is also maintained, visitors take tours while the members of the last active Shaker community go about their daily duties.

(For a list of Shaker museums and libraries and museums with Shaker collections, see page 357.)

Efforts continue to preserve remaining Shaker buildings. In Albany the Shaker Heritage Society seeks to acquire and restore the South Family segment of the Watervliet Shaker Historic District, site of the first Shaker community in America.

Several individual campaigns have tried to acquire Shaker buildings in Ohio.

In Harvard, Massachusetts, since 1963 the Shakerton Foundation has been documenting important Shaker buildings and sites. A private owner is at home and at work on restoration of Harvard's South Family farm.

IN THE "SHAKER WORLD"-AT-LARGE

Shaker furniture went on view in Manchester, England, at a gallery two streets and two centuries from Mother Ann's humble birthplace. The

Photograph by Richard Hong.

show, organized in Munich, traveled on to London and Paris. Shakerism is not widely known in England, but the American Museum in Bath has a Shaker room.

A display of Shaker furniture, dress, and conveniences fascinated Japanese spectators at the 1970 Osaka World's Fair, where it was part of the American exhibition.

Reproductions of Shaker furniture abound, as small workshops and large manufacturers adapt Shaker designs and devices to contemporary living. Inexpensive replicas of "museum pieces" can be assembled from kits.

Books on Shaker antiques and Shaker cooking are popular, and Books in Print has several columns under the subject "Shaker." Forty years ago a library catalog listed one book.

Shaker buildings are periodically measured, photographed, and recorded by the Historical American Buildings Survey, which began the architectural record in the 1930s in Ohio. The former Enfield, New Hampshire, community was surveyed by HABS summer teams in 1978 in cooperation with the residing Missionaries of Our Lady of La Salette. A Shaker visitors' center has been opened at La Salette.

The Library of the Western Reserve Historical Society in Cleveland microfilmed its Shaker collection of more than 1,800 volumes and 10,000 manuscripts. The collection occupies 120 feet of shelf space.

Historical societies and museums with Shaker leanings and holdings are sources of Shaker-related activity from coast to coast.

The Shakers are studied from grade school to graduate school, as well as in courses for continuing education. An Institute of Shaker Studies has been established at the "living laboratory" of Sabbathday Lake, with the cooperation of the University of Southern Maine. A degree in

Shaker Hall (The Great Stone Dwelling) and the Mary Keane Chapel, left, at the Shrine of Our Lady of La Salette, Enfield, New Hampshire. Historic American Buildings Survey photograph, 1970.

Shaker theology can be earned at the United Institute, an ecumenical study center in Bethlehem, Connecticut.

At least ten documentary films have been made about the Shakers, and they are featured in many other films on subjects like women and handcraft.

The Shaker Messenger, *a journal of general interest for Shaker fans, published in Holland, Michigan, has succeeded* The World of Shaker, *published from 1971 to 1977 by the Guild of Shaker Crafts in Spring Lake, Michigan.*

Four books of poetry have been written about the Believers.

Seminars, symposiums, conferences—many meetings of hearts and minds—focus on Shakerism, "visible theology."

Shaker music enjoys a renaissance and is heard in many commercial recordings of early American and folk songs. Choral and dance groups offer Shaker entertainments.

Artists and photographers in the wake of Charles Sheeler are inspired by Shaker themes and the Shaker spirit.

Shaker furniture and artifacts, arts and craftsmanship, attract museum-, gallery-, and auction-goers, while the price of Shaker antiques goes up.

Shaker simplicity
is avidly sought

—Virginia Bohlin, "Antiques for Today," *Boston Sunday Globe,* Aug. 26, 1979

SHATTERING THE SHAKER IMAGE

One day last summer I was preparing to visit the Shaker community at Sabbathday Lake, Maine. The temperature was hovering near 100 degrees, and I was debating what to wear. The practical garb—shorts and a T-shirt—was clearly out of the question. After all, I was visiting a religious community, one with more than 200 years of history and tradition, a celibate community, moreover, that rejects any suggestion of carnality.

Shorts, I decided, had a slightly irreverent, even carnal air about them. So I drove up to Sabbathday Lake wearing a short-sleeved shirt and slacks, and put on a tie just before going in. There I was greeted by my Shaker host—who was wearing shorts.

We all come to the Shakers with certain preconceived notions. . . . We carry an image around in our heads of an austere, highly disciplined, perhaps fanatical sect, living in nearly bare rooms with pegs on the walls, speaking in stilted Old Testament English, refusing to have any truck with the corrupt and worldly twentieth century. . . .

But what we discover, when we arrive, are people, not caricatures. They wear shorts when it is hot, and blue jeans when they work in their herb gardens. . . . They continue to practice their religion, founded in 1774 by the Englishwoman called Mother Ann Lee, which stresses simplicity, possession of all things in common, and separation from the world. But it is separation from "the sense and feeling of the world," not from the world itself. "We can't separate ourselves from the world," one Shaker told me. "God made the world. The world is a good place." They may still say "Yea" and "Nay" instead of yes and no, but it is a fond tradition, not an affectation. The Shakers of today are proud of their past, but they live in the present. . . .

Whenever Shakers read about themselves in newspapers or magazines, they see the words "heritage" and "legacy"—as if Shakerism were the equivalent of a rich uncle in poor health, whose relatives were already eyeing the silver. There is something a little ghoulish about all the articles predicting the extinction of the sect. . . .

And so, not wishing to be numbered among the vultures, I declare that this will not be a premature obituary for the United Society of Believers in Christ's Second Appearance. I believe that the Shakers will be around for quite a good while yet, though maybe not in the picturesque way some of us would like them to be. . . . I want to tell you something about the Shaker present, and its future. But in order to do that we have to look backwards about 20 years, to a time when decisions were made that will determine, for good or ill, what form Shakerism will take in the future.

In 1957 Shakerism was reaching the bottom end of a long decline. For eight decades, Shaker communities had, one by one, been dissolved, consolidated, or sold, as the number of Believers steadily dwindled from a mid-19th-century peak of 6,000 souls in nearly 20 communities. You can check [the] history books for the reasons why, but the first one that might occur to you—celibacy— is not one of them. . . .

As the number of Shaker communities was reduced, much of their property—cash, real estate, and investments—came under the control of Eldress Frances Hall of Hancock, who, when she died in 1957, was the titular head of the Society. Leadership then passed on to Eldress Emma King of Canterbury, along with the Society's assets, which were substantial.

The Eldress in Canterbury was worried about all that wealth, and what to do with it. She consulted professionals outside the Society, among them the distinguished Manchester, New Hampshire, law firm of Sheehan, Phinney, Bass and Green. Upon their advice the money was placed in what is called the Shaker Central Trust Fund, under the direction of what was initially a six-member board of trustees. Each of the three then-surviving communities was represented by a Shaker and a non-Shaker attorney, who were appointed for lifetime terms. In 1960 the last of the Hancock, Massachusetts, Shakers died, so the board now consists of two Shakers—Eldresses Gertrude Soule and Bertha Lindsay, representing Sabbathday Lake and Canterbury respectively, and three attorneys. . . . According to one of the trustees, attorney Richard Morse, of the Manchester firm, the money is actually managed by "a substantial financial institution," acting on behalf of the trustees.

How much money was there? Newspaper reports pegged the amount at either $2 million or $3 million—a figure that Morse describes as "greatly exaggerated." Nevertheless, it was enough money to worry Eldress Emma King, and in the eyes of some Shakers, it was enough to trigger the serious problems that beset the Society today. "I wish they'd never found it," said one Shaker sister.

In the six years following the establishment of the trust fund, the feeling grew in Canterbury that the money was a threat to the purity of the Shaker faith—a threat because it might attract new members more interested in the money than in "bearing the cross," the Shaker term for a life of sacrifice in the Lord's service. In 1965 the Eldress at Canterbury, on the advice of her Manchester lawyers, decided to close membership in the Society. The practical effect of that decision, in a celibate order, was to assure that the living Shaker faith would not survive long, if at all, beyond the end of this century.

Why was this decision, so drastic in its implications, made? Eldress Emma King cannot explain—she died in 1967. . . .

Manchester attorney Richard Morse says the decision to close membership was made "after extensive consultation with all the remaining members of the then two societies," and by joint agreement of the eldress at Sabbathday Lake—Gertrude Soule—and the eldresses at Canterbury.

But every Shaker did not agree with the decision. Sister Mildred Barker of Sabbathday Lake flatly opposed it. . . . "No one has the right to shut the door of the church on anybody who sincerely seeks to enter." She was not alone. Other sisters at Sabbathday Lake opposed the decision, which they say is contrary to the language of the Covenant of the Society, and to the terms of the agreement setting up the Shaker Central Trust Fund. Their disagreement led to open defiance, when, in 1972, they refused orders from Canterbury to eject a man who had been living at Sabbathday Lake for ten years.

Theodore Johnson is a big bear of a man in his late forties, with silver-gray hair and beard, and a light, high voice in which he speaks softly. But he carries a big intellectual stick. A Colby College graduate and Fulbright Scholar, he did postgraduate work at Harvard, and was, for a short time, president of a small college in Lewiston, Maine. . . .

Although Johnson had been living at Sabbathday Lake for several years before the Canterbury sisters decided to close membership, he is not recognized by them as a member of the Society. The Canterbury position, as explained by their lawyer, Richard Morse, is that there are only nine living Shakers, all of them women—three at Canterbury, and six in Maine.

The Shaker sisters at Sabbathday Lake, however, accept Johnson as a brother in their community. Johnson is reluctant to comment on the controversy, except to say that "the important sanction is that which comes from those with whom one is involved in living." He also points out that conflict is not unprecedented in the Society. "On one issue, for example, in the 1870s, when musical instruments began to be introduced into the communities, and the community at East Canterbury bought an organ, Elder Otis, of this (Maine) family, records in his journal his utter consternation over such a move. He wrote, 'The human voice is still a full and sufficient instrument for the worship of God!'

"To be sure," Johnson added after a moment, "the difference of which you speak may be in some respects more fundamental. But in all truth, it does not really affect our daily lives, because we are doing what we think is right, and we do what God has led us to do."

Ted Johnson is not the only man living among the Shakers at Sabbathday Lake these days, but he remains, for some, the most controversial, perhaps because of the increasingly public role he plays, almost as a spokesman for the Shakers. He established the Institute of Shaker Studies in 1967, offering annual courses, seminars, and lectures on Shaker history and thought. He edits and publishes *The Shaker Quarterly*, a periodical of wide circulation in academic circles since 1961. . . .

Regardless of the personalities involved, the Shakers today are a deeply divided community which, throughout its history, has placed a high value on unity. "For whereas there is among you envying, and strife, and divisions, are ye not carnal and walk as men?" wrote one Shaker in

1818. The problem of the Sabbathday Lake community is compounded by the fact that they feel they lack genuine representation on the board of trustees of the Shaker Central Trust Fund. Eldress Gertrude Soule, who is the official Shaker representative of the Maine community, moved to Canterbury in 1971, and still lives there. . . .

The conflict may even have resulted in punitive action against the Sabbathday Lake community by the parent ministry at Canterbury. The sisters at Canterbury live off an income from the Shaker Central Trust Fund, as did the community at Sabbathday Lake until 1973. Then the trust fund cut off the $3,000 monthly payments it had been making to Sabbathday Lake, while continuing to pay taxes, insurance costs, and a small allowance—less than $10 a week—to each of the sisters recognized by the parent ministry.

Ted Johnson says Sabbathday Lake is financially self-sufficient on the income from its herb industry, its agriculture and timber sales, and the proceeds from the museum and tours. Since 1974 the Maine community has also received help from a group of "interested individuals" around the nation calling themselves Friends of the Shakers, which has paid for electronic security systems in several buildings, and for repainting and refurbishing.

The conflict has moved beyond the borders of Maine and New Hampshire as academics and others with interests in the Shakers choose up sides. When the Museum of American Folk Art in New York City announced it would hold a Shaker seminar last fall, featuring Ted Johnson as a speaker, its president Robert Bishop received several "threatening" phone calls and letters from Richard Morse—behavior that Bishop called "appalling." And several of the listed participants in the conference heard from Morse, too. The seminar went on, but was boycotted by the Canterbury Shakers, who were invited to attend.

If the conflict remains unresolved, serious legal questions could arise in the future. The two Canterbury eldresses on the board of directors of the Shaker trust fund are both in their eighties. According to published reports, when the last Shaker dies, the trust fund is to be converted to a charitable trust that would finance scholarships and historical research into Shakerism. But if all three of the Canterbury sisters should pass away before those officially recognized sisters in Maine (as seems likely, in view of the respective ages), would the Maine sisters be allowed to take part in the management of the trust fund?

And who is to decide the future of the buildings and property at Sabbathday Lake, when the last of the "recognized" Shaker sisters living there is gone? In 1972 the entire village of Canterbury was turned over to a nonprofit corporation run by a large board of directors, whose president is Eldress Bertha Lindsay. When the three elderly sisters living there now are gone, it will become what executive director Jack Auchmoody calls "a living museum" where visitors (there were 15,000 in 1978) can see crafts people simulating Shaker works in genuine Shaker dwellings.

If any of these questions should ever be brought before a court (and the courts have in the past tried very hard not to get involved in religious matters), legal precedent has generally dictated that decisions made by church leaders are binding on church members, provided that those decisions are made in the religion's customary fashion. But in this case the debate is not over a church's policy or procedure, but its very definition: who is a Shaker?

What it seems to boil down to is a debate over continuity. Those who favor the decision to close membership seem to think it would be better for the living Shakers to disappear than to risk contamination of Shakerism by the admission of new members. Those who wish the membership rolls to remain open say that change is not something to be feared. . . .

The irony of the whole situation is that while so much grief and tension has been caused by the presence of a few newcomers in the Shaker circle, non-Shakers have become involved in the affairs of the Society to an unprecedented degree. Contamination from within is not a new concern of the Shakers—it is a problem that comes automatically with any organization that must recruit its members from outside. . . .

But never in the history of the Society have worldly persons had so much influence as the Manchester lawyers, or Jack Auchmoody, or Gerard Wertkin. In addition to Friends of the Shakers, there are other nonprofit groups involved in protecting or preserving Shaker villages and artifacts: The Shakerton Foundation in Massachusetts, The Shaker Historical Society in Ohio, the Shaker Heritage Society in New York, the Friends of Pleasant Hill in Kentucky. All are part of a large and growing complex of academicians, museum curators, history buffs, antique dealers, and yes, journalists like me, who interpret the Shaker experience to the rest of the world.

But this complex—call it the Shaker Industry—is not the same thing as the Shakers, and even as it strives to uncover the truth about Shakerism, it warps and distorts that truth in its own interest. . . .

The result is that the picture of the Shakers presented by the Shaker Industry—the Shaker Image—is never quite complete. It is edited, enhanced, packaged. It is made into the curious beast called "Americana," which like all the other "-ana"—railroadiana, baseballiana, Kennedy-ana—is a vain effort to capture some unpossessable spirit. Americana is to America what nostalgia is to history. And the making of the Shakers into Americana is a violation of that Shaker virtue we claim to cherish most—simplicity.

But somehow I am confident that a faith that survived mob violence in the past . . . will survive the corrupting affections of this carnal world. I can say that because I have seen Shaker simplicity triumph even in the midst of one of the most carnal places on earth—New York City.

I saw Sister Mildred's radiant integrity on a rainy night a few blocks from Broadway, when she sang "Simple Gifts" to a crowd of sophisticated New Yorkers, and made their glitter look cheap. She has been a Shaker for most of this century, and a leader of other Shakers, but she is too modest to define her faith. "It took me a long time to find out what Shakerism really meant," she told me. "You don't get it in one reading, in one day's work, in one struggle. You have to go over it and over it again and again. It seems to take more language than I have to really tell you what it has meant to me."

And I saw it again on a Sunday morning in the soaring neo-Gothic vastness of Manhattan's Trinity Church, where the small party of Shakers and their worldly friends gathered for a service—a Shaker service, in a setting so riotously unsimple that the enterprise seemed doomed from the start.

But we got up in turn, and spoke, and prayed. We sang together—the cheerful, childlike tunes, calling on Believers to bow and bend like the willow, and shake, shake out of them all that is carnal.

'Tis the gift to be simple,
'Tis the gift to be free,
'Tis the gift to come down
Where we ought to be.

I watched, and listened, and struggled with my own self-consciousness, which is the great enemy of simplicity. And suddenly my eyes were stinging, and the huge church seemed to shrink to the dimensions of a plain meeting room, and the noise of the city was transformed into the musical silence of Maine, and I felt for a moment that I had come down to where I ought to be.   —Tim Clark, "Shattering the Shaker Image,"
Yankee, May 1980

THE SHAKER REVIVAL

Science Fiction: No Hate, No War, No Money, No Sex

JERUSALEM WEST, N.Y., Thursday, June 28, 1995—The work of Salvation goes forward in this green and pleasant Hudson Valley hamlet to the high-pitched accompaniment of turbo-car exhausts and the amplified beat of the "world's loudest jag-rock band." Where worm-eaten apples fell untended in abandoned orchards less than a decade ago a new religious sect has burst into full bloom. In their fantastic four-year history the so-called New Shakers—or United Society of Believers (Revived), to give them their official title—have provoked the hottest controversy in Christendom since Martin Luther nailed his ninety-five theses to the door of All Saints Church in Wittenberg, Germany, on October Thirty-one, Fifteen-seventeen. Boasting a membership of more than a hundred thousand today, the New Shakers have been processing applications at the rate of nine hundred a week. Although a handful of these "recruits" are in their early and middle twenties—and last month a New Jersey man was accepted into the Shaker Family at Wildwood at the ripe old age of thirty-two—the average Shaker has not yet reached his eighteenth birthday. . . .

It is hardly surprising that so many "feebies"—people over thirty—have trouble with the basic Believers' Creed: "No hate, No war, No money, No sex." Evidently, in this final decade of the twentieth century, sainthood is only possible for the very young.

The "Roundhouse" at Jerusalem West is, in one sense, the Vatican of the nationwide movement. But in many ways it is typical of the New Shaker communities springing up from La Jolla, California, to Seal Harbor, Maine. At last count there were sixty-one separate "tribes," some containing as many as fifteen "families" of a hundred and twenty-eight members each. Each Shaker family is housed in an army-surplus pliodesic dome—covering some ten thousand square feet of bare but vinyl-hardened earth—which serves as bedroom, living room, workshop and holy tabernacle, all in one. . . .

On a typical summer's afternoon at Jerusalem West, with the sun filtering through the translucent dome and bathing the entire area in a soft golden glow, the Roundhouse resembles nothing so much as a giant, queenless beehive. In the gleaming chrome-and-copper kitchen blenders whirr and huge pots bubble as a squad of white-smocked Food Deacons prepares the copious vegetable stew that forms the staple of the Shaker diet. In the sound-proofed garage sector the Shop Deacons are busily

The "New Shakers" as American Gothic. Illustration by Jack Gaughan for "The Shaker Revival," *Galaxy*, February 1970. Courtesy of the artist.

transforming another hopeless-looking junkheap into the economical, tur-
bine-powered "hotrod"—one already known to connoisseurs in this country and abroad as the Shakerbike—and the eight Administrative Deacons
and their assistants are directing family business from a small fiber-walled
cubicle known simply as The Office. And the sixteen-piece band is cutting a new liturgical tape for the Evening Service—a tape that may possibly end up as number one on the federal pop charts. . . . No matter where
one turns beneath the big dome one finds young people humming, tap-
ping their feet, breaking into snatches of song and generally living up to
the New Shaker motto: "Work is Play." One of their most popular
songs—a characteristic coupling of Old Shaker words to a modern jag-
rock background—concludes with this no-nonsense summation of the
Shaker life-style:

> It's the Gift to be simple,
> The Gift to be free,
> The Gift to come down
> Where the Gift ought to be . . .

Background tape. Interview with Harry G [one of the founders of the
New Shakers] . . .

Q: What's your attitude toward the Old Shakers? They died out,
   didn't they? for lack of recruits?

A: Everything is born and dies and gets reborn again.

Q: Harry, what would happen if this time the whole world became
   Shakers?

A: Don't worry, star. You won't be around to see it.

At precisely eight o'clock the two lines of worshippers begin to move
out of the Holy Corridor. They circle the dance floor, the boys moving to
the right, the girls to the left. Actually, it's difficult to tell them apart. . . .
All wear their hair cropped short, as if sheared with the aid of an overturned bowl. . . .

The worshippers have formed two matching arcs, sixty-four boys on
one side, sixty-four girls on the other, each standing precisely an arm's
length from each neighbor. . . . The color of the dome has begun to change
to a darker, angrier crimson. . . . All eyes are turned upward to a focus
about twenty-five feet above the center of the floor, where an eight-sided
loudspeaker hangs by a chrome-plated cable from the midpoint of the
dome. The air begins to fill with a pervasive vibration. . . . And then the

music explodes into the super-charged air. Instantly the floor is alive with jerking, writhing bodies . . . and the music is unbelievably loud. . . .

The tall boy in the center has begun to spin around and around in place . . . now he's whirling like a top. . . . His right arm shoots out from the shoulder, the elbow locked, the fingers stiff, the palm flat—this is what the Shakers call the Arrow Sign, a manifestation of the Gift of Prophecy, directly inspired by the Dual Deity, Father Power and Mother Wisdom. The tall boy is the "instrument" and he is about to receive a message from on high.

His head tilts forward. His rotation slows. He comes to a halt with his right arm pointing at a short red-haired girl. The girl begins to shake all over. . . .

"Everyone's a mirror," the tall boy shouts. . . . "Only a mirror can shine, shine, shine. Let the mirror be mine, be mine, be mine!"

The red-haired girl is shaking so hard her limbs are flailing like whips. Her mouth has fallen open and she begins to moan, barely audibly at first. . . . But it keeps getting louder and louder and still louder, like the wail of an air-raid siren. . . . This is the Gift of Seizure, which the New Shakers prize so highly. . . .

It is unclear whether the eight teenagers—six boys and two girls— who banded together one fateful evening in the spring of 1991 to form a jag-rock combo called The Shakers had any idea of the religious implications of the name. According to one early account in Riff magazine, the original eight were thinking only of a classic rock-and-roll number of the nineteen-fifties *Shake, Rattle and Roll* (a title not without sexual as well as musicological overtones). . . .

On the night of June the first the group arrived in Hancock, Massachusetts, where they were scheduled to play the next evening at the graduation dance of the Grady L. Parker Modular School. . . . There was no room large enough [for all of them] at the local Holiday Inn, so, after some lengthy negotiations, the Modular School principal arranged for them to camp out on the grounds of the local Shaker Museum, a painstaking restoration of an early New England Shaker community dating back to seventeen-ninety. Amused but not unduly impressed by the coincidence in names, the eight Shakers bedded down for the night within sight of the Museum's most famous structure, the round Stone Barn erected by the original Shakers in eighteen-twenty-six. Exactly what happened between midnight and dawn on that fog-shrouded New England meadow may never be known—the validation of mystical experience being by its very nature a somewhat inexact science. According to Shaker testimony, however, the spirit of Mother Ann, sainted foundress of the original sect, touched the Gifts of the eight where they lay and in a vision of the future—which Amelia D later said was "as clear and bright as a holograph"—revealed why they had been chosen: The time had come for a mass revival of Shaker beliefs and practices. The eight teenagers awoke at the same instant, compared visions, found them to be identical and wept together for joy. They spent the rest of the day praying for guidance and making plans. Their first decision was to play as scheduled at the Grady L. Parker graduation dance. . . .

Whatever the reason, the group apparently played as never before. Their music opened up doors to whole new ways of hearing and feeling—or so it seemed to the excited crowd of seniors who thronged around the bandstand when the first set was over. Without any premeditation, or so he later claimed, Harry Guardino stood up and announced the new Shaker dispensation, including the Believers' Creed (the Four Noes) and a somewhat truncated version of the Articles of Faith of the United Society of Believers (Revived): "All things must be kept decent and in good order," "Diversity in Uniformity," and "Work is Play." According to the Hancock newspaper, seventeen members of the senior class left town that morning with the Shakers—in three cars "borrowed" from parents and later returned. Drawn by a Gift of Travel, the little band of pilgrims made their way to the quiet corner of New York State now known as Jerusalem West, bought some land—with funds obtained from anonymous benefactors—and settled down to their strange experiment in monastic and ascetic communism.

The actual historical connections between Old Shakers and New Shakers remains a matter of conjecture. It is not clear, for instance, whether Harry G and his associates had a chance to consult documentary material on display at the Hancock Museum. There is no doubt that the First Article of Faith of the Shaker Revival is a word-for-word copy of the first part of an early Shaker motto. But it has been given a subtly different meaning in present-day usage. And while many of the New Shaker doctrines and practices can be traced to the general tenor of traditional Shakerism, the adaptations are often quite free and sometimes wildly capricious. All in all, the Shaker Revival seems to be very much a product of our own time.   —Gerald Jonas, "The Shaker Revival," *Galaxy*, Feb. 1970

To the End of the World

. . . If there are but five souls among you that abide faithful, this testimony will overcome all nations.

—Father James Whittaker

This gospel will go to the end of the world, and it will not be propagated so much by preaching, as by the good works of the people.

—Mother Ann Lee

Where to Find Shaker Collections in Museums and Libraries*

PUBLIC COLLECTIONS

DELAWARE
The Henry Francis du Pont Winterthur Museum, Winterthur 19735

KENTUCKY
Kentucky Museum, Bowling Green 42101
Shaker Village of Pleasant Hill, Harrodsburg 40330
Shakertown at South Union 42283

MAINE
Shaker Museum, United Society of Shakers, Sabbathday Lake, Poland Spring 04274

MASSACHUSETTS
Fruitlands Museums, Harvard 01451
Hancock Shaker Village, Pittsfield 01201
Museum of Fine Arts, Boston 02115

NEW HAMPSHIRE
Shaker Museum, Shaker Village at Canterbury, East Canterbury 03224

NEW YORK
Metropolitan Museum of Art, New York City 10028
Shaker Museum, Old Chatham 12136

* This list is adapted from the *1979 Guide to Shaker Museums and Public Collections* with the kind permission of its publisher, the Shaker Museum at Old Chatham, New York.

OHIO

Dunham Tavern Museum, Cleveland 44106
Golden Lamb Hotel, Lebanon 45036
Kettering-Moraine Museum, Kettering 45439
Shaker Historical Society Museum, Shaker Heights 44120
Warren County Historical Society Museum, Lebanon 45036
Western Reserve Historical Society, History Museum, Cleveland 44106

PENNSYLVANIA

Philadelphia Museum of Art 19130

VERMONT

Shelburne Museum, Shelburne 05482

WISCONSIN

Milwaukee Art Museum, Villa Terrace 53202

ENGLAND

The American Museum, Claverton Manor, Bath BA2 7BD

SHAKER LIBRARY COLLECTIONS

CONNECTICUT

Connecticut State Library, Hartford 06115

DELAWARE

The Henry Francis du Pont Winterthur Museum Library, Winterthur 19735

DISTRICT OF COLUMBIA

Library of Congress 20540

INDIANA

Indiana Historical Society Library, Indianapolis 46202

KENTUCKY

Filson Club, Louisville 40203
Kentucky Library, Bowling Green 42101
Shakertown at South Union 42283
University of Kentucky, Margaret I. King Library, Lexington 40506

MAINE

Shaker Library, United Society of Shakers, Sabbathday Lake 04274

MASSACHUSETTS

American Antiquarian Society, Worcester 01609
Berkshire Atheneum, Pittsfield 02101
Fruitlands Museums Library, Harvard 01451
Hancock Shaker Village, Pittsfield 01201
Massachusetts Historical Society, Boston 02215
Williams College, Sawyer Library, Williamstown 01267

MICHIGAN

University of Michigan, William L. Clements Library, Ann Arbor 48109

NEW HAMPSHIRE

New Hampshire Historical Society Library, Concord 03301
Dartmouth College, Baker Library, Hanover 03755

NEW YORK

Buffalo and Erie County Public Library, Buffalo 14203
Hofstra University Library, Hempstead, Long Island 11550
New York Public Library, New York City 10018
New York State Library, Albany 12230
Shaker Museum, Emma B. King Library, Old Chatham 12136
Syracuse University, George Arents Research Library, Syracuse 13210

NORTH CAROLINA

Duke University, William R. Perkins Library, Durham 27706

OHIO

Dayton and Montgomery County Public Library, Dayton 45402
Ohio Historical Society Library, Columbus 43211
Shaker Historical Society, Shaker Heights 44120
Warren County Historical Society Library, Lebanon 45036
Western Reserve Historical Society, History Library, Cleveland 44106

WISCONSIN

State Historical Society of Wisconsin, Madison 53706

rINGS, 1987

University, Kentucky Library, Bowling Green, Ky.

aker Inn, Lower Shaker Village, Enfield, N.H. 03748
ciety, Albany, N.Y. 12211
aker Village, New Lebanon, N.Y. 12125
ciety, Columbus, Ohio 43211
brary, Massilon, Ohio 44646
Walter Havighurst Special Collections Library, Ox-
056
iblic Library, Shaker Heights, Ohio 44120

A Selected
Chronological Bibliography

EIGHTEENTH CENTURY

1769   *The Virginia Gazette*, November 9, page 1, col. 3. Published in Williamsburg by Purdie & Dixon. (A very early portrait of the Shakers when they were still in England by the Manchester correspondent of this colonial newspaper, in the collection of the Virginia Historical Society.)

1781   Rathbun, Valentine. *Some Brief Hints Of a Religious Scheme, Taught and Propagated By a Number of Europeans Living in a Place Called Nisqueunia, in the State of New York.* Norwich.

1782   Taylor, Amos. *A Narrative of the Strange Principles, Conduct and Character of the People Known by the Name of Shakers: Whose Errors have spread in several Parts of North-America, but are beginning to diminish, and ought to be guarded against. In Two Numbers. . . .* Worcester: Printed for the Author.

1785   Anonymous letter, dated July 25, 1785, describing the Shaker worship. (A manuscript in the collection of the Connecticut Historical Society.)

1790   [Meacham, Joseph] *A Concise Statement of the Principles of the Only True Church, according to the Gospel of the Present Appearance of Christ. As held to and Practiced upon by the True Followers of the Living Saviour, at New Lebanon, &c. Together with a Letter from James Whittaker, Minister of the Gospel in this Day of Christ's Second Appearing—to his Natural Relations in England.* Dated October 9th. . . . Printed at Bennington, Vermont: By Haswell & Russell.

1796   *The Theological Magazine*, January 1796. Vol. 1. New York: Printed by T. and J. Swords, for Cornelius Davis.

NINETEENTH CENTURY

1807   McNemar, Richard. *The Kentucky Revival; or, A Short History of the Late Extraordinary Out-Pouring of the Spirit of God in the Western*

States of America. . . . Cincinnati: From the Press of John W. Browne. (Reprint) New York: AMS Press, 1974.

1808   Youngs, Benjamin Seth. *The Testimony of Christ's Second Appearing; Containing a General Statement of All Things Pertaining to the Faith and Practice of the Church of God in This Latter-day.* . . . Lebanon, Ohio. Revised and expanded editions: Albany, 1810; Union Village, Ohio, 1823; Albany, 1856.

1813   Wells, Seth Youngs, comp. *Millennial Praises, Containing a Collection of Gospel Hymns, in Four Parts; Adapted to the Day of Christ's Second Appearing. Composed for the Use of His People.* Hancock: Printed by Josiah Talcott, Junior.

1815   *A Declaration of the Society of People (Commonly Called Shakers) Shewing Their Reasons for Refusing to Aid or Abet the Cause of War and Bloodshed, by Bearing Arms, Paying Fines, Hiring Substitutes, or Rendering Any Equivalent for Military Services.* Albany: Printed by E. & E. Hosford.

1816   Bishop, Rufus. *Testimonies of the Life, Character, Revelations and Doctrines of Our ever Blessed Mother Ann Lee, and the Elders with Her; through whom the Word of Eternal Life was Opened in this Day of Christ's Second Appearing.* . . . Hancock: Printed by J. Tallcott & J. Deming, Junrs.

1818   Warder, W. S. *A Brief Sketch of the Religious Society of People Called Shakers,* in *New View of Society* by Robert Owen.

        Dunlavy, John. *The Manifesto, or A Declaration of the Doctrine and Practice of the Church of Christ.* Printed at Pleasant Hill, Kentucky. (Reprint) New York: AMS Press, 1972.

1822   Dyer, Mary Marshall. *A Portraiture of Shakerism, Exhibiting a General View of Their Character and Conduct.* . . . *Certified by Many Respectable Authorities.* . . . Printed for the Author. (Reprint) New York: AMS Press, 1972.

        Dwight, Timothy. *Travels in New-England and New-York.* New-Haven: T. Dwight. (Reprint) Cambridge: The Belknap Press of Harvard University Press, 1969.

1823   Green, Calvin and Seth Y. Wells. *A Summary View of the Millennial Church, or United Society of Believers, (Commonly Called Shakers) Comprising the Rise, Progress and Practical Order of the Society; Together with the General Principles of Their Faith and Testimony.* Albany: Printed by Packard & Van Benthuysen. Revised Edition, Albany 1848.

        Guest, Moses. *Poems on Several Occasions to which Are Appended, Extracts from a Journal Kept by the Author While He Followed the*

Sea, and During a Journey from New-Brunswick, in New Jersey, to Montreal and Quebec. Cincinnati: Looker & Reynolds, Printers.

1824   Sedgwick, Catharine Maria. *Redwood: A Tale.* (Fiction) New York: E. Bless and E. White. (Reprint) New York: Garrett Press, Inc., 1969.

1827   Green, Calvin. "Biographical Account of the Life, Character and Ministry of Father Joseph Meacham, the Primary Leader in establishing the united order of the Millennial Church." New Lebanon, N.Y. Copied from the original by Elisha D. Blakeman May 1859. Manuscript in the New York Public Library.

     Wells, Seth Youngs, and Calvin Green. *Testimonies Concerning the Character and Ministry of Mother Ann Lee and the First Witnesses of the Gospel of Christ's Second Appearing; Given by Some of the Aged Brethren and Sisters of the United Society....* Albany, N.Y.: Printed by Packard & Van Benthuysen, 1827.

1828   Cooper, James Fenimore. *Notions of the Americans: Picked up by a Travelling Bachelor.* Philadelphia: Carey Lea & Carey. (Reprint) New York: Frederick Ungar Publishing Co., 1963. Vol. II.

1832   [Bates, Barnabas] *Peculiarities of the Shakers, Described in a Series of Letters from Lebanon Springs....* By a Visitor. New York: J. K. Porter.

     Trollope, Frances Milton. *Domestic Manners of the Americans.* London: Whittaker, Treacher & Co.

1833   [Hawthorne, Nathaniel] "The Canterbury Pilgrims." (Fiction) In *The Token and Atlantic Souvenir.* Boston: American Stationers' Company. Collected in *The Snow Image and Other Twice-told Tales.* Boston: Ticknor, Reed and Fields, 1852.

     [McNemar, Richard] *A Selection of Hymns and Poems; for the Use of Believers. Collected from Sundry Authors,* by Philos Harmoniae. Watervliet, Ohio.

1837   Hawthorne, Nathaniel. "The Shaker Bridal." (Fiction) In *Twice-told Tales.* Boston: American Stationers' Co. Also published in *The Token and Atlantic Souvenir*, Boston, 1838.

     Martineau, Harriet. *Society in America.* Vol II. London: Saunders and Otley.

     Cushman, Charlotte. "Lines: Suggested by a Visit to the Shaker Settlement, near Albany." *Knickerbocker*, January 1837.

1838   Greeley, Horace. "A Sabbath with the Shakers." *Knickerbocker*, June 1838.

1841   Buckingham, James S. *America, Historical, Statistic and Descriptive.* London: Fisher, Son & Co., 1841. Vols. II and III.

1842 Dickens, Charles. *American Notes for General Circulation.* London: Chapman and Hall, 1842.

The Youth's Guide in Zion, and Holy Mother's Promises. Given by inspiration at New Lebanon, N.Y. January 5, 1842. Printed at Canterbury, N.H. (Reprint) Mother's Work Series No. 1, The United Society, Sabbathday Lake, Maine: 1963.

1843 Lane, Charles. "A Day with the Shakers," *The Dial.* October.

1845 Engels, Friedrich. "A Description of the Communistic Settlements Formed in Recent Times and Still Existing." *Deutsches Bürgerbuch für 1845.*

Grosvenor, Roxalana L., ed. "Sayings of Mother Ann and the First Elders, Gathered from Different Individuals at Harvard and Shirley Who were Eye and Ear Witnesses, the Divine Word of God, Revealed Thro Them at Different Times and in Various Places." Manuscript, Case Memorial Library, Hartford Seminary Foundation, Conn.

1848 Lamson, David R. *Two Years' Experience Among the Shakers....* West Boylston, Massachusetts: Published by the author.

1850 *Extract from an Unpublished Manuscript on Shaker History (by an Eye-witness), Giving an Accurate Description of Their Songs, Dances, Marches, Visions, Visits to the Spirit Land, &c.* Boston: Printed and Published by E. K. Allen.

1853 Elkins, Harvey. *Fifteen Years in the Senior Order of the Shakers.* Hanover, N.H.: Dartmouth Press.

1857 [Lossing, Benjamin] "The Shakers." *Harper's New Monthly Magazine.* July. Vol. XV.

1859 Evans, F. W. *Shakers. Compendium of the Origin, History, Principles, Rules and Regulations, Government, and Doctrines of the United Society of Believers in Christ's Second Appearing. With Biographies of Ann Lee, William Lee, Jas. Whittaker, J. Hocknell, J. Meacham, and Lucy Wright.* New York: D. Appleton and Company. (Reprint) New York: Burt Franklin, Publisher, 1972.

1861 Ward, Artemus. "Artemus Ward on the Shakers." *Vanity Fair*, February 23. In reprint of the 1898 *Complete Works of Artemus Ward* (Charles F. Browne), New York: Burt Franklin, 1970.

1864 Weiss, John. *Life and Correspondence of Theodore Parker.* New York: D. Appleton & Company.

1867 Dixon, William Hepworth. *New America.* 3rd ed. Philadelphia: J. B. Lippincott.

1869 Arnold, Matthew. *Culture and Anarchy.* Reprint, ed. by William S. Knickerbocker, New York: The MacMillan Company, 1925.

Evans, Frederick William. *Autobiography of a Shaker, and Revelation of the Apocalypse.* Mt. Lebanon, N.Y.: F.W. Evans. (Reprint) New York: AMS Press, Inc. 1972.

Munsell, Joel. *Annals of Albany.* 2d. ed. Albany: J. Munsell.

1870   Noyes, John Humphrey. *History of American Socialisms.* Philadelphia: J. B. Lippincott & Co. (Reprint) New York: Hillary House Publishers Ltd., 1961.

1871–   *The Shaker,* official monthly publication of the United Societies and its
1872   "missionary" to the world. Vols. 1 and 2, edited by G. A. Lomas at Shakers [Watervliet] N.Y. Albany: Printed by Weed and Parsons.

1872   Wells, S. R., ed. *The Illustrated Annuals of Phrenology and Physiognomy.* For the Years 1865–1872. New York: Samuel R. Wells, Publisher.

1873   *Frank Leslie's Illustrated Newspaper.* "The Shakers," September 6, 13.

1873–   *Shaker and Shakeress,* second title of the monthly Shaker periodical
1875   published by the United Society at Mount Lebanon, N.Y. Editor: F. W. Evans. Editress: Antoinette Doolittle. Publisher: G. A. Lomas, Shakers [Watervliet], N.Y. Albany: Printed by Weed and Parsons. Vols. 3–5.

1875   Nordhoff, Charles. *The Communistic Societies of the United States; From Personal Visits and Observation: Including Detailed Accounts of the Economists, Zoarites, Shakers, the Amana, Oneida, Bethel, Aurora, Icarian, and Other Existing Societies....* New York: Harper & Brothers. (Reprints) Hillary House Publishers, 1960; Schocken Books, Inc., 1965; Dover Publications, Inc., 1966.

1876   Howells, William Dean. "A Shaker Village," *Atlantic Monthly.* Boston, June. Vol. 37.

1876–   *The Shaker.* Vols. 6, 7. Monthly publication of the United Societies,
1877   edited by G. A. Lomas, Shakers [Watervliet], N.Y. Published by N. A. Briggs, Shaker Village [Canterbury], N.H.

1878   Hinds, William Alfred. *American Communities: Brief Sketches of Economy, Zoar, Bethel, Aurora, Amana, Icaria, the Shakers, Oneida, Wallingford, and the Brotherhood of the New Life.* Oneida, N.Y. Revised edition, Chicago: Charles H. Kerr & Company, 1902. Third edition, Chicago: C. H. Kerr & Company, 1908.

1878–   *The Shaker Manifesto,* Vols. 8–12 of the official monthly publication of
1882   the United Societies. Editor G. A. Lomas was succeeded in 1882 by H. C. Blinn, Shaker Village [Canterbury], N.H. Publisher N. A. Briggs of Shaker Village [Canterbury], N.H. was succeeded in 1879 by Giles

1916   Sears, Clara Endicott. *Gleanings From Old Shaker Journals.* Boston: Houghton Mifflin Company.

1920   Howells, William Dean. *The Vacation of the Kelwyns: An Idyll of the Middle Seventies.* (Fiction) New York: Harper & Brothers.

       La Tour du Pin, La Marquise de. *Recollections of the Revolution and the Empire.* Edited and translated by Walter Geer. New York: Brentano's.

1920–
1921   Briggs, Nicholas A. "Forty Years a Shaker," in *The Granite Monthly,* New Hampshire State Magazine, December 1920, January–March 1921.

1922   Sears, Clara Endicott. *The Romance of Fiddler's Green.* (Fiction) Boston and New York: Houghton Mifflin Company.

1926   Doyle, Arthur Conan. *The History of Spiritualism.* George H. Doran Company, 1926. (Reprint) New York: Arno press, 1975.

1929   Chase, Eugene Parker, trans. and ed. *Our Revolutionary Forefathers: The Letters of François, Marquis de Barbé-Marbois During his Residence in the United States as Secretary of the French Legation 1779–1785.* New York: Duffield & Co.

1932   Hawthorne, Nathaniel. *The American Notebooks.* Edited by Randall Stewart. New Haven: Yale University Press.

1933   Andrews, Edward Deming. *The Community Industries of the Shakers.* New York State Museum Handbook 15. Albany: The University of the State of New York. (Reprint) Philadelphia: Porcupine Press, 1972; Charlestown, Mass.: Emporium Publications, 1972.

       Hedrick, Ulysses Prentiss. *A History of Agriculture in the State of New York.* New York: Hill and Wang.

1936   Carmer, Carl. *Listen For a Lonesome Drum.* New York: Farrar and Rinehart. (Reprint) David McKay Company, 1950.

       Hutton, Daniel M. *Old Shakertown and the Shakers.* Harrodsburg, Kentucky.

       Johnson, Clifton. "The Passing of the Shakers," in *Old-Time New England,* Bulletin of the Society for the Preservation of New England Antiquities. Vol. xxv, No. 1, July 1934; No. 2, October 1934.

       The Peg Board, "First Shaker Number," June 1936. Lebanon School, New Lebanon, N.Y. (Reprint) Darrow School, 1966.

1937   Andrews, Edward Deming. *Shaker Furniture. The Craftsmanship of an American Communal Sect.* Photographs by William F. Winter. New Haven: Yale University Press.

       McCullough, Robert W. *Me and Thee.* (Fiction) New York: Lothrop, Lee and Shephard.

Mansfield, Luther Stearns. "Glimpses of Herman Melville's Life in Pittsfield, 1850–1851: Some Unpublished Letters of Evert A. Duyckinek." Reprinted from *American Literature*, March 1937.

Nichols, Thomas Low. *Forty Years of American Life, 1821–1861.* New York: Stackpole Sons.

1938   Rourke, Constance. *Charles Sheeler: Artist in the American Tradition.* New York: Harcourt, Brace & World, Inc. (Reprint) New York: Kennedy Galleries and Da Capo Press, 1969.

1939   Emerson, Ralph Waldo. *The Letters of Ralph Waldo Emerson.* Ed. by Ralph L. Rusk. New York: Colulmbia University Press.

1940   Andrews, Edward Deming. *The Gift to be Simple: Songs, Dances and Rituals of the American Shakers.* New York: J. J. Augustin. (Reprint) Dover Publications, 1967.

1941   Calverton, V. F. *Where Angels Dared to Tread.* Indianapolis and New York: The Bobbs-Merrill Company, Publishers.

Melcher, Marguerite Fellows. *The Shaker Adventure.* Princeton: Princeton University Press. (Reprints) Cleveland: The Press of Western Reserve University, 1960; Old Chatham, N.Y.: The Shaker Museum, 1975.

1942   Rourke, Constance. *The Roots of American Culture and Other Essays.* New York: Harcourt, Brace & World, Inc.

1943   Leslie, Ann George. *Dancing Saints.* (Fiction) Garden City, N.Y.: Doubleday, Doran and Co.

1945   Cramer, Miriam Ann. *More Love, Brother. A Play in Three Acts about the People Called Shakers, with Incidental Songs and Dances.* (Unpublished typescript)

1947   Neal, Julia. *By Their Fruits: The Story of Shakerism in South Union, Kentucky.* Chapel Hill: University of North Carolina Press.

Roueché, Berton. "A Small Family of Seven," *The New Yorker*, August 23.

1949   Melcher, Marguerite Fellows. *Rose in the Wilderness, a Play in Three Acts with Prologue and Epilogue.* (Unpublished typescript)

1950   Bestor, Arthur. *Backwoods Utopias: The Sectarian and Owenite Phases of Communitarian Socialism in America: 1663–1829.* Philadelphia: University of Pennsylvania Press.

Gottschalk, Louis. *Lafayette Between the American and the French Revolution.* Chicago: University of Chicago Press.

1951   Forster, E. M. "Mount Lebanon" in *Two Cheers For Democracy.* New York: Harcourt Brace Jovanovich, Inc.

Holloway, Mark. *Heavens on Earth: Utopian Communities in America 1680–1880*. London: Turnstile Press. Revised edition, New York: Dover Publications, Inc., 1966.

Piercy, Caroline B. *The Valley of God's Pleasure: A Saga of the North Union Shaker Community*. New York: Stratford House.

1953   Andrews, Edward Deming. *The People Called Shakers*. New York: Oxford University Press.

1956   King, Eldress Emma B. *A Shaker's Viewpoint*. East Canterbury, N.H.

Wagenknecht, Edward, ed. *Mrs. Longfellow: Selected Letters and Journals of Fanny Appleton Longfellow (1817–1861)*. New York: Longmans, Green and Co.

1957   Giles, Janice Holt. *The Believers*. (Fiction) Boston: Houghton Mifflin Company.

1960–   Emerson, Ralph Waldo. *Journals and Miscellaneous Notebooks*, ed. by
1973   William H. Gilman and others. Cambridge: Belknap Press of Harvard University Press. (Vols. III, V, VII, IX, X)

1961   Conlin, Mary Lou. *The North Union Story: A Shaker Society, 1822–1889*. Written for the Shaker Historical Society, Shaker Heights, Ohio. Cleveland: Ontario Printers, Inc.

Randle, William. *The Shaker Heritage*. Ten 12-inch recordings. Cleveland: The Press of Western Reserve University.

1961–   *The Shaker Quarterly*. Sabbathday Lake, Poland Spring, Maine: Pub-
to date lished by the United Society, Portland, Me., Anthoensen Press.

1961–   Bates, Issachar. "A Sketch of the Life and Experience of Issachar
1962   Bates," with an Introduction by Theodore E. Johnson. *The Shaker Quarterly*, Fall, Winter 1961; Spring 1962.

1962   Melville, Herman. *Moby-Dick, or, The White Whale*. Edited by Luther S. Mansfield and Howard P. Vincent. New York: Hendricks House, Inc. (Notes on Chapter 71, "The Jeroboam's Story," explain Melville's references to the Shakers in the 1851 novel.)

1963   Frost, Marguerite. *The Shaker Story*. Canterbury, N.H.

Neal, Mary Julia, ed. *The Journal of Eldress Nancy, kept at the South Union, Kentucky, Shaker colony*, August 15, 1861–September 4, 1864. Nashville, Tenn.: The Parthenon Press.

1967   Jewett, Sarah Orne. *Letters*. Ed. by Richard Cary. Waterville, Me.: Colby College Press.

"The 'Millennial Laws' of 1821," edited and with an Introduction by Theodore E. Johnson. *The Shaker Quarterly*, Summer 1967.

1969   Johnson, Theodore E. *Life in the Christ Spirit: Observations on Shaker Theology.* Sabbathday Lake, Maine: United Society.

Johnson, Theodore E. and John McKee. *Hands to Work and Hearts to God: The Shaker Tradition in Maine.* Brunswick, Maine: Bowdoin College Museum of Art.

Whitson, Robley Edward. *Shaker Theological Sources.* Bethlehem, Conn.: The United Institute.

1970   Jonas, Gerald. "The Shaker Revival." *Galaxy Magazine*, February. (Science fiction)

1970   Miller, Amy Bess Williams, and Persis Wellington Fuller, comps. *The Best of Shaker Cooking.* New York: Macmillan.

1971   Moffat, Goldie Satterlee and John L. Satterlee. *Satterlee-Ley-Ly Allied Families Genealogy.* Perris, Calif.: published by the compiler.

Desroche, Henri. *The American Shakers; From Neo-Christianity to Presocialism.* Translated from the French and edited by John K. Savacool. Amherst: University of Massachusetts Press. (Originally published in France in 1955)

Morse, Flo. *Yankee Communes: Another American Way.* New York: Harcourt Brace Jovanovich, Inc.

1971– *The World of Shaker.* Spring Lake, Michigan: Published by the Guild
1977   of Shaker Crafts, Inc. (A quarterly newspaper)

1972   "All Things Anew." *The Shaker Quarterly*, Winter 1972. Sabbathday Lake, Maine.

Meader, Robert F. W. *Illustrated Guide to Shaker Furniture.* New York: Dover Publications, Inc. (paperback); Peter Smith (cloth).

Phillips, Hazel Spencer. *Richard the Shaker.* Oxford, Ohio: Typoprint Inc.

Swain, Thomas. *The Evolving Expressions of the Religious and Theological Experiences of a Community: A Comparative Study of the Shaker 'Testimonies' Concerning the Sayings of Mother Ann Lee....* Separate from the *Shaker Quarterly*, Vol. XII, Nos. 1 and 2, Spring and Summer 1972. Sabbathday Lake, Maine.

1973   Ray, Mary Lyn. "A Reappraisal of Shaker Furniture and Society." *Winterthur Portfolio 8.* Edited by Ian M. G. Quimby. Published for The Henry Francis du Pont Winterthur Museum by the University Press of Virginia, Charlottesville.

Thomas, Samuel W., and James C. *The Simple Spirit: A Pictorial Study of the Shaker Community at Pleasant Hill, Kentucky.* Pleasant Hill: Pleasant Hill Press.

1974   Pearson, Elmer R., and Julia Neal. *The Shaker Image.* Boston: New York Graphic Society in collaboration with Shaker Community, Inc., Hancock, Mass.

1974   Ray, Mary Lyn. Introduction, *True Gospel Simplicity: Shaker Furniture in New Hampshire.* Concord, New Hampshire: The New Hampshire Historical Society.

       Weis, Virginia. "Women in Shaker Life." A paper delivered at the Shaker Bicentennial Conference, Sabbathday Lake, Maine, August 1974.

1975   Andrews, Edward Deming, and Faith Andrews. *Fruits of the Shaker Tree of Life.* Stockbridge: The Berkshire Traveller Press.

       Filley, Dorothy M. *Recapturing Wisdom's Valley: The Watervliet Shaker Heritage, 1775–1975.* Ed. by Mary L. Richmond. Published by the Town of Colonie and the Albany Institute of History and Art. New York: Publishing Center for Cultural Resources.

       Peters, Robert. *The Gift To Be Simple: A Garland for Ann Lee.* (Poetry) New York: Liveright.

       Sprigg, June. *By Shaker Hands.* New York: Alfred A. Knopf.

       Whitworth, John McKelvie. *God's Blueprints: A Sociological Study of Three Utopian Sects.* London and Boston: Routledge & Kegan Paul.

1976   Lifshin, Lyn. *Shaker House Poems.* Chatham, N.Y.: Sagarin Press.

       Ott, John Harlow. *Hancock Village: A Guidebook and History.* Hancock, Mass.: Shaker Community, Inc.

1977   Aldrich, Jonathan. *Croquet Lover at the Dinner Table.* (Poetry) Columbia, Missouri, and London: University of Missouri Press.

       Richmond, Mary L., compiler and annotator. *Shaker Literature: A Bibliography, in Two Volumes. Vol. I, By the Shakers; Vol. II, About the Shakers.* Published by Shaker Community, Inc., Hancock, Mass. and distributed by the University Press of New England, Hanover, N.H.

1978– *The Shaker Messenger.* A quarterly magazine published by The World
to date of Shaker, Holland, Michigan.

1979   Muller, Charles R. *The Shaker Way.* Worthington, Ohio: *Ohio Antique Review.*

       Patterson, Daniel W. *The Shaker Spiritual.* Princeton, New Jersey: Princeton University Press.

       Ray, Mary Lyn. "Is There a Shaker Aesthetic?" A paper delivered at the Museum of American Folk Art Shaker Seminar, September 1979.

Index

Page numbers in italics indicate illustrations

ten, a Gallery Note," by Homer Eaton Keyes (November 1935; © 1935 by Straight Enterprises, Inc., and The Magazine ANTIQUES). Baker Book House: for excerpt from *The Life of Mary Baker G. Eddy and the History of Christian Science* by Georgine Milmine (pub. by Baker Book House, Grand Rapids, Mich., 1971). Bobbs-Merrill Company, Inc.: for excerpts from *Where Angels Dare to Tread* by Victor F. Calverton (© 1941, ren. 1968 by Books for Libraries). Canterbury, N.H. Shakers: for excerpts from *The Shaker Story* by Eldress Marguerite Frost (1963); *Shaker Music, a Brief History* by Sister Lillian Phelps (196–); *Who Are the Shakers?* by Sister Lillian Phelps (1957); *"A Shaker's Viewpoint"* by Eldress Emma B. King (1956); and the Foreword to *The Shakers and Their Homes* by Charles Edson Robinson (reprint, 1976). Sister Frances Carr: for excerpt from "A Letter to Jennifer." Columbia University Press and Ralph Waldo Emerson Memorial Association: for excerpt from *The Letters of Ralph Waldo Emerson*, ed. Ralph L. Rusk (Columbia University Press, 1939, 1966). Commonweal Publishing Co., Inc.: for excerpt from "American Peaceniks, 150 Years Ago" by Doris Grumbach (*Commonweal*, November 13, 1970; © 1970 by Commonweal Publishing Co., Inc.). Mary Lou Conlin: for excerpt from her *The North Union Story* (© 1961 by Mary Lou Conlin; pub. by Shaker Historical Society). Connecticut Historical Society: for letter dated July 25, 1785. Rosamund Coolidge: for excerpt from *History of Petersham, 1675–1947* by Mabel Cook Coolidge (© 1948 by Mabel Cook Coolidge, ren. 1976 by Rosamund C. Coolidge, Ruth M. Coolidge, Lydian E. Bowley, and Chester D. Coolidge; pub. by Powell Press, Hudson, Mass.). *The Dickensian*, London: for excerpt from "Dickens's Account of the Shakers and West Point: Rhetoric or Reality?" by Duncan A. Carter and Laurence W. Mazzeno (September 1976). Nancy Melcher Diemand: for excerpt from *The Shaker Adventure* by Marguerite Melcher (Princeton University Press, 1941). Doubleday & Company, Inc.: for excerpt from *Dancing Saints* by Ann George Leslie (© 1943 by Doubleday & Company, Inc.); and from *Made in America: The Arts in Modern Civilization* by John A. Kouwenhoven (© 1948 by John A. Kouwenhoven). Dover Publications, Inc.: for excerpt from *Heavens on Earth* by Mark Holloway (1966). Fairmount Presbyterian Church, Cleveland, Ohio: for excerpt from sermon of the Reverend John Schott (1945). Goldie Satterlee Moffatt Fowler: for excerpt from her *Satterlee-Ley-Ly Allied Families Genealogy* (© 1971 by Goldie Satterlee Moffatt; pub. by compiler, Ferris, Calif.). Terry Curtis Fox: for excerpt from review "Simplified Gifts" (*Village Voice*, March 19, 1979; © 1979 by Terry Curtis Fox). Harcourt Brace Jovanovich, Inc.: for excerpt from *Yankee Communes: Another American Way* by Flo Morse (© 1971 by Harcourt Brace Jovanovich, Inc.); and from *Two Cheers for Democracy* by E. M. Forster (© 1951 by E. M. Forster). Harper & Row, Publishers, Inc.: for excerpt, abridged and adapted, from *The Way to Peace* by Margaret Deland (© 1910 by Harper & Row, Publishers, Inc., ren. 1938 by Margaret Deland). Harvard University Press: for excerpt from Edward Deming Andrew's biography of Ann Lee in *Notable American Women*, Vol. II, ed. Edward T. James (1971). Houghton Mifflin Company: for excerpt and illus. from *Susanna & Sue* by Kate Douglas Wiggin. Illus. by N. C. Wyeth (© 1909, 1937 by Houghton Mifflin Company); excerpt from *My Garden of Memory* by Kate Douglas Wiggin (© 1923 by Houghton Mifflin Company); and excerpt from *The Believers* by Janice Holt Giles (© 1957 by Janice Holt Giles). *House Beautiful* Magazine: for excerpt from "The Furniture of the Shakers: A Plea for its Preservation as Part of our National Inheritance" by Walter A. Dyer (May 1929; © 1929, The Hearst Corporation. All rights reserved). William White Howells: for excerpt from *The Vacation of the Kelwyns* by William Dean Howells (© 1920 by Harper & Brothers). Jane Bird Hutton: for excerpt from *Old Shakertown and the Shakers* by Daniel M. Hutton (1936, Harrodsburg, Kentucky). International Creative Management: for excerpt from "The Shaker Revival" by Gerald Jonas (*Galaxy Magazine*, February 1970; © 1970 by Gerald Jonas). Mary Jane Jacob: for excerpt from her thesis, "The Impact of Shaker Design on the Work of Charles Sheeler" (1976). Alfred A. Knopf, Inc.: for excerpt from *The Impecunious Collector's Guide to American Antiques* by John T. Kirk (© 1975 by John T. Kirk). Lyn Lifshin: for excerpt from poem from *Shaker House Poems* (© 1976 by Lyn Lifshin; pub. by Sagarin Press, Chatham, N.Y.). Little Brown and Company: for excerpt from "A Blessing of Women" by Stanley